THE
HIMALAYAN HERITAGE

THE HIMALAYAN HERITAGE

Edited with An Introduction
By
MANIS KUMAR RAHA

GYAN

ISBN : 978-81-212-0082-0

Published, 2018

Published by

Gyan Publishing House
5, Ansari Road
Daryaganj, New Delhi-110002
Phone: 011-47034999, 9811692060
www.gyanbooks.com
E-mail: books@gyanbooks.com

GYAN

Printed at: G. Print Process, Delhi.

In Memory of My
Mother, Usharani Raha
and
Father, Hemlal Raha

ACKNOWLEDGEMENTS

My keen interest on the Himalayas developed after I joined the North Western Regional Office of the Anthropological Survey of India, Government of India, Dehra Dun, Uttar Pradesh, in March 1970 and carried out my research work in the district of Kinnaur, Himachal Pradesh. Since then I have kept myself engaged in studying various aspects of culture of the people of the Western and Central Himalayas. During the course of studying the people of the Western and the Central Himalayas and their cultures, as an officer of Anthropological Survey of India I have been provided with all possible facilities to help me overcoming major difficulties. I express my deep sense of gratitude to our Director. Thanks are due to all my colleagues of the Anthropological Survey of India who helped me in gaining my experience and knowledge about the people of different areas of the Himalayas through personal discussion, seminar etc. Their reports, articles etc. also helped me greatly in consolidating my knowledge of the Himalayas. I am thankful to different officials of the Government of Jammu and Kashmir, Himachal Pradesh and Uttar Pradesh for the co-operation during my fieldwork and suggestions. I am extremely grateful to all my contributors for their enthusiastic co-operation and encouragement without which the book could not be published. Shri Sudip Kumar De, Stenographer, demands all praise for undertaking the very laborious, painstaking task of typing the manuscripts very neatly ignoring his personal difficulties. Shri Surajit Pal, Shri Sunit Mondal, Shri Bidyut Das, Shri Biplab Das, Shri Dipankar Mukherjee, my colleagues and Shri Asit

Basu, Shri Somnath Chatterjee and Shri Partha Pratim Barua require special mention. They all helped me in comparing the typescripts. I am much thankful to them. Thanks are due to Shri Swapan Das who untiringly put his labour to prepare the index for the book and also assisted me in comparing the typescripts. I am also thankful to all others who directly or indirectly assisted me in bringing out this publication.

Finally I shall neglect my duty if I do not express my gratitude to my publisher whose skill and experience made me possible to get this book published in a very short time.

M. K. RAHA

LIST OF CONTRIBUTORS

Dr. P.C. Datta M.SC., LL.B., PH.D.	Director of Research, Govt. of Arunachal Pradesh
Dr. Bhikshu Kondinya M.A., PH.D., Acharya, Sahityaratna, Sahitya-lankar	U.G.C. Research Associate, Jawaharlal Nehru University
Dr. Jayanta Sarkar M.SC., PH.D.	Superintending Anthropologist, Anthropological Survey of India
Dr. B.K. Ray Burman M.SC., PH.D.	Visiting Senior Fellow, Centre for the Study of Developing Societies and Ex-Senior Professor, Council for Social Development, New Delhi, Ex-Professor, Pallicharcha Kendra, Visva Bharati University and Ex-Dy. Registrar General, Ministry of Home Affairs, Govt. of India
Dr. S.K. Chaube M.A., PH.D.	Director and Professor, Centre for Himalayan Studies, University of North Bengal
Dr. Buddhadeb Chaudhuri M.SC., PH.D., P.R.S.	Professor, Centre for South and South-east Asian Studies, Calcutta University and Ex-Reader, Deptt. of Sociology

	and Social Anthropology, North Bengal University
Prof. A.C. Sinha PH.D.	Head of the Deptt. of Sociology, School of Social Sciences, North Eastern Hill University, Shillong, Author of 'Politics of Sikkim'
Dr. A.K. Das M.SC., PH.D.	Director, Cultural Research Institute, Govt. of West Bengal
Dr. C.W. Brown	Department of Anthropology, Lund University, Lund, Sweden
Prof. Allen C. Fanger M.A., PH.D.	Professor of Anthropology, Kutztown State College, Kutztown, U.S.A.
Shri Sunderlal Bahuguna	Famous *chipko* Movement Leader and Freedom-fighter of Tehri and Uttarkashi districts, U.P. Represented *chipko* in different national and international forums. Author of a number of booklets on *chipko* and environmental conservation. Recipient of Shri and Smt. Dashrathmall Singhvi Memorial Award for National Integration
Shri Chandi Prasad Bhatt	Famous *chipko* movement leader and recipient of Raman Magasaysay Award for Community Leadership. Member of various official and non-official committees and author of a number of booklets on *chipko* movement and Environmental Preservation

Professor G.D. Berreman	Professor of Anthropology, California University, Berkley, California, U.S.A.
Shri Ram Chandra Guha M.A.	Fellow, Indian Institute of Management, Calcutta, Doing Ph.D. on 'Forest Movements and Social Change in Garhwal'
Dr. William Hare Newell M.A., PH.D., (Univ. of Manchester), Dip. in Social Anthropology (Oxford University), Dip. in Chinese (New China Union University)	Professor Associate Professor, Deptt. of Anthropology, University of Hongkong and University of Sydney, Australia, Ex-Prof., Deptt. of Anthropology and Sociology, International Christian University, Tokyo
Dr. Manis Kumar Raha M.SC., PH.D.	Deputy Director, Anthropological Survey of India, Government of India
Shri D.B. Negi M.A.	Fellow (UGC), Deptt. of Political Science, Himachal Pradesh University. Submitted Ph D. thesis under H.P. University on Political Leadership in Kinnaur. Shri Negi is a native of Kinnaur
Smt. Puspa Misra M.A.	Fellow, Deptt. of Philosophy, Rochester University, USA, Lecturer, Deptt. of Philosophy, Lady Brabourne College, Calcutta
Professor Anoop Chandola M.A., PH.D.	Professor of Oriental Studies, University of Arizona, Tucson, USA
Dr. M.M. Dahsmana M.A., PH.D., FRAI, FRGS	Squadron Leader, Indian Air Force, Author of the Ramos of Arunachal Pradesh. Currently associated with Institute of Indological Studies, Ambala

Dr. Makhan Jha M.A., PH.D.	Reader, Deptt. of Anthropology, Professor-in-Charge, Centre for Himalayan Studies, Ranchi University, Ranchi, and Associate Editor, Journal of Social Research
Dr. Jagdish Kaur M.A., LL.B., PH.D.	Resident Editor, Tourism Recreation Research and Director, Centre for Tourism Research, Lucknow, Head, Deptt. of Geography, The Avadh Degree College, Lucknow, Author of Studies in Tourism, Wild Life Parks and Conservation, (1982) and Studies in Himalayan Ecology and Development Strategies (1980) etc.

CONTENTS

SECTION TWO

THE CENTRAL HIMALAYAN PERSPECTIVE

SECTION THREE

THE WESTERN HIMALAYAN PERSPECTIVE

LIST OF ILLUSTRATIONS

INTRODUCTION

The vast mountainous tract of the Himalayas in India, with its varying ecological conditions, has not only acted as the centre for meditation for the sages, saints and other holy men, but also has given shelter to a large number of ethnic groups with diverse cultural identity and social formations. These ethnic groups have organised their life and activities in these terrains over a long stretch of time. For centuries most parts of the Himalayas were almost out of reach to the outside world. Thus the inhabitants were able to keep their life style and tradition undisturbed. They could master the difficulties created by the inhospitable environment of the rugged, unkempt, mountainous terrains of the Himalayas they dwell, and could adapt themselves accordingly for their mere survival. The culture built by these sturdy denizens of the Himalayas in such an environment is somewhat different from that prevalent in the plains areas. This difference in their culture exists not only in their material life but also in various other aspects of their life such as economy, social organisation, political activities, religious beliefs and practices and even in their value-judgement. This has happened in spite of the little contact that was maintained by both the mountain dwellers and the inhabitants of the plains.

The human habitations in the Himalayas are spread over different altitudes. Considering the ecological characteristics of different altitudinal position the human habitations in the Himalayas may be classified into three zones—(i) high altitude habitation (above 8000 ft above mean sea level) (ii) middle altitude habitation (between 5000 ft to 8000 ft above mean sea level) (iii) lower altitude and foothill habitations (below 5000 ft above mean sea level).

The high altitude habitations have an arid or semi-arid climate. The vegetation growth here is quite low. The area is inhabited mostly by the Bhot, Bhotia, Bhutia or Bodh or such group of people having Buddhism as their religion. It is a generic name and includes people inhabiting high altitude regions of Arunachal Pradesh, Sikkim, Darjeeling, Chamoli, Uttar Kashi, Pithoragarh, Kinnaur, Lahaul and Spiti and Leh areas. Here settlements are very small in size and situated on the hill slopes or on a small patch of a flat land. The people are mostly mongoloid in character and depend more on pastoralism, but less on agriculture. A few of them are hunters and gatherers. They lead a nomadic or transhumant mode of life. Cultivation is done on small patches of unfertile terraces and inferior cereals are produced. Irrigation mostly depends on snowfall as water sources like springs, streams are very few and rainfall is very insignificant or nil. Earlier, during pre-Indo-China conflict era (1962) many of them had trade link with Tibet, trade was one of their main sources of income. Another interesting character of some of the people here is the seasonal migration. During winter when agricultural activities are suspended because of the severe winter and heavy snowfall, many of them migrate to down hills or even plains with their livestock. They return to summer settlements with the approach of summer season. In the past they used to make tribes to Tibet for trade during summer season. People here are mostly Buddhists as already said, and this area could be treated as the last stronghold of Buddhism in India. Buddhism is surviving here ignoring the threat of the post-Buddhist Hindu renaissance and also the influence of Islam and Christianity. Polyandry and primogeniture are the basic societal profiles of many of them. In pre-independence era they had very little contact with the people of the plains even with the lower hills. With the development of modern communication and transport systems, they are now coming in regular contact with the people of down hills and the plains thereby the long preserved traditions indicate signs of rapid change. People inhabiting this zone include the Monpa, the Khamba, the Ramos, the Pailibe, the Boojar Bori, the Bokar, the Tagin, the Sulung and others of Arunachal Pradesh. In Sikkim the high altitude dwellers are mostly the Bhutia. In the Central Himalayas only the Bhot or Bhotia and the Anwals reside in the high altitude valleys. In Jammu and Kashmir the Bodh or Bhot, the Argon, the Dard, the Mon, the Gara, the Beda and others of Leh and Zanskar areas and the Shia Muslims of Kargil are high altitude dwellers. The Bodh of Spiti, the Zad of Kinnaur, the Pangwala of Pangi valley (Chamba) belong to the high altitude zones of Himachal Pradesh.

In the middle altitude zone reside a large number of tribal groups in Arunachal Pradesh, namely, the Aka, the Apatani, the Miniang, the Sherdukpen and others, both tribal (the Bhotia and the Lepcha) and caste groups in Sikkim and Darjeeling. In the Central Himalayas mostly the Hindu castes and a few tribes like the Jaunsari and the Raji (the Jaunsaris of Jaunsar-Bower area of Dehru Dun district though a scheduled tribe, yet basically include the Brahmin, the Rajput and different lower castes) inhabit in this zone. This zone in the Western Himalayas is resided by the Muslims, various Hindu castes and some non-mongoloid tribals. The caste groups here lack some important caste characters as prevalent among the caste groups of the plains. The people living here follow Hinduism or Islam except a few who have accepted Buddhism. The settlements here are either agglomerated or dispersed type and situated on the hill slopes or on the valleys. The inhabitants are mostly agriculturists. There are some tribal groups (of Arunachal Pradesh) who practise shifting cultivation. Some groups in this middle altitude zone depend on pastoralism and lead transhumant life, while a few others are hunters and gatherers. For irrigation they depend on rainwater though irrigational facilities are also available. Monogamy is the general rule though polyandry is also practised only in a few pockets like Jaunsar-Bower (Dehra Dun), Purula (Uttar Kashi), Rewin-Jaunpur area (Tehri) of U.P. and Sirmur district of Himachal Pradesh. The people of this middle altitude zone always keep contact with high altitude people on one hand and plains on the other. A large number of developmental and constructional works have brought new dimension in this region and have given the people a new meaning of life.

The lower altitude and foothill areas have accommodated a number of tribal groups in Arunachal Pradesh such as the Pasi, the Padam, the Nocte, the Wancho and others, both tribes and caste groups (the Nepalese) in Sikkim and Darjeeling, a large number of caste groups like the Garhwali and the Kumaon castes, tribes like the Bhotia, the Bhoksa and the Tharu and some Muslims in U.P. hill districts, mostly caste people in Himachal Pradesh and both Hindu and Muslims in Jammu and Kashmir. People here are followers of either Hinduism or Islam, of course in Arunachal Pradesh mostly they follow tribal religion or christianity and in Sikkim and Darjeeling both Buddhism and Hinduism. The settlements are built on the flat land, hill sides or on the valleys. The size of the settlement is quite big and usually multicaste in nature. People here are mostly land owners or landless cultivators. Some of them are labourers also. Irrigation depends on rainfall, river and canal water. Shifting cultivators, pastoral nomads and hunter-gatherers are non-existent. Monogamy is the general practice among them though the trace of polygyny is also not wholly uncommon. Polyandry is totally absent. The people here have larger interaction with the people of the plains and this has compelled them to imbibe 'culture of the plains'. The caste groups here bear most of the caste characters as are prevalent in the plains areas.

With his brief observation on the cultural dimensions of the people living in three different altitudinal zones, let us now shift our attention to the cultural variability that exists between the Eastern, the Central and the Western Himalayas and delineate the cultural parameters of the people living there.

The culture of the Eastern Himalayas is basically a 'tribal' culture. The whole of Arunachal Pradesh, where over one hundred ethnic groups (scheduled tribes) live, has a distinct tribal culture. Some of the numerically important tribal groups are the Abor, the Aka, the Apatani, the Bagi, the Bangni, the Bokar, the Dufla, the Deovi, the Karka, the Khampti, the Miji, the Millang, the Miniyong, the Miri, the Mishmi, the Momba, the Monpa, the Nishang, the Nissi, the Nocte, the Padam, the

Simong, the Sulung, the Tagin, the Tangsa, the Wancho and others. Of these tribal people those who live in the high altitude zone are Buddhist by religion though these Buddhists along with other tribal groups follow basically a distinct tribal culture. Some others who have embraced christianity, have also distinct tribal cultural base.

Similarly the Lepchas and the Bhutias of both Sikkim and Darjeeling have distinct 'tribal' base though they profess Buddhism. Of course unlike Arunchal both Sikkim and Darjeeling have a large number of Nepali castes like the Rai, the Limbu, the Newar, the Magar, the Gurung, the Chettris, the Sunwar, the Tamang, the Damais, the Kami, the Sarki and others. The term Bhutia in both areas is a generic name of a number of ethnic groups like the Sherpa, the Yolmo, the Kagate, the Dukpa and others.

But when we reach the Central and the Western Himalayas we find these 'tribal' culture groups living in the high Himalayas do not show the so called 'tribal' cultural features except one or two ethnic groups like the Raji of Pithoragarh. Even the 'scheduled tribes' of both Uttar Pradesh (the Bhotia, the Raji, the Jaunsaris, the Bhoksa and the Tharu) and Himachal Pradesh (the Lahaula, the Swangla, the Jad or Bhot, the Pangwala, the Gaddi, the Kinnaura and the Gujjar) do not bear any major tribal characteristics. Rather many caste characters are distinct among most of them. The Gaddi include different castes like the Brahmin, the Rajput, and the Dom groups who include different artisan untouchables, the Kinnaura or Kinnara similarly do not mean a distinct ethnic group but cover the Khosia or Kanet, the Koli, the Lohars, the Badhi and the Nangalu. Identically the Jaunsaris identify the Rajput, the Brahman, the Kolta and some other lower castes The 'caste system' is prevalent all over U.P. Hills, Himachal Pradesh and some areas of Jammu and Kashmir regions. Even the high altitude Buddhists living in Leh and Zanskar regions of Jammu and Kashmir, Spiti and parts of Lahaul of Lahaul and Spiti district and Pooh sub-division of Kinnaur district of Himachal Pradesh and the Jad or the Bhotia of Uttarkashi are closer to the caste fold. The Bhotias of other two areas, Chamoli and Pithoragarh districts of Uttar Pradesh are mostly Hindus.

It is thus seen that the Himalayan culture bears both altitudinal and regional dimensions; different altitudes, high, middle and low, have distinct cultural entity. The regional culture of the Eastern Himalayas is quite different from that of the Central and Western Himalayas. While the Eastern Himalayan culture is basically a 'tribal' culture, the same of the Central Himalayas bears the 'caste' characters. In the Western Himalayas while we find the same 'caste' feature all over, in some parts both 'caste' and 'Islamic' cultural features co-exist.

II

As our readers have already seen that I have divided the whole of the Himalayas into three distinct regions, the Eastern Himalayas, the Central Himalayas and the Western Himalayas. These divisions have been made basing on the diversity of the culture of the people living there and not purely on geographical or geological consideration. I have included under the Eastern Himalayas, the states of Arunachal Pradesh and Sikkim and Darjeeling district of West Bengal. The Central Himalayas cover all the eight hill districts of Uttar Pradesh, namely, Tehri, Pauri, Uttar Kashi, Chamoli, Dehru Dun, Nainital, Almora and Pithoragarh. Of these former five districts come under Garhwal Division and the latter three form Kumaon Division. Our Western Himalayas have included the states of Jammu and Kashmir and Himachal Pradesh. My classification of the Indian Himalayas is mostly based, as already stated, on the socio-cultural features of the region, and thus may not coincide with the geographical or geological classification of the Himalayas. The geographers and the geologists may dispute this classification.

III

I have incorporated altogether twentyseven articles in this book. Of these I have included seven articles under the heading the Eastern Himalayan Perspective. Of these seven articles four are from Arunachal Pradesh covering four tribes, viz., the Wancho, the Khamti, the Kamang Mishmi and the Sherdukpen. These four articles have focussed various aspects of culture of some Arunachal tribes. The two articles from Sikkim discuss two important aspects of the Sikkimese culture.

One discusses the political activities there while the other is about the traditional arts and crafts which are gradually vanishing. In both articles ethnicity and identity of the Sikkimese have been dealt with. The Lepchas have represented the lone hilly district of West Bengal—Darjeeling. The author has dealt with the Lepcha socio-economic life.

Largest number of articles have come from the Central Himalayas. There are twelve articles in this part. These articles have covered almost all hill districts of Uttar Pradesh except Nainital. A glance in the contents of the articles shows that these articles have covered various aspects of the culture of the ethnic groups like the Bhotia the Kumaoni (the Rajput), the Jaunsari, the Rajput of Rewain-Jaunpur (Tehri) and Purula (Uttar Kashi) and the Garhwali. Though I have covered the varied aspects of culture of this region, I have given stress, for obvious reasons, on the *chipko* movement, the movement that started over a decade ago for the preservation of environment and keeping ecological balance in the Himalayas which later on has stirred the mind of people at the local, regional, national and even international levels. While I have included two articles from two protagonists of this movement, two other articles pertain to two research papers. All these four articles on the *chipko* movement have touched various dimensions of this apolitical movement for the preservation of the Himalayan environment and resources.

Eight different articles have covered the Western Himalayas. Five of these articles are from Himachal Pradesh and three from Jammu and Kashmir. In Himachal Pradesh districts of Chamba, Kinnaur and Lahaul and Spiti have been covered and in Jammu and Kashmir districts of Leh, Kargil and Srinagar have been highlighted. Through these articles three religious groups, the Muslims, the Hindus and the Buddhists have been covered. Ethnically the people covered in these articles are the Gaddi of Chamba, the Khasa (Kanet) and Jad of Kinnaur, the Lahaula and the Bodh of Lahaul and Spiti, the Shia Muslims of Kargil, the Sunni Muslims of Kashmir Valley and the Bodh of Leh and Zanskar of the erstwhile Ladakh.

The contibutors of this volume are all eminent scholars of different disciplines like anthropology, sociology, political science, linguistics, psychology, comparative religion etc. All of them have long experience of the Himalayan regi on and unde-r standing of the Himalayan culture. They have depicted their experience and understanding about the people of the Himalayas and their culture in these thought provoking and interesting articles.

IV

My interest in bringing out this book on the Himalayas is of two fold. One is to fill up the gap on the study of the Himalayan culture and secondly to move a step ahead in building a new discipline of the Himalayan studies.

Though I worked among the Lepcha and the Bhutia of Darjeeling district as early as mid-sixties my actual Himalayan study began in the first quarter of 1970 when I took up a research project in Kinnaur district of Himachal Pradesh under the auspices of the Anthropological Survey of India. Thereafter I was involved directly or indirectly, in different other research projects on the Western and the Central Himalayas. My experience gave me this idea that the Great Himalayas stretching from Jammu and Kashmir in the north-west to Arunachal Pradesh in the north-east are not well represented in the anthropo-sociological literature. The lack of adequate anthropo-sociological materials on the Indian Himalayas has created a gap in professional understanding of this region.

The second reason of my editing this book on the Himalayas is to contribute a little towards building up a new discipline of the Himalayan studies. The Great Himalayas have a distinct culture, a distinct entity, much different from the culture of the plains and even other hill people of other parts of the world. This distinct culture of the Himalayas, surviving in peculiar eco-systems for centuries, requires to be studied thoroughly and methodically. A multi-disciplinary approach would help in bringing out various facts of the Himalayan culture and help in building up the discipline of the Himalayan Studies.

M. K. RAHA

SECTION ONE

THE EASTERN HIMALAYAN PERSPECTIVE

CHAPTER I

SOCIAL ORGANIZATION OF THE WANCHOS OF TIRAP DISTRICT, ARUNACHAL PRADESH

P. C. DUTTA

Introduction

The Wanchos of Tirap District of Arunachal Pradesh are one of the various tribes composing the 3.7 lakhs population of the Territory. Their homeland is the western part of the district on the border of Nagaland. The Patkai hills form the southern border while Sibsagar district of Assam is in the north. To their east live the Noctes, a tribe well known for their frequent contact with the plains since the Ahom days. Upto the time of the British administration the Wanchos were known as the Nagas of the East or the Banforia Nagas. During the Ahom days they were called the Bar Mithunias, Haru Mithunias, Banerias, Bor Banchang, and Haru Banchang and so on. The name Wancho became popular only after the administration of the area was taken over by our own government. The massacre of the Survey party led by Captain Badgley and Lieutenant Holcomb, in the Wancho village of Ninu (also called Nginu) more than a century ago, has brought the Wanchos into prominence even though they were known as headhunters earlier. Closer contact with this tribe was made only when various developmental programmes were taken up by the Government.

The Wancho society is characterized by the existence of class distinction, a system uncommon amongst tribal people.

There are four classes, each one of which is laid on the fundation of clan and sub-clan unity and receives varied degrees of social cognizance. The highest of these classes are the Wanghans, the chiefs, enjoying all the privileges of the society and receiving special honour in every sphere of life. They are the pivots around whom the unity of the tribe revolves. At the lowest level are the Wangpans or the commonalty. Between these two, which are the original classes, are the Wangsas and the Wangsus, two classes sprung up from matrimonial union between the Wanghams and the Wangpans. The Wangsas are the descendants of the Wangham men and the Wangpan women, and are considered next to the Wanghams. The Wangsus are the children of the Wangsa father and the Wangpan mother, occupying the third stratum in the social hierarchy. The growth of these social classes is shown in the following diagram.

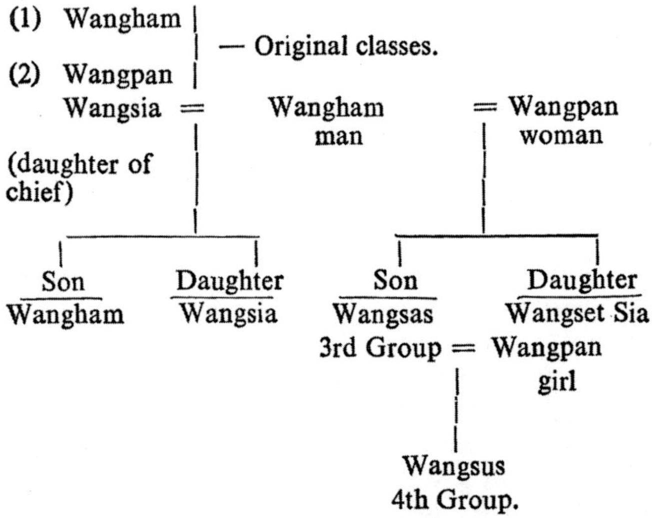

Thus it seems that chief's son, born from a Wangsia, daughter of another chief born of a similar mother becomes the Wangham, and the other sons from a Wangpan wife are the Wangsas. The Wangsas and the Wangsus also possess some royal blood for which, they are entitled to take an important part in social functions, and also they are given some important charges such as looking after the chief's *morung*.

Social distinction between these classes is very clearly recognizable in every sphere of life. For example, in the village festivals, the Wangpans are not allowed to take their meal sitting in the same row with the Wanghams. They are also not allowed to marry girls from the Wangham family, though there is no restriction on the part of a Wangham to marry a Wangpan girl. The Wanghams, Wangsas and Wangsus practically control the village, in which the Wangpans have no say. Leaving aside all these internal classifications the Wahchos in general are a very simple homogenous tribe, having less variation in their general outlook and culture, though the linguistic difference, which is a common factor with the hill tribes, is remarkable.

With this general introduction about the formation of the society we will now go into some of their social institutions.

Family

The smallest unit of the Wancho society is the family, consisting of the father, the mother and their children. This nuclear unit transforms into an extended family when the sons get married and stay under the same roof forming a bigger household.

The grown-up boys of the family sleep apart in the *morung*. There is of course, no separate *morung* for girls who sleep in the houses of some widows not related by blood. An exception to this is found in the chief's families, where girls cannot go to sleep elsewhere but in a separate compartment in the chief's house itself meant for them called *nausa-jip-ham.*

Finally, the family breaks up when the parental roof becomes insufficient to accommodate all the persons including the married sons, their wives and offsprings. In such cases, the married sons establish their individual households except the eldest one who by custom, continues to live in the parental house to support the family and the old parents. Even after marriage, the other sons sometimes stay with the father, till they have two to three issues when they depart. Though the sons establish separate households yet the attachment and the general tie of the of relationship never ceases to exist throughout their lifetime. Girls, however, depart from the family after their marriage and also when they become pregnant. According to the custom the delivery cannot take place in the father's house.

While living in a common household, all the members take their meal from a common hearth. The food is cooked by the mother, or by the wife of the eldest son, if the mother is too old. In case of the chiefs, who generally marry more than one wife, the system is a bit different. There is a particular wife, called *chatonnu*, who cooks for the chief, and the other wives take their meals at individual hearth. Each wife of a chief has her separate accommodation called *noi* in the same house.

All the members work together for the common cause of the family.

In the chief's family also all members except the Wangsia married from another chief's family work in the field to earn their livelihood.

Family Property and Rules of Inheritance

All movable and immovable properties, such as cultivable land, bamboo groves and palm leaf (*tokopat*) gardens, livestock, granary, utensils, ornaments and guns are held in common by the family. The father who is the head of the family, is the sole owner of the property, though the other members can also show their attachment to them. Authority over the property lies with the father and is inherited by the eldest son after his death. The female members have no claim over the family property excepting the articles given to a girl in her marriage, which are her own. Besides the family property, the individual members can possess individual property, which is confined to the bare requirement of a person. Such articles are given as grave-goods after the death of a person. This is to say that the personal effects are one's own and are not left behind to be inherited by others. No property held by the family, can be sold or distributed without the expressed permission of the head of the family.

Primogeniture is the general rule of inheritance, and the eldest son becomes the sole heir of the property. When the family breaks up due to the establishment of separate households by the other sons, the family property is never distributed. The sons also cannot demand or claim any part of the family property. But the eldest brother who inherits the property, generally gives shares till the parting brothers become self-sufficient. At the time of establishing separate households, they are helped with all the requirements, including plots of land for cultivation. Girls do not get any nor can they exercise authority over property. A girl is entitled only to the ornaments, clothings, one basket, one scraper, one iron stick, one *dao* and the grass rain-cover which are given to her at marriage. Even at her husband's house, she cannot claim authority over the property of the husband.

Kinship System

The Wancho society is patrilineal. They reckon their relationship through the male line. But an analysis of the kinship terms reveals that their system of kinship terminology is a classificatory one, where they recognise the cognatic persons, as well as affinal relatives. Most of the terms are applied to persons of both cognatic and affinal relationships. Only a few terms are used to denote some particular persons, which are generally not applied to others. For example, *apa* and *ao* are terms for father and mother respectively which are not applied in case of other persons of one's father's and mother's age. Similarly, *pachong*—father's elder brother, *apasa*—father's younger brother, *nisongnu*—father's elder sister, *nosongsa*—father's younger sister, *hosongsa*—mother's younger brother, *aonu*—mother's elder sister, *konaupa*—younger sisters's husband, *minu*—wife, *mipa*—husband, *nauli*—wife's younger brother, *naupa*—husband's younger brother's wife, are the terms which are not applied to mean any other persons, than those whom they denote.

The terms applied to one's own elder and younger brothers, are also applied to certain other collateral relatives.

Persons, who are junior in age, for example, one's son, daughter, elder or younger brother's or sister's son and daughter, younger brother's wife mother's brother's daughter, wife's younger brother, wife's father's sister's daughter, grand children are generally addressed by name, though they are referred to others by the term. Some persons of both father's and mother's sides are also grouped in one class and a common term is applied to all of them.

Responsibility and behaviour, towards each other in a particular group denoted by a common term, varies according to the degree of affinity and relationship. The term *hosong*, applied to the mother's elder brother, is also applied to the father-in-law of both husband and wife.

Thus it appears that the maternal uncle enjoys similar honour like the father-in-law and is entitled to a certain portion of the bride-price. The existence of cross-cousin marriage of MBD type is hereby indicated.

Again, both parallel and cross-cousins are denoted by common terms, but marriage with the cross-cousin is permitted whereas, parallel-cousin marriage is not only forbidden, but is also considered a crime.

The kinship terms vary to some extent amongst the different *jans*, according to the dialectical variation though all fall within the general framework of classificatory system.

Clan Organization

A study of the clan organization shows that the two original groups or classes, Wanghams and Wangpans, are based on the union of a number of exogamous clans. These clans, locally called *jans*, can more conveniently be called lineage groups, as the very name of the clan signified the names of the families and ancestors from whom the members have descended. It is an obvious fact that most of the tribal people idenify themselves with the name of the ancestors and the families to whom they belong.

Amongst the Maujan group, the two main sub-groups are Wangjans and Panjans, corresponding to Wanghams and Wangpans respectively. The Wangjans have three main clans or lineage groups namely Wangjan (the chief's clan), Khamahamjan and Sanjahamjan. Similarly the Panjans have six different clans, namely, Wangnauhamjan, Nganam(ham)jan, Lo hamjan, Look hamjan, Jo long hamjan and Poi hamjan. Of these clans, the women of Nga hamjan, Lo hamjan, Look hamjan and Poi hamjan cut their hair short.

At Pongchaw also there are two main groups, Wangas and Pansas. The Wangsa group has five clans, namely Wangsa, Wangsu, Dok ham, Wangnauham and Ting loi-sajan, whereas the Pansa group has only three—Wangpanjan, Agihamjan and Wangnauhamjan.

A large number of clans are found amongst the Nijans, the villages under the chiefs of Nimu. At Longkei, the chief's groups has four main clans and the Pansa—seventeen. The clans of the chief's group are, Wangham, Kamsa Wangham, Kamsa Kamsa-ham, and Sinju-ham, and the Pansa clans are—Baunu-ham, Paina-ham, Ganunu-ham, Gannu-ham, Hau fan gan-ham, Khi-ham, Sang-ham, Kham-ham, Gi-ham, Sankoi-ham, Khang-ham, Na-ham, Fangto-ham, Hamoi Napu-ham, Khangnu pa-ham, Nagopa-ham and Khangpa-ham. Of these Khangnu pa-ham, Gannu-ham, Sankoi-ham and Gi-ham are regarded as superior clans amongst the Pansas.

Another peculiarity of the organization is found at Wakka. Here the village has two divisions Singki and Singkhow. Besides the main chief of the village, each division also has its own chief called Singki Gangham and Singkhow Gangham respectively. The people of the chief's group are called Gangsa, and the commoners, Pansa. The Gangsa group has eleven clans, and the Pansa, fourteen.

A study of the different clan groups reveals that the Wancho clans can more conveniently be called lineage groups. An analysis of the different clan names clarifies that the first name indicates the name of the ancestor from whom the family name is derived, the second word *ham* means house, and the last word *jan* means the group rather than clan. For example, Khama ham-jan means people of the Khama's house. Similar is the case with all other *jan* names.

Moreover, if the two groups, Wang-jan and Panjan, are taken as forming two lineage groups, all other smaller groups can very well be considered as sub-lineages. There is sufficient reason also to consider the smaller groups as sub-lineages because one of the important characters found is that marriage between Wangjan males and Panjan females can always take place, but not conversely. Another factor is that these different groups do not also possess a common plot of land—an important feature to be considered in clan organization. Whatever may be the case, it is important to note that these groups regularise the marriage organization of the Wanchos. There are particular groups between whom only, marriage can take place.

Descendants of each group closely identify themselves as relatives and many taboos and restrictions are observed between the members of a particular group.

Life Cycle

A Wancho from the very day of his coming into the world to the last moment of leaving it and even after that, passes through many rituals and ceremonies, performed in different spheres of life for various occasions and purposes. These rituals, ceremonies, feasts and festivities make their life more romantic, charming, virile and picturesque. They are happy and cheerful with their own way of life, content with their mode of living. The rituals and ceremonies performed in different spheres of life together contribute to the formation of the Wancho culture.

Pregnancy and Birth

The security of matrimonial union between a husband and his wife, amongst the Wanchos, depends mostly on the number of children she can bear to him. A barren woman is not only looked down upon, but also divorced soon after she is found to be so, or it will lead to polygyny, if she is not divorced. As a matter of fact, procreation is found to be one of the reasons of marriage to which the Wanchos give more importance.

The idea of conception is common amongst all the different *jans* of the Wanchos, in that they believe that some measure of God's blessings will help in the formation of a baby in the womb of a woman, along with physical intercourse.

Though premarital sexual relationship is not restricted and remains an open secret, yet a girl's pregnancy is socially recognised and considered legal, only when conception takes place after the performance of the usual marriage rites. It is however, a common practice for the husband to cohabit with the wife in her mother's house or in the *morung* where she sleeps, though they never disclose the fact to others. At the time of confinement, however, she goes to her husband's house where delivery must take place.

During pregnancy a Wancho woman has to observe many restrictions and taboos in regard to food and movement. Even after delivery, there are certain restrictions to be observed for a short period.

Ceremonies after Delivery

After the birth of a child, a number of ceremonies are performed.

On the 6th day after delivery a ceremony called *nauman mania o'* is performed, when the hair of the child is shaved. In the early morning the father accompanied by a few male members of the family and clan, goes to the nearby river for fishing and tries to bring at least a few fishes. An expert called *khau gu manu* shaves the hair of the baby before the party returns from fishing.

After hair-cutting, the name-giving ceremony is performed. This is called *nauman.* An old man, called *taikia,* observes the divination with some jungle leaves, uttering the names of the deceased persons of the family, either in the male or in the female line, according to the sex of the child. If the divination is found to be inauspicious with a particular name, several names are uttered, and the one which the divination indicated as good, is kept. The name is disclosed by a particular woman, called *gamnu* who is remunerated with rice beer, meat and a basketful of cooked rice, but the diviner is not given anything. A feast is arranged on this day, with rice-beer, cooked rice and meat, a pig being killed for the purpose.

Then comes the day of *naugam*, the ceremonial visit of the relatives of the girl's side on the seventh day. On this day the relatives of the girl come to visit the house and the new born child. They bring with them about a dozen rats and one fish and give these to the members of the girl's husband's family. The relatives are entertained with rice-beer and meat.

The 8th day called *kanju.* On this day the child is taken out to the front porch of the house. A male child is carried by a boy and a female by a girl.

On the 10th day, the mother can go to the water-point to wash herself properly and to fetch water.

On the 11th day, the child is taken to the nearby cultivable land where the mother offers a little quantity of rice-beer to the deity of the field. But this depends on the result of the divination observed by an expert. If the result is not favourable, the child is not taken outside the house. The period upto 11th day is *genna* for the child. The death of a child within this period is considered abnormal. The *genna* period is called *nan mocha.*

Another ceremony, called *nau thom,* is performed between the age of one to three months when cooked rice is placed in the child's mouth ceremonially by the maternal grandparents for the first time. On this day, the parents of the mother, and the uncle and aunt (mother's side) are specially invited. The uncle brings some cooked rat meat for presentation. They are entertained with cooked rice, rice-beer and meat, for which a pig is killed. The parents of the girl first put the rice in the child's mouth.

On the following day, the girl goes to her parents' house where a feast is arranged by the parents to feed her. It is a great pleasure on the part of the parents to see their daughter becoming a mother. This is called *fong sa wang.* Only after these two ceremonies can the girl eat elsewhere. She returns from her parents' house on the same day.

Marriage

In the Wancho society much freedom is given to young boys and girls; they can mix freely with each other without any reservation, but observing only the rules of clan exogamy. Boys and girls of different clans select their friends freely and meet each other generally in the place where the young girls sleep. This unrestricted mixing helps them in selecting their partners of life. The girls are, however, not allowed to enter the boys *morungs* but the boys usually and regularly meet their girl-friends in private houses where they collect.

In most cases marriage is arranged by the parents, though young people are at liberty to have their own choice.

Rules of Marriage

Clan exogamy is the fundamental and basic rule of marriage. Intra-clan marriage is considered to be a serious crime. If any one violates this rule and marries within his own clan he will not only be ex-communicated but also be exterminated. Their clans are exogamous, but the tribe itself is endogamous, and marriages are mostly confined to the same village excepting in the case of the chiefs, who by custom has to marry at least one wife from another village.

Monogamy in the general rule, but polygynous marriage is also prevalent among the chiefs. The polygynous marriage appears to be to show the importance, personal influence and power of the chief concerned, and to have enough hands to work in the cultivable field. There is no restriction on the part of the commoners in having more than one wife, though this depends mainly on the economic condition of the person concerned. Besides, class-endogamy is also very apparent by which a boy must marry a girl of his own status, else the children will belong to a lower social class.

The children of the chief's families should normally marry into other chief's families in villages outside their own village groups or *jans*. This rule, however, does not apply to any group other than the Wanghams. The commoners are to marry from their own village.

Types of Marriage

Marriage with cross cousins is the most favourite and widely practised type. A man may marry his mother's brother's daughter or father's sister's daughter, who by custom are considered as potential mates. In the absence of a mother's brother's daughter or father's sister's daughter, a youth selects his mate from outside.

Widow marriage is prevalent but sororal polygyny is not allowed. A man can marry the sister of his deceased wife, but not during her life time.

Marriage by exchange of sisters is also prevalent and it is considered to be the best type. This type of marriage is called *songlai-mainlai* (Wakka).

Forms of Marriages

Negotiation between parents is the common form of marriage in vogue amongst the Wanchos. Betrothal is done during the young age of a girl. Examples of betrothal even prior to delivery are also found in many cases, where the father of both the boy and the girl extend their willingness. In such cases, of course, the marriage may not take place afterwards.

Besides negotiation, love marriage is also widely practised. Love marriage takes place as a result of free mixing and free choice of the youthful couples, who make most of the arrangements by themselves. When both the partners decide to marry each other, parents are considered.

Sometimes love marriage leads to elopement, when the young couple fail to obtain the consent of their respective parents. They take shelter in some neighbouring villages; they return to their own village to establish a new household when their parents are found to be agreeable.

Age of Marriage

There is no fixed age of marriage, but child marriage is not prevalent and never practised; only adult marriage is in vogue. Marriage takes place when both boys and girls have become sufficiently grown-up and attained the ability to run a household independently, and to work in the agricultural field.

To confirm the attainment of different stages of life, girls are tattooed in different designs and on different parts of the body. When such tattoo marks are put on the calf, a girl is considered betrothed, and other boys generally do not cut jokes nor mix freely with her.

Marriage Procedure and Rituals

Marriage finalised after the negotiation between parents is performed through the regular procedure, social customs, rituals and ceremonies. In levirate, sororate and love marriages no such ceremonies and rituals are performed, but achieved at the sweet will of the partners, keeping in view the general rule of clan exogamy.

In love marriages, exchanges of gifts of *pan* (betel and nut) is of foremost importance. Acceptance of *pan* offered by a boy or a girl indicates willingness on the part of either person to accept him or her as mate, just as refusal means unwillingness, and marriage cannot then take place between them.

Marriage by Negotiation

Marriage is called *siko asamle* or *minulam* and the process of negotiation, *onupa kakole* or *nausa kam*. Negotiation is carried out between the parents after the betrothal in the young age of the boy and the girl. At first the betrothal remains limited to verbal discussion only and when the girl attains the age of five years or so the mother of the girl puts tattoo marks of two cross lines over the umbellious. After the girl becomes sufficiently grown up, a ceremony called *hawanle* or *toi-mon-mok* is performed. A day is selected by the parents in consultation with the diviners. The girl accompanied by some of her friends goes to her proposed husband's house on this day carrying a basketful of fuel. A feast is arranged at the boy's house for the occasion. After the feast she comes back to her own house. From this day onward, she can freely talk to and associate with the boy and on all festival days can visit that house and even spend a night or two. She is considered, earmarked for the boy, and cannot be married by any other person. Similarly, the boy pays frequent visits to the girl and they may indulge in sexual intercourse also. When the girl conceives tattooing known as *be-huta* on the thigh is done. A feast is arranged on the occasion to which relatives are invited. After this the girl is taken to the boy's house, accompanied by relatives and friends. There too, a feast is arranged and for this, articles such as cooked rice, fish, rice-beer and cooked pork, etc., are taken from the girl's house. Tattooing on the breasts of the girl is done on this day at the bridegroom's house. This tattooing is called *kha-huta*.

The articles are carried by four persons of the girl's family. The parents of the girl also go together. The bridal party returns but the bride stays behind. After staying for about a week or so in the groom's house, the bride pays a visit one day to her parents. She brings with her some articles of food such as cooked rice, rice-beer and meat, etc. from her husband's house. These articles brought from the boy's house, are shared by all the relatives of the girl. Thus, exchange of articles of food continues for three times, after which only the marriage is cemented. Every time the girl visits her parents she takes such articles from her husband's house and also carries back similar articles of equal quantity from her parent's house.

At the time of marriage the girl takes with her the following articles from her parents—bead necklaces, *endi* (silk) cloth, a few pieces of white 'markin' cloth, armlets, bangles, a basket, a *dao*, a sleeping mat and seeds of arum, millet and paddy.

There is no ritual performed to indicate the marriage, other than tattooing done at different stages. The days are selected by a ceremonial process of divination.

The marriage procedure is a bit different in case of the chiefs and involves some more rituals. The chiefs and their sons and daughters by custom take their partners from villages other than their own village group.

The negotiation between two chiefs' families is undertaken after observing divination, performed by *opa* with an egg. If only the portents are good, the negotiation starts, otherwise the case is dissolved. The process is called *chule*. Thereafter a party is sent to the chief's house to negotiate for the Wangsa—which is called *wangsa kaje yang*. They meet the parents of Wangsa and express their desire. If the girl's parents also agree, a day is selected to send out the Wangsa, which is called *ham nap Wangang*. On this day a feast is arranged at the groom's house. A buffalo or a mithun and a pig are killed for the feast. Sufficient-rice beer is prepared. The bride is accompanied by a large party, and the whole village accompanies her up to the village boundary. A mithun or a buffalo with several *chungas* or rice-beer is taken to the groom's house along with the bride. The villagers from the groom's village also come forward to the village boundary to welcome the bride. From the point where the groom's party welcomes the bride, all articles brought from the bride's house are carried by the groom's party. Before entering the groom's house, a dog is killed just at the entrance by an old man from the bride's party. He utters some ritual incantations at the time of sacrificing the dog. He is presented with a *dao* by the groom. The groom offers a feast to all the members present on that occasions. After the feast the inhabitants of both villages dance and sing in the night. Next day the bride's party returns and the bride stays in the groom's house for a day or two more, during which dancing and feasting continue.

A presentation of *dao* and *endi* cloth by the groom to all persons both male and female, who accompany the bride symbolises the grooms respect for the guests. Moreover the *wangsampa* or the persons who carry out the negotiation and perform all other functions for the chief are also presented on this day. The one who does all the work when the chief dies is the *wangda*.

The girl after this ceremony, continues to visit the groom's house, and every time she pays a visit, she is accompanied by a few girls who carry articles of food such as rice-beer, rice and meat.

Tattooing, in case of the chief's daughters does not signify the different states of marriage though it is done at different stages of life.

Among the Wanchos, there is no system of paying brideprice or dowry but presentation of articles such as *endi* cloth, rice-beer, *pan* and meat is made at the time of negotiation and actual marriage. But in case of love marriage and elopment, where the parents do not agree, some amount of fine in cash as well as in kind is imposed on the boy who marries the girl. There is also a custom of giving presents to the girl by the boy. The presentation is made after negotiation and before actual marriage, and is continued for three years consecutively. Articles such as baskets for paddy and fuel, and armlet made of coloured cane, are included in the present. In return the girl also gives ear ornaments of wool and chains of the fine slip of reed made by herself.

After completion of negotiation with due observance of the usual customs, the girl concerned, cannot be married by any other person. If the girl elopes with some other person than the one for whom she has been negotiated, the matter takes a very serious turn and may lead to a feud. If such a thing happened in the case of a chief's daughter it used to lead to head hunting, in the old days. Nowadays, the village council imposes a heavy fine on the offender which amounts to payment of a portion of cultivable land, gun, gong, and palm groves. Instances of such offences are very rare nowadays but in the old days it was one of the causes of head hunting.

Illicit connection with girls, if exposed, is dealt similarly but it is more seriously viewed when a person has such relations with a married woman or a negotiated girl.

Divorce

Divorce is allowed on payment of a fine and is permissible only in some justified causes such as the wife is barren, or not active and cannot help the husband in cultivation, or if she is quarrelsome or possesses an immoral character and indulges in illicit sexual connections with another person. A wife can also divorce her husband on such grounds and if she is not happy. But cases of a wife divorcing her husband are very rare. The case is put up before the village elders who decide it and give their verdict. The fine imposed varies according to the nature and degree of the case. The fine is paid to the chief and compensation to the agrieved party only after which the divorce can be achieved.

Death and Disposal of the Dead

The Wancho idea about death, varies according to its nature. When a person dies in old age, it is considered as natural, but death due to illness is attributed to the evil action of the earth god, Baurang who, they believe, devours the person in the shape of illness. Accidental or sudden death is always taken as due to bad luck.

The funerary custom varies from village to village insofar as the minute details are concerned, but in general it appears to be similar.

Custom in Normal Death

A dead body in normal cases, such as in death due to old age is called *mang* (Pumas), *mangjiga* (Longkai), *mi due* (Wakka) and so on.

The corpse is kept inside the house for about twenty-four hours during which the relatives assemble and express their sorrow. In case of a chief, a wooden coffin is made but a commoner's corpse is wrapped in cloth and matting. The disposal is called *manggu.* Relatives, both men and women together, go to the cemetery, which is generally near some path, leading out of the village. The place is called *jak kha.* There the wrapped corpse is placed on a platform constructed at a height of about five to six feet from the ground. A small shed is made over the platform. An effigy either of wood or bamboo is made where the possessions of the dead are kept hanging. Sometimes the possessions are hanged on the tomb itself. The effigies or images made for the purpose are disposed of in various ways. Sometimes these are placed in front of the tomb, sometimes several such images are kept together under a small shed.

In many cases, it has been found that the relatives of the dead keep guard near the tomb for a few days.

After disposal of the dead, a feast is arranged at which a pig or a *mithun* is killed. Till the skull of the corpse is finally placed under the earth, members of the family offer a share of each meal they take in the name of the deceased.

After about a month when the dead body has complelety decomposed, the skull is detached by an old man called *taisongpa* (Pumao). It is washed carefully, wrapped with a piece of red cloth and put under a stone. The skull-placing day is a great festival and is called *rapolev* or *ja foatle.* Before the ceremony, a number of people go out to catch fish, they cook the fish caught with rice and take the food to the ceremony. They tie a bundle of fish and rice to the skull saying: "We give this to you; eat and go away, O Lumpu ! Go and do not return, do not let us see you again."

In many villages, the skull is put inside an earthen pitcher before being placed under a stone.

Every year at the *poatakle* festival (a festival for taking new rice), the villagers offer rice-beer and other cooked food to the skulls of the deceased members of every family. On this day the whole village collect near the cemetery and the skulls are taken out.

The custom of disposal of the dead body in Longkai and Wakka area is slightly different. At Longkai when a man dies, during the days of dearth the corpse is kept only for about twenty-four hours, otherwise it is kept for two days. The dead body is called *mangjiga.* During these two days, the relatives come and weep near the dead body. On the third day which is called *manggu,* it is taken to cemetery. Relatives and other mourners, both men and women, join in the procession.

The *gampa,* a ritual expert, does all the work of disposal. The corpse is placed on a bamboo platform called *liatan,* over which a shed (*gangsi*) is constructed. The disposal platform is constructed by the *gampa*. The corpse is wrapped in a piece of cloth and the mat on which the dead person used to lie down. An wooden effigy called *sapa* is fixed near the tomb on which the belonging of the deceased such as beads, hat, loin cloth, *dao*, gun and spear are hanged. The articles of foods and utensils are hanged on the tomb itself. On the day following the day of disposal, a ceremony called *latau* is performed. A feast is arranged with rice, rice-beer and meat. A pig or a *mithun* is killed for the purpose. All relatives and other persons who attend the disposal are invited. On the day following the *latau* ceremony, called *guntai*, the relatives sit near the tomb for the whole day. In case of the chief or his wife, the whole village sit near the tomb.

After about one year, the skull-placing ceremony called *go-chau* is performed. The skull is taken out of the tomb, washed carefully and burried underground at a place called *galong*. Before burial, it is put inside an earthen pitcher.

Rice-beer and other items of food are offered to the skull on this day. Valuable articles such as gong, elephant tusk and beads are put in the pit along with the skull. The pit is covered with a stone, over which a gun, a *dao* and a spear are kept.

Disposal of a Chief's Dead Body

The dead body of a chief is first kept near the house for about seven days. On the eighth day the skull is removed with a *dao*. The body part is taken to the common cemetery and the head to a place called *ruk tran khra*, situated in the centre of the village. It is then boiled in water in an earthen pitcher. The flesh is removed and placed with the body in the cemetery.

After the removal of the flesh, the skull is washed, cleaned and kept on a stone. The whole village dance and sing around the skull. Side by side, a feast is arranged. Pig, buffalo and *mithun* are killed. All village under the chief come to join the festival. Each village brings pig or buffalo, rice-beer, rice, vegetables and the like. Heads of the sacrificed animals are kept hanging at the *ruk-tram*. After the ceremony the skull is buried in a stone pit. Valuable articles are buried along with the skull.

In case of the chiefs of the big villages of each *jan*, another ceremony called *lung pong wan*, is performed after six or seven months. In this ceremony all the neighbouring villages, including big villages of other groups, are invited. This is a very big festival performed for a deceased chief. Each village sends presents of pig, buffalo and rice-beer and join the festival. Feasting, dancing and singing continues for several days. The dancers put on their ceremonial dresses.

Disposal in Abnormal Deaths

In abnormal, unnatural and accidental death, no ceremony is performed. The corpse is disposed of in the jungle. It is wrapped in a mat and tied to a tree in the jungle. All the personal belongings of the deceased are thrown away or placed together near the corpse. Nothing of his belongings is kept in the house. No offering is made to him afterwards. In such cases, the corpse is generally disposed of as soon as possible. In some villages, after disposal of the corpse the fire in the hearth of the house is extinguished and the fire is lit afresh.

At Wakka, a feast is arranged on the day following the disposal even in abnormal cases. This is, however, not done in other villages. This day is called *gunku.* A pig is killed, and the *gampa* and *taikia* offer a portion of the meat and a share of the meal to the deceased. The clan members are invited for the feast.

The third day is called *guntai.* On this the whole village observes *genna* and refrain from work. The members of the deceased's family do not move out of the house.

A woman who dies at the time of delivery is disposed of in a similar manner. No precaution is taken in case of abnormal deaths.

The Soul after Death and its Destination

The Wanchos do not have a clear idea about the soul and its destination after the death of a person, but they believe that there is some place where man goes to live after death. This imaginary place is called *junpu*, *lompu* or *yumpu* where, they believe, all the dead forefathers are living. According to some, *junpu* is in the sky but the majority believe it to be under the earth. The soul is called *sab.* It lives inside the human body. If one sees in a dream the *sab* of ones forefathers or deceased relatives coming home, one will die very soon, or at any rate some one of the village will die.

At Wakka, the people believe that the shadow of a man is his soul. It vanishes as soon as the person dies. The shadow which they think to be the soul, is called *sab*. It dwells inside the body so long a man is alive and at death goes to *junpu*, a place under the earth. There are two paths through which the *sab* goes. In normal cases the path is good but in abnormal cases it takes a very bad path.

The *sab* comes out from *junpu* on the day after disposal to meet the parents, friends and relatives. At first its comes out from *junpu* in the shape of a man, but while crossing a small river which they believe is on the way, it slips on a mossy slippery stone and becomes a kite. So, when they see a kite flying over the village after the death of a person, the members of the particular family throw some rice grains outside. In case of a child the bird is very small.

There is a village at *junpu*, called *aujum sia* or *chu-sa* where the *sab* of different persons construct individual houses and live, just as they lived in the earth. At *junpu*, there are three rivers from where the *sab* takes water. The *amai si jin* is the good river meant for the *sab* of good people, while the *ganma si jin* is for bad ones and the *angon si jin* is for disceased ones, specially lepers.

There is a story about the existence of the village at *junpu*. Once upon a time a man went to bring paddy from *Aujum sia* village. While coming back he saw his pig was going towards the village following an old woman. He went near the woman who was just like his mother, and in fact he could recognise her as his mother. She, however, did not talk to him. He was surprised to see his mother there and at her not talking to him. On reaching home he found his mother had died. Then he told the whole story to the villagers. Since then people believe that after death the *sab* of a person goes to *junpu* and lives in *aujum sia* village.

Morung Organization

The Wanchos have well organized *morung* system for men which, in the good old days, when the people were ardent headhunters, was the centre for training for the youths in the art of fighting, or for holding meetings and discussions with the villagers and also serving as guard houses to protect the village. Since the abolishing of head-hunting, these *morungs* are becoming centres of recreation and sleeping houses of the bachelors. In the old days each *morung* was equipped with all the available arms for fighting. The young boys of the village used to stay there in ever-ready position and guard the village from the attacks of the enemy.

Pa or *Pau* is the Wancho word for the *morung*. Each village has several *morungs*. It has been mentioned previously that the Wancho villages are divided into two main divisions. In many villages these divisions are again subdivided into a number of smaller zones consisting of a few houses. These smaller zones are called *jong* which is similar to the Assamese word *chuburi*. Each *jong* in the village has got a *morung*. Thus the number of *morung* in different villages varies from six to eighteen, depending on the size and the number of houses in the village. The chief's *morung* is called the *wangham-pa*, below which are two *morungs*, *panu* and *pass*. The *panu* is the biggest *morung* in a village. In the *wangham-pa*, important discussions and meetings are held whereas at the *panu*, all the heads collected during head-hunting days are kept. In fact the chief's *morung* is a sort of 'Darbar hall' (assembly house) of the chief. The *panu* is the main *morung* where community meetings and similar other gatherings are held. The different *morungs* are named after the name of the *jong*.

Each *morung* of the Wanchos is well decorated with various wood-carvings and heads of buffalloes and other animals killed on various occasions. But all the people give more attention to decorate the *wangham pa* and the *panu*.

There are small raised bamboo platforms constructed for sleeping purposes. In many *morungs* small compartments are made where the sleeping platforms are arranged in rows and stairs, one over the other just like a shelf. This can, in fact, be called sleeping shelf.

There are several fire places around which the youths and in many cases the old men also sit and gossip in groups. They exchange their thoughts and experiences, hear adventurous stories from the old people and learn different arts and crafts in the *morung*. On the rear side of the *morung* is a well screened place which serve the purpose a latrine.

In the *panu morungs*, the human skulls are kept in a particular place, some times arranged in rows on some bamboo shelf, and sometimes dumped in a heap.

During day time, the youth of the *morung* stay there in batches, to guard the *morung* as well as the village. If any accident occurs during the watch of a particular batch of young men, either in the village or in any of the houses under that *morung*, all the guards are severelly dealt with and heavily fined.

There is no age limit for entering the *morung*, but generally young children do not stay in the *morung*, though there is no restriction to their entering it. Women of any age, excepting children, are not allowed to enter the *morung*. Only on the day of construction of a *morung* can young girls and women enter for the purpose of distributing food at the feast arranged on this day.

The *morung* is constructed generally by the members of the particular *morung*, but in many villages members of one or two neighbouring *morungs*, also help in the work, if they are invited. The chief's *morung* and the *panu* are, however, constructed on a cooperative basis by the whole village. The *morung* construction is community work, and at the completion of the work, a big feast is held at night, followed by dancing and singing, sometimes throughout the whole night.

A big long-drum called *kham* is kept in each *morung* on one side of it. The size of the drum varies from 12 to 30 feet in length. Sometimes the drum is decorated with carvings of the human head, and motif's depicting various animals, snakes and birds. In the old days, when head-hunting was in full practice, the drum was mainly used to give the alarm to the village to be ready for a fight. Nowadays also, besides being used as a musical instrument, it is used on many other occasions as when some accident takes place in the village or some big animals have been killed or to invite people to any gathering and on festival days. There are different ways of playing the drum each indicating a different meaning. The villagers recognize the different sounds, and accordingly they can understand the purpose for which the drum has been played. Each sound has its particular name. For example, when it is played on festival days—the sound or variety of tones is called *kham chu u.* Similarly, there are others like *khou kham tap, tham sayu, khong khan tup,* etc., which indicate sudden outbreak of fire or accident, killing of animals like the tiger or the bear and approaching of an enemy, respectively. The *khong khan tap* is not played nowadays.

The chief of each big village has a long drum of his own, kept at his house. To bring this drum, a festival called *kham dak le* is performed by the chief at which the whole village and sometimes neighbouring villages too, join. It is one of the grand festivals of the Wanchos. Each chief, after he is declared as chief, has to perform this festival. The *kham dak le* festival is performed on the day when the drum is finally brought to the village, but smaller rituals are performed at every step of the making of the drum, right from the selection of the tree.

There is no separate *morung* for the young girls of the village. But according to the custom, the girls generally congregate in some houses, perferably those of old widows and sleep there. Young men come to meet the girls in these places, gossip with them, make exchanges of gifts and some times pass the night with the girls. The place where the girls sleep together is called *nausa jup ham,* which means young girls' sleeping house. Though there is not even a rudimentary *morung* for the girls in the true sense, yet the custom indicates the existence of a rudimentaiy *morung* organization, because the girls who sleep together, work on many occasions in a cooperative way. They collectively go out to bring fuel and supply to each house under the *morung.* They also celebrate their own festival for bringing firewood.

Boys of a particular *morung* also work collectively on a cooperative basis, helping widows in cultivation, in constructing houses and on occasions of need. They together clean village paths, water points and do such other works in the village.

There is a particular person called *wangsam-pa,* who is incharge of the *morung* and is responsible for all works required to be performed by the *morung.* He directs the youths to do different kinds of work, as conveyed to him by the villagers or the chief. It is his duty to see that the *morung* boys regularly bring firewood and water to the *morung*. He is the only man who can touch the skulls and other valuable articles kept in the *morung*, other people are not allowed to touch them normally. Thus the *wangsam-pa* is the acknowledged leader of the *morung*.

Though there is no system of the *morung* exogamy and the organization does not exert direct influence on marriage, yet the girls do not usually sleep with the boys of their own *morung* whom they consider as their own brothers.

Previously the *morung* were generally constructed near the entrances to the village to guard it against the attack of the enemy, but nowadays *morungs* are constructed within the village itself.

The *morungs* are also centres of arts and crafts. The boys while talking with their friends may make baskets, weave mats carve on wood and gather many useful experiences from experts and old persons. Thus the younger generations learn the different activities of life through association with others in the *morung* which are nuclei of the society and the basic and fundamental institutions of the people to guide the new generation for the well-being of all.

CHAPTER II

ROLE OF BUDDHISM IN THE KHAMTI SOCIETY

BHIKSHU KONDINYA

The Khamtis are a Buddhist tribe with Theravada (Khampti=*to-ni*) faith living mainly in the Lohit District of Arunachal Pradesh. They are also to be found in the Tirap District of Arunachal Pradesh as well as in the districts of Dibrugarh and Lakhimpur of Assam.

The Khamti priests (Khamti=*chaw-mun*) are men of great importance, and their influence is greater even than that of the chiefs. No undertaking is commenced without first consulting them. They also teach the Khamti youths who are compelled to attend school in the temples where they learn to read and write in his own language.

Every Khamti village has a *vihara* which they call *kyong* or *chang* and which is prominent among the houses of the village by its height and sometimes, Burma-like roof. Describing the ordinary house, Dalton writes: "The temple and the priests' quarters are also of timber and thatched, but the temples are elaborately carved, and greatness and taste are evinced in the arrangement of the internal fittings" (1960 : 10). On a high pedestal are placed a number of Buddha images. Pictures of scenes from the Jatakas and Vimanavathu and Petavatthu (Khamti=*phung-chen*) also adorn the inside of the *vihara*.

Almost all Buddhist temples are built in the eastern part

of the village, mostly situated on the bank of local rivers. One cannot think of a Khamti village without the *vihara* and *bhikkhu*. The *bhikkhu* helps in fulfilling the spiritual needs of the people and guides them in the religious festivities. He also controls the social life of the villages.

It is the responsibility of the villagers to provide food to the *bhikkhu* and *samaneras* who may also receive gifts of the barest necessities and accept invitations to meals.

Many of the ceremonies and festivals of the Buddhist cults, like those of other religions, are tied to the calender—the lunar calender in the case of Buddhism. This being so, they are cyclical: they are performed on predictable occasions, at fixed periods and periodic intervals. The Buddhist ceremonial cycle, however, as in case of other religions, consists not of one but of a series of cycles, each of a different duration. Specifically in Buddhism there are daily, weekly (and biweekly), monthly and annual cycles. Participation in them is voluntary; failure to participate is in no sense sinful or demeritorious.

For a pious Khamti, therefore, the first and last acts of the day consist of devotions performed in front of a small shrine found in almost every Khamti household, and always on the eastern side of the house above the head level which is considered auspicious. To place the shrine below one's head level is a grave insult to the deity while to place it above is the sign of respect. The shrine consists minimally of a vase (Khamti =*nang-le*) on a shelf which usually contains fresh flowers to honour the Buddha. In some cases a Buddha image or a polychrome picture of the Buddha (Khamti=*hang-phra*) is found on the shelf.

In addition to the floral offerings, candles are lit and/or food offerings are placed on the shelf as part of the daily devotions. Typically, these are brief, consisting only of the famous Buddhist common prayer, *okasa* (properly calls it) and the five precepts, *sin ho* (Pali=*panca-sila*). The former, named after its opening phrase—*okasa* ! *okasa* ! *okasa* !—has two parts. The first part is an expression of reverence:

> "I beg leave ! I beg leave ! I beg leave ! By act, by word and by thought, (Khamti, *kayakam, vacikam, manokam* and

Pali, *kayakamma, vacikamma, manokamma*). I raise my hands in reverence to the forehead and worship, honour, look at, and humbly pay homage to the three gems—the Buddha, the Dharma and the Sangha—one time, two times, three times, O Lord (Buddha)."

The second part is more strictly a prayer:

"By this act of worship may I be free from the four states of woe (rebirth in hell, as an animal, a ghost, a demon i.e. a monster with a huge head and slender body), the three scourges (war, epidemic, and famine), the eight wrong circumstances of birth (rebirth in hell, as an animal, a ghost, a brahma-deva, or a human remote from human habitation, with heretical views, incapable of understanding the Buddhist doctrines, or outside Buddhism), the five enemies (king, thief, fire, water, foe), the four deficiencies (tyrannical kings, wrong views about life after death, physically deformed, dull-witted), and the five misfortunes (loss of relations, wealth, health, proper belief, morality) and may I quickly attain *nirvana*, O Lord !"

In reciting the *tiratan* and *panca-silas* the devotee pledges to :

"Adoration to the Blessed one, Arahant, Supreme Buddha."[1]
"I take refuge in the Buddha,
I take refuge in the Dharma,
I take refuge in the Sangha"
Second time, third time, etc.[2]

(1) from taking life, (2) from stealing,
(3) from sexual immorality, (4) from lying and
(5) from drinking intoxicants.[3]

The recitation of the *gunas* (virtues) of Buddha, Dharma and Sangha :

I. "The exalted one, Arahant, supremely enlightened,

proficient in knowledge and in conduct, the blessed one, who understand the world, peerless tamer and driver of the hearts of man, the master, the Buddha for gods and men, exalted one"[4]

II. "Well proclaimed by the exalted one is the norm, relating to the present, immediate in its results, inviting all, giving guidance, appealing to each, to be understood by them that an understand"[5]

III. "Well practised is the exalted one's order of Disciples, practised in interity, in intellectual methods, in right lines of action—to wit the four pairs, the eight groups of persons—this is the exalted one's order of Disciples worthy of offerings, oblations, gifts, salutations, the world's peerless fields for merit."[6]

Especially the pious Khamti Buddhists—typically, the elderly—conclude their evening devotions by saying their beads. The beads are said while reciting *anicca, dukkha, anatta* or Buddha, Dharma, Sangha or some other such *prarthana* (Khamti =*sutang*), in minimal units of mine. Some say that these units represent the twenty-seven planets. Others, that the three represent the three gems (Buddha, Dharma, Sangha) (Khamti= *fala, tala* and *sangkha*), nine merely being its square. On *satang* (Pali=*uposatha*) days, some pious Khamti Buddhist wear rosary (Khamti=*paya-men*) on the wrist or around the neck. Sitting on the monastery or in the shrine compound, the faithful Khamtis move their lips (in silent litany) and click their beads even while listening to or participating in the day-long conversations.

1. Permission to worship the Buddha :
"May the incomparable Buddha, who possesses supermundane powers beyond all other creatures, whose wisdom is greater than that of the sun and the moon, who has six kinds of holos, thou, the discoverer of the four Noble Truths and the Noble-Eight-Fold path, permit us to worship thee."

Prayer—"As a result of worshipping the Buddha we pray

that we may enjoy *nirvana* and the higher abodes."

Offering of flowers, candles, and water :

The offering is accompanied by the following words :

"We possess name and form ; therefore, we offer water, flowers, and candles unto thee—water for cleaning and drink, flowers and candles for whatever thou mayest desire."

Recitation of the objects of worship :

"There is no object more venerable than the Buddha. We give endless veneration to the Buddha, the law, the order, our parents and our teachers, by worshipping these five objects may we attain *nirvana* (Khamti=*nik-pan* or *nipan*) and be free of all hindrances."[7]

The recitation is believed to protect the Kamti worshiper from all evil creatures.

The dissemination of love :

"May all creatures, all living things, all beings, all persons, all individuals, all males, all females, all aryans, all non-aryans, all gods, all mankind, all spirits be free from enmity, and from oppression. May they all live happily! May they all be free from trouble and adversity! May they all enjoy prosperity ! May they all help themselves through the *Kamma*." (Recited in Pali)

Water libation rite (Khamti=*ye-nam* or *likvoi*).

While water is poured drop by drop from a glass (Khamti =*nang-ley*) into a vase and thence onto the ground, the congregation recites:

"We have offered candles, flowers and alms-food to the Buddha, we have observed the Triple-Gem, Five Precepts (*panca-sila*) and have practised giving and meditation. May the Deva...bear witness to our meritorious action.

May I, as a result of this merit, attain *nirvana*, and may all intoxicants (*asavas*)[8] be destroyed."

This water libation ceremony, as the Khamtis call it, is an intrinsic part of all public ceremonies and public acts of meritorious giving.[9] As the formula indicates, it calls the merits of the worshippers to the attention of an earth goddess, known in Khamti as Nang-Vasunduri Devi, and in ancient India as Vasundhara. Although little known in ancient Indian Buddhism, this goddess is widely known among the Buddhists of Southern Asia. Indeed, it is myth associated with her that provides the Buddhist charter for the water-libation ritual, which is no doubt older than Buddhism in South-east Asia. This myth is known to every Khamti temple school student.[10] The Nang-Vasunduri's summary is as follows :

When Mara the Evil one arrives with his hosts to oust the Buddha from under the Bodhi-tree, he points to his army as validation for his claim. The Buddha, in turn, points to the Earth, as witness to his many meritorious deeds, to validate his claim. Thereupon, the earth appears in the guise of a woman, and to display the Buddha's accumulated merit she squeezes from her hair. The water that had been poured on the earth, commemorates his meritorious deeds. They are so numerous that the water creates a flood, causing Mara and his hosts to flee.

Like the Buddha, then the Khamti commemorate their meritorious acts by pouring water on the ground, calling upon Nang-Vasunduri to witness them. As in many rituals, however, the symbolism is over determined. The 'intoxicants' for whose destruction the worshipper prays while performing the libation, are also compared to floods which, if not controlled, wash one away (from the path).

Although to the Khamtis, the year is solar, the month is lunar, and four days in each lunar month—the full and new moons and the eighth days after each of these—are duty days, as the Pali, *uposatha*, (Khamti=*satang*), is variously translated. Canonically based, these devotional days were appropriated by Buddhism from the religion of pre-Buddhist India in which the days of the full and new moons were regarded as sacred. They were, appropriately, the sacrificial days, the day preceding the sacrifice was a sanctified day, the sacrificer observing abstinences of various kinds—from food, labour, sexual intercourse and so on. The day of sacrifice (the *upavasa*) became the Buddhist *uposatha*, known in Khamti as *satang* (originally from *sattaha*).

Typically, the Khamti *uposatha* observer arrives in the monastic compound early in the morning and spends most of the day in the rest house (Khamti=*chalap*). If he or she observes the day at a remote place he or she arrives on the *uposatha* eve, and the rest house is his lodging for the night. As in any Buddhist ceremony, his or her first act of piety and merit is to offer almsfood to the monks, after which he joins the other laymen assembled in the rest house for his own meal. Following their meal the faithful enter the monastery, where the important rituals take place. First in the presence of a monk, the Khamti laymen chant the common prayer. By repeating after the monk, they chant the Buddhist Confession; then the monk offers them the Eight-Precepts (*attha-sila*; Khamti=*sin-pet*)[11] and he chants the precepts, and they repeat them after him and vow to observe them.

The rest of the day thel aymen spend quietly in the monastery compound, the rest house, or the temple compound, where they observe the *uposatha* i.e. life in accordance with the precepts they have vowed to observe. Some spend the day in conversation with the monk (Khamti=*chow-mun*) who sometimes discusses various aspects of the Buddhist doctrine, or more rarely delivers a sermon. Others may spend the day saying their beads, intoning silent prayers, or reading one of the many popular Buddhist homilies. Mostly, however, they rest and talk.

For Buddhism the *uposatha* day is not primarily a day of rest and abstention from secular activity—although it is that as well—but chiefly an opportunity for the layman to live according to the rule of the Buddha; to observe the *uposatha* means to observe not only the five lay precepts (*panca-sila,* Khamti-*sin-ha*) which prescriptively govern the daily routine of the faithful, but also the additional five precepts. These include abstention from food, after midday, from worldly amusements (such as plays, sports, gambling, and so on), from the use of perfume and other ornaments, from the use of high beds for sleeping, and from bodily the handling of money. These five, unlike the first, are incumbent upon the layman for the duration of his or her vow only i.e. for the twenty-four-hour *uposatha.* They may, of course, observe them for a longer period—even for life—if they choose, and there are laymen who, unwilling or unable to observe the 227 rules of the monastic order, lead the semimonastic life entailed by perpetual observance of the ten, or if they live in world and must handle money—nine precepts.

Although *uposatha* observance is an important source of merit, as we have seen, on a regular basis it is not widespread. This is related not only to the situational factors discussed above but to certain motivational factors related to the very desire for merit as discussed above. This variable is demonstrated most easily when *uposatha* observance is related to age, sex, and economic status; the resultant correlations show that those who most desire merit are the most regular *uposatha* observers.

Not only do the elderly persons in the Khampti society observe *uposatha* much more frequently than the young, but females here observe it much more often than males. Women are more concerned with merit because, among other reasons, they aspire to rebirth as male. Their greater concern is shown not only in ritual, but also in meditational activity.

Paritta (Khamti=*pilik*) are the core of the Khamti crisis ritual, (this generalization holds for Thailand, Burma, Sri Lanka as well and most probably for all other Theravada traditions), constituting an indispensable element in the Khamti's personal security system. No crisis can be faced without them, and all crises can be dealt with by them. The changing of these spells (together with the public recitation of the precepts) constitutes one of the few ritual acts which the Buddhist monk performs on behalf of the laymen. For a monk to refuse an invitation from a layman to perform a *paritta* (Khamti=*pilik*) ceremony would be as inconceivable as for a doctor to refuse to attend a patient in his care.

Taught as part of the core curriculum of the village monastery-school, many *paritta* (Khamti=*pilik* or *tra* or *tala*) are known to the laymen. Memorized in Pali, however, a language which the students do not understand, they are only barely grasped. Their ritual use is nevertheless justified by some monks on the ground that even if the students knew Pali they would still not understand the texts because Buddhist concepts are too difficult for them to comprehend. Most of the *paritta* have been translated into Khamti, however, and it is in that language that they are recited in the lay devotions held in the village school.

With this general discription of their rituals we may now consider, in translation, a sample of the main *paritta*.

In studying these texts it will be noted, as has already been indicated, that although they are used for magical protection, a few of them have either the form or the content of a spell, and in any event their cognitive meaning almost or the content of a spell, never has any relation to the specific protective function they are intended to serve.

Metta Sutta (Khamti=*Metta Suk*)

The Khamtis believe that their recitation is especially efficacious for protection from evil spirits because as one monk put it, "for reciting the *metta sutta* all the Brahma and Samma Deva will love (and therefore protect) you", when recited in the house all the windows are opened, so that all creatures may have the love (*metta*) that is being expressed for them.[12]

Mangala Sutta (Khamti=*Mankala Suk*)

The *mangal sutta* is believed to have been composed by the Buddha when requested by a Deva to tell him what the "highest blessing" might be. The Buddha's answer, which comprises the text of this *sutta*, is probably the most famous of all *paritta* in Khamti. It is recited not only for protection from danger, but as a means to attain almost any problematic end—a good harvest, good grades in victory, in competition, and so on. Together with the *ratana* and *metta suttas*, it is always chanted by the monks after they are feasted by the faithful.[13]

Ratana Sutta (Khamti, *Latana Suk*)

The *ratana* (jewel) *paritta* was taught by the Buddha to his disciple, Ananda, when the *Row* asked him to rid their city (Vesali) of the many calamities that had been brought upon it by evil spirits. The Buddha instructed Ananda to recite the jewel *sutta*, a hymn in praise of the three Gems, while walking round the city and sprinkling water from the Buddha's bowl.

When Ananda followed his instructions the evil spirits fled, and the people recovered from the famine, flood and other difficulties that had befallen them. The *ratana sutta* is a very long *sutta.* This sutta is recited in any situation of danger, but especially for those that are supernaturally caused.[14]

Mora Paritta.

The *mora* (peacock) *paritta* is taken from the Mora-Jataka. According to the story, a monk informed the Buddha that he had broken his vow of chastity because he had seen a woman dressed in 'magnificent attire'. Sympathetic, the Buddha said that even the holiest of men are tempted by and succumb to the seductive attraction of a woman. Even he, as a Golden Peacock, had so succumbed to as the following tale reveals. As a Golden Peacock (incarnated Buddha) he used to pray, morning and evening, to the sun and the various other Buddhas for the safety and protection of all creatures including himself. When at the command of six successive kings of Banaras (Varanasi), a hunter attempted to trap the peacock, he was unsuccessful because the peacock was protected by these spells. Finally, having observed the peacock's habits, the hunter brought a peahen with him, and before the peacock had recited his morning spell the hunter had her utter her cry. On hearing the cry, desire was awakened in the peacock, forgetting to recite his spell, he went toward the peahen and was captured by the hunter. The spells recited by the peacock comprise the contemporary *mora paritta*:

"There he rises, king all seeing,
Making all things bright with thy golden light.
Keep me safe, I pray,
Through the coming day.
All saints, the righteous, wise in holy love,
These do I honour, and their aid implore;
All honour to the wise, to wisdom honour be,
To freedom and to all that freedom has made free."[15]

Angulimala-Paritta (Khamti, *Ankulimala-Suk*)

The *angulimala* (garland of fingers) *paritta* is named after an infamous robber and killer, who took his name from the fact that he wore a garland comprised of the fingers of whom he had murdered. Although the Buddha had been warned that he would pass through the country where Angulimala lived at the risk of his life, he deliberately ignored this warning. Seeing the Buddha, Angulimala attempted to seize him, but (the Buddha having performed a miracle) was unable to catch Him even when walking in slow motion. Recognizing thereby the greatness of the Buddha, Angulimala became a convert; and when the Buddha ordained him a monk, he became His attendant. One day Angulimala went to Sravasti to collect his alms, and seeing a woman in difficult labour he became disconcerted. Telling the Buddha of his distress, the latter said he should return to the woman and tell her (presumably as a magical means for saving her life) that he had never intentionally taken a life and that "by truth may there be well-being for you, well-being for the unborn child". Angulimala replied that he could not say this to her since he would be telling a lie. The Buddha said that he should then go to her and say instead that from the time he had become a monk he had never intentionally taken a life, and that "by this truth may there be...etc." He did so, and the lives of woman and child were saved by this *paritta*.[16]

There are other, even more famous *paritta* in Theravada Buddhist societies, which, however, (although consisting of canonical *sutta*) are not based on historical or legendary events.

The *paritta* are spells consisting of chapters or section of chapters taken from various books of the canon mostly from the *sutta*, which are chanted for protection against danger. Although all the *sutta* which are used as *paritta*, were composed for that purpose, at least one of them was (allegedly) composed as a spell by the Buddha himself, and with only two exceptions, all the other *sutta* that comprise the classical collection (Pali=*mahaparitta*) must have been used as spells very early in the history of Theravada Buddhism.

Although the ornate and complex ritual system of Buddhism has often been remarked upon, Theravada Khamti ritual has been less frequently described. Indeed, for those who conceive of the later form of Buddhism as a precursor of modern humanism (or even of analytic philosophy !), its rich ritual system comes rather as a shock, or is viewed as a degeneration from a pristine state of ritual purity.

Either attitude is consistent with the major premises of nibbanic Buddhism, viz., the Buddhism is a salvation religion; since here is no saviour (the Buddha is dead), salvation must be attained by man's unaided efforts; and these efforts consist of three types of action : charity (*dana*), morality (*sila*) and meditation (*bhavana*).

These three concepts—instrumental, commemorative and expressive ritual—are the cultural dimensions of rituals, that is, the goal or purpose of ritual action. Although religions differ in the relative weight, there is probably no religion which does no include all these three.

(I) The commemorative ritual is performed in remembrance or in celebration of some event, historical or mythological, second in the annals of the religious tradition. Many Buddhist rituals, for example, commemorate on events in the life of the Buddha.

(II) The expressive ritual serves as a vehicle for manifesting emotions, attitudes and sentiments felt toward the religious sacrament. In Buddhism, for example, the Buddha, the Dhamma and the Sangha are objects of intense reverence, and the performance of many Buddhist rituals is a means for expressing veneration, homage, and devotion to these three jewels (*tiratana*), as they are called in Buddhism.

(III) The instrumental ritual, performed to achieve some goal or end, is rather more complicated. The end may be some extrinsic goal—physical (health, beauty and so on), social (wealth, honour, fame, power and so on), natural (rainfall, plentiful crops and so on)—which could be attained either in the present life or not until after death. In Buddhism, future goals are achieved by meritorious action, while present goals are attained by a combination of meritorious and ritual actions. Sometimes, however, the end to be achieved by instrumental ritual is an intrinsic goal i.e. a spiritual or psychological change in the self.

Although even instrumental ritual is sanctioned by scripture, the rituals of nibbanic Khamti Buddhism are essentially expressive and commemorative in character. Offering to the Buddha, His relics and His symbols, *stupa* (Khamti=*kangmu* or *bo*-tree or images) are certainly encouraged, but these offerings (flowers, incense, water, food) can in no way affect one's hope for *nibbana.* They are expressions of *vandana* (veneration) and of *puja* (honour) to Him who has discovered the way. Prayer, if that term may be used to designate a simple expressive statement, consists of the following confession of faith, the *buddham sarnam gacchami,* a confession which is ancient as scripture itself:

> I take refuse in the Buddha
> I take refuse in the Dhamma,
> I take refuse in the Sangha.
> For the second time, I take refuse in the Buddha (etc.)
> For the third time, I take refuse in the Buddha (etc.)

This confession of faith is the one indispensable ritual of nibbanic Buddhism.

This ritualistic attitude of nibbanic Buddhism is represented in Khamti (in Arunachal and Assam) by a small minority. Worship of the Buddha's relics, at least, is widely practised not only a form of homage to the Buddha but as a means for a better rebirth and contrary to some interpreters of Theravada Khamti Buddhism this practice is explicitly legitimized by scripture. The Suttapitaka especially abounds in passages referring to the efficacy of worshipping the Buddha, the *stupa, bo*-tree and the relics of the Buddha. Thus whereas in the Dhammapada *puja* refers to an attitude of reverence, in these later works it means an instrumental act producing future fruits.

The Buddhist rituals include some form of offering. Daily devotions before the Buddha image, prayers at the *stupa* and so on, almost invariably include the offering of lighted candles, flowers, water and food.

For seven of the fifteen, the motive is soteriological—to obtain *nibbana,* to achieve a better rebirth, to avoid hell, to acquire merit (for their next birth). Some of them mention the conventionally ascribed soteriological benefits of the offerings: flowers are a means to health and beauty; water is a means to a "cool" mind—peaceful and free from worry; food assures adequate nourishment; the lighted candles are a means to enlightenment and glory. Those Khamtis who hope for rebirth in a higher abode, admit that these offerings in themselves are not sufficient to guarantee the outcome; still, their importance, they say, cannot be minimized. To make offerings is the duty of a Buddhist, because it is a Buddhist custom. Whatever their conception of this ritual may be, when the Khamti devotees make their offering, they recite a standard prayer.

> "I offer this good food in honour of the lord of the world;
> May I, by this meritorious act, avoid the pains of hunger.
> I offer this good water...the torture of burning.
> I offer this good light...a great darkness.
> I offer these fragrant flowers... the smell of raw flesh."

Although a Khamti performs the act of worship by means of prostration, other forms of motor behaviour are also required to be performed by him in the presence of Buddhist *sacra*. To remove shoes and sandals at the entrance to the monastery compound is a must for him. In the presence of the Buddha image or a monk a Khamti either sits or rests on his haunches so that his head does not remain above the head of the image or the monk. Under no circumstances may his feet be pointed in the direction of any sacred object; the legs are always turned backward, away from it. When reciting or listening to the *dhammadesana* (discourses), his hands and palms touching each other, are held to the forehead in the case of men and to the chest in the case of women. The completion of the *dhammadesana*, like its inception, is marked by physical prostration performed three times.

SOME RELIGIOUS FESTIVALS

1. *Samkyen Festival*

There are several festivals in the Khamti society round the year. The *samkyn* (origin, *samkranti* or New Year) festival is another great occasion for the Khamtis. It comes at the juncture of the months of *Caitra* and *Vaisakha*. The village youths make preparation for the festival from some fifteen days ahead of it by rehearsing the songs of the festival (*lik-samkyen*) and setting up a temporary temple for images (*kyang-fra*) with an indigenous mechanism for spraying water around from a boat (*hang-lin*). The Buddhas of the *vihara* (*chang*) are taken out by the priests and kept for bathing in the *kyang-fra*. In the first morning of the festival the priests recite the *metta sutta, mangala sutta* and other traditional Pali *gathas*, and young men and women of the village sing the Holy books. The priests are given a wash, and the pouring of water on the Buddhas in the *kyang-fra* goes on as the boys and girls throw water and colour and mud at each other. In the evening the villagers come to the *chang* and light innumerable lamps. On the following day the washing of the Buddha (*san-fra*) continues, and there are much of *khow-sam-dana* (*annadana*) and *magya-dana* (*puppha-dana*). At the end of all this the priests give the last wash to the images and put them back in the *vihara*. There are much decoration, feasting and prayers. All people take *tisarana* and *panca sila* and also listen three or sometimes four days. This celebration is a mixture of religious piety and boisterous fun.

2. *Buddha Purnima* (*Paya Puthikham*)

The Khamtis commemorate the full moon of May (*paya-puthikham*) as the day on which all Buddhas attain enlightenmented and on which the present Buddha, Gautama, was born, attain enlightenment, and died. In addition to the central ritual of any *uposatha*, the observance of the precepts—they mark day by watering the *bo*-tree, the tree under which enlightenment bestowed to the Buddha.

3. *Khauwa* or *Vassavasa*

To the Khamtis the three-month period from the full moon of July to the full moon of October is called the Buddhist lent (Pali=*vassavasa* and Khamti=*khau-wa*). In addition to its monastic importance the Khamti monks may not travel for that period—it is a solemn season for laymen; marriages cannot be performed, plays and other forms of public entertainment are forbidden and pious Buddhists attempt to observe the *uposatha* as frequently as possible during this time.

4. *Kathina Civara Festival*

After three months of *vassavasa*, the Khamtis remain busy with the celebration of *kathina* ceremonies (*paya-kathing*) in the month of November. Scripturally based this ceremony consists of the public offering of yellow robes to the monks. Needless to say, these and all other public offerings are accompanied by a large feast for the monks. Although individual monks are supplied with robes throughout the year by the faithful, those offered during this season, fall into a special cetegory.

Although originally conceived as a robe offering ceremony exclusively, this robe ceremony in the Khamti society has become an occasion for providing the monks with all their needs and wants, such as canned food, medicines, umbrellas, begging bowls, toiletries, tobacco, blankets, money, etc. Rather than being offered in the usual manner in the begging bowls or on trays, these are hung from, or placed under an artificial 'tree'. In Pali text it is known *Kalpataru* (Khamti=*tunputesa*). This 'wishing tree' as it is called, is reminiscent of the trees found in the mythical southern island which, according to Buddhist cosmology, supply its inhabitants with all their wants merely for the plucking.

Besides the above festivals, the Khamtis also celebrate a number of other Buddhist festivals, time to time in their villages. These are as follows:

1. Kham chow-san (Pali, *Pabajja*)
2. Kham chow-mun (Pali, *Upasampada*)
3. Pung vot (Pali, *Parivasa*)
4. Paya-leng (*Parinibbana* ceremony)
5. Nohwa (*Pabarana* ceremony)
6. Tun-putesa (*Kalpataru* ceremony)
7. Lu-lik (Book offering ceremony)
8. Lu-fra (Buddha offering ceremony)
9. Lu-chang (Temple offering ceremony)
10. Mai-ko-sum-fai (*Magha-sankranti* festival)

FOOTNOTES

1. *Namo tassa bhagavato arahato sammasambuddhassa.*
2. *Buddham Saranam Gacchami*
   Dhammam Saranam Gacchami
   Sangham SaranamGacchami
   Dutiyampi Buddham Saranam Gacchami...
   Tatiyampi Buddham Saranam Gacchami...
3. (*1*) *Panatipata veramani sikkhapadam samadiyami*
   (*2*) *Adinnadana veramani sikkhapadam samadiyami*
   (*3*) *Kamesu micchacara veramani sikkhapadam samadiyami*
   (*4*) *Musavada veramani sikkhapadam samadiyami*
   (*5*) *Surameraya majjapamadatthana veramani sikkhapadam samadiyami*
4. *Itipiso Bhagava araham sammasambuddho vijjacaranasampanno sugato lokavidu anuttaro purisadammasarathi sattha devamanussanam Buddho Bhagavati*
5. *Swakkhato Bhagavata dhammo Sanditthiko akaliki ehipassiko opanayiki paccattam veditabbo vinnuhiti*
6. *Supatipanno bhagavato savakasangho ujupatipanno bhagavato savakasangho, nayapatipanno bhagavato savakasangho. samicipatipanno bhagavato savakasangho, vadi-dam cattari purisayugani atthapurisapuggala esa bhagavato savakasangho, ahuneyyo pahuneyyo dakkhineyyo, anjalikaraniyo anuttaram punnakhettam lokassa ti.*

7. Some *sutta* recited in Pali and some in Khamti known as *sutang* in the Khamti language.

8. Asavas are four in number—*Kamasava, Bhavasava, Ditthasava*, and *Avijjasava.*

9. It is found most probably in all Theravada traditions.

10. This myth is found in the Khamti 'Tra' although it is recorded in Thailand and Combodia in a Pali text. At Chowkham Raja-vihara Nang Vasundari image was found by the writer. This image is very attractive. In Arunachal or Assam the writer could not see this type of Nang Vasundari image People worship this image.

About this Rev. Silavamsa explained to me, when I was at Chowdham.

11. (*1*) *Panatipata veramani sikkhapadam samadiyami*
    (*2*) *Adinnadana veramani sikkhapadam samadiyami*
    (*3*) *Abrahmacariya veramani sikkhapadam samadiyami*
    (*4*) *Musavada veramani sikkhapadam samadiyami*
    (*5*) *Surameraya majjapamadatthana veramani sikkhapadam samadiyami*
    (*6*) *Vikalabhojana veramani sikkhapadam samadiyami*
    (*7*) *Nacca-gita-vadita-visuka-dassana-mala-gandha-vilepana-*

dharana-mandana vibhusanatthana veramani sikkhapadam samadiyami

(*8*) *Uccasayana-mahasayana veramani sikkhapadam samadiyami*

12. This *sutta* is found in '*Khuddakapatha*' N.D.P. Ed. pp. 11-12.

13. This *sutta* is also found in the '*Khuddakapatha*'. In Khamti, a book containing explanation of the '*Mangala-sutta's* stories is also available and is known as 'Lik-mankala-suk'.

14. The text of this *sutta* is also found in the *Khuddakapatha* and N.D.P. Ed., pp. 6-7-8-9.

15. *Mora-Jataka*, Vol. 2.23.

16. The middle length sayings (*Majjhima nikaya*), (Vol. II, Ch. 86). *Mora* and *Angulimala paritta* are recited by lay devotees also.

REFERENCE

Dalton, Edward T., 1960, (Ori. 1872), *Descriptive Ethnology of Bengal* Indian Studies: Past and Present, Calcutta.

CHAPTER III

AVOIDANCE OF DIRECT EXCHANGE OF BRIDE AMONG TWO TRIBES OF ARUNACHAL PRADESH[1]

JAYANTA SARKAR

The avoidance of direct exchange of bride between certain lineages in the North-Eastern part of this country was first observed by late T.C. Das as early in 1936 (Das 1945) among the Purum of Manipur. There are at least four other tribes namely the Khamti, the Kaman Mishmi, the Singpho and the Tangsa of Arunachal Pradesh who have similar custom.

The Khamtis are mainly concentrated on the bank of the Tengapani (Namsoom) river of Lohit district while the Kaman Mishmis are inhabiting the high hills in the northern part of this district. The main concentration of the Tangsa population is in northern part of Tirap district and the Singphos are distributed both in Tirap and Lohit districts. A few of them have also settled down in Dibrugarh district of Assam.

The 1971 census records the population of the Khamti, the Kaman Mishmi, the Tangsa and the Singpho as 4,078, 8,233, 6,941 and 1,567 respectively. The Khamtis are the followers of Buddhism which a large number of the Singphos have also adopted. The other two tribes are animist.

The present exercise is an attempt to give an account of the avoidance of the direct exchange of bride among the Khamti and the Kaman Mishmi and to examine how the kinship terms reflect this system.

All these four societies are divided in a number of exogamous clans. Though the clans play important role in regulating marriages, the lineages are considered more important because they impose restriction on exchange of bride between two lineages. Before giving a girl's marriage it is first ascertained whether the groom's lineage is eligible to take a girl as wife from the girl's lineage. It is customary for a boy of these tribes to marry his mother's brother's daughter who is the first preferential mate for him. The other type of cross-cousin marriage i.e., with the father's sister's daughter is strictly tabooed. It is an obligation for a marriageable boy's mother to see that her brother's daughter is brought to her family as wife of her son or a person of equal position. The mother's brother gets offended if his sister's son refuses to marry his daughter.

Besides the mother's own brother's daughter they also marry the girls whom they consider at par with the mother's brother's daughter. Members of a specific lineage of the Khamti call those of their maternal uncle's lineage, real or classificatory, as *lungta*. A marriage with a girl of *lungta*, real or classificatory is considered as a marriage with the mother's brother's daughter. Among the Kaman Mishmis the mother's brother's lineage and also the lineages where from a girl can be brought as wife, are categorised as *yook* while the Tangsas bring a girl as wife from the mother's lineages, real or classificatory, which they classify as *rifan*. Das has mentioned about a similar type of marriage among the Purum. He says, 'the mother's brother's daughter is the most suitable bride for a man, and after her, any girl from the mother's brother's sib may serve the purpose'. (1945 : 153).

Though mother's brother's daughter is a preferential wife, there is no specific Khamti kinship term of address for her or for the girls of her category to separate them from the girls who are to be avoided for taking as wife. One's own elder sister, MoBrDa, MoSiDa, FaBrDa, FaSiDa, elder than ego, are addressed by the same term and the younger sister, MoBrDa, FaBrDa, FoSiDa, younger than ego, are similarly referred to by a single term. However, terms of reference for these relatives are different to indicate the exact consanguineal and affinal relations. Among the Kaman Mishmis both terms of address and reference

FIGURE - I

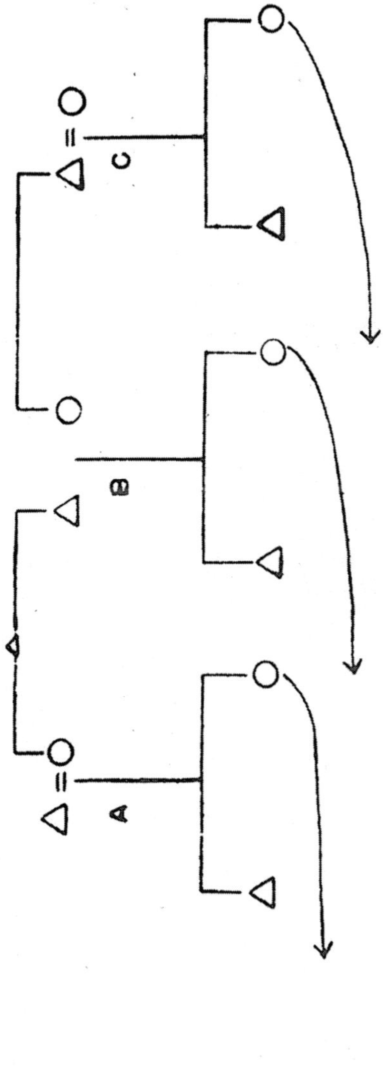

for younger sister, MoSiDa, FaBrDa, FaSiDa, younger and elder than ego, are same (*chamai*) but the MoBrDa is referred to by prefixing *yook* to *chamai* indicating her separate social position than ego's other sisters. She is the potential wife of the ego.

In the marriage system of the Khamti and the Kaman Mishmi, members belonging to ego's one ascending and one descending generations generally form a unit for either taking or giving wife to another such unit. One such unit where a girl from another unit has come as wife, normally is not expected to give a girl as wife to the wife-taker unit. This has been illustrated in Figure—1.

Here unit A has taken wife from unit B. So at least for three generations unit B's consanguineal relatives are not expected to take a wife from unit A. Similarly when unit C gives wife to unit B, its members avoid taking any one as wife from unit B. Like the Purums the Kaman Mishmi and the Khamti clans are not subdivided into named lineages, but each lineage is tied to some other lineages for the purpose of marriage. In case of the Khamti, the lineage from where a man and his family members can take wife is known as *lungta.* To a man the lineages from where his father, his own brothers, himself or his own sons can take wife, are categorised as *lungta,* whereas to a woman's consanguineal relatives, the members of her husband's one ascending and one descending generations are referred to as *khuithaw* indicating a lineage from where husbands can be taken. This is also reflected in their kinship terms, where the FaSiHu, SiHu and DaHu are refererd to as *khui* prefixing *po, nong* and *luk* as the indicators of generation. Though FaFaSiHu is also a wife-taker from ego's lineage, he is not categorised as a man of *khui* group by the ego as the avoidance of direct exchange of bride is observed within one ascending and one descending generations of the ego. To a man his MoBr, WiBr and SoWiBr are referred to by using the term *jao* categorising their families as non-recipient of girl as wife from the ego's lineage.

Kinship terms for wife-receiver and wife donor lineage.

	Relations	*Khamti*	*Kaman Mishmi*
Wife receiver from ego's lineage	FaSiHu	Po *Khui* Chao	*Komou*
	SiHu	Nong *Khui*	*Komou*
	DaHu	Luk *Khui*	*Komou*
Wife donor to the ego's lineage	MoBr	*Jao* Chao	*Yook*
	WiBr	*Jao* Chee Man	*Nang*
	SoWiBr	*Jao* Noi	?

From the above listed kin terms of the Khamti one can easily group certain categories of the kins like the *khui* and *jao* to whom females can be given and from whom females can also be obtained as wife. The kinship terms of the Kaman Mishmi also have a single term *Kamou.* FaSiHu, SiHu, DaHu and BrDaHu are all referred to as *kamou.* The term *kamou* indicates a non-consanguineal relative and his family where a girl has been given as wife and from whom no female can be taken as wife. Since FaSiSo can also take a girl from the ego's family as wife they are referred to as *kamou* classifying them as potential wife-taker. But like the Khamti, for MoBr, WiBr and DaHu there is no common term to indicate their families from whom wife has been taken. Though the term *yook* is referred to one's mother's brother and his descending generations, it always means the family which is supposed to provide a girl as wife to the ego's family. The customary law of the Kaman Mishmi prohibits marriage of a person with his father's sister's daughter and permits marriage with mother's brother's daughter. This automatically imposes restriction on the direct exchange of bride between certain families at least for three generations, if not more. The kinship term for FaSiDa, FaBrDa, Si and MoSiDa is *chamai* classifying them as non-marriageable but MoBrDa is referred to as *yook chamai* indicating that the girl is not as par with other sisters.

Though the direct exchange of bride between two units is tabooed, deviation from such norm is not totally absent among the Khamti. In a village near Chowkham out of 75 married men only two had direct exchange of bride. In one case a man of a lineage of Namsoom clan married to a girl of a lineage of Manjee clan which is supposed to be a wife-taker lineage from the former's lineage. Both the bride and the bridegroom had non-traditional education, and the villagers did not take it as violation of rule as within two ascending generations of the boy no girl was given to his lineage. In another case a man of a lineage of Namsoom clan married to a girl of a lineage of Manpoong clan of Manmow village. As per the norm the same lineage of Namsoom clan cannot give a girl to that particular lineage of Manpoong clan at least for three generations. But the girl's younger brother has married to his sister's husband's elder brother's elder daughter. This was also not taken as an offence; and the couple and their children are enjoying the same socio-religious rights as others. Needham in his analysis of the Purum society has dealt with such problems of departure from the norm. He says, 'For one person or another, difficulty arises in marrying a woman of the eligible category. Must there then be departure from the norm ?' Will a man have to marry a woman of the category of 'tu' ? 'Tu' is the category of wife-taker. The answer to judge by the common practice in other such societies and particularly by a report from the related Chaute, is that he will not. What typically happens is that a woman is removed from a marriageable one. Her genealogical connection e.g., as father's sister's daughter is entirely disregarded and she is ritually assigned to the appropriate category in the classification which in fact orders social life'. (1960 : 87) In the two marriages of direct exchange mentioned above no such removal of girl from her 'non-marriageable' category was done. They were accepted and recognised as exceptional cases. The villagers, however, feel that the offsprings of such marriages face difficulties in getting wives from the recognised wife-giver unit. They are to go to find out a new unit for obtaining wife. Among the members of a lineage of Manpoong clan living at Manmow it has been observed that in one generation girls have been given to Namsoom clan of different lineage distributed at Sengsap, Chowkham and Momong villages. They have also taken wife of clan of different lineages distributed at Dikrong, Momong and Chowkham. Such exchange of bride between two clans have also been found in a Kaman Mishmi village where the Kri clan has taken both the wives and husbands from three clans, namely, Yiun, Ngaton and Pull. These clearly indicate that the clan as such has no role to play in controlling wife-giving or wife-taking. The families and the lineages actually avoid taking wife from another family or lineage whom it has already given wife during last three generations.

Acknowledgement

I am grateful to the Director, Anthropological Survey of India for extending all facilities for undertaking field works in Lohit and Tirap districts of Arunachal Pradesh.

REFERENCES

Chari, B.R.	1971	*Census of India*, Paper 1 of 1975. Series 1, *Scheduled Castes and Scheduled Tribes*, Table C-VIII, Part A and B.
Das, T.C.	1945	*The Purums: An old Kuki Tribe of Manipur*. University of Calcutta, Calcutta.
Needham, Rodney	1962	*Structure and Sentiment: A Test case in Social Anthropology*, University of Chicago Press.
Sarkar, J.K.	1975	Society and Culture in Three Villages of Arunachal Pradesh (Unpublished report).
	1977	A note on avoidance of direct exchange of bride among the Khamtis of Arunachal Pradesh, *Man in India*, Vol. 57, No. 3.

CHAPTER IV

MARKET, RECIPROCITY AND SYMBOLISM AT RUPA—A SHERDUKPEN VILLAGE IN ARUNACHAL

B. K. ROY BURMAN

The village Rupa is situated in the south-west of Bomdila, the headquarters of Kameng district of Arunachal. It is situated at a height of about 4,700 feet above the mean sea-level.

In 1964 when the study was conducted Rupa had a nuclear settlement known by the same name. Besides, the people of Rupa claimed eight hamlets (Thaungreo, Gnau, Gomiam, Mukhuthing, Chellen, Gecham, Brokpoblang, and Smugchi) as their satellites. These hamlets are at different distances from the main core, the further one being 16 km away. The administration, however, does not recognise all the eight hamlets as part of Rupa. In the sixties only the last four were considered to be part of the village organisation of Rupa.

There are also several other ways in which Rupa means different things to different people. Previously Jigaon, situated not far off from the main residential cluster of Rupa, was considered to be a part of the village. But the people of Jigaon did not like to remain clubbed with Rupa, under the same administrative polity at the village level. This unwillingness was more related to the social distance between the people of Rupa and Jigaon, than to the physical distance between these two places.

Though to the outsiders, the people of Jigaon are also the

Sherdukpens, to the Sherdukpens of Rupa and other villages of the tribe, they are the Sherdukpens of lesser shade; they are more commonly known as the Yanlaks. They are supposed to be persons of the Bhotia origin, who were adept in smithy, and were settled by the Sherdukpens of Rupa within their territory a few generations ago. They were required to carry out smithy work and also to render certain ceremonial services during the seasonal migration of the Sherdukpens to the foothills. The Yanlaks were thus a satellite community and the land occupied by them was a sub-village. In the fifties, with the extension of effective administration in this part of the country, a social upheaval took place. The government recognised Rupa as a separate village as early as that time, and the Sherdukpens of Jigaon, who were second class Sherdukpens as it were, became equal along with other Sherdukpens. But it appears that the newly gained equality tended to push the community in two opposite directions: first to become full-fledged Sherdukpens and second to become full-fledged non-Sherdukpen. At present there is a tendency among some in Jigaon to claim the Yanlak to be a distinct community. But Jigaon has not been able to cut off its umbilical cord altogether. Even now, on certain ceremonial occasions of the tribe, Jigaon is not recognised as a separate entity. It is dealt with as a part of Rupa social complex.

Thus Rupa is one in many. This is at the same time a source of flexibility as well of tension, in the social and political relations of the villagers with the outside and also among themselves.

The social world of Rupa has several other complex features. Shinchang, the village of the Khawas, stands on a separate footing from Jigaon. Until recently the Khawas of Shinchang, were subjugated to the Sherdukpens of Rupa. They were required to pay an annual tribute in service or in kind, but their distinct civic identity was not merged. They had a separate village authority of their own. Hence when with the extension of effective administration, the Khawas were exempted from the payment of annual tribute, Rupa did not feel that its identity was being mutilated. The Sherdukpens knew that any claim that they might have over the Khawas belonged to the political order and not the normal order.

More complex, however, was the relationship of the Sherdukpens with the Kacharis of the plan. In the past, the Sherdukpens used to collect tribute from the Kacharis living in between the Dhansiri and the Belsiri rivers. It does not appear that the Sherdukpens considered the Kacharis as their subject or the land of the Kacharis as their subjugated territory. The tribute that they used to get from the Kacharis, has been described by many as blackmail money. Perhaps it was so. But this was commuted into annual stipend during the later phase of the Ahom rule; and the same system continued during the British rule. It continues till now. It is, however, significant that even after the commutation of the so-called quit money into stipend or *posa*, the Kacharis have continued to give some sort of tribute in kind. But why?

It appears that there were two elements in the payments made by the Kacharis to the Sherdukpens. First was the military consideration, second was the consideration of economic and political relations. At the tribal level, the Sherdukpens, because of the strategic location of their habitat, were in a position to carry on raids on the Kachari territory, cause devastation and then turn to their mountain retreat. But it is obvious that, neither by number nor by superiority of arms, they were in a position to continuously rule the Kacharis. Therefore it was only quit money they could impose on the Kacharis. But then there were also other matters of mutual interest. The Sherdukpens required supply of food grains, metallic wares and cotton textiles from the plains; on the other hand they had sheep and goat, woollen goods, musk, borax and other jungle products to offer. In this circulation of commodities, there were two alternatives. After coming all the way to the foothill, the Sherdukpens could as well sell all their wares in the nearby markets in the plains of Assam. But till recently, the bulk of the wares do not appear to have been transacted in this manner. Most of the transactions used to be carried on through the Kacharis. Thus, the Kacharis served as the middlemen between the Sherdukpens and the agriculturist population of the plains of Assam. This role of middlemen was sanctified through a number of rituals at the place of the Sherdukpens and the Kacharis both.

The rituals symbolised the principle of circulation, which appears to be basic to the social structure, not only of the Sherdukpens, but also of most of the hill tribes of Arunachal Pradesh. The tributes paid by the Kachari households to the Sherdukpen households were indicators of another principle, which was in a nebulous state, in the context of primitive political and economic organisation; the principle of earning profit during the course of commodity transaction. But before discussing the same, it is proposed to examine the symbolism of circulation in some detail.

For ages, the most important source of livelihood of the tribal communities of the region has been shifting cultivation. It used to be supplemented by collection of jungle products. There were also some household crafts at various levels of technology, but in most cases the technology was low. The population living in the area was, therefore, perpetually haunted by the spectre of starvation. But at the same time, the diversity of the terrain, the differences in the proximity of the more or less stable food producing region of the plains of Assam in the south, and the fairly sophisticated handicraft producing centres of Tibet and Bhutan in the north and the west, created conditions where reciprocity was an imperative need for survival. It was this principle of reciprocity, which promoted circulation. It was symbolised in two forms; one in the form of ceremonial friendship, the other in the form of circulation of sacred bells and sacred plates made of brass, which did not have any use value. The bells and the plates were transferred from family to family as bride wealth. Again, these were returned to the family concerned, through the institution of marriage with the father's daughter. These were also bartered for minimum and other valuables. The possession of these conferred status to the household, as a recognition for the service rendered to the community, by upholding the principle of circulation.

The ethos of circulation is even expressed in the lamentation of the father when the daughter takes leave after marriage. He tells her that it is part of the principle of circulation that he should give her away, even though it rends his heart.

Circulation on the basis of reciprocity presupposes a world view, where accommodation and compromise constitute basic organising principles in human relationship. This is symbolised in their myth, where the demon who had abducted the princess, was forgiven as soon as he apologised to her spouse, whose hire was roused. He was even befriended and the princess, her spouse and the demon danced together.

A question arises as to how Rupa could become the place for exchange in cash, if reciprocity was the basic principle, not only for circulation of articles, but also for organising the human relations.

To examine this question, one is to consider what are the antimonies of circulation and reciprocity respectively.

The antimony of circulation is extortion and ıhat of recıprocity is market.

Both the antimonies have been symbolically represented among the Sherdukpens. At Rupa they have built up a *chhorten* in honour of a gaonburah, who oppressed them and extorted goods and services for years, and asked for their forgiveness in his deathbed. This narration brings out two processes, first, the symbolic enunciation of the self-destroying character of extortion and second, reiteration of the principle of reciprocity, even to the extent of deifying a repentant oppressor. In fact, one may wonder, whether it is really the ex-oppressor who is deified or whether it is the principle of reciprocity or the fact ot his repentance which is extolled. Perhaps, the collective act here communicate different things to different persons; or even to the same persons in different contexts.

In any case, this narration and the *chhorten* associated with it, also bring out the fact that extortion as a method of control of services and goods, is within the mental focus of the community, though its limited validity is also recognised.

In fact, the Sherdukpens as well as other tribes of Arunachal Pradesh practised extortion quite considerably, both in their internal social relationships as well as in their external relationships. But at the same time, they did not allow the acts of extortion to supersede the overall process of circulation through reciprocity. May be sometimes, extortion was a short term *handmaid* of reciprocity, but not its substitute. One can even visualise situations when the social organisation of reciprocity would be out of gear and extortion would be required to restore the balances. Such situations would be caused by failure of crops in the plains, or in the hills; dynastic changes or shifts in the centres of power in the plains or in Tibet or Bhutan; introduction of improved technology in any sector of production; expansion of transport and communication and so on. But unmitigated extortion could not be a long term process; in that case the whole political structure of the hills would have required a complete reorganisation and the loosely connected tribal entities would have been wedded into a state structure. But there were two constraints to this; first the nature of the terrain and the low level of technology did not provide the economic base for sustaining the state structure; second it would have reduced the flexibility of a larger system of economic and political relationship which involved North East India, Tibet and Bhutan during the pre-British period. The loosely linked up tribal entities of Arunachal allowed the organised state to operate their spheres of influence without directly confronting each other, and at the same time to ensure that commodity transactions from one area to another took place through diverse, but fairly stable channels. Thus it is in the interest of maintaining a larger system or systems of relationship that the tribes of Arunachal remained in a state of perpetual flux in their internal relationship and were not integrated into a single polity. It is easy to perceive that a single polity would have subjected it to pressures and pulls of cultures of entirely two different orders—one primarily based on settled agricultural economy, the other having more diversified and at the same time technologically more simple base, particularly drawing upon agriculture, animal husbandry and forestry. It would have been required either to ally with one and confront others, or to merge completely with one of them. Any of these developments would have complicated the mutual relationships of the organised states of this part of the world, which by virtue of the differences in the nature of their economy, were partially interdependent on one another. Conversely it follows that, had the wider system of symbiotic relationship not been there, or had it broken down, conditions conducive to the integration of the tribes of Arunachal into a single state structure might have prevailed.

This analysis brings out the fact that the loose ensemble

of tribal communities in Arunachal served both as buffer as well as bridge in between the organised states. It, however, requires to be explained why the bridge role or the system of circulation was primarily organised on the principle of reciprocity.

As observed earlier, the antimony of reciprocity in the circulation of articles is market. But did conditions prevail for the market to operate ? Market would require security, minimisation of the role of tradition in determining the exchange values, continuous responsiveness of the exchange values to supply and demand, political sanction to the infringement of the norms of transaction and so on. Looked upon in a different way, market enshrines the kings, while reciprocity enshrines the gods.

This, however, is a figurative statement. There is no pure market and there is no pure reciprocity. Market relations cannot continue for long without cogitation of a minimal of empathy. On the other hand, as already indicated, there are always possibilities of stalemate being created in reciprocity and thus paving the ground for extortion.

This analysis takes us back to the question raised earlier about the role of Rupa as a place for exchange in cash. Is it possible that Rupa was a market only symbolically and not in an empirical sense? Or is it possible that Rupa was partly a market and partly a strategic area in the system of circulation based on reciprocity ? For gaining more insight, it would be useful to examine two institutions connected with the Sherdukpens of Rupa.

At Rupa there is a *chhorten*, which was constructed by the Sherdukpens as a mark of repentance for killing a large number of the Kacharis during an encounter. Obviously there was an occasion when the system of reciprocity broke down. But the *chhorten* symbolises the anxiety of the Sherdukpens to restore the system. Is it possible that a short spell of exchange through market economy is associated with this break down?

The other institution is the existence of a *chhorten* in the foothill in honour of a Tibetan Lama, who is supposed to have taught how to carry on trade with the people of the plains and then to have disappeared mysteriously. This legend is of particular importance. It is significant that the *chhorten* is located in the foothill, where the Lama met the Sherdukpens. It is obvious that the Sherdukpens believe that they used to come to the foothill and carry on the transactions with the Kacharis, even before the Lama taught them the principle of trade. The innovation which was introduced by him, was to carry on transactions directly with the plainsmen in the markets situated in the plains. This new practice, however, did not completely replace the transactions with the Kacharis based on the principle of reciprocity. It only supplemented the former practice. The mysterious disappearance of the Tibetan Lama is also interesting. The legend symbolises the introduction of the new principle of circulation, by a Tibetan entrepreneur bypassing the system of reciprocity; it also symbolises the discontinuation of the direct role of the Tibetan in the new system. The location of the *chhorten* at the foothill, where the Sherdukpens migrate mainly to carry on the reciprocal transactions with the Kacharis also symbolises the subordination of the new principle of market transaction, to the old principle of reciprocity. At the same time to the people of the plains, a new image of the Sherdukpens also began to emerge. They were taken to represent that section of the people of the western sector of Arunachal who were involved in market economy. Thereafter it was an easy transition to consider the main village of the Sherdukpens as the centre of cash transactions. Thus though Rupa might not be much of a rupa (centre for transaction in silver coin), its reputation was fixed.

A question that still remains unanswered is how the new principle of market transaction was subordinated to the old principle of reciprocity? It appears that the answer to this question will bring out the true character of the tribute ceremonially paid by the Kacharis to the Sherdukpens. This tribute, represents at least part of the profit that the Sherdukpens would have earned had they carried on the entire trade directly in the market. It is an archetype of profit in the peculiar institutional complex of the region, a compromise between market and reciprocity.

It is not the only compromise that the Sherdukpens have to make in their pursuit of the principle of reciprocity. One can see it in their internal social relations as well.

The social organisation of the Sherdukpens symbolises the syntheses of two opposite principles, namely, extortion and reciprocity, in a dramatic manner. The Sherdukpen community is divided into two primary categories, the *thongs* or the master and the *chhaos* or servants. Each *thong* family has a *chhao* family attached to it. But the *chhaos* live in separate households and own property including landed property. They are, however, required to render certain services to the masters on various occasions and are not entitled to certain rights which go along with the membership of the community. For instance, they do not have a share in the *posa* paid by the government, or again they cannot expect to receive any tribute from the Kacharis. The extortion of certain services or the denial of certain rights is, however, one side of the picture. There is the other as well. Each *thong* family has a secret treasure of its own. Its location is known to the head of the family and his head *chhao*. Ordinarily the head of the family does not visit the secret place; whenever he requires anything, the *chhao* fetches it for him. When he dies, the *chhao* shows the hidden treasure to his son.

It appears that if the *thong* extorts services from the *chhao*, he reciprocates by investing the *chhao* with great dignity. He is not a servant in the ordinary sense of the term; he is servant-cum-trustee-cum-conscience-keeper of the family. From the point of view of the cultures within the orbits of industrial or industrialising societies, this institution seems to be ridden with a number of paradoxes. Functionally one can perceive it as a prototype of modern bureaucracy in a primitive setting. But perhaps it also symbolises a deeper structural principle of differentiation in the ownership and accumulation of wealth on the one hand and custody and protection of wealth on the other. It is easy to see that in the context of involvement of the Sherdukpen and other tribes of Arunachal in the circulation of goods cutting across political boundaries and cultures, such differentiation is a reiteration of the principle of reciprocity and at the same time curb to uninhibited accumulation through extortion or through other means, not sanctioned by the norms of the community.

CHAPTER V

ETHNICITY AND POLITICS IN SIKKIM

S. K. CHAUBE

The Demographic Profile

Sikkim joined the Indian Union as its youngest and smallest state on May 16, 1975. Its total territory (7,299 km) constitutes 0.22% of India's total territory, its population in 1981 (315,682) being 0.04% of India's population. As against the average density of population in India of 221 per sq. km.. Sikkim has a density of 44 (Padmanabha, 1981).

It will at once appear from a study of the population map of India that all the low-density states and Union territories are on the fringes of the Indian Union. Except the Andaman and Nicobar Islands, further, they are all located on the Himalayan ranges or their extension in north-east India. Of course, Sikkim is surpassed by Himachal Pradesh (density: 76), Manipur (54), Meghalaya (59) and Nagaland (47). However, it leads the Andaman and Nicobar Islands (23), Mizoram (23), Jammu and Kashmir (22) and Arunachal Pradesh (7).

Table—1

Low Density (less than 100) States and Union Territories in India

State	*Density*
Himachal Pradesh	76
Manipur	64

State	Density
Meghalya	59
Nagaland	47
Sikkim	44
Andaman and Nicobar Islands	23
Mizoram	23
Jammu and Kashmir[1]	22
Arunachal Pradesh	7

The explanation of this low density is easily furnished by nature, the inhospitability of the Himalayan mountains. Sikkim is entirely a mountainous state, its elevation ranging from 800 ft. to 28,000 ft. Its land-use pattern in 1971 can further illustrate the inhospitability of its territory.

Table—2
Land-use Pattern in Sikkim

Type of land	Proportion to total land (%)
1. Cultivation and Agriculture	11.14
2. Reserved Forest	26.66
3. Private Forest	4.24
4. Khasmahal and Garucharan (Pasture) Forest	5.30
5. Area Under Snow and Glaciers	28.29
6. Alpine Pastures	14.14
7. Settlement, Villages, Roads, etc.	10.23
Total	100.00

Source : Report of the Technical Team on the Fourth Five-Year Plan of Sikkim (cyclo), Gangtok, 1971, as quoted in Dasgupta (1980: 135).

The Cultural Frame of Reference

The theoretical frame in which the Sikkimese society can be understood is partly provided by the 'bridge-buffer role' of the borders provided by Roy Burman (1972). Sikkim's strategic location between India and Tibet has rendered her civilization certain special features which cannot, however, be fully appreciated without a reference to her historical evolution. One needs to look into Sikkim as much as at her environs. The sweeping assumption of the Tibetan influence on the Buddhist faith of most peoples on the southern slope of the Himalayas (in Nepal, Sikkim and Bhutan), for instance, needs to be qualified by the fact that the sects which predominate in these areas are 'heretical' in Tibet. Tibet is under the Gelukpa sect (identified by their yellow hats). Buddhists in Nepal, Bhutan and Sikkim are identified by their red hats.

In fact the red hat sects were the originally prevalent sects in Tibet until the ascendancy of the Gelukpa, under the Dalai Lamas, and with the support of the Mongol emperors of China (Shakabpa, 1967: 96-111). During the two earlier centuries of conflict over political hegemony in Tibet the defeated sects seem to have dispersed and founded their own niches around Tibet. Subsequently, however, they appear to have established a functional relationship with Tibet without foregoing their autonomy.

It will also be necessary to take into account the century of impact of British imperialism on the Himalayan states in general and Sikkim in particular before the transfer of power in India. But it is no less important to note the socio-economic tensions that developed *internally* partly through such impact.

The Ethnic Profile

It is difficult to ascertain the 'original' inhabitants of Sikkim. Apparently the two oldest groups, the Lepchas and the Limbus, are believed to have migrated into the present-day Sikkim, from outside Sikkim. The Bhutias are believed to have entered Sikkim later than the above-mentioned groups and were originally called Khampas by themselves (Shukla, 1976: 7-8). The indigenous name of the Lepcha was 'Rong' and of Limbus 'Chong' (Tsong). The Lepchas used to call this land 'Neliang' (literally the country of caverns). The name 'Sikkim' was probably given by the Limbus who came via Nepal (and are still there in a large number). The indigenous name of the country is Denzong (valley of rice). Both the Lepcha and the Limbu are believed to be of the Kirati stock of Indo-Mongoloid group distinguished from the Tibeto-Mongoloid Bhutia.

In the past in Sikkim the local people are believed to have been ruled by their chiefs (*pano/punu*) (Shukla, 1976: 7). Mainwaring speaks of a Lepcha *ano* ruling about 1425 A.D. when a Bhutia patriarch—Khye Bumsa—came to Sikkim from Kham (1876: X). Khye Bumsa came across a Lepcha chief—Thokung Tex—whose blessings led to Khye Bumsa having a child. The last Lepcha *ano* was born in 1886 and ruled for twenty-five years (Sinha, 1975: 12).

The legend about perpetuation of Khye Bumsa's dynasty from which the first Bhutia ruler of Sikkim—Phuntshog Namgyal —emerged was the first attempt at racial assimilation by the immigrants. The story about the killing of Turue by the Limbus (Shukla, 1976: 7) suggests frequent clashes between these two early inhabitant groups of Sikkim. Yet, there was no social bar to their marriage and intermixture. The Bhutia rulers made conscious effort to promote intermarriage with the Lepcha chiefs (Sinha, 1975: 7; Basnet, 1947: 14).

Such intermarriages must have been selective enough to restrict an effective intermixture with the result that the 1971 census showed clear demarcation between the major ethnic communities of Sikkim.

Table—3

Indigenous Linguistic Groups of Sikkim 1971

Linguistic Group	*Total Strength*	*as % of total Population*
Tibetan	4,627	2.20
Bhutia	8,064	3.84
Sikkim Bhutia	10,891	5.19
Lepcha	22,316	10.63
Gorkhali/Nepali	134,275	63.99
Others	29,670	14.14
Total Population	209,843	99.99

Table—4

Dominant Religious Groups in Sikkim 1971

Religious Group	*Strength*	*as % of total Population*
Hindu	144.544	68.88
Buddhist	62,617	29.84
Others	2.682	1.28
Total Populations	209.843	100.00

(Source : Chandra Shekhar : Census of India 1971)

The above statistics reveal the fact that 18.55% of Sikkimese people not belonging to the Bhutia category, are Buddhists. Their strength is accounted for by the Nepalese-speaking Buddhists, mostly Tamang, Sherpa and parts of the Newar, Limbu and the Lepcha communities. Among the Lepchas Buddhism predominates due to the historical reason of the Bhutia political hold. Recently, a section of the Lepchas have embraced Christianity. Yet, both the Buddhist and Christian Lepchas have retained considerable tribal elements in their religious practices (Sinha, 1975 : 6).

The Lepcha-Limbu-Bhutia triangle

The place of the Limbus in the Sikkimese life demonstrates a significent impact of politics on ethnic relations. Most of the Limbus are animists (followers of ancient *bon* religion) but now broadly considered to be either Hinduized or Buddhist. They have a distinct dialect, but are mostly considered to be Nepalese speaking. They are supposed to have been immigrants, but are identified with a region covering eastern Nepal and Western Sikkim and traditionally called Limbuan.

All these dichotomies point to certain hypotheses about their history. They are : (1) The Limbus probably had come from the Tsang valley in the wake of politico-religious disturbances; (2) They probably settled in a region under small chiefships but could not develop a full-fledged state; (3) While consolidation of the Bhutia rule in the fifteenth century led to the formation of the state of Sikkim emcompassing a part of the Limbu country, the subsequent consolidation of the Gurkha rule led to the formation of the modern state of Nepal encompassing the bulk of the Limbuan. Finally, when the Sikkim-Nepal border was determined at the Donkhya range, the Limbus became divided under two sovereignties.

The Lepcha-Bhutia-Limbu interaction thus taken on an interesting pattern. The Lepcha society has in the past been permissive. While the Bhutia rulers and their retenues took Lepcha wives, the privilege of entering such matrimonial alliances must have been restricted to the Lepcha elite and we find a few Lepcha Kazis (the governing class of traditional Sikkim), while no Limbu could emerge to such position. On the other hand, Lepcha-Limbu inter-marriage appears to have been more frequent and at the level of the commoners.

Nepali immigration

The biggest linguistic group in today's Sikkim is the Nepali. The bulk of the Nepali population in Sikkim, i.e., those excluding the Limbu, the Magar, the Gurung, the Rai and the Tamang—are immigrants from Nepal since the late eighteenth century, following the Gurkha invasion of 1788-89. But the Gurkha immigration was officially allowed in Sikkim after the 1860 war with the British government, and under the British pressure. In 1867 the first formal lease of land was granted to two Newar brothers (Basnet, 1947 : 44). The Bhutia aristocracy including the king opposed such immigration. This led to ethnic tension and court intrigues.

'By the early twentieth century tension over the Gurkha immigration ceased' (ibid : 66). Though some Bhutia landlords opposed immigration, the strength and influence of the Nepalis grew fast due to their energetic drive. Though no Nepali acquired the status of Kazi, many of them become substantial landowners with the title of 'Thikadars' (lessee landlords). On the whole, however, the Bhutias predominated as both Kazis and Thikadars (ibid : 67). By 1947

> The Lepcha-Bhutia tussle had disappeared almost completly due to cultural and social integration of both ethnic

groups to a large extent through inter-marriage and a sort of combined aristocracy and landlordship of the other communities had emerged. The problem of Lepcha peasants and that of Nepali peasants has however remained the same and they continued to be exploited by the landlords without ethnic distinctions. Some of them also migrated to neighbouring British territory (Shukla, 1979 : 46).

Class and ethnicity

Class and ethnicity intertwined in the chequered political process in Sikkim about the time of the transfer of power in India. Sikkim was categorized as an 'Indian state' under the Government of India Act, 1935. When the Constituent Assembly of India started working out the Indian Constitution representatives of the princely states were sent there. Himmatsingh K. Maheswari represented the Sikkim and Cooch Behar group of states. On December 5, 1947 the first political party was organized in Sikkim with the name of the Sikkim State Congress and with a multi-communal leadership. Its chairman was a Bhutia commoner, Tashi Tsering (Ibid : 47)

The Sikkim State Congress demanded (1) abolition of landlordism, (2) formation of an interim government to have the way for a popular ministry and (3) accession of Sikkim in India. The Sikkim Maharaja accepted the first two demands and rejected the third. The Maharaja founded an interim government with three secretaries—nominees of the State Congress—who quickly changed side and defied the party's mandate to resign. The then Crown Prince (subsequently the last Chogyal), Palden Thondup Namgyal, got a National Party organized in April 1948, under Sonam Tsering, one of the renegades, emphasizing the Bhutia-Lepcha distinctiveness and opposing merger. This rendered a militancy to Sikkim State Congress on the one hand and created bad blood within it on the other.

The Maharaja formed the first ministerial government with five ministers, on May 9, 1948. Three of them were the nominees of the State Congress and belonged to the three different communities: Tashi Tsering, who acted like the Chief Minister, was a Bhutia, Dimik Singh, a Lepcha, and C.D. Rai, a Nepali.

The official nominees were Dorji Dadul (a Bhutia) and Reshmi Prasad Alley (a Nepali). The Chief Minister had no control over the Sikkim durbar, made of the Maharaja's supporters. This led to such an unhappy situation that the Indian Government had to intervene and dismiss the ministers. A new system of a Dewan—deputed by the Government of India—with total administrative power took its place.

In May 1951 the Maharaja entered into negotiation with the National Party and the State Congress and hit upon a 'parity formula' over the election of a state council whereby the Bhutia-Lepcha population would have six seats, the Nepali population six seats and the Maharaja's nominees five seats in a 17-member council. Tashi Tsering refused to sign the agreement calling it 'unjust and communal' (Ibid : 57). The Nepali and Lepcha representatives of the State Congress, however, accepted it.

Acceptance of the parity formula by the State Congress was the watershed of inter-ethnic politics in Sikkim. Tashi Tsering, being a Bhutia 'commoner' himself, symbolized the Nepali-Lepcha-Bhutia democratic unity against the monarchy. The parity formula pushed the Bhutias into the royal camp. Tashi Tsering was replaced in the State Congress by Kazi Lhendup Dorji Khangsarpa, who claims to a be Lepcha, but whose name strongly suggests a Bhutia background. Tashi Tsering soon died as a frustrated man.

Factions and power

In the first election held, on August 7, 1953, to the State Council, the palace-backed National Party won all the six Bhutia-Lepcha seats. The palace had its five nominees besides them. The State Congress has won the six seats open to the Nepalese. In the new situation the Dewan, as the chief executive, was in charge of the reserved subjects. Besides the Dewan, there were two executive councillors, dealing with the transferred subjects: Kashi Raj Pradhan, representing the State Congress and Sonam Tsering representing the National Party. The experiment proved to be a 'farce' (Sinha, 1975: 28). As the ethnic demarcations were becoming increasingly prominent, Kazi Lhendup Dorji's own position was becoming untenable.

He resigned from the State Council and the Sikkim State Congress party leaving the latter entirely to the Nepalis. He formed first the Swatantra Dal and later, the Sikkim National Congress.

During the second election the strength of the State Council was raised to 20: 6 Nepali, 6 Bhutia-Lepcha, 6 nominated, 1 reserved for the Sangh (monastery) and 1 general. In 1958, election of a number of winning candidates was declared void on the ground of malpractices. Bye-elections were held in those seats in 1959.

Table—5

State Council 1959

	Bhutia-Lepcha	*Nepali*	*Sangh*	*General*	*Total*
Sikkim National Party	5	—	1	—	6
Sikkim National Congress	1	3	—	—	4
Sikkim State Congress	—	3	—	—	3
Total	6	6	1	—	13

The Maharaja nominated six members while the general seat remained vacant (Shukla, 1976 : 62). The life of the second State Council was short and, on the pretext of the 1962 India-China conflict, election for the third State Council was deferred to March 1967. In that election the strength of the Nepalis and Bhutia-Lepchas was each raised to 7. 2 seats were allotted to the Tsongs (the Limbus) and the Scheduled Castes. One seat each remained with the Sangha and General. The strength of the nominated members remained at 6. The total strength rose to 24. In this election Dorji's Sikkim National Congress emerged as the biggest party with 5 Nepali, 2 Bhutia-Lepcha and 1 General seats, but was soon split into two factions. The

Sikkim State Congress having won 2 Nepali seats, was also split into factions and power remained with the pro-palace National Party which had won only 5 Bhutia-Lepcha seats and the nominated councillors.

"The period between the third and the fourth general elections was one of a pathetic betrayal of democracy by the old guard among the popular leaders" (Sinha, 1975 : 31). Largely due to the machinations of the ruler all the political parties were split. Even the pro-palace National Party was split when an Executive Councillor, was manoeuvred out of not only the government but also the presidentship of the party for demanding more power for the Executive Council; (Shukla, 1976 : 76) In the fourth election of April 1970, the two factions of the National Party won 7 seats and the National Congress 4 seats. The two other elected seats remained with the independents. Yet, in this election, the Sikkim National Congress showed itself to be a multi-ethnic party having captured not only the all-Sikkim General seat, but also Nepali, Bhutia-Lepcha and Tsong seats.

The National Congress joined the multi-party Executive Council as a minor partner (with one seat, while the National Party got three and the State Congress two seats), but continued in the anti-monarch stance. This led to the exit of Lhendup Dorji from the Executive Council. Dorji fled the country and returned on the eve of the State Council election of 1973. Meanwhile the Sikkim State Congress had merged with the Sikkim Janata Party to form the Sikkim Janata Congress.

The critical absence of the Kazi from the scene during the latter half of 1972 had boosted the National Party which won all the seven Bhutia-Lepcha and two Nepali seats. Two independents elected by the Sangha and the Scheduled Castes joined hand with it. The Lepcha-Bhutia supporters of the National Congress had meanwhile either joined the National Party or become inactive. It won the General and Tsong seats along with three Nepali seats (1+2+3=6). The Janata Congress won the two other Nepali Seats.

The 1973 was a critical year in the ethnic politics in Sikkim. Acute tension arose with the Nepalis being pressed for adopting the Lamaist way or to quit Sikkim (Sinha, 1975 :

33). The situation was aggravated by the firing on the Nepali crowd by a Bhutia police official on April 4, 1973. This started a confrontation which was resolved only with the signature of an agreement on May 8, 1973, at the intervention of Indian officials heralding constitutional government for Sikkim and introducing one man one vote formula within the continued framework of separate electorate, on the basis of which there was a fresh election in April 1974.

Democratic Politics

It was the force of the mass movement that stemmed the rot. The palace lost all control over the politics of the state and even failed to effectively back the National Party as a result of which that party could fight only 6 out of the 32 seats in the State Council and win only one seat. The Sikkim Congress, born out of union of the Sikkim National Congress and the Sikkim Janata Congress, swept the poll and started negotiation, backed by agitation, that ultimately led to the merger of Sikkim with India. It appears that Kazi Lhendup Dorji, himself claiming to be a Lepcha, was not only able to unite the Nepali political elements, but also mobilized at least the Lepchas, who had so far been combined with the Bhutias in the elections. Most of the pro-palace Bhutias were thus neutralized.

The Kazi's exit from power was a subsequent development flowing from wider Indian politics as well as a sharpening of a kind of class contradiction over the question of land reform. Sikkim joined India on May 16, 1975. The Sikkim Congress joined the Indian National Congress at the end of the same year, the government of Kazi Lhendup Dorji was so much powerful, specially during the emergency, that during the Lok Sabha election of 1977 the ruling party won the seat without contest. The predicament of a small state, however, forced the Kazi's party to join the Janata Party *en bloc* shortly after the 1977 Lok Sabha election.

Such change of side as well as internal contradictions discredited the Kazi to the extent that in 1979 the Sikkim Parishad, with a programme of protecting Sikkimese interests and traditional institutions, was swept to power. The Sikkim Parishad was led by a Nepali but included more Bhutia-Lepchas than the Kazi's party did. Ironically, within one year of the electoral victory the Sikkim Parishad merged itself with the Congress (I). On the other hand, in 1982, B. B. Gurung—a Nepali and a formerly close lieutenant of Kazi Lhendup Dorji, led a batch of 10 MLAs, six of them belonging to the ruling party, with the support of the monks from Sikkim's premier Buddhist monastery at Pemeyangtse, to 'consecrate' the son of the deceased former ruler as the Chogyal (*Statesman* : February 22, 1982).

Thus, while under the monarchy ethnicity appeared to be the prime determinant of factions, in the republican system factions take the upper hand over ethnic alignments.

NOTE

1. In working out the density of population in Jammu and Kashmir, the area occupied by Pakistan has been excluded. (Source : Padmnabha, Census of India, 1981, Provisional).

BIBLIOGRATHY

Basnet, Lal Bahadur 1947 *Sikkim : A Short Political History*, New Delhi, S. Chand & Co.

Chandra Sekhar, A. 1975 *Census of India 1971, Series 1, Part II C(ii) Social and Cultural Tables.*

Dasgupta, M. 1980 'Structure of Sikkim's Economy', *Indian Journal of Regional Science*, Vol. XII, No. 2.

Mainwaring, B.D. 1876 *Grammar of Rong (Lepcha) Language*, Calcutta, Baptist Mission Press.

Padmanabha, P. 1981 *Census of India 1981, Series 1, India, Paper 1 of 1981 : Provisional Population Totals.*

Roy-Burman, B. K. 1972 'Integrated Area Approach to the Problem of the Hill Tribes of North-east' in K. Suresh Singh (ed.), *Tribal Situation in India*, Simla, Indian Institute of Advanced Studies.

Shakabpa, Tsepon W.D. 1967 *Tibet : A Political History*, New Haven and London, Yale University Press.

Shukla, Satyendra R. 1976 *Sikkim : The Story of Integration*, New Delhi, S. Chand & Co.

Sinha, Awadesh Coomer 1975 *Politics in Sikkim : A Sociological Study*, Faridabad, Haryana, Thomson Press (India) Ltd.

CHAPTER VI

CRAFTS OF SIKKIM AND SOCIAL IDENTITY

BUDDHADEB CHAUDHURI

The history of our crafts is as old as the history of man. From time immemorial the techniques of handicrafts have been handed down from parents to children, and the artisan families perserved the same in spite of many trials and tribulations. The innate strength of handicrafts has withstood the onslaught of mechanization. In richness of design, artistic excellence and inimitable workmanship, handicrafts hold their own against machine-made goods.

Below the Khangchendzonga, world's third highest mountain, lies Sikkim—a mountainous state bounded by Tibet in the north, Bhutan in the east, Nepal in the west and West Bengal in the south. A tongue-shaped southward project of Tibet, the Chumbi Valley, is driven like a wedge between Sikkim and Bhutan for more than half the length of Sikkim's eastern border. On the south lie the hill areas of Darjeeling district of West Bengal.

The present paper is based on a study made on the crafts, particularly wood-carvings of Sikkim. Besides discussing the history and background of the region and communities practising the various types of arts and crafts, it has been examined how far arts and crafts are based on religion and thus, through arts and crafts,t he socio-ritual boundaries are often maintained and internal solidarities of these communities are strengthened.

Sikkim is the 22nd State of India, with an area of 7096 sq.

km. encompassed in varying elevations ranging from 224 to 8,534 metres (800 to 28000 ft) above mean sea-level. The whole of Sikkim is mountainous, especially the north, east and west regions. There are many high ranges and lofty peaks, eternally under snow and the loftiest of them all is the famous Khang-chendzonga which is also intimately connected with the socio-religious life of the inhabitants and is supposed to be the protecting deity of Sikkim. But even the existence of these high ranges forming the physical boundary of Sikkim, it was not isolated to that extent as expected due to the presence of numerous passes, including the Jelep-la-Pass and the famous Nathu-la-Pass through which people traditionally used to migrate or visit Sikkim regularly.

The name of Sikkim is an appellation of Nepalese origin —Sukkim meaning peace and happiness. The Tibetans called it *Denzong*, the hidden valley of rice. It was also known to the Lepchas, one of the early inhabitants of Sikkim, as Nye-Maed or heaven.

Sikkim was under feudalistic order for about three centuries and a quarter and remained relatively isolated from the developed and developing countries. Again, because of the severe climatic conditions and hilly terrain, the only popular means of transport is road. Infact, a few years back, transport and communication systems were in a very bad shape. However, at present, Gangtok, the state capital, is well connected by roads with different nearby places of West Bengal like Darjeeling, Kalimpong and Siliguri and all the district headquarters of Sikkim. Besides the Sikkim Nationalised Transport which ply regular services connecting these places, private buses and taxis are also available. The nearest air port is Bagdogra in West Bengal situated 124 km. from Gangtok. The two closest railway stations are Siliguri (114 km) and New Jalpaiguri Junction (125 km). The river Tista and its tributaries are perennial rivers, but they are not safe for nevigation. This relative isolation, however, has helped this region to maintain its tradition and culture to a great extent.

In the past, a large number of communities with varied socio-cultural background migrated to Sikkim. The earliest settlers in Sikkim were the Lepchas who are supposed to have migrated from the Assam Hills during the 13th century along with other ethnic groups like the Tamangs and the Rais. The tradition of the Lepchas shows that they practised the Tantric version of Buddhism which was prevalent in the eastern parts of India. It may not be out of context to give the community-wise population of Sikkim in 1891, which may give some idea about the ethnic composition of Sikkim in the past.

Table—1

Community-wise Population of Sikkim—1891

Community	*Male*	*Female*	*Children*	*Total*
Lepcha	2,362	2,399	1,001	5,762
Bhotia	1,966	1,960	968	4,894
Limbu	1,255	1,159	942	3,356
Gurung	1,108	1,047	766	2,921
Murmi	801	778	1,288	2,867
Rai, Jimdar etc.	742	691	587	2,020
Khambu	726	648	589	1,963
Kami	626	464	580	1,670
Brahman	521	372	521	1,414
Mangar	363	346	192	901
Chetri	303	253	273	829
Newar	240	183	304	727
Slaves	124	99	103	326
Dirzi	102	92	93	287
Miscellaneous including troops	350	72	99	521
Total	11,589	10,563	8,306	30,458

(Source : Risley, H., 1894, *The Gazetter of Sikkim*)

This sensitive and strategic region of the country became a full-fledged state of India with effect from 26th April, 1975, in order to meet the increasing socio-political and economic aspirations of the people of the area. It has a population of 3,15,682 according to 1981 census living in 215 villages and 7 towns, falling in four districts, East, North, South and West. About 83.77% of its inhabitants live in villages and Gangtok, the biggest town of this state has a population of 36,768. In Sikkim, the average general density of population is 44.

The present population of Sikkim is composed of the Lepcha, who are supposed to be one of the early inhabitants of the state, the Bhotias, who came some centuries ago and the Nepalis—who are more recent immirgants and now constitute the majority covering about 75 per cent of the total population. The Lepchas and the Bhotias are roughly 13 per cent and 12 percent of the population respectively. The three groups speak their own languages, namely Lepcha, Sikkimese (Bhotia) and Nepali.

In Sikkim, two-thirds of the population are Hindus and a little less than one-third are Buddhists. The rural urban differential in the distribution of the Hindus is quite marked in Sikkim. The number of the Hindus per 100 of the population is 67 for all areas, 69 for rural areas and only 24 for urban areas. In Sikkim, the proportion of the Hindus to the total population declined substantially from 71.06 per cent in 1951 to 66.69 per cent in 1961, the growth rate among the Hindus being 10.53 per cent only against a general growth rate of 17.76 per cent. The Muslims, Jain and Sikh population in Sikkim is insignificant and less than one per cent. The Christians account for 1.7 per cent of the population. The Buddhists have registered a growth rate of 26.64 percent against a general growth rate of 17.76 per cent only.

An overwhelming majority of the population (89%) are engaged in cultivation, the cultivated area is estimated to be only 11% of the total area of the State. About 1/3 of the area of the state is covered by forests. Naturally, woods are avaiable in plenty. The staple food of the people of Sikkim is rice, grown along with millet, cardamom, oranges, apples, potatoes, ginger, etc. Sikkim exports cardamom, oranges and potatoes. Besides agriculture, animal husbandry, pig-raising and poultry are followed by many either as primary occupation or to supplement the need. Only a very few local persons are in business;

trade and commerce are mostly controlled by the outsiders. The extent of industrialisation is very limited.

The unique geographical position of the State has many interesting consequences. Historically, this region was largely influenced by the cultures and traditions of the neighbouring countries. Again, its relative isolation has helped to preserve its cultural traditions to a great extent.

Mahayana Buddhism, being the religion of the ruling family, enjoyed a privileged position. The Buddhist monasteries were given aid from the general revenue. The Bhutias are all Buddhists. A large number of the Lepchas are also Buddhists, the rest being divided between spirit-worshippers and Christians. The Nepalese barring a small Christian and Buddhist population, are all Hindus. The Buddhists in Sikkim belong to the "Red Hat" sect, so called because of the colour of the headgear worn on their ceremonial occasions. The "Red Hat" represents the older schools including the *nyingma-pa* (ancients) and the *kargyu-pa*.

The mysticism of Sikkim is evoked partly by the grandeur of its natural beauty, but mostly from the prayer flag, the *stupas* and the 67 odd monasteries. Inside these monasteries are the facinating Buddhist murals, images of hundreds of deities from the Tibetan Buddhist pantheon. The gentle chant of the Lamas reciting the *mantras*, the glow of the butter lamps on the altar, complete the setting. It may be pointed out that it is mostly the Buddhists, who have encouraged the various arts and crafts of Sikkim including woodcarving and, in fact, most of these crafts are actually done by them. In all these monasteries one may find the beautiful evidences of handicrafts and all of them like Rumtek monastery (one of the oldest monasteries where lived the 16th reincarnate His Holiness Gyalwa Karmapa, head of the *kargyu-pa* sect of Tibetan Buddhism). Pemayangse monastery (the second oldest monastery in Sikkim belonging to *nyingma-pa* sect and is the head of all other monasteries of this sect in Sikkim), Tashiding and Enchay monasteries have real beautiful pannels of wood-carving.

The Tusklakhang, the royal chapel, is also a repository of monastic art, rich mural pointings and lavishly decorated altars holding the images of Buddha, Bodhisattvas and Tantric deities.

Beautiful wood carvings in the chapel demonstrate the markedly impressive craftsmanship of the artists. One may also find such examples in other places, the most important of which is the Sikkim Research Institute of Tibetology, a world famous institute having the third largest collection of Tibetan books on Manayana Buddhism in the world. There are also over 200 icons, prized objects of art and a number of rare *thankas* (tapestries) which are internationally acclaimed. This is also a centre for study of the Buddhist scholars from all over the world. In the monasteries, wood was largely used not only to decorate or preparing altars or images of the deities, in many places preachings were also written in the beautifully decorated wood.

Now the different arts and crafts of Sikkim, the nature of involvement of the different communities in them and the present condition of the different crafts will be discussed. In this context, a discussion on the history of crafts of Sikkim may be useful.

The earliest known art forms in Sikkim do not go back before the 15th-16th century A.D. This partially explains that the Lepchas did not have the culture of art. However, the earliest forms were rather crude carvings in relief placed on the *chhorten* (receptachles of worship). A *chhorten* is a kind of miniature *stupa* whose origial function, that of housing relics of the Buddha or other Great Teachers, was later combined with religious significance. The *chhortens* also marked the route of pilgrims found for the holy places of Buddhist legend. More than a thousand years after King Ashoka built the first *stupa*, this architectural design reached Tibet in its maturity in the 8th century A.D. The first *chhorten* in Sikkim were built after Tibetan models and other shapes were fixed by definite measurements and designs. The earliest forms of stone reliefs used for outer decoration of the *chhortens* go back to a period perhaps before Phuntsog Namgyal (born in 1604 A.D.) who was the first consecrated ruler of Sikkim.

The ascendency of the Namgyal house marks the begining of the Sikkimese art, the cultural influences of which can be traced to the origin claimed by the rulers of Sikkim. The Namgyals claim to be the descendents of the legendary king, Indrabodh who, according to one tradition, was the king of Zahor, or what is now Mandi in Himachal Pradesh.

But Sikkim was not only exposed to other parts of India but also to other countries. So the arts and crafts of Sikkim reflect an interesting admixture of the cultures of these different countries. However, the influence of the Tibetan arts and crafts seems to be considerable.

Now a brief review is made on the different arts and crafts of Sikkim.

The *thankas* (i.e. religious scroll paintings) which depict Buddhist scenes or motif, are not only very beautiful but are rich in colour and entirely traditional in composition. They are bordered often with rich *Banarasi* silk, with heavily engraved silver knobs at either end, which enhance the exquisite beauty of the *thankas*. A *thanka* is regarded as a sacred object. The central figure in a *thanka* is always a Buddha, or any other deity, or Bodhisattva of Mahayana Buddhism, and the motif is invariably the predominance of (Mahayana) Buddhism over other forms of religions. Other figures depicted around the main deity have their mystical significance, but all, in essence, are represented to support the dominant faith. These paintings truly represent the Sikkimese art and culture.

The Sikkimese carpets are woven using wool in piles of knots. They are woven in beautiful traditional Sikkimese designs. Their workmanship, attractive colours and durability are all world-renowned and are much in demand. The vegetable dyes prepared locally are mostly used to produce a variety of matching colours and in different sizes and designs. The traditional motifs and designs of the Sikkimese culture are mostly made on the carpets.

The Lepcha cloth woven in traditional designs with rich colours may be used for variety of purposes like curtains, bags, table-mats, belts, shawls, bed-covers, cushions, jackets, tray-cloths, etc. It is manufactured in cotton, staple, silk, and woollen yarn. These handloom designs demonstrate the very sensitive and distinctive marks of the Sikkimese culture, mood and mind, representing the creative and artistic mind of the Sikkimese people.

Of the various metal objects, jewellery is an important item. The Sikkimese jewellery depicts the different tastes of the three ethnic groups of Sikkim, namely the Lepcha, the Bhotia and the Nepali. The "Dragon" jewellery made in Gangtok, is famous and is made in cuff-lings, rings, earrings, necklaces, etc. The gold and lead jewellery of the Nepalis is also very popular. Articles, such as ash-trays, nut-bowls, spoons, and religious artifacts in the Bhotia pattern are often made.

The metal objects that are most attractive, are pots and jugs of various beautiful shapes and types. They reveal best of all that mysterious, ancient culture which is the most characteristic and most basic contribution of native origin to the mixture termed Lamaist art. Some times they do not look very artistic, worked less precisely than the other objects, but they have what is called a touch of folk art, and thus has a certain beauty any iconographic treatment which makes them all the more attractive.

Arts and crafts on stone and clay do not seem to be very popular with the craftsmen. However, small stones are often inserted to decorate a particular object.

Crafts made of bamboo and cane are often seen, but they are less popular and less honourable.

Wood carving is one of the most important crafts of Sikkim. The different articles or objects produced by the wood carvers may be either movable or immovable. The difference between immovable and movable objects is not of design. The same designs are used both on movable and immovable objects. The designs on wood are first carved and pointed. After this, if it is fixed on a movable object, it will be movable, and if it is fixed on a wall or a window or a door, then it becomes immovable wood-craft. The immovable wood-crafts are mostly seen in the *gumphas* and in the houses of well-to-do persons. The common movable objects prepared by the craftmen are discussed below. It may be pointed out here that some of the objects are traditionally prepared, some, however, have newly emerged considering the commercial demands of some of the articles and are mostly prepared by some of the commercial firms emerged recently.

Type	*Approximate time required to make (days)*	*Price of the article (Rs.)*
1. Table :		
(a) Choktshe—Small, medium and large sized	5-19	135-385
(b) Bagchu—or four-sided table	19	600-700
(c) Two sided Coffee table—large, medium, small	5-34	300-600
2. Screen having different designs	50-57	750-1000
3. Altar or Choesum	80-85	2500
4. Almirah	18	1285
5. Stands	6-20	65-185
6. Wall decoration—bird, dragon, flowers, etc.	2-5	25-85
7. Sitting place or Bhodin	35-42	1200-1600
8. Mask	1	15-20

(It may be added here that the price depends on nature of design, whether the article has two-sided, three-sided or four-sided designs, painted or not and even on the nature of colour).

Raw materials for wood carving : The raw materials required for making a wood-carving are mainly two; (i) Wood; (ii) Paints.

Each of these materials has again sub-types :

(i) Wood happens to be the main raw material for producing any article. They use mainly three types of wood.

(a) local timber
(b) Magnolia or *chap*
(c) Tuni variety

(ii) Paints : The wood-carvers have certain preference about the use of colours. Thus they use only five colours namely green, blue, yellow, red and white. These are supposed to be the auspicious colour. In fact they never use certain colours, particularly black.

Besides these, among the subsidiary raw materials required, the notable ones are connected with paints, namely

(a) Varnish
(b) Tarpin

Sources of raw materials: The local variety of wood and paints are purchased by the wood-carvers from the local market. The other varieties of wood which are not grown locally, are brought from outside The carvers often find some difficulty in getting the raw materials particularly for the varieties brought from outside.

Cost of raw materials

1. *Wood* :
(i) Timber — Rs. 28 per cubic feet
(ii) Magnolia — Rs. 26 per cubic feet
(iii) Tuni — Rs. 24 per cubic feet
2. Paints — Rs. 33.60 p. per litre (Price as existed in Jan. 1980)

Tools used for wood carving: For wood-carving, the carvers use either sixteen or eighteen tools. But there is no separate name for each of the tool. However, there are three broad tool-types each including more than five tools.

1. *Tikyon*
2. *Akan Chren*
3. *Dhunshedhung*

Their English equivalents are difficult to mention, and there is every doubt that there are Engligh counterparts for their names. In one word the functions of all the different types of tools are the same—wood carving. But different tools are used at different place to project different shapes. For example, to carve a flower a tool with a curved blade is required The tools used are accordingly of three sizes—large, medium and small.

The carvers said that the types of tools they have at their disposal are not adequate. Beautifying the edges often becomes very difficult. Moreover, the tools get blunted very soon and the carvers have to spend money everytime for sharpening their tools.

The tools required for carving the wood are generally obtained from the local blacksmiths who also do the repairing and sharpening. After making a wood carving, sometimes paints are applied and for that brushes are required. Generally the craftsmen use brushes of two size (a) thick and big size and (b) thin and small size. These brushes are usually brought from local markets.

Cost of tools and other articles :

Tools : (1) Large-sized : Rs. 5/- each
(2) Medium-sized : Rs. 4/- each
(3) Small-sized : Rs. 2.50/- each

Repairing or sharpening charges for all the sizes is Re. 1/-; for each brushes : (1) Thick and big size Rs. 3.50/- each
(2) Thin and small size Re. 1/- each

Design: The Buddhists are the only skilled craftsmen so far as the wood carving is concerned. In the context of other crafts, the Nepalese are also equally skilled. Whatever may be their ethnic background, most of the arts and crafts are used for religious purposes. They often produce articles such as monk's thunderbolts, three-edged ritual poignant with steel blade and bronze handles on which three heads are shown, candlesticks and altar decorations representing symbols of happiness. Further there are symbolic badges of the church hierarchy, knives, hammers, axes, etc. A large number of metal objects are made in connection with the religious worship like amulet shrines, prayer wheels, food dishes, etc.

The most common decorative elements found on these objects are lotus flowers, heads of monsters (*kala* heads) with their paws in front of their muzzles, the Serpent gods, heads of monsters (*makara*) with elephant trunks, all of them are ancient Indian motifs. Further, the prayer—

Om nami padme hum or
Oh thou Jewel on the lotus (Buddha)

in decorative writings, various spells, symbols of happiness or of protective gods are also found. But the dragon is the most popular object. Frequently surface decorations are composed of popular semiprecious stones.

Caste/Community Participation: The Sikkimese population is generally divided into two broad religious groups, the Buddhist community including the Bhotias, the Lepchas and a part of the Nepalese (Newar group) and the Hindu community including the Nepalis. The representation of other groups except the tribals is rather insignificant. Only the Buddhists, the Lepchas and the Bhotias, follow wood-carving. The status of the craftsmen may be low individually due to economic reasons, but if viewed from the community angle, they enjoy quite high status and position in the local social structure. The Lepchas and the Bhotias are since time immemorial, professing Buddhist religion. Since they are Buddhists, they are familiar with the traditional pictures, designs and motifs mostly associated with Buddhism, which they carve on wood. Thus these craftsmen are historically associated with a particular religion and wood carving. Even the Buddhist section of the Nepali group, the Newars, are known for the craftsmenship.

The preparation of a single article requires the cooperation between the carvers and the carpenters. For example, the different pieces of wood required for making a table, are at first smoothened by the carpenters. These smoothened pieces are then brought by the carvers. Designs are drawn over the wood with the help of a drawing made on a paper earlier and after the drawing is complete, the craftsman starts carving. The carved pieces are again taken to the carpenters who fix up these pieces and give the required shape. After that, the carving are again brought to the carvers' house where the paintings are done if required. Except this broad division of work, there is no other fixed division of work. The carvers generally want to do the paintings by themselves as it is less difficult, time-consuming, hard but more profitable. Normally, a carver goes through the whole operation alone and only after a number of wood carving are made he starts the painting work. All the carvers are males and so there is no division of labour on the basis of sex.

In the recent past, Sikkim has been exposed to outside influence to a great extent and this has affected even their traditional crafts particularly wood-carving At present, craftsmanship is being more and more commercialized and so is the craft. If the earlier crafts had only religious significance, the modern crafts are often taken more for decorative purposes than for religious. Wood-craft is one of the traditional crafts of Sikkim and still now it has great demand, both for traditional (ritual) and decorative purposes, though certain other crafts like metal crafts, bamboo craft, etc., are decaying.

Considering the importance of handicrafts in the economy of Sikkim, various measures were taken for the development of different traditional crafts of Sikkim particularly wood-carving and carpet-making. In this context, mention may be made about the Government Institute of Cottage Industry located at Gangtok. It was opened in March, 1951 as a Centre for both preservation and development of the traditional arts and crafts of Sikkim. The Centre has been imparting training to the local boys and girls in the traditional arts and crafts of Sikkim. The two notable areas of its activities are carpet making and wood carving. The beautiful carpets mostly have the dominating figures of the dragon and the eight auspicious motifs or designs. The Sikkimese wood-carving, again a traditional craft has been brought to a high level of artistic efficiency. Besides training, it also helps the craftsmen in promoting business.

Even in the context of these chages and facilities, due to religious implications attached to a number of wood-carving, they are never done commercially, though many of them have great attractions. This situation, no doubt, creates some problems in the commercial development of the craft. It was told by the authorities of the Cottage Industry that in many cases, the craftsmen are reluctant to make some designs which might have great market demand only because of the fact that magico-religious beliefs are traditionally associated with certain designs. It was also told that a Buddhist craftsman of Tinkitam village, who makes beautiful wooden masks, have declined the offer of making them on a large scale or to teach some students that craft with the financial assistance from the Institute of Cottage Industry. Even though this Cottage Industry has played a great role in the development and growth of crafts in Sikkim in the recent past, it was pointed out by some authorities of Sikkim art that the various crafts and specially the wood-carvings done at the instance of the Industry are not as beautiful and unique as were done in the past. This is because of the fact that they are done commercially, to meet the need of the outsiders, whereas, in olden days and even to-day in other places, since they perform some traditional rites mostly associated with religion, more attention is always given to the details. It was said that, there has naturally been a decline in the quality even though more facilities are now extended and available.

An authority of the Sikkim Research Institute of Tibetology, Gangtok pointed out that the traditional crafts of Sikkim are more related or rather absolutely related to religion, but recently crafts have been commercialized considerably and often serve the decorative purpose. This is true not only for the wood crafts, but also for other crafts like metal craft, bamboo-craft, etc. The colours painted on the crafts, however have religious significance. Still now they use certain prescribed colours only and avoid a few others.

Some former advisor to King Chogyal pointed out that even though the craftsmen are getting more facilities and various efforts have been made to develop the crafts particularly wood-carving, the result is not very encouraging. The depth, colour and as a whole the perfection of earlier wood-carvings are definitely more praiseworthy. He feels that this is essentially due to commercialization. Even some of the authorities of the Institute of Cottage Industry pointed out its association with religion and emphasized that it would not be too much commercialized and felt that even through traditional arts and crafts, the identity and cultural traditions of Sikkim can be maintained.

Some of the wood-carvers were also against large scale commercialization of the craft and felt that traditional norms and crafts should be maintained.

In this paper, the crafts of Sikkim particularly wood-carving have been discussed. The handicrafts can play a very important role in the economy of Sikkim due to its ecological background and cultural tradition. The unique geographical position of the State has many interesting consequences. Its relative isolation has helped to preserve its cultural traditions.

It has been noted that all the wood-carvers were the Buddhists, belonging to the Lepcha and the Bhotia communities. Traditionally the Lepcha and the Bhotias are Buddhists by religion and as such, they are familiar with the pictures and designs which they carve on wood. Even the Buddhist section of the Nepalis, the Newars, is known for the ceaftmanship. The wood-carvers produce a variety of articles traditionally used for religious purpose and now even for decorative purpose. Due to religious implications attached to a number of wood carvings, they are never done commercially even though many of them have great attraction. Again, in the choice of colours also, they are very particular, and certain traditionally prescribed colours only are used and some colours, traditionally believed to be unauspicious, are always avoided even for the articles produced commercially. This traditional attitude, no doubt, is a problem for the commercial developments of crafts of Sikkim.

It may not be out of context to discuss one very interesting aspect of handicrafts of Sikkim. Here, art is largely based on religion. Many symbols or designs have religious implications, wood-crafts are traditionally used for religious purpose and only certain communities belonging to a particular religion practise it. This is true even for the government controlled Cottage Industry, which is also known as Preservation-cum-Production Centre implying that the Institute helps in maintaining the tradition and identity. All the wood-carvers here are Buddhists. Thus in Sikkim art, religion and community are all related and in a sense, art has a functional role in the boundary maintenance mechanism.

REFERENCES

Bulletin of Tibetology, Gangtok, Sikkim.

Maharaj Thutob Namgyal & Maharani Yeshey Dohna 1980 *History of Sikkim*, (unpublished mimeograph)

Rao, P. R. 1972 *India and Sikkim* (1814-1970), Sterling Publishers (P) Ltd., New Delhi.

Risley, H. 1981 *The Gazetteers of Sikkim*, H. K. Kuloy (ed.), Manjushri, New Delhi (Reprinted, original, 1894)

Sukla, S. R. 1976 *Sikkim, the Story of Integration*, S. Chand & Co., New Delhi.

Sinha, A. C. 1975 *Politics of Sikkim, a Sociological Study*, Thompson Press Ltd., Delhi.

Stock, C. De Beauvoir 1975 *Sikkim's Customs and Folklore*, Cosmo Publications, Delhi.

CHAPTER VII

SIKKIM'S SEARCH FOR IDENTITY

BETWEEN LAMAS' PRAYER-WHEEL AND THE NEPALIS *KHUKHRI* AND BEYOND

A.C. SINHA

It is a healthy symptom of an open society such as ours to examine the various issues associated with Sikkim's identity into the Indian melting pot. Perhaps the time has come for a deeper analysis beyond the individual manipulations and historical accidents. Possibly one may look into the quality of social forces that led to the events of mid 1970's. It is also imperative to delineate the social base of the ethnic politics. Associated with the ethnic issue is the problem of choice. Has Sikkim got a choice between Lamas' prayer wheels and the Gurkhas' *khukhri* in a symbolic sense ? Or it is an absurd question: Why can't both co-exist in a tolerant, happier and prosperous Indian nation? It is a fact that ultimately the Sikkimese have to make a choice and see to it that it works to their maximum satisfaction. However, an academic analysis may project such courses of choice, options open and their implications for the common masses.

Had there been a line drawn to delineate the northern boundary of the British empire in the Eastern Himalaya, east of the river Mechi in 1826, it would have rarely touched the Himalayan foothills. Purnea, Dinajpur, Rangpur, Goalpara, Kamrup, Darang and Lakhimpur—all in the plains—were the frontier districts. The British got a foothold in the Himalayas in 1817; got an ally in the form of the Gurkhas (Nepalese) and also took tne vulnerable *Sikkimpatti* under their wings. The process began in 1835, when the grant of Darjeeling was secured from Sikkim. All through the treaty of 1861 between the two, the process was complete in 1868, when Sikkim became an Indian princely state within the British Empire. Kalimpong, Jalpaiguri, parts of Goalpara, Kamrup and Darang were acquired after the Duar was with Bhutan in 1864-'65 and a pliable principality was established in Bhutan in 1907 with acknowledged British support. And subsequently, the two Maharajas attended the Delhi Durbars knowing fully well that only the British feudatories did so.

Thutub Namgyal was consecrated as the ruler of Sikkim in 1874. In contrast with the Bhutan scene, the Sikkimese ruler had lost everything—his kingdom, his crown and thc Crown Prince—and spent years in captivity at Kurseong. All these happened mainly because of his style of functioning was contrary to the then dominant British emperical forward policy to the Himalayan region. The *paharias* (The Gurkhas or the Nepalese) played a significant role in execution of this policy and that's how the present international boundaries in the Eastern Himalayas come to be established within three decades of the Sikkimese takeover. Slowly but steadily, the *paharias* emerged as the dark horse of the British metropolitan economy in the entire Himalayan foothills. They were encouraged to reclaim the malarial *tarai* and *duars* at farmers. They were engaged in cattle rearing, animal husbandary and dairy products. They were first hired to clear the forest and then employed in the flourising timber industry. With the introduction of tea plantation they turned to be reliable plantation hands. All through they were employed in the armed and para-military forces, so much so that by the turn of the 19th century, they emerged as a very dominant ethnic force in the Eastern Himalayan foothills.

They were seen by the British as the most reliable forward columns of the British interests, Herbert Risely who wrote the Gazetteer of Sikkım, identified the Sikkimese scenario in the context of the Nepalese :

> "The Lepchas are rapidly dying out; while from the west the industrious... Gurkhas of Nepal are pressing forward .... Here also religion will play a leading part in Sikkim as in India Hinduism will assuredly cast out Budhism and the praying wheel of Lama will give place to the sacrificial implement of the Brahmin. The land will follow the creed;.... Thus, race and religion... will settle the Sikkim difficulty for us in their own way". (1894 : XXI)

This was the phase in the Sikkimese history, when Sikkim was administered by Claude White, the then Political Officer in Gangtok. The royal couple spent better part of their rule in exile and imprisonment and they lost two of their elder princes —the eldest one in voluntary exile and the younger one was killed by a callous medical diagnosis. Tashi Namgyal, the third prince of the Thutubs, was entirely a British creation as the next ruler. He was tutored, groomed and guided by the Political Officer. If his father was recalcitrant and indolent, he was weak, ineffective and of retiring nature. He was nominally the ruler and even his family affairs such as education and marital alliances were arranged by the Political Officers. Under such a strong British paternalistic care, the state emerged from the subsistence slash-and-burn and forest economy to the settled wet peasant economy. The Marwari and Deswali merchants had already established the strong roots of the British metropolitan economy. The earlier communal land-owership was changed into contractual lease system on the feudal pattern, the Sikkim was well integrated into the British colonial system. As a result of all these, Sikkim occupied the most significant place in the chain of the buffer-states on the northern border af India ranging from Afganistan to Burma.

After the two World Wars the British policy towards the Himalayan states underwent sea-change because of the nationalist movement in India. Nepal and Afganistan were recognized as the independent entities. Bhutan was advised against the earlier efforts to show its distinctive character separate from India. And the British empire cautioned the new Indian rulers not to add to their communal problems by integrating Sikkim into India. As the strategic elites in Delhi had given a little thought to the relationship between the Himalayan states vis-a-vis India such advices came handy to them.

The movement for democratization in the Himalayan states was addressed to the British empire as well as the feudal rulers. It was primarily a movement of the Nepalese peasants, which was led by semi-educated lower middle class leaders as a whole. They did neither the ideological sophistication, nor the organizational skill nor the larger political perspective. As a whole, it was a confused ad-hoc movement against some vague targets. Their slogans, symbols, and action programmes were not much relevant to their local situations. And that is why when the first Government in Sikkim was dismissed in May 1949 after its 29 days existence, the State Congress leadership was not only demoralized, but was also much confused because the State Congress drew inspiration from the Indian democratic ethos and leadership. It happened because the Indian Union under the Congress had changed its previous preference. In the new situation, Sikkim meant the Maharaja of Sikkim rather than the people of Sikkim. Thus, the administration was once more handed back to the paternalistic care of the bureaucrats. Perhaps this might have helped the staggering feudal structure to get strengthened at the cost of the democratic forces.

What resulted on the Sikkimese political scene came to be known as the democratic fraud of the *parity* formula, a concession to the feudal authority. The then Crown Prince got the Sikkim National Party, an anti-thesis to the Sikkim State Congress, floated with his fund and personnel. The *durbar* getting encourged, started its manoeuvre against the State Congress, which had been espousing the anti-feudal democratic cause. It was a vulnerable movement because of its weak social base. Thus, it was divided on the communal and factional lines. Consequently, politics as a means to do away with the feudal oppression came to be identified with political horse-trading, manipulations, defections and fragility of the political parties.

Among the other reasons for 1973-74 happenings the unreasonable and inflated international personage of Sikkim propped up by the then ruler and some courtriers may be identified. And that is why what happend in Sikkim in 1973-'75 was neither an invasion nor a revolution. It was simply a matter of changed priority from point of view of New Delhi. The then ruler had possibly overplayed his limited role; gone beyond his brief; and was already nursing an inflated internatlonal stature for himself. This should be restrained for greater interest of India. Give it any name, but that's what actually happened.

This could have also happened in 1949, had there been a positive democratic movement against the colonial and feudal structure. Because of the ethnic complexity, such a movement was also vulnerable to dissention. The Bhotias had identified themselves with the ruling dynasty, Kazi aristocracy, lamaist monastic privileges and an overall feudal-cum-theocratic anachronism. The autochthonous Lepchas were too weak and oppressed to assert themselves. Because of their mild, indolent and conflictless temper, they are normally clubbed with their coreligionists—the Bhotias. The Nepalese immigrants, broadly divided into the Kirati, Newari and the Gorkhali stocks, are further divided into various social segments of castes and tribes. They may be Hindus, lamaists or even the animists. Hindus are broadly divided into *tagodhari* (the refined) and *matwali* (those who may drink intoxicant drinks). However, the language, dress, food habits and a largely common cultural tradition unify them into an identifiable Nepali stock. It is an industrious perseverent and gregarious community. It is a mobile stock which had been expanding from its Nepalese base to Darjeeling, Sikkim, Bhutan and then to eastern frontier states. It is slow but steady flow of humanity from the impoverished and over-populated Nepalese hills to the low density but plentiful untapped resource potential eastern hills.

With the above ethnic background, it may be easier to survey the Sikkimese democratic movement. Though it was led by the non-Nepali Sikkimese, it had always been effectively organised by the Nepalese younger activities. As their social base reflecting their own operational sphere, was always weak, these functionaries had sometimes been changing their political affiliations. In the process, none of them had a consistent image of a fighter for the cause of the oppressed masses. They also suffered from the neo-rich pretensions. In this way the present problem is not of selling or mortgaging the soul or body of Sikkim, but availability of an organizationally skilled and experienced political enterpreneur, who could galvanize the Sikkimese belaboured mass into an effective force.

The muddled political scenario of theocratic feudal Bhotia inwardedness, the Lepcha's loss of nerve and the Nepalese propensity to manupulative politics and organizational unpredictability has created a number of paradoxes. These may be identified as three inter-related levels.

The actual status of the Nepalese, a large immigrant community from another sovereign state, has to be determined. How do they belong to the Indian commonwealth of various cultural nationalities as others do ? In what ways their language, culture, traditions and history are Indian ? Will the efforts of the Nepalese to seek for the Indian indentity be construed as the extention of the genuine policies, programmes and traditions of Nepal ? Before one tries to answer the above issues one must be frank enough in accepting certain reservations in India about the Nepalese. Firstly some of the leaders of the Indian freedom movement had thought a section of the Nepalese as the faithful British allies. Secondly, the Nepalese belong to a country which claims to be the only Hindu country in the world; while India proclaims from the house-top her recently acquisitioned secular political culture. Will these two genuine strands of the traditions not lead to a possible conflict of the values ? Thirdly, the issue of the Indian Nepalese may be linked with the problems of the immigrant Indians in Nepal. During the last two hundred years the Nepalese rulers encouraged the peasants from the Gangetic plains to clear the hot, humid and malarial *terai* forests. While the hillmen from the interior and eastern Nepal were migrating eastward in India, the Deswalis were engaged in turning the negative *terai* into the most precious economic bastion. It is also a fact that the Deswalis and the *Paharis* fought shoulder to shoulder against the feudal oppression. Both have their kinsmen across the border and share some common cultural and religious tradition. Not only that; more privileged among them, educated at Varanasi, Lucknow, Patna and Calcutta, saw little difference between Hindi and Nepali written in *devnagri* script.

Since 1960, much water has flown in the Bagmati. The resurgent ('Rising' as they call it) Nepal has changed its priorities. Instead of the past common heritage of culture, religion, and history, she emphasizes her distinct identity. On the other hand, Nepal considers herself as the natural custodian of the larger Nepalese interests. And that is why the real and putative problems of the Nepalese immigrants in the North Eastern Frontier of India are not easily acceptable. This is a complex issue. The Bhotias in Sikkim invariably inform their visitors that most of the Sikkimese Nepalese have multiple identities—Sikkimese, Bhutanese, Indian and Nepalese. Many of them are reported to have immovable properties in Nepal and also perhaps voting rights. However, thus atmosphere of unreal, mukey suspicion, and past reservation has to be changed with something positive. We have to face the problem squarely : How far have we been able to accomodate the aspirations of the Nepalese in the body politic of India ?

Because of its past experience the Sikkimese regionalism is similar to that of Manipur, Tripura and other eastern states. There is a very small white collar (or blue coat) middle class professionals, who actually provide base to the political parties. Similarly, traditional system of landownership based on communal holdings provides bastion for ethnic base for or against a political party. In such a situation a political party is floated by some one who has resources of his own commands (ethnic, religion or communal) followers, and political ideologies may be turned to demand for or against certain privileges. Consequently, such political activitists (or operators) are in a great hurry to achieve a position of power, authority and eminence. In case they are out of position of power, they tend to join the club of powerful quickly because they cannot afford to survive for long politically without access to distributive sphere of governmental activities. And in such a situation small, fragile and shapeless regional political parties, which are the means (and not an end in themselves) to achieve the position of power, come handy. For such politicians the national political parties are cumbersome, inconvenient and are something like obstacles. For them the national politics, ideologies and political structure remain vague, opaque, mysterious and too much impersonal. One does not know for sure what type of contribution the Sikkimese politics will make to enrich the national political culture; however the present political scenario of conflicting regional and national perspectives has yet to be provided with a settled pattern.

This leads us to the third dilema in the sense that much of the regionalism is addressed to the ethnic issues. As per the constitutional provision to safeguard the interests of the weaker section of the society, localized ethnic groups tend to forge their solidarity. This solidarity is claimed on the basis of subjective, putative and objective criteria of culture, language, history, etc. The articulate among the ethnic elite may raise the issue of their exploitation by the non-ethnics, could be some of them, may also be the exploiters of their own brethern. Being a tribal (or local) ensures certain access to resources such as lands, reservations in the jobs and preferential opportunity for admission to certain professions. It is conceded that an indulgent preferential treatment may go against the principle of the equality.

What is happening in Sikkim is very much similar to the above scenario. The Nepalese, who constituted about 70% of the total population, were equated by the Chogyal with the 25% Lepcha-Bhotia combine for representation to the State Council. This principle of parity between the two continued till 1979. That was the year in which Sikkim was brought on all India pattern of democratic representation. Out of 32 seats in the State Assembly, 12 were reserved for the Lepcha-Bhotia, two for the Scheduled castes and one for the monastic bodies and rest of 17 seats were left open to be contested by any Indian citizen. Some Sikkimese Nepalese feel deprived by this stipulation. They declare that their status as the Sikkimese (and Indian) has a chequered saga of suffering, humiliation and struggle against the feudal and colonial rule. They claim to be the Sikkimese.

The above analysis may provide a way to understand the complex problem. Too much reliance on the historical background may lead to draw wrong lessons by putting the lamas' prayer wheel agaist the Nepalese *khukhris*. However, like many colonial predilections, we have been able to prove the above prophecy wrong. Sikkim has come to stay as an Indian state. The Bhotias and the Lepchas have got their secured constiutional status. It is the turn of the Nepalese to make their final choice as a community. As the dominant ethnic group of Sikkim they require to demonstrate their political maturity and rise above the parochial issues and integrate themselves with national political structure.

REFERENCES

Risley, H. H.	1874	*The Gazetteer of India*, Calcutta, p. XXI
Sinha, A. C.	1975	*Politics of Sikkim*, Thomson Press, p. 8

CHAPTER VIII

THE LEPCHAS OF WEST BENGAL

A SOCIO-ECONOMIC AND CULTURAL PROFILE

A. K. DAS

I

The Lepchas, popularly known as the 'Children of Kanchanjunga' are concentrated in the border State of Sikkim and Darjeeling district of West Bengal. Numerically, though a less dominant community, but from the socio-cultural point of view their position is quite unique in view of the fact that they represent a synthesis of different religions, beliefs and practices; cultural norms and values; economic stages of development and possess a typical psychology of an 'isolated' group with a defeatist mentality of a loosing race. This little known community of our border area has covercome different invasions and natural calamities through ages and was under the control of alien rulers at different stages of history. Though their life style and thinking have been moulded to a great extent due to the impact of alien cultures still they maintain a continuity in their culture which is quite worthnoting.

The outsiders call them as the Lepchas but they prefer the term *Rong*, meaning thereby the mountain dweller. The *Rong* means 'peak' or mountain peak. There still remains a good deal of confusion about their original homeland. Many believe that the Lepchas are living in Sikkim from long past and they are the autochthones of the region, there is uncertainty about the country where from they have migrated. One of their legends indicates that at first they used to live in a valley called 'Ma-el' in the neighbourhood of the Kanchanjunga. In other legends other peaks in the neighbourhood of the Kanchanjunga are indicated as their original habitation. With the increase in number they slowly spread over the whole area. Some believe that the Lepchas migrated from the Assam hills and entered Sikkim as early as the thirteenth century.

The literature dealing with the Lepchas are meagre in number and information furnished in majority of them, excepting a few, are mostly piecemeal in nature, travelogue in character and rather unscientific in approach. Some of these writings of the nineteenth and twentieth century authors provide us with some basic information on the Lepchas, their life and activities, etc. Most of these writings have given indications that the Lepchas are a type of people with such personality that attracts one who come in touch with them. They are extremely simple, amiable, cheerful, helpful, cooperative, carefree and lack in spirit of conflict.

II

On the basis of the writings of different authors five phases of development of the Lepcha culture can be constructed.

I. The first phase represents the condition of the Lepchas prior to any invasion from outside. The Lepchas then were the original and sole inhabitants of Sikkim and led a semi-nomadic life subsisting mainly on collection of roots and tubers, fishing, hunting, etc. Shifting cultivation whenever present, was very rudimentary in form and the technology was very crude. They had a good deal of traditions relating to mythology, folklore, knowledge of plants, herbs, animals, etc. based on a very simple social structure with primitive technology and crude animism. Isolation due to natural barrier and typical Himalayan ecosystem played a great role in the development and retention of such a type of simple culture during this earlier phase.

II. The next phase of development of the Lepcha culture is marked by the first major contact with the Tibetans. Although the Lepchas settled in Sikkim sometimes between ninth and thirteenth century it became a political entity in the fifth decade of the seventeenth century, when the people of Sikkim were converted into the Buddhist faith and Phuntsog Namgyal was appointed as the first king. Since then a number of kings came into power in Sikkim. This contact with the Tibetan resulted in large scale migration, dominance of ruling class and subjugation of the conquered, gradual replacement of the traditional Lepcha scriptures and introduction of Buddhism, emergence of Sikkimese Bhutias due to intermarriage, infiltration of newer ideas and values.

III. This phase may be regarded as the most critical phase in the Lepcha life in view of the fact that hordes of the Bhutanese, surged into Sikkim from the east, plundering the settlement and carrying off the inhabitants as slaves to Bhutan. Territorial integrity was threatened to a great extent due to frequent attack by the Bhutanese and the Gurkhas on the Kingdom's eastern and western frontiers.

This phase is characterised by unrest with conflicts and tensions. Side by side, this era is remarkable for the Lepcha heroism. Many heroic tales are associated with their fightings with the Bhutanese and the Gurkhas. Different types of newer ideas and values got infiltrated into ther culture due to their contact with the Bhutanese and some other caste people of Nepal. This contact further led to the destruction of the Lepcha scriptures, increase of inter-marriage as also increase in number of slaves.

IV. Contact with the British may be regarded as another phase of development of the Lepcha culture. With the outbreak of the Nepal War help was sought by the king of Sikkim from the British for the protection of his territory against the Nepalese attack. The British force came to the aid of Sikkim and the Gurkhas were defeated and the subsequent peace treaty established the Nepal and Sikkim boundary. Out of friendship the Raja of Sikkim granted the site of Darjeeling to the British. Gradually, the relationship of the king of Sikkim with the British became strained and in 1850 the serious punitive action taken by the British was the withdrawl of grants to the Raja of Sikkim and the annexation of the Terai and the positions of the Sikkim Hills. Kalimpong sub-division was annexed after the Bhutan war of 1865.

The area in general was under forest, uninhabited and a primitive system of Government existed which countenanced slavery, but did nothing to encourage development and increase population over the handful of the Lepchas, the indigenous population of the area.

Some of the significant characteristics of this phase, that deserve special mention are as follows :

(i) Introduction of a new type of administration, (ii) Adoption of certain policies for protection of hillmen from exploitation, (iii) Interest taken by the British administration for the development of the area, (iv) Immigration of communities from outside who took part in the development, (v) The Lepchas becoming minority in the land of their own due to the heavy influx of the Nepali population, (vi) Reservation of forests and imposition of taxes, (vii) Impact of Christian Missions and their activities in the life of the people.

Further, this phase is worthnoting for the beginning of the settled cultivation, opening of different avenues for earning livelihood, exploitation of the Lepchas by different communities, etc. The Lepcha life and cuture were gradually exposed to the outsiders through writtings of travellers, missionaries, administrators, etc., till that time these people were rather unknown to the outside world.

V. The last phase through which the Lepcha are now passing is the phase of the development of their life and activities during the post-independence era. Special safeguards have been provided in the Constitution of the Republic of India for the protection and socio-economic and cultural development of the Scheduled Tribes at a rapid pace. This phase is specially remarkable for implementation of different welfare and developmental schemes by the official as well as non-official agencies aimed at towards over-all betterment of the life condition of the people therein improving the quality of their life. Impact of all these have exerted quite a good deal of influence on the socio-economic and cultural life of the Lepchas.

III

A common belief that is quite current among the general mass, is that the Lepchas are at the verge of extinction, their number being gradually decreasing. This notion has been created from the writings of some of the earlier authors who, while dealing with the Lepchas of Sikkim, have also tried to trace out the reasons for the same. Gorer observed the presence of a fear complex associated with sterility amongst the Lepchas of Sikkim. Out of 56 married women over twenty years of age, he found 18 of them completely sterile and one had produced only a still born daughter. Premature population and some sort of genito-urinary deseases (*tanji*) were considered to be the possible cause for such sterility. In Gorer's own words:

> "as a society with its unique conglomeration of attitudes the Lepchas are certainly disappearing for in their culture presupposes a homogeneous interlocking community and this as well as their complete suppression of competition and aggression, cause an inevitable break down of culture in any mixed community." (1938 : 36)

Hutton while introducing Gorer's book remarked that the whole complex of want of aggression, sex obsession and sterility arises from the effects of a long period of undisturbed isolation in an uncoveted terrain where necessity for self-defence against external enemies was not experienced. He concluded by saying that if the situation be so there might be possibility of tracing out the parallels of Lepchas psychology in some island communities of Oceania (*ibid*). Certain amount of sterility, according to Morris, was due to the custom of very young girls cohabiting with grown up men. To Morris, the reason for dying out of the Lepchas appeared to be psychological to a great extent, associated with the habit of too much of drinking. (1938 : 284-238)

It appears from the accounts of the two authors, Gorer and Morris, that the Lepchas are dominated by a strong sex complex and it is a big question whether the consciousness of sex can be attributed to be the cause for declining Lepchas population, about which the Lepchas themselves are quite aware.

To me it appears that the problem is rather psychological than sex oriented and Morris' analysis may hold true to some extent.

The situation that has been emerged through the above writings may hold true to a considerable extent about the dying out of the Lepchas of Sikkim, more particularly of those living in Jongu, a reserve but so far as it concerns the Lepchas of Darjeeling District the demographic situation reveals quite a different story. In addition, my field study in Darjeeling reveals that the Lepchas are neither conscious of any sort of decaying population like Sikkim Lepchas, nor are aware of any sort of chronic sterility among them. It has been noticed that they lack competitive zeal and this, in an indirect way, is influencing their psychology as they think they are losing in day to day struggle and a lack of confidence is overwhelming these people. This sort of psychological depression has not yet become a chronic affair to that level of thinking themselves to be decaying. At present educated Lepcha leaders are very much conscious about the lack of competitive zeal among their community and are devoting much time to improve the condition of their community individually or through different organizations (1978 : 162). The following census figures of the Lepcha population of the State would also convince that there is a steady rise of the Lepcha population from decade to decade.

The Lepcha population has increased by 49,92 per cent in West Bengal during the period 1891 (9,717) to 1971 (14,568). There was a slight decline in the growth of population during the period 1911—1921. From 1921 onwards the Lepcha population has been steadily increased except in the year 1941 and 1971 wherein a fall in the rate of increase is noticed.

Variaiion of Lepcha Population in West Bengal during different decades

Year	*Total No. of Lepchas*	*Over all Percentage variation since 1891*	*Percentage increase/ decrease over the preceding decade*
1891	9,717	——	——
1901	10,052	3.44	3.44
1911	9,842	1.28	2.08
1921	9,669	—0.49	—1.75
1931	12,719	30.89	31.54
1941	12,468	28.31	—1.97
1951	13,430	38.21	7.70
1961	15,309	57.54	13.99
1971	14,568	49.92	—4.08

Almost similar type of trend is noticeable among the Lepcha of Darjeeling District also.

IV

The district of Darjeeling in West Bengal consists of two distinct tracts—the ridges and the deep valleys of the lower Himalaya and the level country at their base. The district has four sub-divisions Sadar, Kurseong, Kalimpong and Siliguri. In the first three hill sub-divisions the Lepchas of the state are mainly concentrated. Out of 14,568 Lepchas in the State of West Bengal as per 1971 census, 13,536 (92.92%) reside in Darjeeling district alone and of the rest (7.08 per cent), Jalpaiguri district shares 901 Lepchas and the remaining Lepcha population (131) are scattered in other districts. The distribution of the Lepcha population in different districts of the state are as follows :

Calcutta—31, Cooch Bihar—3, 24 Parganas—44, Jalpaignri—901, Darjeeling—13,536, Nadia—2, West Dinajpur—Nil, Purulia—6, Burdwan—6, Bankura—Nil, Birbhum—Nil, Malda —Nil, Murshidabad—4, Midnapur—23, Howrah—2 and Hoogly —10.

Of the thirteen police stations of Darjeeling District the

Lepchas are mainly concentrated in three police stations (Rangli Rangliot, Kalimpong and Kurseong) where about 78 per cent of the total Lepcha population of that district are found.

About 90 per cent of the total Lepchas are inhabitants of rural areas. Male and female ratio stands 57.01 : 42.09; 8,305 being males and 6,263 females.

The following table gives an idea about the proportion of the Lepcha population to the total population of Darjeeling District.

Year	*Total Papulation*	*Lepcha Population*	*P.C. of the Lepcha to the total population in each decade*
1891	2,23,314	9,717	4.35
1901	2,49,117	9,972	4.00
1911	2,65,550	9,706	3.65
1921	2,82,748	9,669	3.41
1931	3,19,635	12,101	3.78
1941	3,76,369	12,468	3.31
1951	4,45,260	13,164	2.95
1961	6,24,640	14,910	2.38
1971	7,31,777	13,536	1.73

The table reveals that though the Lepcha population show an increasing trend through decades, in general their proportion to the general population is gradually decreasing (except in 1931), the lowest being in 1971. This might be creating an atmosphere of the Lepchas being gradually becoming extinct. But this decreasing trend is mainly due to the heavy migration of other groups of people in this tiny hill district bordering Nepal, Sikkim, Bhutan and Tibet. The British exploitation was mainly in the development of tea, engineering, trade and education and did not result in permanent British population here. The impact of the British administration resulted in the heavy influx of the Nepali population who were considered more useful as labourers in tea gardens and more efficient and thrifty as cultivators than the Lepchas. Development of trade and communications brought further exploitations through immigrants like the Marwari, Behari and the Bengalee traders and professional men, many of whom have started permanently settling in this part of the State. Economically these groups dominate over the Nepalis inspite of their strong numerical position. All these migrations at subsequent streams have resulted in a very mixed population of the Lepchas, Nepalis, Bhutias, Tibetans, Marwaris, Biharis, etc.

V

Karan and Jenkins have observed that the Mongoloid tribes from Tibet, the Indo-Aryan people from northern India and the Lepchas from Assam and Upper Burma have settled in the Himalayan valleys and developed separate cultural pattern, since long past (1963: 14). While dealing with the migration of the Lepchas, Risley observes that the tribe has its origin in two successive waves of immigrants of the Mongoloid race, the last one coming in the middle of seventeenth century (1891:7). Hermanns noticed two basic types among the Lepchas, one with the long head, small face, high forehead, high narrow nose and prominent eyebrows, eye almost without any epicanthic fold, cheek bones not so prominent, light yellow skin colour while the other type has a broad face with prominent cheek bones and supraorbital ridges, broad nose, with prominent epicanthic fold, broad head, colour of the skin being light yellow. The former group is taller than the latter one. Hermanns could associate these two physical types with two different religions and economic status, the hunters and the farmers. The hunters with their hunting religion, sociology and economy represent the tall *Rong* (Lepcha) type and the farmers on the other hand, with shorter physique. Thus according to him the Lepchas represent a mixed culture. Some believe that they have connections with the Tibetan, others say that they wandered from the east along Burma, Assam mountains. The hunting component of the Lepcha are believed to be the primitive indigenous inhabitants of the forests of Sikkim and the farmers migrating at a later stage having connection with such people as the Naga, the Lolo, the Miau (1954: 105-106).

The Lepcha villages, generally situated on the slopes of the hills, constitute important socio-political units and play dominant part in their life and activities. The selection of the site of the villages (*bustee*) in this part of the country is mainly guided by the proximity to the water sources and abundance of suitable cultivable land. The significant characteristics of the Lepcha village that deserve special mention, are stated below:

1. The Lepcha houses are generally spread over a wide area throughout the length and breadth of the hill slopes.

2. The village is divided into the number of hamlets in accordance with their position in the hill slopes (upper, middle, lower etc.), Sometimes hamlets are known by the name of major community of the hamlet or by the name of an import characteristic of the hamlet such as '*mandir*' (temple), etc.

3. The Lepchas generally classify two types of cultivable land—(i) *panikhet* and (ii) *sukhakhet*. In the upper portion of the hill slope the cultivable land is of *sukhakhet* type (dry land) and in the lower portion it is of *panikhet* type (wet land).

4. The composition of the hamlets in general is of multi-ethnic type. The people professing Christianity irrespective of their community affiliation, try to reside in a particular hamlet, where the presence of a Mission church is a major characteristic. This is not the case in general with the people of other religious groups.

5. Homesteads are in general of dispersed type on the hill slopes. Clustered homesteads are sometimes visible at the lower hill slopes where patches of table land are visible. Cultivable land is situated around the homesteads or in between them. There is no well-defined lane or bye-lane. One has to approach the homesteads through hilly track.

6. The main sources of water supply are *jhoras* (water falls), *simsarmul* (water logged areas), rivulets, etc. From running *jhora* water is brought to the homesteads for domestic consumption or to the kitchen garden or cultivable lands for irrigational purpose, by joining a number of bamboo pipes through hill slopes.

7. The village life is centred to a considerable extent

round the churches, monasteries, etc., which are the major features of the settlement. Some of the other important places are *manes* (memorial pillars), schools. clubs, etc. The Christians have their separate graveyard whereas this is not the characteristic with the people professing other religious faiths (Buddhism, Hinduism, Animism, etc.). In their cases land near the homestead or a portion of cultivable land is utilised for burial/cremation purpose.

Economic condition of the Lepchas is not at all satisfactory. Of the total Lepcha population more than half (51.60 per cent) are workers and of the total workers (7,899), 81.91 per cent are cultivators and 3.01 per cent agricultural labourers. The remaining 15.08 per cent workers are engaged in other types of occupation. Though cultivation is their primary occupation, they are regarded as poor agriculturists. In addition, majority of the cultivating families have small land holdings, most of which are of *sukhakhet* type i.e. dry land. Possession of *panikhet* (wetland) is meagre. When the Britishers took possession of this tract of land, the hill portion was almost under forest. The Lepchas used to practice *jhum* (i.e. shifting cultivation) with crude type of implements. With the reservation of forests, appropriation of land for tea cultivation and extension of plough cultivation, the Lepchas were bound to adopt plough cultivation. At present they practise terrace cultivation which forms the principal subsistence activity. But they are poor agriculturists and the skill and the hard labour that are required for the various operations in this hilly area, are generally lacking in them. Due to this they do not get the full benefit out of this subsistence activity. Contrary to this, the Nepalese being hard working and having efficient labour force, get much more benefit from whatever land they possess. The Lepchas cultivate paddy in the *panikhet.* Maize and millet are primarily grown in the *sukhakhet*. Cardamom which constituted one of the major crops a few decades back, has now almost been abandoned by the Lepchas. Fruit and vegetable cultivation go side by side, though to a very limited extent.

Handicrafts now-a-days do not play a major role in the Lepcha economy. The materials they use for expressing their artistic tendencies are brass, iron, bamboo, stone beads, silver, etc. The traditional Lepcha handicrafts is weaving by hand. Some of them entirely depend on carpentry and masonry works while a few of them are good painters. Some of them are at present engaged in different types of white colour jobs (office assistant, teacher, etc.) and are also found in police and military services. Thus the Lepcha economic system in general may be grouped into the following five categories—(i) agriculture, (ii) agricultural labour, (iii) daily labour, (iv) service, (v) craftsmanship.

It has already been mentioned that the economic condition of the Lepchas is not at all satisfactory. Apart from low income the Lepchas are spendthrift in nature. Whenever they get money they spend lavishly. The drinking of *chi* (homebrewn liquor) is a curse to them. Their socio-religious functions also compel them to spend a lot. Each ceremony from the birth of a baby to the death of a person is a costly affair to the Lepchas. Moreover, they are accustomed to spend a lot on the sacrifice of animals and associated ceremonies in order to appease innumerable evil spirits of whom they are afraid of throughout their life. (Das 1978:77)

In Sikkim, the Lepchas who live primarily in a reserve set aside for them by the then ruling kings, manage to grow rice, wheat, millet, maize, as well as varieties of fruit, vegetables and spices, including the cardamom. The reserve Jongu is located in the precipitous valley of the high Himalayas. There is probably not a 100 feet sequare piece of flatland in the whole region and cultivation often takes place at a 60 degree angle. The Lepchas find it impossible to use even mules for porterage and are obliged to carry all baggages on their own backs. They greatly fear famine and to ward off hunger and disease they perform a good number of religious rituals. (Lindholm 1960: 50)

The Lepcha life style is communal and the ideal of cooperation, unselfishness and sharing are the basic characteristics of their society. Lindholm observes:

> "The Lepchas redistribute their resources to alleviate poverty and sharing with the poor is considered a very good custom because, as one village headman explained, 'It makes everybody realize that the happiness of one is...

> the happiness of all'. Both children and adults are extraordinarily unselfish and always share things. Children are taught to help others, so that others in their turn will help them and they are told that no one will help a thief. They are instructed to receive a gift in cupped hands and always to give a small gift in return. Gift giving, which is a continuing motif in the Lepcha life, is always an exchange, never simply one-sided receiving.
>
> Among the Lepchas, relations are based on exact reciprocity and mutual obligations and the individual who fulfils those obligations, is automatically a good person and will be well liked. It is interesting to note that the stomach, not the heart is considered to be the center of emotions and that past events are often remembered in terms of menus. Male and female work roles are not greatly differentiated, both work in the fields and men will take over the cooking if necessary. Although the society is patrilineal with women unable to inherit land, the only real difference the Lepchas see between men and women is in the genital organs which are considered to have a sort of independent life very much of their own." (1980 : 54)

The Lepchas had three social divisions based on three geographical regions. These were *tamsang* or *damsang* (this area falls in Sikkim, Darjeeling and Bhutan), *rinjong* or *daudjung* (area falling on the other side of the Tista river in Sikkim) and the last one is the *Ilam* district of Nepal. In the past the Lepchas belonging to each of the regions, formed well knit social groups with surnames adopted from these groupings but nowadays these divisions do not exist. It is believed that of the three social divisions *rinjong* held the upper most position, *ilam* coming next and *tamsang* at the bottom of the social hierarchical order. People of *rinjong* and *ilam* groups used to establish matrimonial ties amongst them whereas the *tamsangs* had to restrict their marriages within their own group. It is believed that when Bhutan had conquered *tamsang*, the people of that region most ignorably submitted themselves to the Bhutias and imbibed to a considerable extent their dresses, manners and customs and that is the reason of their placement at the lowest of the social hierarchy.

At present among the Lepchas of Darjeeling there exists nothing of the sort of slave as a class or the conception of nobles or commoners as classes. The Lepcha society is regarded as a casteless—classless society not only by the Lepcha themselves but by the neighbouring communities also such as the Rais, Limbus, Tamang, Bhutias and others. Further, the Lepchas are acceptable to all the societies and vice versa. There is a proverb quite common in the area which states that from a Lepcha plate every one can take meal and the Lepchas are also allowed to take meal from others' plates.

The Lepchas cannot be treated as an endogamous community in view of the fact that marriages quite often take place between different ethnic groups. In case of intercommunity marriage the couple belong to the particular community to which they affiliate themselves.

The family (*tiyum*) is the smallest and most fundamental social unit and characterised by common residence, economic cooperation and reproduction. Majority of the Lepcha families are at present small/medium sized. Family life is not particularly warm. For the child, the world is a place of pervasive anxiety and adults remember their childhood as times of fear, hurt and obscurity. Though infants are given much attention, that attention is rather impersonal and the older child, though desired for his labour, is treated with some sort of neglect (Lindholm 1980 : 55). Next to family the consanguineal type of kingroup is *putso* (sib) the members whereof trace descent from their original ancestor associated with a particular landscape feature. The Lepcha *putso* does not play any significant role now as it did in the past, excepting in the regulation of marriage. Practically, it has lost all its influences on the economic and political spheres of activity of the people. The characteristics of the Lepcha sib are that these are exogamous, associated with place names instead of plants, animals, etc. as in the cases of majority of the Indian tribes, unilineal in nature but sex linked in character. The sex linked character of the sibs is being gradually diminished due to the influence of neighbuoring communities.

and prominence to father's line has already gained ground in some areas.

Among the Lepchas relations are based on exact reciprocity and mutual obligations and the individual who fulfills those obligations is automatically a good person and well liked. The Lepchas do not have large number of kinship terms; different types of kinsmen are grouped under a few broad kin terms in each of ascending, decending and ego's generations. In this connection Lindholm's observation is quite worth nothing. He mentions,

> "Communal life among the Lepcha ignores individual differences and stresses obligation rather than affect or feeling. People exist only as a part of a larger whole. They are liked and accepted according to their fulfillment of obligations, not according to their individual personalities, which are not really recognized among the Lepchas. This lack of individuality is reflected in the fact that individual names are of almost no consequence in the Lepcha culture; people are called by kinship terms and if even possible for a man to forget the actual name of his own wife. Arranged marriages are thought to work out well since they are merely a relation of mutual obligation such as might be set up between any two people. Provided both parties fulfill these obligations, they will automatically grow to like each other" (1980 : 55).

The institution of marriage among the Lepchas as in the case of other human societies, deserve special considerations as it reflects some unique features. The census figures of 1971 reveal that more than 99 per cent of the married Lepchas belong to the age group 15 and above indicating that early marriage is not the norm of the society. However, the accounts of Hooker (1955), Morris (1938 : 80-112), Gorer (1938 : 316) etc. reveal that early marriage was once the pattern of the Lepcha of Sikkim. Accounts furnished by Gorer and Morris reveal that the Lepcha girls are betrothed and occasionally married from the age of eight onwards and the boys from the age of twelve. The social customs though modified to a certain extent, are responsible for the high incidences of late marriage as well as unmarried persons among the Lepchas. That is the reason as to why 98 per cent of the unmarried Lepchas belong to the age group 0-44. On the other hand, the incidence of divorce is quite meagre (0.9 per cent) unlike other tribal groups of the plains areas. The high incidence of late marriage and unmarried persons and occurrence of less number of divorced persons among them are due to high bride price, costly marriage custom, and the mode of acquiring bride by rendering service in father-in-law's house (though this custom has mostly been abandoned at present).

The present day cultural axiom is monogamous type of marriage which is favoured and tried to be followed strictly by most of these people. According to the cultural norm polyandry is prohibited, even polygyny is not usually practised but only in very rare cases. Factors such as barrenness of the wife etc., lead to polygynous union. Marriage is generally arranged through negotiation by employing a *pibu* or marriage go-between and sometimes service is rendered to the future father-in-law in the hope of marriage. Incidences of love marriage are on the increase due to traditiodal marriage customs involving high costs and service. Junior levirate is permissible but the incidence of occurrence is negligible unlike in the past when it was customary for a widow to marry the younger brother of his deceased husband, whatever his age might be. Simultaneously sororate was also practised after the death of the wife by marrying her younger sister.

In the past, bride price as well as rendering service to the bride's house were the main consideration for marriage. The bride price involved payment of money in cash and also different types of animals as well as costly utensils and clothings. But now-a-days due to economic harships such bride price is not so strictly demanded as in the past. Now a groom is allowed to pay the bride price in two or three instalments to the parents of the bride. Some amount of money with bull, pig, clothings and utensils are given as bride price now-a-days. This costly custom has not only compelled the Lepchas to marry late or to remain unmarried or to go for love marriages but it on many occasions, has led them to choose partners from out side theri own community. It has also led to the credit system of marriage. Here the girl remains in her father's house and the husband lives with her till he can pay the bride price or earns the money which entitles him to take her home. There are other considerations also—star observations for life, body, etc., consulation of horoscope and a twelve year cycle by a lama. (Das 1978: 134-139)

The rituals followed in connection with marriage, vary from area to area. The rituals reveal a mingling of the traditional Lepcha as well as Buddhist or Lamaist faiths and these are performed by religious functionaries like *bongthing* and *mun* (priest and pristess) of traditional faith as well as Lama of Buddhist faith. The rituals have so nicely been blended that there exists no conflict at any stage of their performance. The marriage in general, constitutes two broad divisions *asek* or betrothal and *bri* or bringing home the bride. In Kalimpong area of Darjeeling district the Lepcha marriages constitute of five parts (1) *lagto*, (2) *chamu*, (3) *tung-gung*, (4) *ashek* and (5) *nomchum*. In Kurseong area *sigiyang* is the first phase of marriage and Phase II and III consist of *asek* (giving marriage) and *niyom chum* (to give everything to the daughter). A good number of the Lepchas after performing the first phase of marriage, do not even care to perform the next two phases due to the very poor economic condition. This sometimes results in instability of marriage as the girl's father often tries to take back her daughter to his own house as he does not consider *sigiyang* to be a fullfledged form of marriage.

The incidence of divorce in the Lepcha society is still very limited. According to Census Report of 1971 less than one per cent is divorced or separated. Formerly, this percentage was almost nil because of their painstaking endeavour involved in getting a partner. In the past most marriages were stable and divorce or separation was very rare. (Gorer, 1938 : 157)

Lindholm has observed that the sex life of the Lepchas is very active. Inpotence is unheard of and sexual activity continues until quite late in life for both men and women. (1980: 52). Gorer has found that sexual activity is practically divorced from emotion. Sexual jealousy is not considered a normal emotion and there is no word for jealousy in the language. (1938 : 327).

Lindholm states:

> "This is not to say that the Lepcha society is totally promiscuous. In fact, the range of partners prohibited by incest taboo is extremely wide : sex is forbidden with a partner related back at least seven generations on the father's side and at least four on the mother's... Marriage and sex partner must come from some distance away." (*ibid*)

Siiger notes that "real ingenuity has to be exercised in order to find a suitable partner for one's son or daughter and perhaps this is the reason for allowing the sharing of women within the village." (1956 : 34)

It has been found that the marriage circle of the Bhutias, Nepalis etc., tends to include a fairly large area from hill to hill while marriage among the Lepchas takes place within fairly limited neighbouring areas. Nakane has observed that the degree of social distance or discrimination between the Lepcha and the Bhutia appears more strongly among the peasants and tends to decrease in professional circles. Thus in the upper-strata aristocrats inter-marriage has taken place to a surprising degree. In Nakane's own words:

> "Professional priests and aristocrats form one community based on their common intellectual, social and political activities the value of which is far stronger than the ethnic differences. Thus elite consciousness and the common ground of intellectual, social and political activities, diminish ethnic consciousness." (1966 : 235)

To the Lepchas death is the real enemy of life. To them it is nothing but the separation of the soul from the body. The soul of a living body is called *apil* and it changes at the time of death into a spirit named Muknyam. The common causes of death as believed by them, are diseases and accidents and these two are also believed by them to be due to the influence of evil spirits. To protect individuals from the attack of various evil spirits (Sand grong mung, Dut mung, Sum, mungo etc.) the Lepchas perform different rituals and ceremonies which are costly affairs for a poor community like them. The Lepchas have also a number of benevolent spirits. (Abo a moisa rum, Musikung etc.) who protect them from the attacks of the malevolent spirits. Traditional priest/pristess *bongthing/mun* and Buddhist Lamas perform their duties side by side following both the indigenous as well lamaist rites and ceremonies.

The Lepchas practise both burial and cremation for disposing dead bodies. Three types of graves are generally recognised, pit grave with a circular base (*kok*), pit grave with a square base (*kokden*) and oblong grave (*kokblee*).

Rites connected with dead before and after burial/cremation are quite elaborate in nature following both traditional and lamaist customs. The existence of traditional beliefs and practices side by side with Buddhistic ideas, somewhere there exists a blending of ideas and practices instead of total replacement.

> "The balanced role of the *mun/bongthing* and the Lama of different religious groups in different ritualistic performances of the Lepchas concerning death and other associated rites, further strengthens this blending of two cultural values in a unified manner thereby strengthening integration in cultural as well as psychological level." (Das, 1978: 183)

As in the case of social life, the religious beliefs and practices of the Lepchas also represent a balanced blending of their traditional indigenous beliefs and practices as also Lamaism, the newly adopted religion. The co-existence of these two different belief systems and their integrated functioning in a balanced and effective way in minimising life crises is possible due to the nature and chatacter of the Lepchas and their society, which is non-aggressive in nature and tolerant in character.

Siiger while discussing about the Lepcha religion states:

> "The problem of the origin of the Lepcha religion is complex and rather difficult because Tibetan Bon and Red Sect Lamaism for centuries have influenced the religious practices, but I am inclined to join Risley's suggestion that

the original Lepcha religion was closely connected with old Central Asian Shamanism." (1956 : 45)

God among the Lepchas is known as *rum* meaning thereby the spirits which are benevolent, that is, those who give protection to the Lepchas and are favourable to them. By the term *rum* itself the Lepchas indicate or rather express the idea on the Supreme God. Words expressing the special attributes of the Supreme God are often joined to the term *rum.* Pum-rum or Pong-rum is regarded as the god of hunters. The god of hunters is worshipped exclusively by the men, while the women do not participate in the worship. It is believed that the god has given them bows, arrows, knives, etc., and taught them how to shoot fish. Sa-dju is another god venerated as the god of agriculture. Rum-fat is the family or the household god and is the protector of the domestic animals. Ayek-rum and Alat-rum are regarded as the gods of procreation. In addition, an individual may have one or more spirits who render protection into the individuals (Hit-rum, Darmit-rum, Monlam-rum, Bong-thing rum, Dang-mu rum etc.). Side by side, the Lepchas also believe in the existence of a number of evil spirits known as *mung*. These malevolent spirits cause harm to men and animals, fields, etc. Each one of the human illness is caused by an evil spirit Rumung (Consumption), Dom-mung (leprosy), etc., and these constitute the great flock of disease round demons. These evil spirits hover round in the mountains, woods, gorges etc.

Numbers of traditional Lepcha priests and pristess (*mun* and *bongthing*) have come down considerably in Darjeeling area due to varied modern forces. They act as the intermediaries between the god and the man. They are regarded as powerful religious functionaries who are meant for expelling demons and appeasing the gods through sacrifices. They choose spirits as their servants. Important sacrificial offerings made by them in their propitiation are bullock, ox, pig, goat, fowl, etc. The *mun* and *bongthing* are not allowed to practise any black magic as such, for their vocation is precisely to help people and to ward off all harm.

It is clear that the chief function of the *mun/bongthing* is to ward off the misfortunes and illness caused by the evil spirits, which is done by animal sacrifices as well as by direct communication with the supernaturals, and on certain occasions the *mun* becomes possessed by the guardian spirit and prophesies. In Lamaism, on the other hand, priesthood and sanctity are acquired by learning and not by inspiration and they personally never carry out sacrifices which are regarded as a sinful act on their part. The future is depicted by them not by inspiration but by consulting holy books and they believe in individual destiny and a sense of sin. Gorer, however, states in this connection about the Sikkim Lepchas that they have a word for sin (*la-yo* borrowed from Tibetan) but have no idea of sin. The word is commonly used in the killing of animals. (Gorer, 1938 : 182-183)

The Lepchas have adopted the very core or essence of Lamaism to varied extent in their day to day life. They have accepted the ritual, the validating mythology and organisation of Lamaism to some extent but could not accept its ethics to the fullest extent because according to them, Lamaism like other higher religions is individualistic in conception, it concerns mainly with the spiritual welfare of the individual concerned and this is quite alien to the Lepchas and rather contrary to their traditional religious conception.

The Lepcha religion in characterised by the presence of a number of ceremonies. Some of these ceremonies held on family level, are performed by the head of the family, some are on village level, *mun/bongthing/lama* acting as the priest and some are performed on monastic level. The ceremonial place is consecrated and altar structures of bamboo, mats and the like are arranged. The main functions are comprised of offerings and sacrifices or both, invocations of gods and conjurations of *mungs*, or both and some times, of entrance by a *mun*. The ordinary minor offerings consist of rice, local beer (*chi*), a coin, some small birds and small fishes, but on more important occasions, *tormas*, i.e. conical figures made of rice, maize, etc. are used in addition. The Lepchas distinguish between cultic performances to the gods and the *mung*. While the *mung* requires sanguinary sacrifices, the gods usually get vegetable offerings, but sometimes also sacrifices of animals, depending on the character of the god. The rituals accompanying the offerings to the gods, consist of requests for protection and fertility, whereas in the rituals accompanying the sacrifices to the *mung*, the people beseech the *mung* to accept the meat and the blood of the sacrificed animal instead of devouring the bodies of human beings. Here the sacrifices to the *mung* indicate a kind of substitute, the meat and the blood of the sacrificial animal replacing the human body or bodies, (Das, 1978 : 201)

The socio-economic and cultural life of the Lepcha have undergone a good deal of changes through different historical phases due to various external and internal forces. The Tibetan influence helped spreading of Lamaism and the neighbouring Nepali groups of people influenced their socio-economic life. With the advent of the British rule vigorously Missionary activities started and the Lepchas were gradually exposed towards different forces of modernization. With the attainment of Independence different welfare and development schemes were specially designed for the hill people with the intention of overall development of the area and the people. All these factors have helped in accelerating the process of acculturation and making them well conscious about their identity at community and national levels. Changes in the material and cultural levels have not only helped them in improving their standard of living but also in broadening their mental horizon and to a great extent in creating a confidence among them to overcome the fear complex of a loosing race which haunted them through generations.

REFERENCES

Campbell, Archibald 1840 Note on the Lepcha of Sikkim with a vocabulary of their Language *Jr. of the Asiatic Society of Bengal*, Vol IX, Part I.

Dalton, Edward Tuite 1872 *Descriptive Ethnology of Bengal*, Calcutta, Office of the Superintendent of Government Printing.

Das, Amal Kumar 1978 *The Lepchas of West Bengal*, Calcutta, Editions Indian.

Donaldson, Florence 1900 *Lepcha Land or Six Weeks in the Sikkim Himalayas*, London: Sompson, Low, Marsten.

Gorer, Geoffrey 1938 *Himalayan Village : An account of the Lepchas of Sikkim*, London : Joseph.

Grierson, George A. 1927 *Linguistic Survey of India*, Vol. III, Tibeto-Burma Family, Calcutta : Superintendent of Government Printing.

Grunwedel, Albert 1892 *A Rong-English Glossary*, T' Oung Archives (Series I), III.

Hermanns, Matthiss Fr. 1954 *The Indo-Tibetans : The Indo-Tibetan and Mongoloid Problem in Southern Himalaya and North East India*, Bombay : K. L. Fernandez.

Hodgson, Brian H. 1847 On the Aborigines of the Sub-Himalayas, *Jr. of the Asiatic Society of Bengal*, XVI.

Hooker, Joseph Dalton 1855 *Himalayan Journal* : *Notes of a Naturalist in Bengal, the Sikkim and Nepal Himalayas, the Khasia Mountains* etc. Vol. I & II, London : Murray.

Hunter, William Wilson 1868 *A Comparative Dictionary of the Languages of India and High Asia*, etc., London : Truebner.

Karan, P.P. and Jenkins, W.W. 1963 *The Himalayan Kingdom : Bhutan, Sikkim and Nepal*, Princeton Van Nostrand.

Latham, Robert Gordon 1859 *Descriptive Ethnology* : Vol. I, Eastern and Northern Asia-Europe, London : Van Voorst.

Lindholm, Charles and Lindholm Cherry 1980 What Price Freedom, *Science Digest*, Nov.-Dec.

Mainwaring, George Byres 1876 *A Grammar of the Rong (Lepcha) Language as it Exists in the Darjeeling and Sikkim Hills*, Calcutta: Baptist Mission Press.

Morris, John 1938 *Living with Lepchas : A Book About the Sikkim Himalayas.* London : Heinemann.

Nakane, Chie 1966 *A Plural Society in Sikkim in Caste and Kin in Nepal, India and Ceylon,* ed. Christoph von Furer-Haimendorf, Bombay : Asia Publishing House.

Risley, Herbert Hope 1891 *The Tribes and Castes of Bengal*, Vol. 2, Calcutta : Bengal Secretariat Press.

Rock, Joseph F. 1953 Excerpts from a History of Sikkim, *Anthrops*, XLVIII.

Siiger, Halfdan 1956 Ethnological Field Research in Chitral, Sikkim and Assam, *Hidyotidk-Gilolo-gishe.* Meddeleser, XXXVI.

—— 1967 *The Lepchas : Culture and Religion of a Himalayan People.* Part I and II, Copenhagen : National Museum Ethnographic Series.

Stocks, C. de Beauvoir 1925 Folklore and Customs of the Lepchas of Sikkim, *Jr. of the Asiatic Society of Bengal* (New Series), XXI.

Waddell, Lawrence Austine 1899 *Among the Himalayas,* London: Constable.

White, J. Claude 1909 *Sikkim and Bhutan : 21 Years on the North-East Frontier. 1889-1908*, New York : Longman Green.

SECTION TWO

THE CENTRAL HIMALAYAN PERSPECTIVE

CHAPTER IX

ECOLOGY, TRADE AND FORMER BHOTIYA IDENTITY

C. W. BROWN

All people are obliged to solve basic problems of subsistence. The solutions confront them in different ways according to the conditions into which they were born and under which they live. For some people in the modern world there are special institutions designed to make the articles of subsistence available to be packed into shopping bags in exchange for a certain sum of money then transferred a relatively short distance home by car and stored until needed for relatively short periods of time in specially designed refrigerators. Most people, however, can only imagine such solutions. Although the basic problems are the same, the solutions for most people involve a labour input which is more closely associated with the very production of subsistence goods. For whatever reasons this state of affairs comes about, for a large number of peoples their close association with production means a simultaneously closer integration with the ecological conditions which thus act with a greater finality on their behaviour. Needless to say, the mountain ecology of the Himalayas confronts its inhabitants with special problems and each of its different ecological zones reflects a concomitant local adaptation in the integration of subsistence production and ecological finality. Since the people of these areas have of course not yet been confronted with conditions that make supermarkets and cars a solution, their ecological conditions tend to act with a greater finality the more so the higher the elevation above sea level.

It is the people inhabiting these higher levels that is the concern of the present chapter. It will be shown that the effects of ecology has led to consequences cutting into the very processes of identity that impose on groups of people even to extents exceeding their own wishes. In these higher reaches, we are in fact confronted with an interface of two major ecological zones—on the one hand one conducive to the production of goods such as those of the Indian lowlands and on the other one in which products of high elevation zones and the Tibetan plateau are available. This interface has resulted in a combination of problems for its inhabitants. Its semi-desolate nature has presented a problem in subsistence which the two zones in fact make solvable in a very special way—namely by generating a potential trade situation which confronts products of each zone with the other in a market which itself is only possible if its practitioners assume very specific modes of exchange. The people with whom we are now concerned occupy this interface zone and have traditionally exhibited a specific socio-economic practice which reflects the interface demands. As we look closer at these people, we witness also the curious twist of human logic in which, without the as yet relevant a prior identity of nations or even kingdoms, a society becomes consolidated around the articulation of an external identity according to features of its socio-economic practice and an internal, "centripetal" tendency to reproduce itself. This chapter will be concerned with this process of identity in the "ethnogenesis" of a group of people known as "Bhotiya". In fact, the association of ecological-economic "niche" to "Bhotlya" is so profound that the term is applied traditionally to all peoples along the interface from the Sutlej to Bhutan associated with the now disappearing Indo-Tibet trade, but so dispersed and varied that the term tends to become somewhat randomly applied. But a look at this traditional application of "Bhotiya" will lead us through some very central features both in Himalayan ecology and history and in the ethnogenesis of some of the Himalayas' most interesting people.

"Bhotiya" is the term applied to the people associated with the area called "Bhot" especially in the central Himalayan area. It seems that a popularization of the term is in some way connected to British expansion from Bengal past Nepal to the western Himalayan area in the 18th and 19th centuries A.D. The earliest British references to the "Booteas" associated them with Bhutan. Thus concerning the British-Bhutan War, the British records speak of an "invasion of Cooch Behar" by the Booteas (Bhutanese) in 1772. In fact during the time of Hastings when contacts were first made by the British with Tibet proper, Bhutan and Tibet were conceptualized together as "Boutan", and the inhabitants called "Boutans" or "Booteas" (cf. eg. on Hastings and Bogle in Markham, 1879). As British expansion pushed into the Himalayan regions of modern Uttar Pradesh, the administrators were confronted once again with a problem. This time the issue was further confused by the term "Hundes" which referred to western Tibet (mNga-ris) and forced the administrators to differentiate the Bhot of British territory from the Hundes of Tibet. R. Strachey (1851 : 85) follows Atkinson's interpretation of Hundes as the "country of Huns" as opposed to "Undes" (wool-country) or even "Huindes" (snow-country, which is Traill's interpretation and probably the most sensible). It may be noted that Traill in an "enclosure" to the Broad of Revenue of the Ceded and Conquered Provinces, 25 July 1817 refers to western Tibet as "Northern Bhote" in speaking of the Bhotiya trade system in general (No. 13A in *Board of Revenue,* 1817). It is probably quite true as D.N. Majumdar once noted:

> "The part of the country inhabited by the Bhotiyas, is known in Kumaon as Bhot while the Kumaonese call Tibet as Hundesh and the Tibetans are known to them as the Huniyas. The Bhotiyas also use the same appelation for the Tibetans and for the country of the Tibetans, they use Hundesh. According to popular belief, the words Bhot and Bhotiya were mainly popularized by the British administration, due probably to the cultural similarity with the people of Sikkim and Bhutan states..." (1949 : ii-iii)

The generality of the term even when used today can be exemplified by Bagchi who, in describing some characteristics of the eastern Himalayan area, refers to certain groups of Nepal, Sikkim, Bhutan and even to some Tibetans as the "Bhutias" (1977 : 366). Sastry interprets this identity more precisely in noting the generic character of the name as applicable to certain non-Tibetan peoples of the border region who have traditionally been practitioners of the trade between India and Tibet. (1975 : 19) This brings us quite near to the one of the central conditions inherent in the process of the Bhotiya identity which sometimes unfortunately is underemphasized. This is the influence of the Hindu caste system on the process of the Bhotiya identity especially as the system articulates within both the process of British expansion and the ecological determination of the interface niche. This caste-orientation is emphasized by R.P. Srivastava in his excellent article of 1961-62 (1979). Srivastava notes the general confusion of applications of the term "Bhotiya" but emphasizes a common association with the Tibet trade. He also notes the influence of the British administration in both intensifying the Bhotiya loyalty towards British India and officially categorizing them according to specific physical and social features. (Srivastava, 1979 : 174, 186-187) In connection with this latter factor, Srivastava correctly follows the tendency to centralize "Bhotiya" to those people less associated with a Buddhism which is in many ways a characteristic of the groups of Nepal and eastwards and more an integral part of the Hindu society as in characteristic of those groups of the central Himalayan area of India. We will follow this lead but not continue an investigation of the sometimes complicated problems associated with the tribe-caste situation and the important but, for our present purposes, study of the historical development of caste and British expansion. Thus we will emphasize that material aspect of the traditional, ecological, socio-economic reality which seems to permeate local history to a great extent independent of external global "political" situations. This will be emphasizing former economic conditions which may not be of central relevance today but have played a role in establishing the "Bhotiya" identity. At the same time we will be aware of the very important repercussions the concept of the "Bhotiya" may have for its modern occupants.

The geographical area of central concern to us then extends from east of the Sutlej to east of the Karnali river basins, and between a line running approximately between Karnaprayag and Darchula and on the Jumla in Nepal, and a line running between Gartok and Taklakot in old mNga-ris, Tibet. Although obviously only a small part of the whole of the chain of the great Himalaya mountains, there are some special features in the ecology, geology and geography of the area that generate a niche-like local potential which is reflected in the Bhotiya practices in its specificity. This is generally speaking characterized in part by the relative isolation of their higher level valleys and by the overall nature of the Indo-Tibetan interface. If one were to imaginc travelling from the plains into the lower foothills towards increasingly higher elevations, one would witness concomitant changes in the ecology at different levels. Food grains are cultivated in both the plains and lower foot-hills regions and form one basic link in the chain of trade that draws these necessary items towards areas in which they are more scarce due to the decreasing productivity of the soil. Items of trade have since time immemorial been borne along the roads and paths that more or less follow the courses of the great rivers and emerge intermittently at smaller market centers such as the hill towns of Srinagar, Rudraprayag, Joshimath, Bageswar, Almora, Pithoragarh etc.

What essentially a central feature of the higher elevations is the very lack of the cultivable areas that characterize the fertile lowlands. At higher elevations, settlements cling to the steep hillsides around what cultivable ground there is available along the rivers which now flow rapidly through the narrow valleys. Some of these valleys are nestled among some of the highest mountains in the world, the best known of which are the Nanda Devi, (7817 meters) and the Kamet (7735 meters), the eighth and ninth highest respectively. The area not in cultivation, which increases at increasingly higher elevations, is characterized by a ruggedness and expanse amendable only to the passage of caravans from the cultivated zones at the lower levels to beyond the mountain backbone over passes which range from

5099 meters (Lipu-lekh Pass) to 5505 meters (Chorhorti Pass) and which are open only during the warm season June to October. According to traditional usage, the area inhabited by the people who not only are obliged to trade for their own subsistence but are able to take advantage of their situation and transport the goods from the lower regions over the passes to the areas beyond is called "Bhot" and the people themselves are called the "Bhotiyas".

Beyond the passes were the high-elevation plains of an area earlier known as mNga-ris a part of greater Tibet. These plains consisted of vast grasslands inhabited mainly by nomadic herdsmen, and dotted here and there by more or less permanent settlements along trade routes and/or river valleys. These trade routes of mNga-ris ran from Ladakh in the west eastwards to Lhasa as well as from north to south, some of which of course were the routes monopolized by the Bhotiya. Salt was to be found in great quantities in certain areas of mNga-ris and was of sufficient scarcity in the middle hill regions at least to be exchangeable even at a small profit against the grain which was grown there or brought up from the lower areas. In a sense, this simple exchange formed the core around which other items also passed in transaction. G.W. Traill, one of the early British administrators most versed in this economic system, described mNga-ris in the system's perspective thus:

> "Subjected, by the rigor of its climate, to perpetual sterility.../ mNgar-ris/ depends on the surrounding countries for almost every commodity, both of necessity and of luxury; to remedy these deficiencies, it has, at the same time, been amply furnished by nature with a variety of valuable products; its rivers and deserts abound with gold, in its lakes are produced inexhaustible supplies of salt and borax, while to its pastures it is indebted for wool of an unrivalled quality.../etc. and it/has naturally attracted the resort of numerous traders from every quarter, and has, in consequence, become a general mart..." (1851 : 94-95)

In fact, quite a large number of items were once a part of the north-south trade network effected by the Bhotiyas. Earlier accounts mention, in addition to the central staples to which we shall return shortly, the following items of export from India to Tibet; calicoes, hardware, broad-cloth, pearls, *gur* (an item of cooking), sugar candy, spices, dyes, wooden vessels, timber, cabinet ware, beads, chintz, sugar, and such other miscellaneous items as could be produced by the British and the British inspired Indian industry. Of the imports to India from Tibet are mentioned: salt, tincal (raw borax), wool, shawl wool, gold dust, shawls, silks, cowtails, ponies, drugs, dried fruits, saffron, cured leather, and the important item of musk (Atkinson, III; 1886: 129; Mehra and Tiwari 1955: 14; Traill 1825 and 1851: 98-101). Traill notes that trade is probably the "sole consideration" which makes the Bhotiyas remain in their inhospitable habitat. The fact of their remaining there meant for them a virtual monopoly in the carrying trade, since the Tibetans would not visit the cis-Himalayan areas and the hillmen would not visit Tibet (Traill, 1851: 94, 96). Srivastava summarizes the situation quite well:

> "The Bhotias are thus situated in the middle of two regions of contrasted production. Their own valleys being unfit for agriculture or large-scale sheep-rearing, they had to look to.../ the adjacent/two regions for their livelihood. By virtue of their location they were in a position to meet the requirements of the people in these two regions by simply transporting the required commodities from one region to the other. Through their medium, the trade thus became not only a form of ecological adjustment between the two regions, but for the Bhotias it also became the mainstay of their economy." (1963 : 138)

The salt-grain trade, which we have called the core and which has probably been the stable feature of the Bhotiya economy for hundreds of years, can be described in the following terms together with a parallel system, from the ecological point of view, of a residential transhumanence. The semi-nomadic residential cycle itself is also a function of the demanding ecological conditions of the interface regions. There are two main domiciles of the Bhotiyas. One is occupied between June and October, the warm months when the snows have melted from around their homes, which by the way the Bhotiyas consider their proper homes and which are exclusively Bhotiya, near the passes along the upper reaches of the rivers of modern Chamoli and Pithoragarh districts. Their other residence forced upon them by the cold climate is further down the rivers near the middle hill region and shared with other groups of peoples permanently living there. At both locations a few crops are raised, usually tended to by the women, and supplemented by the food items that earlier were brought in by the men on their trading missions.

The traditional trading system of the Bhotiyas was one of the central features of their identity. Even if the traditional Tibetan trade has now ended, the basic residential pattern is still followed by many of the people, and the identity of the Bhotiyas still leaves marked traces of the traditional way of life. Even C. Von Furer-Haimendorf has described a parallel trade-domicile cycle among the peoples of the upper Karnali basin in Nepal who represent a counterpart group to the Indians. Although different in some important ways, the basic pattern followed there is an equivalent and should be referred to for its details (Von Furer-Haimendorf 1975: 222-285). Concentrating only on the people of the Indian borderlands then we can follow their cycles beginning in their moving out of their summer residence nearer the passes and taking salt from Tibet with them which is transported on the backs of up to a total for all these areas of about 30,000 sheep and goats. The Tibetan salt is bartered for grains in areas even nearer the lowlands from their newly re-established cold-weather residences. These residences are established in areas where other groups of people of the hills areas permanently reside, even sometimes taking the form of house rentals. The sites were originally chosen to maintain a close proximity to the respective valley of each Bhotiya group but in areas in which some cultivation could take place where the snowfall was at least much less than was typical of the higher level valleys.

Items such as borax were once exchanged as far afield as at Ramnagar (by the Johari Bhotiyas at least) in the plains although most of the bartering took place more or less locally to the cold-weather domiciles. The grain collected first at distances farthest from these domiciles was returned there to be stored and salt was collected from the same depots to be exchanged for more grain in the surrounding areas, etc. By March the flocks reached the areas most adjacent to the winter residences. The grain collected then up to and during this time was then shifted to the warm-weather residences when the main residential shift in May-June took place. This shift could feasibly take place when trade was made possible by the opening of the passes into western Tibet. Once the men crossed the passes into the mNga-ris plains, the grain was exchanged in its turn for the local salt and wool at markets established for the purpose in the areas. The salt collected was then deposited at the summer residences awaiting the future transfer to the areas in the lower areas when the people moved once again to their cold-weather quarters in October. And so on, the cycles were repeated (see Atkinson, III: 1886: 131 and Traill 1851: 97 for some descriptions of the traditional Bhotiya trade-residency cycles).

The description we have given so far of the Bhotiya society is extreme in the sense that only the albeit central ecological constraints are mentioned. We have not dealt with the conditions that would be theoretically relevant for an understanding of the development of the Bhotiya society itself visualized as a social phenomenon unfolding in time. The ecology of the interface has, of course, left a severe imprint on the identity of "Bhotiya" which it was our intention to discuss, but it is reflected in the "Bhotiya" of a society parameterized both by the intricacies of a necessary closeness to Nature as well as by a social setting that posited it into a global, general system. Thus, in the terms of an ecological extremity, there is a certain reflection of external conditions on the social behaviour of the "Bhotiyas". But these social conditions reflect also the conditions of those peoples in the greater society of India into whose overall structure and "world outlook" the Bhotiyas were forced to fit themselves, and in the end whose development they were intimately dependent upon.

The social life of the Bhotiyas then when viewed from its traditional aspects is as much reliant on the economic demands of the interface as on the Hindu society which it came more and more to find itself a part of. For purposes of closer social analysis, it is necessary to distribute the Bhotiyas according to the different mountain valleys their villages are found in. One approach is to follow the traditional geographical classification which centres on Indian Bhot and the six areas of Mana, Niti, Johar, Darma, Byans and Chaudans which correspond roughly to the upper reaches of the river valleys from above Joshimath in the west to the upper Kali River basin in the east. A second, more systematic approach centers the Bhotiya people around the larger now extinct trade system of the mNga-ris plains. This represents a more realistic dimension since it concentrates on the very features (trade) which have traditionally defined the peoples in question. This approach assigns to the Bhotiya domain the peoples east of Byans to the Humla Karnali river basin of north-western Nepal. Beyond the extremes of Mana and Humla are peoples less centered on the same trade systems, and if conceived as "Bhotiya" are done so only in terms of general categorization by similarity to the Bhotiya.

Traditionally, each valley of the Bhot had certain associations in the minds of its inhabitants. According to early British sources, Johar was considered the richest and Darma the poorest and least "modern". Accordingly, the Joharis intermarried with the Mana and Niti Bhotiyas, but looked down on the Darmas and refused to eat together with them and the Byansi. The people of Darma, Byans and Chaudans intermarried apparently rather freely. The main exogamous rules were to exclude members of the same village as marriage partners or, this failing, to exclude members of the same lineage within the village. Although the older accounts are quite unclear from an anthropological point of view, it seems that cross-cousin marriage was the preferred type and the most common from practised (Lall 1911: 190-198; Sherring 1906; Traill 1851:85). It has been noted in several places that the women of the Bhot were generally more free in their behaviour than their counterparts among the Hindu population at large. Whether or not this and the marriage system are in keeping with the necessities of the trading economy or is a point of view from the Hindu side could be contested. Selection of marriage partners at any rate was often a fairly open choice by both persons involved, and among the "exotic" institutions associated with the Bhotiyas of Darma, Byans and

Chaudans was the *rang-bang* a staged meeting of young men and women for courtship purposes (see for example Srivastava, 1953).

One fact that seems totally to effect many of the features of the Bhotiya social praxis is the tendency to become more and more an integral part of the surrounding Hindu society—a process sometimes referred to as "Hinduization". Generally, it refers to the tendency in which traditional activities tended to be supplanted by those more in line with Hindu ethics. Traill, the earliest of the British administrators of the Bhot, noticed this tendency to amalgamate Hindu practices especially in the Mana, Niti and Johar regions (Traill, 1851 : 86). Sherring noted Traill's contribution and added that the process of Hinduization had in fact led to many changes in the Bhotiya life by his time and the general tendency of the western group to be more influenced than the eastern group had been maintained (Sherring, 1906 : 93-95). It can be noted that there is a very pronounced association of "modern" to "rich" to "Hinduized" in this connection, Majumdar noticed that the Joharis referred to themselves exclusively as Hindu and refused in fact to be identified by the term "Bhotia" since it was all too reminiscent of Tibetanism (Majumdar 1949: iii). This is a point made today by some of the Mana and Niti peoples as well who emphasize their Hindu connections and find the term "Bhotiya" to be quite a misnomer. An interesting parallel has been noted among the Thakaali of the Kali Gandaki River area of Nepal. Several interesting articles have been written in this regard from an anthropological point of view (see for example Bista, 1971; Iijima, 1963; Von Fürer-Haimendorf, 1969). According to these authors, there seems to have been a strong association of behaviour to either the Tibetan or Hindu side of the Indo-Tibetan trade cycle depending on which side the traders were to be found. The increasing relevancy of the Hindu society for the traders has led to a desire on their part to raise their Hindu status.

To modern groups referred to as "Bhotiyas" may not reflect all of the aspects of the traditional formative boundaries, but these features have all played their role in forming a sense of a "Bhotiya" community. Today, the Tibet trade, one of the most important features of this tradition, has ceased to have its effect (since 1962 in fact), and the huge flocks of sheep and goats once used in this trade have almost totally been decimated. Still the people keep up a regular annual cycle of transhumanence, and their high elevation homes are referred to with tenderness as their real homes. They have also maintained an old tradition of woollen carpet weaving which today represents their main source of income. In 1967, they were included among the five Scheduled Tribes of Uttar Pradesh under the name "Bhotiya". For the Bhotiyas, as well as for others, in the end, as modern times witness the submergence of more people in a general mass of non-identity, there are pockets of the human race as well as individuals in their own way, which find an identity defined for them by conditions in their own historical panoramas. Hopefully, this brief description of "Bhotiya" has given one dimension of this process.

RFFERENCES

Atkinson, E.T. 1882 1884 1886 *The Himalayan Districts of the North-western Provinces of India*, 3 volumes, Allahabad.

Bagchi, Gourchandra 1977 Miscellaneous note : Some socio-economic aspects of stratification in the East Himalayan society. *Man in India* 57 (4) 363-367.

Bista, Dor Bahadur 1971 Political innovators of upper Kali Gandaki. *Man* 6(1).

Board of Revenue 1817 Ceded and Conquered Provinces. 25 July, Furruckabad. Nos. 9-13B (Uttar Pradesh State Archives, Lucknow).

von Fürer-Haimendorf, Christoph 1969 A case of Hindu-Buddhist contacts in Nepal. *Proc. of the 26th Congress of Orientalists 3(1)*.

von Fürer-Haimendorf, Christoph 1975 *Himalayan Traders: Life in Highland Vepal.* Murray, London.

Iijima, Shigeru 1963 Hinduization of a Himalayan tribe in Nepal. *Kroeber Anthropological Society Papers*, vol. 29.

Lall, Panna 1911 An enquiry into toe birth and marriage customs of the Khasiyas and the Bhotiyas of Almora District, U. P. *The Indian Antiquary*, XL 190-198.

Majumdar, D.N. 1949 The social economy of the Bhotiya in KS. Pangtey, ed. *Lonely Furrows of the Borderland* Folk Culture Series No. 3, Universal, Lucknow.

Markham, Clements R. 1879 *Narratives of the Mission of George Bogle to Tibet and of the Journey of Thomas Manning to Lhasa*, Trubner, London (2nd ed)

Mehra, J.D. and S.C. Tiwari, 1955 The Bhotias of Almora District *Vanyajati* III (1) 10-16.

Sastrp, S.S. 1975 The Bhotiya of U. P. Hill Districts (Central Himalayas) *Vanyajati* 23(4).

Sherring, C.A. 1906 Notes on the Bhotias of Almora and British Garhwal. *Memoirs of the Asiatic Society of Bengal*, 1 (8).

Srivastava, R.P. 1953 'Rang-bang' in the changing Bhotia life. *Eastern Anthropologist* 6 (3).

Srivastava, R.P. 1963 Bhotias—the frontiersmen of Kumaon. *The Modern Review* CXIV (2).

Srivastava, R.P. 1979 Tribe-caste mobility in India and the case of Kumaon

Bhotias in Christoph Von Furer-Haimendorf, ed. : *Caste and Kin in Nepal, India and Ceylon. Anthropological Studies in Hindu-Buddhist Contact Zones* East-West Pub. London, The Hague.

Strachey, R. 1851 On the physical Geography of the provinces of Kumaon and Garhwal in the Himalaya Mountains, and of the adjoining part of Tibet. *Journ. Royal Geographical Society:* 21.

Traill, G.W. 1825 "Letter" of Traill to Board, No. 3, 25 April 1825, *Proc. Board of Revenue in the Western Provinces* 1822-1829, 8 July—30 July, 1825 (Uttar Pradesh State Archives Vol. 55, Lucknow).

Traill, G.W. 1851 "Statistical report on the Bhotea Mehals of Kumaon" (Original in: *Asiatic Researches* 17, 1832) in: Batten, J.H. ed., *Official Reports on the province of Kumaon.* Secunda Orphan Press, Agra.

CHAPTER X

BRIDEPRICE DOWRY AND DIVERTED BRIDEWEALTH AMONG THE RAJPUTS OF KUMAON

ALLEN C. FANGER

Introduction

This paper will examine the changing patterns of marriage and marriage prestations among the Rajputs of the Himalayan region of Kumaon. Fieldwork on which this paper is partially based was conducted in PakhuRa[1] a Kumaoni village about eighty-five road miles west of Nepal, sixty-three road miles north of the Indian plains and about six trail miles northwest of Almora, the district capital. The high caste. Ksatriya Rajputs are the numerically dominant *jati* in Kumaon (about fifty per cent) and constitute about eighty per cent of Pakhura. PakhuRa Rajputs, like nearly all of the Rajputs in rural Kumaon were formerly known as Khas-Rajputs, Khasiya or Khasiya. But as these are terms of derision and insult today, I will avoid using them further. However, these Rajputs are not to be confused with the few remaining higher-ranking Thuljat Rajputs who are descended from the plains and from the royal families of the ancient Kumaoni *rajas* (e.g., Chand, Katyuri, Mankoti, etc.).

Although Rajputs make their living primarily by the cultivation of terraced fields, most households supplement their agricultural income with cash earned from employment outside the village. As we will see, this external employment is an important factor in the changing pattern of marriage prestations.

Marriage Prestations in the Indian Context. The question of brideprice (or bridewealth) has long fascinated anthropologists; yet, until recently, most discussion of the topic has been confined to the continent of Africa. Moreover, the considerable interest in brideprice has not nourished a parallel concern with dowry. While this situation may reflect the relative infrequency of dowry in most non-western societies, this explanation does not apply to India. Until Tambiah's seminal essay (1973: 59-169), there has been very little theoretical attention focused on this subject for India. Hopefully, this article will help fill the gap, especially as it relates to the Kumaoni area.

Both brideprice and dowry involve the transmission of property at marriage. In the case of dowry, the kin of the bride provide her with property "...as a type of pre-mortem inheritence..." (Goody, 1973: 1). Technically, this property is under the wife's control, although her husband may have the right to manage it. According to Tambiah:

> A husband cannot transfer the dowry to his sister, partly because he requires his wife's consent, but more importantly because it is against the spirit of the dowry institution, which is that the dowry given a wife and in her legal possession should form part of the conjugal estate, to be enjoyed by husband and wife and to be transmitted in time to their children (1973: 62).[2]

Brideprice, in contrast, is a transaction in which property passes from the kin of the groom to the *kin* of the bride. I want to emphasize that in brideprice the property ideally ends up with the *kin* of the bride rather than with the bride herself. Brideprice can be distinguished from what Goody has called "indirect dowry" by which he means "...marriage prestations (that) are made by the groom or his kin... (in which) the ultimate recipient of these gifts is the bride and not her kin" (1973: 2). While I find Goody's distinction between "indirect dowry" and bridewealth useful, I consider his phase, "indirect dowry", to be inappropriate. As the wealth and gifts are given by the groom's family, the term dowry is inconsistent. Barbara Miller (personal communication, 1980) suggested to me the phrase "diverted bridewealth". I prefer this, as it more accurately reflects the direction of these prestations. This distinction is particularly relevant to marriage payments in India, and as we shall see, for Kumaon. While many ethnographers of marriage payments in India have described prestations from the groom's side to the bride's side,[3] these gifts often end up as "diverted bridewealth" rather than brideprice. According to Tambiah, because brideprice payments in India are considered degraded and immoral, they are "...under pressure to be converted back into dowry..." 1973: 71). It is apparent from Tambiah's analysis of marriage exchanges in India that prestations from the groom's side often consist of jewelry and clothes *for the bride.* When cash is given by the groom's family, the bride's family usually is expected to use it to purchase jewelry *for the bride.* While such prestations may be reported or interpreted in the literature as brideprice, it appears to be more akin to our concept of "diverted bridewealth."

Many anthropologists would agree with Karve's observation that "...all over India there is the custom of giving brideprice among the poorer castes and of receiving dowry among the higher castes" (1965: 132). (Miller 1978: 218-224) has found that brideprice is relatively widespread among unpropertied groups throughout India and that dowry is prevalent in north India, especially among upper class groups. However, she also found that reciprocity (relatively balanced prestations in both directions) characterizes marriages among many propertied groups in central and south India and that there are exceptions to all of these patterns. My interpretation of Miller's examples is that many of the "reciprocity" and "brideprice" exceptions among the higher castes may be understood as "diverted bridewealth", as most of the groom's prestations end up as gifts to the bride. However, there are examples of brideprice (as defined here) among higher castes (e.g., Madan, 1965: 114-118; Sanwal, 1966) and landowning peasant castes (e.g., Burkhart, 1969: 220), and of dowry among lower castes. The latter is increasingly so, as many low caste *jatis* have been giving up their distinctively inferior caste customs for the more prestigious ways of higher castes (e.g., Cohn, 1955: 75).

Some authors have emphasized the view that brideprice

and dowry are conceptually opposite and that they function differently in different social systems. Nur Yalman illustrates this point of view as it relates to marriage and kin in Ceylon and south India: "...dowry stands in radical contrast to bride-wealth... the differences between the kinship systems that utilize one or the other type of payment are fundamental..." (1967: 303). However, as we have seen, throughout India there are communities which practice both brideprice (or diverted bride-wealth") and dowry, or *jatis* which are changing from bride-price to dowry. This seems to indicate that the distinctions between the two do not reflect radical differences in the marriage systems associated with them. Perhaps it would be more helpful to view brideprice and dowry as variant emphases on a pattern of marriage exchanges and to ask what variables may be associated with one emphasis or the other. I will now address this question for the region of Kumaon.

Marriage Prestations in Kumaon. In the Kumaon Himalayas, the highest ranking Thūl-jat Brahman and Rajput castes always has practised orthodox dowry marriages, while the majority of the Rajputs traditonally practised marriage by brideprice. However, in the last fifty to seventy-five years, there has been a gradual movement among the Rajputs to the orthodox dowry marriages. In the most acculturated areas, especially in villages where large numbers of Rajputs males work in service, the dowry has become more of a cultural expectation than an exception. Nevertheless, brideprice may be required secretly in these dowry marriages and used as a diverted bride-wealth. Conversely, in the early twentieth century when brideprice marriages were still supreme, token dowries also were given (Joshi, 1929 : Chapter 3). Clearly we are not dealing with two polar types of marriage systems, for within the same *jati*-cluster, both dowry and brideprice have been operating together for at least fifty years. What I will be discussing, then, is not a movement from one polarity to another, but rather from an emphasis on brideprice to an emphasis on dowry.

It is clear from a broad range of historical materials (discussed below) that prior to the twentieth century, the marriage customs of the Thul-jat Rajputs and Brahmans on the one hand, and of the Rajputs on the other, were quite different. The Thul-jats continued to maintain plains standards of orthodoxy in the hills, with great emphasis placed on marriages involving *kanya-dan* (i.e., gift of daughter) and dowry. Such marriages always were performed by Brahman priests according to the rules of Hindu orthodoxy. Presumably, all marriages involving Thul-jat females conformed to these standards; any exceptions resulted in nothing less than expulsion from caste. The Thul-jats did not allow remarriage of widows or divorcees. Thul-jat Rajput males, however, could take women as concubines or secondary wives from the Rajputs. Presumably, these "marriages" were done according to Rajput customs. I might point out here that what was marriage for the Rajput may have been merely the acquisition of a concubine for the Thul-jat.

Rajput marriage, on the other hand, required no standardized ceremonial performance to make a union legitimate. Ceremonies often (but not always) were performed in the first marriage of a woman, and some of these were conducted by a Brahman priest. The latter ceremonies usually were an abbreviated portion of one of the sections of the orthodox pattern, but never the section involving *kanya-dan*. The ceremonies mentioned most frequently by older informants were the *amcal*, *saptapadi* and Ganes *puja*, all of which are sections of the orthodox marriage. Some informants said all they did was hold a *jagar* (spirit possession seance) so that the household deity could bless the bride. All of these ceremonies could be performed (and often were done) after the bride entered the groom's village. These ceremonies did not, in themselves, contribute to the jural completion of the marriage nor the legitimization of the offspring. Indeed, I would agree with Sanwal that the "...primary purpose of these religious ceremonies...is to reaffirm their claim to be 'good Rajputs" (1966:50).

Traditionally, there were two necessary conditions for the completion of a legitimate Rajput marriage. The guardians of the bride must be paid a brideprice (*dam*) and the bride must be taken to the residence of the groom. Feasting and ceremony were probably common (although not required) in the first marriage of the bride, but not in cases of her remarriage.

The payment of the brideprice seemed to take on the

nature of a commercial transaction. Sanwal reports that traditional Rajput marriage

> is that union (it need not be marked by any religious ceremonial) between a man and a woman of the recognized socio-ritual categories, which has been created by a formal transfer of power over the woman from her legal guardian to another man in consideration of a "price" paid on behalf of the latter by his guardian...to the woman's guardian (1966:50).

In 1929 Joshi, a keen observer of Kumaoni social organization, remarked that among the Khasa (i.e., Rajputs), "A woman is a chattel, who is purchased for one of the sons by the father of the family. The nature of the transaction is more the acquisition of a valuable article for the family than a contractual relationship between a man and a woman" (1929:108). Prior to British rule (from 1815), a husband acquired almost complete control over his wife and her offspring. Indeed, a husband or his heirs had the right to sell her and her children into slavery. During the period of Gurkha rule over Kumaon (1790-1815), a tax was levied on the sale of wives and widows, and a duty was placed on their export (Joshi, 1929:110; Walton, 1911: 132-133). This right to sell a wife, a widow or her children eventually ceased under the British, but the custom was not completely eliminated. Berremen has reported this kind of "traffic in women" in the nearby district of Garhwal among the culturally similar Garhwali Rajputs (1963:74-75), and in the 1960s I found this practice still occurring in a village near Bargaon.[4]

The nature of marriage negotiations involving a bride-price or a dowry with a diverted bridewealth has all the signs of a commercial exchange. The price is not fixed and depends on whatever the traffic will bear. Considerable haggling is expected, especially if questions of gifts and food exchanges are involved. There usually are three negotiators from each side, and local tradition says that when five of six negotiators agree on a point a decision is made. This enables the leader of each delegation to compromise on an issue without actually giving in himself.

Perhaps most important in our judgment of brideprice as a commercial affair is the fact that the Rajputs themselves see brideprice marriages in terms of a sale. To illustrate this, I give the following paraphrase of a quotation from a fairly well off middle-aged Rajput. I regard these comments as generally typical.

> Of my three wives (not simultaneously) all were purchased but in the marriages of my six children there was only *kanya-dan*, charity of daughter. If I took money, it would mean I was selling my daughter. We do not do this anymore.

While the veracity of this statement is unsubstantiated, the important point is that the speaker regards the paying of bride-price as amounting to a sale and he regards such sales as immoral, although he implies that his wives were acquired this way.

Another important dimension of traditional Rajput marriage by brideprice is that the transaction was not irrevocable. A woman could return to her home or marry another man. The original husband might protest, but he had no recourse provided his brideprice was returned. If a woman ran off with another man, the union was not legitimate until the first husband had been reimbursed for the brideprice.

In cases where the husband died, the usual expectation was that a young widow would marry her husband's younger brother. Informants acknowledged that the primary purpose of this was to save the cost of another brideprice. Both the widow and the younger brother had the right to reject the union. However, if she returned to her natal home or married someone outside her husband's lineage, her husband's heirs had the right to demand the return of the brideprice.

Since the beginning of the twentieth century, there has been a significant trend toward the adoption of orthodox Hindu marriages based upon the ceremony of *kanya-dan* and the giving of a dowry. The decision to have this kind of marriage usually also means the sponsoring of a rather expensive orthodox ceremony and the providing of a feast for the groom's marriage party (*barat*) and village kin. According to orthodox ideology, when one does *kanya-dan*, he must not accept any money;[5] however, in the past, this rule frequently was broken surreptitiously. In the traditional non-Sanskritic marriage, a feast was not expected, although sometimes the marriage party brought its own food or, perhaps, paid an extra portion for its share of a feast. With dowry marriages a feast is considered obligatory, and the cost is supposed to be borne entirely by the bride's family. However, money or grain may be given to provide the cost of the marriage party's portion of the feast. Informants who admit to this practice insist that such a payment is not a brideprice, as they do not keep any of the money for themselves. However, others insisted that it was wrong to take anything and that to do so was to destroy the purity of the *kanya-dan*. In 1967, some informants said that "a few unscrupulous people" still take a large brideprice and perform *kanya-dan* anyway. However, by 1982 such diverted bridewealth-*kanya-dan* marriages in the first marriage of a daughter were becoming increasingly rare. Only poorer Rajput families would accept grain or cash payments in their daughter's dowry marriage, and such unions are not easy to find. If a poor Rajput could not afford a dowry marriage for his daughter, he would now look toward his *biradri* (patrilineage) for assistance.

All of the discussion so far has been in regard to the first marriage of Rajput females. Rajputs know very well that divorce, levirate and widow remarriage are frowned upon by orthodox Hinduism, yet they recognize the legitimacy of all these practices. A widow is greatly praised if she stays in her husband's village without remarrying, but she is not expected to do so. While *kanya-dan* marriages probably are more stable than marriages based on brideprice,[6] the former occasionally do break up, and women who once were given in marriage may then remarry. The second marriage of a woman, whether widowed or divorced does not matter, is never done with a dowry or Brahmanical ceremony, and a brideprice usually is paid[7] either to the former husband, his heirs or to the woman's father. Although such marriages suffer some stigma, and women so married (called *nolis* or *dhantis*) bear some ritual and commensal restrictions, there is no question that these are valid, legitimate unions.

How, then, do we explain this movement from brideprice to dowry marriages ? My first reaction was to view the data in terms of Srinivas' model of Sanskritization. The village of study is only six trail miles from Almora, the district capital, and is situated in an area of relatively high concentration of immigrant Rajput and Brahman *jatis*. Local Rajputs have been long exposed to models of Sanskritic Hinduism, and they are well aware of the gaps between their behavior and what is expected of Thul-jat Rajputs. This seemed to be an ideal environment for Sanskritization. Furthermore, over the past few decades large numbers of village Rajputs joined the military or had gone to the plains or other hill towns in search of employment. Inevitably, this further sensitized the Rajput population to the marginal nature of their form of Hinduism, and increased their feelings of inferiority versus orthodox plains standards. Although aspirations to identify with plains Rajput standards is certainly a factor, Sanskritization is an insufficient explanation for the trend. First of all, Khasa long ago had achieved Rajput status[8] as is clear from the fact that they generally are acknowledged to be Rajputs rather than Khasa or Sudra. Thus, the local Rajputs are not claiming a position or title to which they are not freely acknowledged be being entitled. Secondly, the trend, toward Sanskritic Hinduism is not occurring on a *jati*, or even on a village-wide basis. There is no corporate *jati* action involved here. Third, those who take to Sanskritic marriage rituals do not necessarily follow Sanskritic values in other religious contexts. For example, two weeks after a *kanyadan* dowry marriage, a Rajput family held an unorthodox spirit possession seance (*jagar*) to bless the new bride. In another case, a man who married his daughter with a substantial dowry bought a second wife for his son when the latter had no children from his first wife.

While the Rajput's increasing exposure and sensitivity to orthodox values is a likely factor in the observed trend, by itself it is an incomplete explanation. I would suggest that a significant additional factor is to be found in the economic forces that surround the widespread employment migration outside the village that I mentioned in the introduction. This seems to be a likely path to pursue when we realize the enormous economic implications in the shift from a brideprice to a dowry marriage. Whereas the typical brideprice may cost the groom's family between three hundred and one thousand rupees, a dowry marriage often will cost the bride's family over a thousand rupees. This can result in a net difference to the father of a bride of at least Rs. 1,300.

The population of the village has expanded rapidly in the past few decades so that the size of most land holdings is barely sufficient to meet the peasant's normal consumption needs. Largely due to this economic pressure, village men have taken to the military and other forms of service in large numbers. In 1967, some sixty-one percent of the Rajput village households studied had a total of seventy men involved in full-time employment. By 1982, employment migration had expanded to the point where eighty-five of the ninety-three Rajput house-holds surveyed (ninety-one percent) had at least one man employed in the external cash economy. A total of 105 men were employed outside the village as opposed to forty-one who worked in the village as farmers. The few families that had no men in service were headed mostly by widows with no adult sons, or elderly men who had retired from service. Moreover, of the forty-one village farmers in 1982, many received cash income locally on a seasonal or daily wage basis. Thus, although village land holdings appear insufficient to meet the subsistence needs of most peasant households, villagers have been very successful in gaining income through employment migration.[9]

There are two relevant consequences of these developments. First, the simultaneous reduction in land holdings and increase in population has reduced considerably the heavy burdens of women in the village economy. Kumaoni women have been long famous in Uttar Pradesh for the incredible amount of work that they perform in the Pahari domestic economy. They do almost all of the agricultural work except the plowing, and gather huge loads of pine needles, oak leaves, grass and green branches for the cattle's shed and fodder. In addition, they do the usual household chores of cleaning, tending the cattle. cooking and so forth. Their importance and high value was clearly reflected in the brideprice form of marriage. Today, they continue to perform all of these tasks; however, the amount of work done per female has been reduced considerably due to the decrease in the size of the average land holding. There are more women to work less land and, thus, their economic value has been reduced proportionately. This observation is consistent with the findings of Boserup who noted that when the major part of agricultural work is done by women there often is a higher incidence of brideprice, but where women do less agricultural work than men, dowry is more prevalent (1970:50).

The second point is that although the agricultural economy has been reduced in its relative importance to each household's production, this has been more than offset by the wages earned by men in service. Indeed, many families appear to be financially better off today than they were just a generation ago. Although my stay in 1981-82 was brief, I was struck by a considerable improvement in village prosperity. Many new houses had been erected and older houses had been expanded and improved, new *pakka* irrigation canals had been constructed and a large irrigation scheme was in preparation. A new village temple and a new water source had been built and people had many more household and personal possessions. The number of students in school was greatly increased, and students were achieving much higher grade levels of education. Whereas in 1967 only four students had reached the ninth grade, in 1982 this was common place, and one student had just completed his M.A. All of this inevitably has had its effect on marriage and marriage prestations. While in the past a man hardly could afford not to sell his daughter in marriage, today he is ashamed to do so. Indeed, with his new-found financial security, he is motivated to express his wealth in an idiom that not only manifests his material success, but also increases his prestige and asserts his identity as a good Rajput. Dowry marriages, with the accompanying orthodox rituals an expensive feasts, are an ideal form of conspicuous consumption. In one stroke he establishes his reputation as a religious man, and good Rajput and a wealthy, generous person.

Summary. Up to the nineteenth century traditional Rajput marriages were largely brideprice arrangements with little attention paid to Brahmanical rituals. Sometimes around the beginning of the twentieth century, Rajputs began to adopt dowry marriages, although they often continued to accept brideprice. Gradually, the brideprice was converted to a "diverted bridewealth" as the bride's family used the brideprice to pay for the dowry and the wedding feast. Within the last generation, the brideprice has become a rarity except among poorer Rajputs or in the remarriage of widows and divorced women. Simultaneously, dowry and *kanya-dan* have become standardized in the first marriage of a woman among most Rajputs in the village of study.

Three possible factors were considered to help explain this process of change. First, we explored whether the movement toward dowry was part of a broader Sanskritization-like mobility movement. Although the Rajputs of today were formerly classified as Khasa and Sudra, there is little evidence of a *jati*-wide social mobility movement. In fact, they long ago successfully achieved their current Rajputs status and rank. Nevertheless, opportunities to observe orthodox role models of Rajput and Hindu behaviour have dramatically increased in the twentieth century and undoubtedly constitute an important consideration.

Secondly, it was observed that the expanding population and decreasing size of per capita land holdings has reduced significantly the agricultural labour of women. Simultaneously, as male employment migration has increased, the importance of agricultural labour in the village economy has declined as well. Perhaps the brideprice form of marriage reflected the enormous importance of women in the traditional economy, whereas the emergence of dowry suggests her decreased role in the expanding cash economy of employment migration.

Finally, we noted that the Rajput's increasing participation in the cash economy through employment migration brought considerable improvement in village prosperity. Although Rajputs are not trying to change their position in the caste hierarchy, they do aspire to recognition as good, proper Rajputs. With their new success and increased awareness of plains Rajput behaviour, they can *now* better afford many of the ceremonies and customs of a Rajput position in society. Accordingly, dowry and *kanya-dan* have become important means to express their new prosperity as well as their traditional Rajput identity.

FOOTNOTES

1. Initial fieldwork was conducted in 1966-67 under the auspices of a grant from the Fulbright Foundation and the United States Educational Foundation in India. A return visit to PakhuRa and Kumaon was made in December, 1981 and January, 1982 and was partially funded by the Kutztown State College Research Committee and the Department of Anthropology and Sociology.

2. Tambiah is expressing here the ideal principles of dowry; in practice, a husband or his family may be able to appropriate a wife's dowry for use by other family members (e.g. the husband's sister or mother). However, this usually would be done secretly and is a violation of the principle of the institution.

3. See Miller for a compilation of several dozen examples of this pattern (1978:227-244, 1981).

4. See also Hasan (1971; Chapters 10, 11).

5. According to the classical *Code of Manu:* "No father who knows (the law) must take even the smallest gratuity for his daughter; for a man who, through avarice, takes a gratuity is a seller of his offspring" as quoted in Tambiah 1973:68).

6. Sanwal found that "...it is generally agreed that three decades or so back, the number of marriages which ended in divorce amongst the rural Khasi (Khas-Rajput) had increased alarmingly and that...at the present time divorces are...becoming less common" (1966: 56). It is my interpretation that when marriage is done by *kanya-dan*, the participants are making a public commitment to the "great tradition" values of a permanent marriage. A woman who is given in *kanya-dan* cannot be returned to her natal home without embarrassing her family. However, there is no such embarrassment associated with

brideprice marriages as the family is not making any pretentions. Admittedly, in such cases, the woman's parents or a future husband is expected to return the brideprice.

7. In 1982 some informants said this might be waived because a father is embarrassed to take money for a daughter whom he already had given in *kanya-dan*. Also, a husband or his heirs may not claim compensation for a woman who was given to them rather than purchased.

8. Sanwal (1976:43-44) reports that the Khasa were elevated from Sudra to Rajput status during the reign of the Chand *rajas* (which ended in 1790). Pauw (1896:12) and Berreman (1963: 130) indicate that the Rajputs of Garhwal were without the sacred thread until the twentieth century.

9. This employment migration has taken them throughout the plains of north India, mostly to the large urban centers or into the Indian military and police services.

BIBLIOGRAPHY

Berreman, Gerald D. 1963 *Hindus of the Himalayas*. Berkeley: University of California Press.

Boserup, Ester, 1970 *Woman's Role in Economic Development*. New York: St. Martin's Press.

Burkhart, Geoffrey L. 1969 *Agnatic Groups and Affinal Relations in a South Indian Caste : UDaiyaars of Salem District, Tamil Nadu*. Ph. D. dissertation, University of Rochester.

Cohn, Bernard S. 1955 "The Changing Status of a Depressed Caste" in *Village India*. McKim Marriott, ed., Chicago: University of Chicago Press.

Fanger, Allen C. 1980, *Diachronic and Synchronic Perspectives on Kumaoni Society and Culture*. Ph. D. dissertation, Syracuse University.

Goody, Jack. 1973 "Bridewealth and Dowry in Africa and Eurasia" in *Bridewealth and Dorty*. Jack Goody and S.J. Tambiah, eds., New York: Cambridge University Press.

Gray, Robert F. 1960 "Sonjo Bride-price and the Question of

African 'Wife Purchase' " *American Anthropologist.* 62: 34-57.

Hasan, Amir. 1971 *A Bunch of Wild Flowers.* Lucknow: Ethnographic and Folk Culture Society, U.P.

Joshi, L.D. 1929 *The Khasa Family Law in the Himalayan Districts of the United Provinces of India.* Allahabad: Superintendent, Government Press, U.P.

Karve, Irawati. 1965 *Kinship Organization in India.* Bombay: Asia Publishing House.

Madan, T.N. 1965 *Family and Kinship : A Study of the Pandits of Rural Kashmir.* Bombay: Asia Publishing House.

Miller, Barbara D. 1978 *Sexual Discrimination and Population Dynamics in Rural India.* Ph. D. dissertation, Syracuse University,

——1980 Personal communication.

——1981 *The Endangered Sex: Neglect of Female Children in Rural North India*, Ithaca: Cornell University Press.

Sanwal, R.D. 1966 "Bridewealth and Marriage Stability Among the Khasi of Kumaon" *Man, Journal of the Royal Anthropological Institute.* 1: 46-59.

——1976 *Social Stratification in Rural Kumaon.* Delhi: Oxford University Press.

Tambiah, S.J. 1973 "Dowry and Bridewealth and the Property Rights of Women in South Asia" in *Bridewealth and Dowry.* Jack Goody and S.J. Tambiah, eds., New York: Cambridge University Press.

Walton. H.G. 1911 *Almora: A Gazetteer, comprising Vol. XXXV of the District Gazetteer of the United Provinces of Agra and Oudh.* Allahabad: Government Press.

Yalman, Nur. 1967 *Under the Bo Tree.* Berkeley: University of California Press.

CHAPTER XI

BELIEF IN SUPERNATURAL AMONG THE JAUNSARIES—A PSYCHOANALYTICAL APPROACH

PUSHPA MISRA

Introduction and Background

As a student of psychoanalysis two questions intrigued my mind from time to time. One—how far is Freud's theory of Oedipus complex justified under changed family configurations ? —a question was raised but not satisfactorily answered by B. Malinowski. (1979) Two—how far the archaic and primitive form of thinking which constitutes the core of mental symptoms characterises the so-called normal thinking process ? The questions are not new, but my desire to have a first-hand answer led me to seek the help of the Anthropological Survey of India in choosing the place which I may visit in persuance of my enquiry. The place must satisfy two criteria: (1) it should have a family structure other than monogamous; (2) the people should be relatively uninfluenced by the scientific and rational way of thinking. I was advised to visit the Jaunsar—Bawar area of Uttar Pradesh.

Jaunsar—Bawar is situated in the cis-Himalayas forming the northern half of the district of Dehra Dun of the state of Uttar Pradesh. Jaunsar and Bawar are the two constituents of which Jaunsar roughly forms the lower half of the areas. (Majumdar, 1962: 3)

A combination of polygyny and polyandry prevalent in the area satisfies my first criterion. Extremely limited means of communication with the civilized world and the consequent psychological isolation provided me with the apportunity of seeking an answer to my second question.

Data were collected during 1976-1977 from sixteen villages of Khat[1] Baunder. While collecting data I was struck by their widespread belief in supernatural entities. On deeper enquiry it seemed to have direct relevance with my second question posed above. In this paper I have dealt with their belief in supernatural from psychoanalytical viewpoint.

In treating the subject, I have divided my paper in three parts. I have presented the data briefly in Part I. In Part II, I have tried to clarify my idea of the two terms, 'supernatural' and 'belief'. Part III has been devoted to the psychoanalytic interpretation of the data.

Part I

Data

The supernatural entities can be divided into two groups—(1) malevolent and (2) benevolent. In this paper I have discussed only the malevolent supernatural entities. Most important among these entities are : (i) *Daag, Daak, Dankan or Daagi,* (ii) *Matri,* (iii) *Cheda* and (iv) *sins commited by people which become alive.*

(1) *Daag, Daak, Dankan or Daagi*

A *daag* or *dankan* is a living female human being supposed to have "evil eye". Such a woman casts her evil eyes on any thing she likes and her evil eyes have the power of making an individual fall ill. Every village has a good number of such females who possess evil power of wide range. Such women are stamped as the *dankan* and are avoided by the people of the village though they continue to reside in the village in normal way. A *dankan* is almost invariably a female and it is only on rarest occasions that a male is considered as a *dankan*.

The activities of a *dankan* are various though we may try to categorize them under two heads.

(1) Casting 'evil eyes' on the food, clothes and other belongings of the people and thus making them fall ill or causing some harm to the owner. Such activities are committed by a *dankan* in her natural form of an ordinary living woman.

(2) The *dankans* have another form also which they show during nights only. At night they leave a replica of their bodies on their beds sleeping normally and go out of the houses in search of prey. They are very fond of eating *jhikudi* i.e. the heart of a living human being. They can enter the house through a small hole and can take out the heart of the person without cutting open the body or shedding a drop of blood. Even after the heart has been eaten by the *dankan*, the person lives normally for a few days and then falls ill or meets with an accident and dies. During this intervening period the person either lives without a heart so the belief goes—or with the heart of an animal which has been transplanted in his body by the *dankan*. The disease or the accident is merely a pretext to give the death a normal appearance so that people may not suspect the role of the *dankan* in the death of the person. Actually such a person is dead before he dies. Almost all diseases are believed to be caused by the evil power of the *dankan* or other spirits and almost all deaths with a few exceptions—are, in some way or other, related to them.

Varieties of mischiefs which a *dankan* can do, will become clear from the anecdotes related to me by various people residing in different villages. Some of them are mentioned below:

(1) Once three *dankans* decided to eat the *jhikudi* of a boy who was living in his *chhani* (a place away from the village where cattles are kept). When the *dankans* arrived at *chhani* the boy was awake and was smoking tobacco. They threatened the boy but left him unharmed and ate the heart of a cow instead. Next morning, the cow was found dead.

(2) A boy was found dead one morning and it was believed that a *dankan* must have eaten his heart though the body was intact.

(3) Mrs. S. of Lakhamandal village related that during the Baisakhi festival a woman took her one-year old boy in her lap. Immediately after, the eyes of the boy turned upward and his face became pale. Mrs. S. snatched her child from the

woman's lap immediately and circled a few breads around the head of the boy and the boy became alright. The mother condemned the woman as a *dankan*. Otherwise why, she asks, should the child behave in such peculiar manner as soon as the woman touched her child.

(4) Mrs. T. of Lakhamandal village related the following stories:—

An old lady was completely blind. Therefore, she could not do much of household works and used to spend her time sitting in one corner of the room. This old lady and her daughter-in-law both were the *dankans*. On the new moon day of every *bhadrapada* (August-September), an assembly of the *dankans* is held on the top of a hill. This date is considered particularly inauspicious for the mortals. The daughter-in-law advised her husband to go to the hill and to see his mother in her true colour. The son went to the hill and watched his mother coming with an ox between her armpits wearing two big stone-wheels of grinder in her two ears. He watched the entire proceedings throughout the night. When he came back home in the morning, he found his mother seated in the corner of the house in her usual manner. He took a sword, beheaded his mother and sent his wife to her *mait* (father's place).

5. A Brahman Pandit was going somewhere. On his way, he reached a village and entering a house belonging to a *dankan* asked her permission to sit. The permission was duly accorded to him. The woman of the house then climbed the chimney and stuck out a long tongue to devour the Pandit. The Pandit uttered some *mantras* (sacred words having special power) and the tongue became struck to the floor. The *dankan* became extremely upset and pleaded the Pandit not to kill her. She offered him her nose-ring in lieu of her life. At least, the Pandit agreed to her proposal. Next day, he produced the nose-ring before the master of the house, related the incident and instructed him to send the wife away which he promptly did.

6. Four *dankans* killed an ox and were distributing the meat among themselves. A quarrel ensued over the distribution of meat. One *dankan* belonging to superior caste was demanding the *jhikudi* to which the others were not agreeing. (The *jhikudi* or the heart is considered the most prized part of a meat. It

always goes to the eldest male member of a family. He may give it to any other male member of the family but never to a female). During this quarrel the Bajgi (the beater of the drum) came to beat the drum. On seeing the *dankans* he caught hold of one of them but the others fled. He shouted and other people from the village came out and started beating the *dankan*. She started crying and said, "I am not alone, there are three others". The villagers found out the other three and beat them up severely. (A song has been composed around this theme and is often sung by the villagers.)

7. One day Mrs. T. had a very severe quarrel with a *dankan* of the village and then became afraid that the *dankan* would come to eat her at night. And her apprehension proved correct. The *dankan* came at night. But just as the *dankan* entered her room, Mrs. T. was possessed by her God. She caught hold of the *dankan* and kicked on her chest. "And then my sleep was broken." (A dream?) After this the woman remained ill for many days. She used to complain of pain in her chest.

8. Mrs. S. of Lakhamandal village related the following story :

After the birth of her second son Mrs. S. suffered from profuse bleeding which could not be cured by any treatment. The Pandit declared that the *dankan* who was causing this mischief would leave her, if a cock was sacrificed to her. The day her husband started for the town to buy a cock, her bleeding became so profuse that she thought that she was going to die and asked for butter-milk and rice as her last meal. As soon as she ate it, the bleeding stopped as though it had never occurred. Next day, her husband came and sacrificed the cock.

9. Mr. M. of Lakhamandal village related the following incident :

He went to attend the marriage of one of his cousins at Nada village. As per their custom the *ryanties* (woman married to the village) are to be invited for lunch on the day of marriage. Among the invitees was an old woman, almost completely blind, who was being served every item twice. He was also instructed to do the same because the lady was believed to be a *dankan*. He was serving *halwa* (a delicacy, prepared by a mixture of flour, refind butter and sweet). Since there was enough on the plate of the old lady, he did not serve it again. At night when he was sleeping with four of his companions a strong gust of wind suddenly extinguished the lamp. The old woman was inside the room. But one of his companions got up from the bad. He was possessed by his God. He proceeded towards the *dankan* but could get hold of her cloth only. Next morning, they found that the old woman had the same part of her cloth missing. This proves conclusively that she was a *dankan*.

10. Mrs. G. of Lakhamandal village related that a *dankan* —a particular woman of the same village—had entered her room at night when Mrs. G. was asleep. She woke up and on seeing the *dankan* inside the room became immobile with fear. The *dankan* came forward and touched her heart. She groaned in fear and her parents woke up. The *dankan* left the room. Mrs. G. refused to reveal the identity of the *dankan* because it is believed that if anyone reveals the identity of a *dankan* he/she becomes a sure target of the evil activities of the *dankan*.

11. Mrs. C. of Kandi village reported the following incident:

A man used to have spells of god upon him. During this period he could tell many mysterious and unknown facts. So the *dankan* of the village became afraid that he might expose her real identity to the villagers. So one night she entered the room of the man with the hide of a cow in her hand. The man immediately woke up. His god came upon him. He caught hold of the throat of the *dankan* and pressed it with all his force. The *dankan* became afraid and managed to run away with difficulty. But by that time her throat had become swollen. Next day the man showed it to all villagers.

The *dankan* invariably harms the person who has spell of god upon him.

12. Mr. D. of Mothi village reported :

"The *dankan* clung to my goat at night and she (the goat) was found dead next morning. The stomach of the goat was found full of chaff."

According to the people of the area a strong evidence in favour of the existence of the *dankan* is that the government also recognises the existence of the *dankan*. Once a case against a *dankan* was instituted in a court and the magistrate enquired of the *dandan*, 'How do you kill a man ?' The *dankan* asked for two lemons and covered them with a piece of cloth. She asked to be left alone for 1/1½ hours. After the expiry of the period the lemons were cut and squeezed but were found to contain not a drop of juice. The *dankan* had sucked the juice of the lemons without even touching these.

(This story was related to me in almost every village I visited. On enquiry, it was found that the story relates to a woman of Shirpa village who was believed to be a *dankan*. The judge had ordered that the woman was not be beaten or disturbed in any way. Violation of the order would bring about at least six months of rigorous imprisonment to the offender. The above-mentioned anecdote is obviously a fabrication of the villagers to whom a belief in the *dankan* seems almost to be a psychological necessity.)

13. Miss P. of Bhatar village says :

The *dankans* are galore in this village. Many houses in this village have the *dankans*... My own grandfather was eaten up by a *dankan*. Our *chhani* and most of our village is in Guthar village. This grandfather of mine was very timid and diffident and rarely went out after dusk. That day he had gone to Guthar to give some ghee (refined butter) to his sister. At about dusk he went to cut some grass in spite of his sister's insistence not to go out in dark. When he did not return after a considerable lapse of time people went to the *danger* (high, steep places of the mountain) and found his dead body. His heart was found in the *chhani* of our uncle. The *dankan* had eaten it.

14. One day Mr. B and Miss P.'s aunts were sitting near the temple and talking together. It was dark. They saw a tall woman and the next moment the woman became a parrot. It was a *dankan*.

15. Mr. M's mother of Kandoi village said :

The *dankans* definitely exist. One day she was going to some other village along with her daughter. When she was at the out skirts of the village, she came upon two women who were suspected to be the *dankans*. She became apprehensive that some evil would definitely befall her. And so it happened.

As soon as the two women crossed them, her daughter fell and injured her knees.

16. Mrs. C. of Lakhamandal village says :

"Before coming to this village, there was no end to my troubles. Two *dankans* had their eyes on me. There was constant pain in different parts of my body. My whole body had become thin and emaciated... It is only after coming to this village that my sick and dried body could bear fruit. Ref. birth of her son after coming to this village); the *dankan's* eyes are very evil. Nothing happens to the people of plains. But here in the hills, some women are bad. They cast their evil eyes on everything... Because of this we always wear dirty and ragged clothes. Anyone wearing nice and clean clothes would invite the *dankan's* eyes on him."

The same lady reported that they had two buffaloes who used to give bucketful of milk. When, after the death of her husband, the people started milching them, their evil eyes affected the buffaloes. As a result their peaceful and quiet buffaloes became very arrogant and unmanageable. Ultimately, they had to be sold away.

The lady continued : "A woman's evil eyes can be managed by rebuking and scolding, but a man's evil eyes cannot be managed. If they are cast towards anyone, they would rest content only after taking away his life."

Mr. T's wife who died yesterday was eaten by the *dankan*. She was pregnant. But the child was brought out safely from the womb, so there is no reason why she should die. It means that the *dankan* had eaten her. (The lady referred to here had died of septic infection. She was carrying full months. Due to certain complications the foetus died in the womb. She was removed to the nearest hospital where due to inadequate medical facilities, she could not be saved.) Some women are so bad that they cast their evil eyes even on the faces of the person. If they see good feces, they think, "Oh! he must have eaten good things", and their eyes will be on him, reports Mrs. C. "We do not take our children out till they are at least one year old"—said Mrs. C.

17. A Bejgi woke up one night and came out in the open to see whether it was nearing dawn. He saw one Domni (a

woman belonging to Dom caste—the lowest in the stratum of caste—hierarchy) standing outside the house. A little afterwards two Brahmin women also came and expressed their desire to eat the child of the house. The Domni pleaded them to spare the child because he was the only child of the family. But the Brahmin women were adamant and ordered the Domni to bring the child out of the house. The Domni entered the house through a small hole and brought the child. The Bramin women decided that the child would die after a few days by falling from the staircase of the house. They kept the *jhikudi* and the better parts of the meat for themselves. At this the Domni became angry and hid her portion of the meat in the cowdung. The Bajgi saw every thing. Next morning, he showed the hidden game to the villagers who called the Domni first and the two Brahmin women later. The Brahmin women came, looked at the Bajgi and the Bajgi died instantly. The child, of course, is living. The *dankan* had eaten up an ox and had replaced the heart of the child by that of the ox.

18. Mrs. C. of Kandoi village :

A Kolta (the lowest caste in Jaunsar area) and three Rajput women decided to eat an ox belonging to one of the Rajput women. The husband of the Kolta women heard their conversation. When, at night, the Rajput women came and called the Kolta woman, the husband came out wearing the clothes of his wife and went along with the Rajput women. On reaching the *chhani* the Rajput women asked the Kolta to enter the *chhani* through a hole. He replied that he had forgotten his magic, and hence was unable to enter the room. The Rajput women said, "Put on a mark of face on your forehead and you will be able to enter the room." The Kolta refused. One of the Rajput women entered the *chhani* through a small hole and opened the door and others entered. An ox was killed and its meat was distributed among themselves. Since it was approaching dawn they asked the Kolta to fix the hide of the ox and its body. The Kolta deliberately fixed it in the wrong way and hid his own portion of meat without eating. In the morning, the Rajput women who owned the ox created a scene before the dead ox. The Kolta came out of the house, caught hold of her hand and shouted, "You yourself have eaten the ox. Why are you abusing others?" He called others from the village, related the entire story and showed them the portion of the meat given to him the previous night. Then the villagers recognised them as the *dankans.*

19. In the assembly of the *dankans* one *dankan* caught hold of the husband of another *dankan* and wanted to eat him up. His wife arrived in the meantime and rebuked the other *dankan*, "Why are you eating my *malik* ? I have only one *malik* (husband) and if he dies how am I to rear up my children."

20. There was a *dankan* who ate her own husband and another one who ate up her own daughter.

Methods for the Appeasement of the Dankan

There are prescribed methods for the appeasement of the *dankan.* The intitial or primary method can be adopted by the members of the family themselves without the aid of the Brahmin Pandits. But if the malady continues the help of the Pandit is sought.

Method : I—When a person falls ill and it is suspected that the person is suffering from the evil eyes of the *dankan*, the people at home beg a little amount of flour from every house of the village or from three houses belonging to the three different castes of the village. The three houses obviously represent all the people of the village belonging to three different castes of the village. While begging flour every house is to be informed about the illness of the person and thus the entire village comes to know of the affliction of the person. This is supposed to make the *dankan* afraid. A bread is prepared with the begged flour which is known as the *dhinkudi.* This *dhinkudi* is circled round the head of the ill person seven times. The bread is to be kept on a leaf with uneven number of veins. Even numbers are considered impure. This *dhinkudi* then is torn into pieces and thrown into all directions at the outskirt of the village. During this activity, the performer blames and abuses the *dankan* with all the vehemence and force he can command, such as, "Why don't you eat your own husband and children ? Why have you cast your eyes on my child ? Eat up every one of your family and leave my child," etc. The blaming and abusing must be done with full force since it is supposed to make the *dankan* afraid.

If the person is not cured after this, the Brahmin Pandits are consulted, and if they find that the disease is due to the *dankan* following measures may be adapted :

Method II :—The iron blade of a used plough is removed and the wooden shaft which holds the iron blade (known as the *naas*) is half-buried in the ground with proper religious ceremony. The tip of the *naas* should remain pointed upward. The *naas* is to be buried preferably at a junction of four ways from four directions. If such a junction cannot be found, the *naas* is to be buried at a two-point crossing at the outskirt of the village.

In some cases thorns are also attached to the *naas*. Seven different kinds of thorns are taken and circled around the head of the ill person seven times and are attached to the front portion of the *nass* which is then buried in the ground. The Brahmin also ties specially powerful strings to the *naas* known as the *bramhaphansa*. During all these procedures, breads and sweets are strewn in all four directions which are meant for evil spirits.

Method III—Another version was that if the Brahmin finds after calculation that the illness is due to a *dankan* and the *dankan* wants the sacrifice of any particular animal, he advises the family as such. Accordingly, such a beast is taken and circled round the head of the ill person thrice, five or seven times and then is taken to the temple. A little water is sprinkled on its body and someone asks, "Are you a *dankan* ?" If the beast trembles then only it is sacrificed, not otherwise. The sacrifice is usually done at the place where the *naas* is buried. Part of the meat is given to the Brahmin and the rest is eaten by the members of the family including the sick person.

A slightly different version is that the beast which the *dankan* desires is circled round the head of the ill person and then is kept reserved for the *dankan* till the peron is cured. If the person is cured within a specified period then only the sacrifice will be made, not otherwise. This procedure was not confirmed by many. In most cases the sacrifice is made on knowing what the *dankan* desires. Obviously the motive is to appease the *dankan* so that the sick person is relieved. In the former case as if a contract is entered into with the *dankan* and if she keeps her part of the contract, the family will keep their part of the contract.

Method IV :—A less resorted to method is to fix specially sanctified nails on the wheels of water-mill. When the water-mill is not operating, nothing would happen to the *dankan*. But when it is operating the *dankan* would constantly moved round in circle just as the nails on the wheels are moving round. When the *dankan* will agree to release the afflicted person the punishment will be stopped.

Matri

It is difficult to find an exact synonym of the term, *matri*, but they come very close to our concept of fairies. The *matries* are supposed to be spirits residing at the top of high mountains which is their territory. Anyone entering their territories must seek their prior permission by worshipping them properly.

There was a difference of opinion regarding their sex. Some said emphatically that they are females while other believed that people who die young irrespective of sex, become the *matries*.

All serious and permanent physical disorders are ascribed to the *matries*. Blindness—both one and two-eyed, stammering, loss of limbs, paralysis etc. are all believed to be caused by the *matries* and can be remedied by properly worshipping them.

Some of the different stories and beliefs prevalent in the name of the *matries* are given below :

1. A very old story says that once a European gentlemen and his wife who were good hunters camped on the hill for hunting. The hill-people who were escorting them requested them to worship the *matri* before starting for hunting. The Europeans refused but the hill-people performed the *puja*. Each and every shot fired by the hill-people was successful but the Europeans failed to get even a single game because they did not worship the *matri*. On the high hill-tops there are temples for the *matries*.

The influence of the *matries* in curing diseases and deformities was narrated by some :

2. A veterinary doctor from Khubau village related that he

was not a believer in 'these things' but his wife was cured of a long standing menstrual trouble after proper worship and sacrifice to the *matries*. Since then his disbelief has lost much of its strength.

3. *Baki*—a *baki* is a person—usually Brahmin but can be of any caste—who is believed to have communion with supernatural entities. People suffering from various afflictions and troubles of any kind consult the *baki* who calls upon different spirits on himself and in this possessed state informs the people of the causes of their sufferings and ways of getting relief. The *baki* of Kuan village reported that of all the evil spirits the *matries* are worst. They are invariably women. In a house, after the *puja* of Lord Satyanarayan, a little girl of 7/8 could not be traced. After three months the dead body of the girl was found on a very high hill of Himachal Pradesh near the temple of the *matri*. The *matries* had taken away the girl.

4. The Pradhan (the chief of the village) of Laudi village reported that the face of one of his friends started twisting (a case of facial paralysis subsequent to a cerebral attack?) and he was removed to Dehra Dun hospital but nothing happened. He was cured when offerings were made to the *matri*.

5. One woman was very much in love with her husband. One day two *matries* saw them together hand in hand and said, "Oh! she is very much in love with her husband." Just then the woman happened to look above and the *matries* immediately took her with themselves.

6. A famous legend regarding the *matries* is narrated below : This legend has been composed in the form of a song and is known as the *dangudi*.

The river known as the Bhagirathi or the Ganges was originally seven sisters who had one brother. One day the seven sisters had gone to graze the goats. Suddenly it started raining and they took shelter is an *adar* (the cave of a hill). By noon they felt very hungry. Their own mother was dead and the step-mother sent food in a basket which was brought by their brother. The brother left the basket at the entrance of the cave and went away. Hungry and exhausted they opened the basket and found that their step-mother had sent basketful of ash for them to eat. Tears rolled down their cheeks. The rain became heavier and the hill toppled and the seven sisters were buried alive. All these seven sisters have become the *matries* and often come out in their chariot. They are known as the *dangudia.* (It could not be properly ascertained what is the relation between these seven sisters and the river Ganges).

7. The *baki* of Kuan village related that two persons had gone for hunting to the hill top and had defecated in front of the temple of the *matri.* The *matri* ordered them twice in their dreams to clean the place but they did not pay any heed to it. They were killed by their own buffaloes who was constantly looking at the high hills and bellowing loudly.

8. Two relatives of the persons mentioned in anecdote 7 went to high hills and killed *ther* wnich is a particular kind of deer often the size of a young buffalo. The *matries* residing on the hills started crying, "Oh Jamaraja! (God of Death in Hindu pantheon) How are we now to feed our children? We shall punish these people." When these men reached home, a storm came and their house was blown away.

Fear is one of the chief causes of being afflicted with the *matri.* If a strong wind blows and someone becomes afraid, the *matries* will afflict him; if a pot full of water falls from the hands of a young girl and she becomes afraid, she will be afflicted with the *matri.* Nothing will happen to her if she is not afraid.

Another cause is good and clean living. People wearing good and clean clothes and eating good food make themselves more vulnerable to the attacks of the *matri.*

The *baki* of Kuan village emphatically related that only females dying an unnatural death at a young age having unfulfilled desires at their hearts, become the *matries.* Pregnant women are exempted from this rule because they are considered impure. A worse fate awaits them.

A *matri* herself declares who she is and what does she want. When a person is ill a rupee is placed inside a pot on the advice of the Brahmin and the pot is then covered with a plate and a number of cloths. This is an invitation to the *matri.* After a few days, the sick person starts trembling as if possessed by some spirit. The spirit will declare who 'she' (*matri*) is and what kind of sacrifice 'she' wants. In giving her identity the spirit will use the name she had when she was alive.

Other versions are that either a Brahmin or a *baki* will be able to tell whether the affliction is due to the *matri*. A *baki* will follow the same method as mentioned above. In the morning an invitation will be extended to the supernatural entity through the *baki* by offering him Rs. 1.25 and little bit of rice tied in a piece of cloth. During afternoon the *baki* will start worshipping the deity and in this process he will become 'possessed' by the *matri*. The *matri* will reveal her identity and will make her desire known.

A *matri* always wants a hen or a she-goat, never a cock or a he-goat. While offering the sacrifice the Brahmin must pronounce the name of the *matri*. One leg, the heart and the head are given to the Brahmin and the rest of the meat is eaten by the members of the family of the afflicted person including the sick person himself.

Pushu of Kandoi village emphasized that a *matri* must be a female which seems plausible because the description of the *matries* is very much similar to our concept of fairies who are supposed to reside in heaven and move about independently in their chariots and their shadows fall on earth. The *matries* can visit even the palace of Indra Raja who is the king of heaven. It is said that anyone who looks at the fairies of Indra Raja gets his house burnt as punishment. Women of any caste can become the *matries*, even the animals can become the *matries*.

The *matries* are of two types—(i) those who wear white cloths and (ii) those who wear coloured clothes.

A classification of the *matries* can be made on the basis of sacrifice and worship required to appease them :

(i) Those who demand sacrifice of beasts.

(ii) Those who do not touch meat but eat different kinds of animals made of flour.

(iii) Those who are satisfied by the offerings of flowers only.

(iv) Those who can be prevented by wearing a sacred talisman around the neck prepared by the Brahmin.

The last one is the most common safeguard against the *matries*.

Sin or Paap

The concept of sin or *paap* may not appear supernatural at first glance. But the reason for categoriziag it as supernatural lies in its functioning.

The sin of a person becomes 'alive' and afflicts any member of the family. The affliction is usually in the form of some disease.

There are certain specific types of activities which are considered sinful and the gravest among them is the sudden or unnatural death of any member of the family at a young age. Jagatram of Bhatar village said, "If someone falls from the high hills or if child dies, i.e. when people die at an age when they should not die, we call it a sin." Tikaram of the same village said, "Such a sin is our sin and as a result members of family may fall ill or may suffer from various diseases." In other words, the responsibility of the unnatural death of any member of the family goes to the family as a whole and inability to protect a member of the family from unnatural death is primarily a sin of the family. Pushu of Kandoi village said, "Sister, you are roaming about from village to village But if anything happens to you, if we do not give you food and shelter and if you die, its sin will not be ours. It will be the sin of your family." This sin becomes 'alive' i.e. acquires a power and dynamism to afflict a person with disease or misery.

Whether the disease is due to 'sin' is found out either by a Brahmin or by a person who can 'call God upon him'. The latter expression in used to mean a trance—like state of the person during which he is 'possessed' by supernatural power who will deliver the required information.

In cases where the diseases is on account the 'sin' a replica of the dead relative is carved out of wood or iron and propitiated as an idol. It may be decorated with streak of gold or silver. The idol is preserved and worshipped with all the sacredness of a deity and is especially worshipped during the *pitripaksha* or the 'ancestral fortnight' (the dark-half of the months of September-October is specially devoted to the worship of the ancestors in Hindu religion). But he is considered powerful or sacred only when the disease is cured. In the words of an informant, "We say to him, 'If you are a god, do some good to us, otherwise why should we worship you ?'

Cheda: The *chedas* appear to be pet spirits owned by individuals. They can be males and females both, and unlike the *matries* are found in the company of big gods, like Lord Shiva etc.

The *chedas* are utilised by the owner to cause affliction to the person the owner desires. They silently 'cling' to the person and he falls ill.

It is the task of the Brahmin to find out whether the disease is due to the *cheda* and what kind of sacrifice he wants. Accordingly, a he-goat or a ram, or a cock or grains are offered to him. But the sacrifice made to the *cheda* are not to be eaten by anyone except the owner of the *cheda* or the *cheda* will 'cling' to the eater also.

Part II

Definition: It is difficult to give a wholly acceptable definition of the term 'supernatural' because of the ambiguity involved in the two conjuncts 'super' and 'natural'. Literally speaking, it means that which transcends natural. Hence a supernatural entity is to be understood in relation to a natural entity. The characteristics of a natural entity are that it is not miraculous, it acts according to an established order, it is governed by certain laws and is comprehensible by human mind. The fact that many natural phenomena have not yet been comprehended by human mind, does not prove that they are beyond the comprehensive ability of human mind. Hence, the falling of an apple downward, the ebb and tide of the rivers, the eclipses, the day and night are all natural phenomena. As opposed to them, ghosts, fairies, demons and even gods are supernatural phenomena. Their activities are miraculous, not necessarily controlled by established laws, and the human mind cannot comprehend them fully. The functioning of the supernatural entities involves everything that is natural but transcends it beyond human comprehensibility. Thus, a fairy possesses a human body, has wings like birds but is "something more" which is superior and cannot be reached by human beings.

In this last respect, supernatural should be clearly differentiated from unnatural. Anything which is not—inbeing or function—according to nature, is unnatural. If water ceases to quench our thirst or fire ceases to burn, it is unnatural. Similarly, a baby born with two heads or a tail is unnatural. In other words, if a particular natural entity fails to behave or function according to its established laws, the phenomenon may be termed as unnatural. Therefore, an unnatural phenomenon does not transcend human comprehension because it is essentially natural phenomenon which has failed to come up to the mark due to reasons supposed to be within the comprehensibility of human mind.

One more point should be noted here. Supernatural power may be possessed by a natural being also. Such a power may or may not remain restricted to a particular field of activity. This enables the person to transcend natural functioning with reference to that particular field or fields. For example, from the above data we find that a *dankan* is a normal human being in form and behaves normally in all the fields of life like an ordinary Jaunsary woman. But she possesses the supernatural power of making an individual fall ill if she so desires simply by looking at him or eating the heart of a living being without cutting open the body. Therefore, the form of the entity is not of importance as such. The differentia of 'supernatural' is the power or the capacity to function in a way which transcends the natural laws and becomes miraculous.

After getting a workable definition of the term 'supernatural' we now proceed to define the term 'belief'. In Psychology, a belief is defined as an "enduring organisation of perceptions and cognitions about some aspect of the individual's world". (Crech and Crutchfield, 1948: 150-151). This makes beliefs dependent upon the perception of an object or situation. But a single perception in itself is not sufficient for the formation of a belief. Perceptions are reorganiged to give us a cognition of the object, and the totality of such organisations is belief. It should be noted here that the term 'perception' is used in a very broad sense to mean that all forms of cognitions have perception at their bases.

The organisation of perceptions in the form of belief is not deliberate on the part of the perceiver. It is spontaneous and a psychological necessity for the individual. Without the formation of beliefs the psychological continuity of the individual is hampered, and he feels helpless in his encounters with the external world. Since beliefs provide him with the meaning of the objects he can organize his reactions beforehand with regard to specific stimuli.

The foregoing account brings belief very close to knowledge. In fact, in common parlance, the two terms are often used interchangeably. When one says, "I believe Mr. X to be a good person", one means that one knows that Mr. X is a good peason. This knowledge is the result of reorganization of a number of previous cognitions about Mr. X at different times; such as, he may have heard an account of the goodness of Mr. X from a reliable source, he might have personal experience of the good activities of Mr. X on different occasions etc. Psychologically speaking, a belief is synonymous with knowledge. A belief may be objectively false but for psychological purposes it is the knowledge of the individual about the object of belief because it determines his reactions towards the object of belief.

The date narrated in Part 1 clearly reveal a system of beliefs which guides, controls and determines the attitude of the Jaunsaries towards diseases, deaths, physical injuries, and consequently conditions their behaviour in these fields. Any continuation of this study will invoke the legitimate questions: Why do the Jaunsaries believe what they believe ? In other words, are the beliefs of these people determined in any way ? A philosophical off-shoot of this problem will take us to the age-old problem of determinism versus indeterminism. But since our enquiry is directed more towards psychological point of view we shall try to see what psychology has to offer us as an explanation.

Since a belief is the reorganisation of perceptions and cognitions it does not involve any new psychological factor which are not present in perception. If, therefore, our perception of a thing is determined, the belief regarding the thing is also determined in the same way.

Psychologists have agreed that our perception of an object is determined by two types of factors: 1. structural and 2. functional. The structural factors are those which are 'derived solely from the nature of the physical stimuli and the neutral effects they evoke in the nervous system of the individual, (*op. cit.*). Thus, the structural factors are determined mainly by the sensory factors and are responsible for whatever objectivity is present in our perceptions.

The functional factors, on the other hand, are those which 'derive primarity from the needs, moods, past experiences and memory of the individual' (*op. cit.*). Experiments performed in this field have proved that all our immediate perceptions are determined to a very great extent by our needs, moods, emotions and past experiences. This fact emphasizes that all our perceptions will have a subjective colouring too. The functional factors will also explain why certain beliefs are held even in the absence of supporting structural factors and why 'facts are even created by individual to support a strong belief'.

We should not forget, however, that the structural and functional factors are interrelated in the psychic world of the individual. Any segregation of these facts is always done for the sake of our own convenience and for a better understanding of these processes. Therefore, all our perceptions are partly objective and partly subjective.

Two points should be noted in this connection: (1) when perceptions are organised into a higher order of beliefs, this higher order itself turns into a functional factor and determines our subsequent perceptions. In other words, our previous beliefs also determine our subsequent perceptions. Hence comes the influence of culture on our perceptions. Particular belief-patterns are sometimes preserved and propagated through the cultures in which they are prevalent. Therefore, in addition to the subjective needs, moods, mental set up and emotions of the individual, his perceptions and beliefs will also be determined by his previous beliefs, social ideals, moral ideas etc., which have largely a cultural frame of reference. Culture also determines our beliefs by determining the 'real' environment of the individual, i.e. by determining the kind of physical stimuli the individual will be exposed to, the needs induces in him etc. Since these are more or less uniform in case of all the individuals belonging to a culture, uniform belief-patterns are sustained in particular cultures.

Cultural determinants of beliefs, in ultimate analysis, can hardly be distinguished from functional factors. Not all beliefs, ideals and moral ideas prevalent in the culture are accepted by the individual and made part of his own belief-system. There is a selectivity present in this respect which is governed by the individual's subjective needs, moods and motions. Because of this I have considered the cultural factors as part of functional factors.

(2) The functional factors may not always be consciously known to the individual. There may be unconscious motivational factors determining our perceptions and consequently our beliefs. Sigmund Freud in his 'Psychopathology of Everyday Life' (1948) has tried to prove with the help of numerous examples that 'nothing in the psyche is uncaused'. What appears as uncaused appears so due to our ignorance of the cause which may not always be consciously known to the individuals. There are various unconscious motivational factors which determine, to a very great extent, our activities, perceptions, beliefs and consequently our attitude towards a thing or a person. Even when a belief becomes a part of a particular culture and is handed down from generation to generation, there must be some sustaining motivational force behind it. In majority of cases, such beliefs are sustained because they fulfil a certain purpose which, if not consciously known, must be functioning from an unconscious level of mind providing the necessary psychic energy for the sustenance of such beliefs.

A criticism of Freudian principle of 'psychic determinism' will take us far a field and is not required for our purpose. If we accept that our perceptions and thus our beliefs are functionally determined it will be difficult to keep unconscious motivational factors out of the sphere of determining forces. Therefore, we shall proceed on the assumption that the beliefs of the people are determined by motivational forces—conscious and unconscious.

PART-III

Interpretation

In persuance of our task we are now faced with the question : What are the structural and functional factors which determine the above-mentioned beliefs of the Jaunsaries?

Structural Factors

Since the structural factors are strictly determined by the nature of the physical stimuli they are conspicuously absent in the subject-matter of our discussion. By its very definition a supernatural entity is not necessarily amenable to senses and cannot always act as a physical stimulus. But we have accepted 'supernatural power or capacity' as the differentia of the term 'supernatural'. A power or capacity is not given to the senses but its existence can be inferred from the activities which can be traced as causally connected with it. If the causal connection is proved the belief will be justified. We shall accept here Mill's (1967) definition of a cause that it is the immediate, invariable, unconditional, antecedent toth e effect and shall try to find out how far the supernatural entities are causally connected with the incidents of deaths, diseases and physical infirmities. In other words, how far the beliefs of the Jaunsaries are structurally justified?

In the present case, a number of events—diseases, deaths, and physical deformities are given to the senses. These are natural events and should be explainable by natural laws. If a person falls from high hills, he may meet with his death. The fall itself may be caused by a number of factors, like, poor visibility, or the slippery condition of the road or the drunkenness of the victim etc. which are all natural phenomena. But to explain such natural phenomena by believing that they have been caused by a *dankan* or a *matri* and the person was dead before he was dead is contrary to all accepted natural laws.

An analysis of the anecdotes will show that all the stories lack logical coherence and the belief is totally unsupported by any objective evindence.

It can be analysed as:

(i) A disease, physical deformity or death has occurred;
(ii) It is considered as the activity of the *dankan*, *matri* or *paap*;
(iii) A Brahmin is consulted who always makes a corroborating diagnosis;
(iv) Sacrifice is offered;
(v) In some cases the disease is cured, in others, not;
(vi) In the latter case the same process is repeated. If after the sacrifice the disease is cured, the belief is reinforced and subsequent similar events are interpreted in the same way.

There is no need to point out that there is no casual connection between the sacrifice and the cure of the disease. It is neither an invariable nor unconditional antecedent to the cure of the disease. It might have been cured in its natural course or due to whatever medicines have been taken by the sick person. Moreover, many diseases are not cured even after the sacrifice is made, but such contrary instances are not taken into consideration. The fallacy of non-observation is too obvious here.

But the interesting point to note is that when an event happens, no attempts are made to find out the cause behind it. The cause is already determined and the event is merely an opportunity to confirm the belief. Someone finds one's ox or goat dead in the morning, one finds support to one's belief that the *dankan* must have eaten the heart of the animal. Someone apparently healthy dies, therefore, his heart must have been eaten by the *dankan*. An event is almost an excuse for the exercise of an already existent belief. The other explanations are nothing but superstructures built around this primitive belief, to rationalize it and to give it an intelligible structure. Such a process is comparable to the process of 'secondary elaboration' in dreams where disconnected and fragmentary elements of dream—thought are woven together to give it a logical appearance. The core of all the anecdotes related here is that evil spirits exist and are out to do harm to them. The anecdotes do not prove the existence of the evil spirits but revolve round the belief of their existence giving them additional pep and vigour.

That the stories are largely confabulations, will become clear if we take into account the important features of the *dankan, matri* or *paap* (sin).

Daag or *Dankan*

(i) Ordinary living females acting through casting 'evil-eyes' on individuals.

(ii) Good food, clothes, prosperity of an individual etc. form the bases of being afflicted with the *dankan.*

(iii) Like ordinary human beings they have husbands and children and feel concerned about their safety.

(iv) Caste difference is not forgotten.

(v) Like human beings there is dissatisfaction and quarrel over the distribution of meat.

(vi) Ordinary human beings can catch them in their acts and can beat the truth out of them.

A few more supernatural elements are :

(vii) A *dankan* has the power of taking any human form she likes though outwardly she is of normal human appearance.

(viii) She has special power of entering through small holes presumably by minimizing the size of her body.

(ix) She has the power of eating the heart of the person by keeping the body of the person intact.

(x) She can replace the heart of the person by that of an animal—the body of the person remaining intact.

(xi) She can enlarge her tongue to abnormal proportions.

Matri

(i) The main difference between the *matri* and the *dankan* is that the former are spirits while the latter are living human beings.

(ii) They live in the high hills with their husbands and children and have households like ordinary human beings.

(iii) Fear and cleanliness form the chief bases of being afflicted with *matries*.

Sin (*Paap*):

(i) The family of the dead person is guilty of committing the sin of 'allowing' the person to die.

(ii) As a result the wrath of the dead person afflicts, misery, usually in the form of some disease, to members of his own family.

The above analysis will show that this supernatural world of the Jaunsaries is nothing but a replica of their own social and psychological world. Just as a story, poem, or a novel often represents the thoughts, feelings and social environment of the author, these anecdotes also reveal that they must have originated from the minds of the Jaunsaries. In spite of possessing supernatural power a *dankan* behaves like an ordinary Jaunsari woman, and her supernatural powers become totally ineffective when she is caught and beaten by people. A good number of ancedotes rotate round this topic, making the idea of supernatural powers in the *dankan* limited and contradictory. The ancedotes, thus, are a peculiar mixture of rational and irrational thinking and are similar in nature to the thought-process of a child guided by 'primary process of thinking'. The characteristics of primary process of thinking are that it is pre-logical, "relatively unorganized, tolerates and condenses contradictions and is ruled by emotions and hence is full of wishful and fearful misconceptions.' (Fenichel, 1945: 35) Needless to say that later rationalisations have tried to give the belief a logical appearance. Such, as when confronted with the task of explaining how a person can have an intact body after his heart is eaten by a *dankan*, the *dankan* were ascribed the power of eating the heart of the person without cutting open the body of the person; but if the heart is eaten away, the person must die. Therefore, the belief does not get an opportunity to function till there is a death. If and when a person dies for reasons beyond their understanding the belief gets an objective support. In other words, the process of reasoning is just the reverse of normal process of thinking. Death is the proof that the person was alive, but the Jaunsaries believe that death is a proof that the person had already died because his heart had been eaten away by a *dankan.* Sometimes the person is endowed with the heart of an animal—again to explain why a person is living for the period he is living after being eaten by a *dankan.* That such a person lives up to the average age of the animal heart had been transplanted in his body is another proof of the pre-logical form of thinking which is essentially based upon similarities and analogies, and where similar things are taken as identical. It is also believed that a person also incorporates some of the essential qualities of the animal whose heart has been transplanted in his body; such as, if a person is endowed by the heart of a donkey he will work incessantly like a donkey.

All cases of causal connections are based upon two events following each other in succession. A female is suspected to be a *dankan* if a disease or mishap occurs just after her departure or arrival. If such a thing happens in a number of cases, the suspicion turns into a belief. The only basis of joining the two incidents as causally connected in the extremely superficial condition of their being antecedents and consequents in a number of cases only. No other causal factor is sought and no other proof is required. Such a process of reasoning involves a common logical fallacy known as the fallacy of *post hoc argo propter hoc*, (after this, therefore because of this).

By pointing out the above contradictions in the stories, we wanted to emphasize that no causal connection is established between the incidents of diseases, deaths and physical deformities and the supernatural entities believed to be causally connected with these incidents. Hence, objective factors have not prompted the formation of these beliefs and their contribution in this respect is almost nil.

This leaves us with the only alternative of finding out the source of these beliefs in the functional factors—conscious and unconscious.

FUNCTIONAL FACTORS

When a belief is held in the absence of all or on the basis of little objective evidence as has been shown here and is gradually built up into a system, it must be determined by strong motivational factors. Apart from giving an illogical and inconsistent explanation of diseases, deaths and physical deformities, no conscious need seems to be fulfilled by these beliefs. Hence we shall have to look for unconscious motivational forces determining these beliefs.

If we take into account the main features of these beliefs we may get a glimpse of the motivational forces working behind.

The most striking feature seems to be the wide-spread evil propensities prevalent among human beings. A *dankan* is a living human being but whenever she finds anyone wearing good clothes, eating good food and enjoying life in any way, she afflicts him with the misery of disease. In the language of Mrs. S. of Lakhamandal village, "Some girls, are very bad. If they see even good feces, they think that the person must have eaten good things and 'cling' to him". This clearly indicates that jealousy and anger are the motivating forces behind the activities of a *dankan*. The same holds good in case of *matries* too. One old man said, "If we see good food and clean clothes we like it. So also the *matries* and they 'attach' themselves to him". The anecdote where the *matries* took away a woman because she was very much in love with her husband and was loved by her husband also is a clear indication of why *matries* afflict people. If a person dies at a young age his anger and wrath causes physical affliction to other members of his family. In other words, the world of Jaunsaries is full of evil-doing forces.

Another important feature is that death is seldom equated with total extinction. Any person dying at a young age, having unfulfilled desires becomes *matri* and keeps on living in some other form.

Since our contention is that in this case the beliefs are determined by the functional factors, i.e. the needs, moods, emotions, past experiences and the cultural factors, we now have to find out the needs of these people operating behind the belief that the world is infested with evil forces. The objective experiences of the people surely do not warrant such conclusions because every group or community life is largely and basically sustained through co-operation between people belonging to the group. Hostility and aggression are definite evidences and the relations between people are also characterised by these tendencies to some extent. But a disproportionate belief in its all-pervasiveness to the utter disregard of the reverse aspect of the picture forces us to find its causes in the deeper region of the psychic world of the people.

The only plausible explanation seems to be that these evil forces are the hostile and aggressive impulses of the individuals themselves which have been projected on outside agencies like *daags, matries* etc., due to sense of guilt associated with such tendencies. To substantiate this conclusion we shall have to take a brief excursion into the theory of psychoanalysis.

Psychoanalysis has shown us that the infant, in the process of development has to modify many of its instinctual demands on account of pressure from outer-reality.

The instincts which undergo greatest amount of modification, are sexual and aggressive. Every instinctual need is endowed with some amount of psychic energy. The non-fulfilment of the needs results in an accumulation of psychic energy creating a tension within the organism. This tension is experienced as highly unpleasant by the organism and threatens its homeostatic equilibrium. The ego, faced with the uphill task of mastering the tension, takes recourse to a number of defensive or economic measures. The defence-mechanisms are directed towards releasing this accumulated energy through various means and thus maintaining the desired state of equilibrium within the organism by lowering the tension. All the defences are unconsciously adopted by the ego. Hence, the individual is not conscious that these warded-off impulses are getting partial satisfaction through defensively oriented activities. Repression, projection, denial, reaction formation, isolation etc., are some of the pathogenic defences. The successful defences may be summed up under one heading—sublimation.

There is still a controversy among the psychoanalysts regarding the exact nature and function of aggressive tendencies. But there is a consensus of opinion that 'in part, they are reactive in character, i.e. they are the response to frustrations and have as their goal the overcoming of frustrations' (*op. cit*). The innumerable frustrations which the child has to experience as the inevitable consequence of his uninhibited demand over reality lead to the repeated stimulation of this tendency. But the manifestation of this tendency is strongly decried by the external authorities. Since the helpless child is dependent upon the external authorities for the satisfactions of his basic needs, he cannot afford to lose their love and approval. In his attempts to master the aggressive impulses the child takes the help of defensive measure. During the process of the formation of super-ego popularly known as the conscience, the aggressive and hostile impulses experienced towards the forbidding authorities are transferred to the internalized image of the parental authorities. Thus the aggressive tendencies which were primarily directed towards the external world are returned to the ego. This part is detached from the ego and functions as the super-ego exercising the same aggressiveness towards the subordinate ego which the ego directed towards the external world. The ego's need to fulfil its desire and the super-ego's restrictions on them creates a tension which is experienced as the sense of guilt and manifests itself as the need for punishment' (Freud, 1957: 105). Freud in his 'Civilization And Its Discontents' (1957) has discussed elaborately, how aggressive impulses internalized give rise to the formation of the super-ego whose severity is enhanced by each successive act of suppression. When the ego is forced to renounce any instinctual gratification, the aggressive tendencies stimulated due to frustration, become a part of super-ego making it more severe. The severer the super-ego the greater will be its demands on the ego and the greater will be the sense of guilt. Mere renunciation, therefore, cannot generate a sense of guilt unless the aggression directed towards the forbidding authorities is transferred to the super ego and created tension between ego and super-ego.

An exaggeration of such tension, i.e. an aggravated sense of guilt creates anxiety in the organism and threatens its psychic equilibrium. The ego again takes the help of defence mechanisms in order to preserve homeostasis.

With this account in view, we are now in a position to understand why for the Jaunsaries evil has become such an all pervasive force and why diseases, deaths etc., are viewed as manifestations of these evil forces.

The hostile and evil forces which these individuals experienced as the consequence of frustrations, become internalized and form part of their super-ego. Due to tension beween the demands of the instincts and the commands of the super ego the resultant sense of guilt necessitates further defences to be adopted by the ego. In this case, the ego adopts the defence of projecting its own hostile impulses on the outside agencies and thus by transferring part of these tendencies to other agencies a partial instinctual gratification is effected.

One point should be borne in mind in this connection. A child initially cannot distinguish between ego and non-ego. It is gradually through the process of deprivation that the infant comes to realise that certain of his needs cannot be fulfilled because the objects of gratification are not parts of his body. He cannot get them as and when he desires. If all the needs of the child are taken care of it is doubtful whether he will ever develop a sense of reality. The outer reality, therefore, is initially seen as part of the ego, behaving like the ego. This is the source of primitive anthropomorphic tendencies in us. As the child grows up through knowledge and experience, the distinction between ego and non-ego becomes sharper and the infantile anthropomorphic ideas are rectified.

Deprivation gives arise to frustration which generate aggression aimed at removing frustration. This is true in case of all individuals irrespective of culture. But they do not give rise to such beliefs among the civilized people as held by the Jaunsaries. This is explainable by a number of facts.

Firstly, frustrations are comparatively greater among these hill people. In civilized societies most of the needs of the individuals are taken care of. On the other hand, the environmental condition of the Jaunsaries deprive them of such fulfilments. Extreme proverty, an unkind nature and an infertile land unite to make their lives miserable. Good clothes and good food are luxury items to be envied and never to be obtained. Hence, the *dankan* or the *matries* afflict people who eat good food and wear nice clothes. The reactions of a child on seeing some desired object beyond his reach are these of jealousy and aggression. The same appears to be the case with the Jaunsaries.

Secondly, supernatural beliefs become rarer in civilized

societies because of increased scientific knowledge which helps in the proper understanding of the reality. If it is proved that diseases are caused by bacterial infections and can be cured by proper application of medicines, it is difficult to maintain that are not so. In other words, a belief cannot sustain itself if it is in direct contradiction to the structural factors except in extreme cases where it may be considered pathological. In case of Jaunsaries no such modifying factors are present. Lack of education and ignorance of scientific reasons behind diseases, deaths and physical deformities have helped them to pin their faith more in supernatural.

These beliefs have become part of the culture of the Jaunsaries. A Jaunsari child grows up amid such beliefs and knows of no alternative explanation. These beliefs become part of his psychic world and inturn are handed down to thc succeeding generation. But the basic sustaining force of such beliefs remains essentially related to the psychic needs of the individual.

The picture which we have obtained till now is that the Jaunsaries remain in some aspect of their psychic development more infantile than the normal people. That part of their infantile age, unable to cope up with instinctive aggressive demands projects them on some external agencies, and thus obtains a partial gratification. The belief is built up into a system with a pre-logical process of thinking—characteristic of an infantile mind. To the infantile mind aggressiveness appears all pervading and indestructible, because the child is unable to handle successfully his aggressive desires, and the hostile impulses raise their heads again and again.

The infantile nature of their thinking is manifested in the predominance of oral tendencies in the activities of these supernatural forces. The first reaction of the child towards external objects is to put them in the mouth. This reaction becomes the prototype for the mastery of all external situations later on. Fenichel says, 'Taking-into-the-mouth or spitting out is the basis of all perceptions and in conditions of regression one can observe that in the unconscious all sense organs are conceived mouth-like.' (1945 : 37) The *dankan* eat the hearts of the people; even when they inflict diseases on the individuals the linguistic expression used by the Jaunsaries is; 'The *dankan* or the *matries* are eating him away.' Death is also considered as 'being eaten away by the *dankan* or *matri*'. This predominance of oral incorporation indicates a strong regressive tendency characteristic of very infantile stage of psychic development. The defence-mechanism of projection is also very infantile in nature. It owes its origin to two infantile biological tendencies—one of spitting out which is oral in character and second of elimination of feces which is anal in character. In both these cases the basic idea at work is to externalize the undesirable tendencies. That which threatens the organism from within his excreted out and the organism feels comparatively safer. Like oral incorporation, oral and anal ejection is also a very infantile process. The Jaunsaries make an extensive use of this defence-mechanism. When the repressed hostile impulses threaten to break through the barrier and enter the consciousness the ego adopts more drastic measures by attributing them to outer agencies. In other words, instead of saying 'I want to kill him' he says, 'He wants to kill me : The entire fear of the Jaunsaries of being attacked by the *dankan* etc. can be expressed verbally as such : 'I am not jealous of her beautiful clothes and the nice food she eats, she is jealous of my clothes and food.' The hostile impulses generated through jealousy and hatred are directed towards the object of jealousy. Because of guilt they are projected on imaginary (*matri*) or non-imaginary (*dankan*) entities. Verbally expressed it amounts to saying ; 'I do not want to cause this death, he does'. Hence, the *dankan* and *matries* cause diseases and deaths which is nothing but the fear of being attacked by one's own aggressive tendencies projected on outer agencies.

We have one more fact to explain. Why is not death equated with total extinction ?—a point which we raised at the beginning of our discussion.

The answer to this question lies perhaps in the inability of an infantile mind to conceive total negation. A clinical example will make the point clear. One of my female patients having prominent paranoid trends, aged 8/9 years but having a mental age of 4/5 years expressed her hostile attitude towards her cousin of approximately the same age but much advanced in mental abilities in the following way : "I will take a sword and cut his head off. That will be very nice because after cutting his head he wo'nt be able to eat even if he feels hungry". Obviously the infantile mind could not conceive that cutting the head means death which is total extinction. Similar beliefs prevail among the Jaunsaries when they believe that the *dankan* eats the *jhikudi* of the person but the person continues to live for some more days. Only later the demands of reason forced them to realise that the person must die and he dies due to some insignificant cause to give the death a natural appearance. Moreover, death is seldom viewed as a natural end of the life-process. It is considered as an act of aggression on the part of some unknown force. Similar beliefs also lie at the core of civilized mind which become manifest through expressions as, 'death has snatched him away', etc. This might explain the belief that the sin of the death of any member of the family afflicts other members of the family. Death itself being an act of aggression, the aggressive desires of people towards other members of the family get an unconscious fulfilment. Hence arises the sense of guilt which is expiated through the punishment inflicted on the family in the form of diseases.

The analysis of the above materials brings out one more point to the fore. The evil forces are predominantly females and they can be prevented by worshipping gods who are predominantly males. Why have females been chosen for the projection of evil tendencies ? Some objective factor must be present behind such consistent projection. Since a female is a mother-image, one may naturally wonder whether there is something wrong with the mother-image of the Jaunsaries. Freud as quoted by Reik in his book 'Myth and Guilt' (1970) had once pointed out that the primitive evil forces were predominantly females is indicative of an aggressive and authoritative role of mother in the matriarchal system of family which remained imprinted in the tribal mind and gave rise to this idea by projecting their own mother-image as supernatural evil forces. (1958 : 137) In the absence of date in support of this view among the Jaunsaries, we may look for another explanation. The mother-image of the Jaunsaries is certainly not of a very high order. People there usually consider their women in a different way on account of their frequent divorces and desertion of their families. It should be kept in mind, however that an image is not always a true representation of the person. It is not possible to say how far this mother-image of the Jaunsaries has determined their belief that evil supernatural forces are predominantly females. But this is a point which certainly merits consideration.

In conclusion, I would like to point out that there are many minor points which need explanation. But within the limited span of this paper it will not be possible to do justice to them. Therefore, I have not tried to take them up for discussion and interpretation.

From the foregoing discussion, one question conspicuously raises its head : Can the removal of the ignorance of the Jaunsaries regarding the real causes of deaths and diseases totally eradicate such beliefs ? The answer is not difficult to find. A civilized person does not believe that diseases are caused by the *dankans* and *matries* but by infections. He is not afraid of being eaten by the *dankan,* but he is afraid of being infected with germs. A pathological manifestation of this fear is found in some forms of obsession and compulsion psychoneurosis, which show on analysis all the infantile psychic processes present in the beliefs of the Jaunsaries. So long as the inner necessities determining the belief are not adjusted the environmental change may bring about change in the form of belief only, the content remaining the same.

REFERENCES

Fenichel, O. 1945 *The Psychoanalytic Theory of Neurosis* Routledge & Kegan Paul, Trench Trubner & Co., London.

Freud, S. 1948 *Psychopathology of Everyday Life,* Ernest Benn Ltd., London.

	1957	*Civilization and Its Discontents*, The Hogarth Press Limited, London.
Krech, David & Richard S. Crutchfield	1948	*Theory and Problems of Social Psychology*, McGraw Hill Book Co., New York.
Majumder, D.N.	1962	*Himalayan Polyandry*, Asia Publishing House, Bombay.
Malinowski, B.	1927	*Sex and Repression in Sevage Society*, Routledge & Kegan, Paul, London.
Mills, C. Wright	1967	*Sociological Imagination*, Oxford University Press, London.
Reik, Theodor	1970	*Myth and Guilt*, G and D, New York.

CHAPTER XII

SYMBOLISM AND MYTH IN GARHWALI RELIGION: THE HOT LADLE LICKING RITUAL

ANOOP CHANDOLA

A myth contains symbols that represent values of a culture. Symbols are metaphorical in nature. All metaphors evolve from literal, human experience of objects or items and their interrelationships. The values associated with a metaphor continue as long as they are literally reinterpreted or acted out.

In this paper[1] our focus is on the function of myth and its symbolism in the religion of Garhwali speakers. This religion is part of the complex of Hinduism. It is best classified as the *Smarta* type of Hinduism. This type allows various social groups to alter the contents of standard myths. Thus a myth may have two versions—one standard and the other folk. Both versions co-exist with mutual exclusiveness in actual social contexts. Each version is utilized to create social harmony. These are the main points which will be elaborated below in the context of the Garhwali hot iron ladle licking ritual.[2]

General Background

The term 'Garhwali' (pronounced in my dialect as *gadwali*) is derived from 'Garhwal' (pronounced as *gadwal*). The word 'Garhwali' refers here to the people and the associated language of the following hill districts of the Utter Pradesh state of India:

Garhwal, Tehri, Chamoli, and Uttar Kashi. A huge population of Garhwali original so resides in Dehradun and Mussoorie and other areas adjacent to the plains south of these four districts. Traditional Garhwali society is divided into two major groups, namely, *bit* and *silpkar* (or *silipkar*). The word *bit* seems to be derived from Old Indo-Aryan *dvi-stha, *dvistha and Middle Indo-Aryan*bittha meaning 'twice-born' (Sanskrit *dvi* 'two' and *stha* 'situated', equivalent to Sanskrit *dvija*).[3] Two sub-groups called *baman* and *jajman* (respectively from Sanskrit *brahmana* and *yajamana*) form the *bit* group. The Rajputs (*rajput* in Garhwali) are in the *jajman* class. The traditional *varna* or classes of *brahmana* and *ksatriya* (*rajanya*) are represented by these two *bit* sub-groups. The *vaisya varna* or business class does not exist as a clear sub-group in traditional Garhwali society. The *sudra varna* is sometimes erroneously associated with the *silpkar* group (the term is from Sanskrit *silpakara* 'artisan').

It is possible that the *baman* and *jajman* caste formerly called the artisans *dum* (Sanskrit *doma, domba*) with a derogatory connotation. In return the artisans might have called the *baman* and *jajman* together as *bit* with a derogatory connotation. In such a case the etymology of *bit* could be Sanskrit *dvit* or *dvista* meaning 'enemy, hostile, unlikeable' from the verb root *divs* 'hate, be unkind or unfriendly, etc.' The same historical reflex is found in the Garhwali word *bitmanu* or *bitmano* 'to say unkind or abusive words' where the verb root has *bit*.

Many *baman* and *jajman* castes came to settle in present day Garhwali and Kumauni speaking areas between the thirteenth and seventeenth centuries A.D. Their movement was due to Muslim rule in other regions of the Indian sub-continent. The Gurjars (Sanskritic *Gurjara*), who might have been in Garhwal as early as the tenth century A.D., should also be considered new settlers viewed from the position of the people of *Khas* or *khasa*, origin. (The Garhwali word *khasya* is related to the Sanskrit *khasa* or *khasa*, applied to people who were in Garhwal before the Gurjars.) The later settlers, whoever they were, might not have found the earlier settlers' practices up to their expectations. So these earlier settlers, might have been classified as *dum* like the ancient *vratya* groups. In turn, the new settlers might have been branded as *bit* by the older ones. But this is only a conjecture, since the historical background of social stratification is not quite clear.

The influx of several ethnic groups in historical times has resulted in the adding of new myths and symbols; well-known older Hindu myths kept getting modified and non-Hindu elements were even integrated with the Hindu traditions. Such an enrichment is in line with the *smarta* view of the Hindus[4]. The result was that this Pahari area became a culture area in the sense of Berreman (1972). There are some differences between the practices of Pahari Hindus and non-Pahari Hindus. Some Paharis who are in contact with the non-Paharis do not like even today to openly admit that such differences exist. This is an attempt on the part of such Paharis to match their socio-cultural values with or even show their superiority over the cultural values of the Hindus of the plains. We who work in social sciences are not much interested in value judgments. For example, we cannot regard Sudra as 'the group of low caste people' and Brahmana as 'the group of high caste people,' or the *khas* Rajputs as inferior to non-*khas* Rajputs in any way. I am writing this because recently a popular Garhwali writer reviewing my book "Folk Drumming in the Himalayas" (1977) identified the Garhwali folk drummers as artisans from the 'lowly caste.' It is true that the traditional local Hindus do interact in terms of caste hierarchies in certain contexts where 'high' and 'low' distinctions are significant. What actually is more important in our view is the role of castes in ritualistic performance in which no role is considered 'high' or 'low,' but where castes are treated rather as components needed for the evolution of the whole event or performance. In the context of the following religious performance, the Brahman priests and the silpkar drummers, for example, interact on a functional or role basis, not on a scalar basis.

The Ritual

This religious service or *puja* is performed in a village near Pauri (administrative headquarters of Garhwal) in the month of June for four days. The last day is the sacred of *ganga dasara*. We were present for one such service one evening. I was accompanied by Sudha (my wife), Manjul (my fourteen year old son), and my father. The ritual is performed in a house near the temple of *debi.*[5] The morning and daytime services are performed in the temple, whereas some evening services performed in a home as well as in the temple.

People from this village, as well as from other villages began to assemble in the front yard of the host family around 9 p.m. The home belonged to the relatives of BH, our host. Then a bonfire was prepared in a corner of the yard. Two Shamans stood beside the bonfire. The leading Shaman had the drum *dhol* and the assistant Shaman had the drum *damau.* They started playing the drums while singing songs in praise of the *debi.* The song language was Garhwali. There was intermittent use of Hindi also, mainly in the invocation part of the song. (See Chandola 1977 for more details of the Garhwali music of the Shamans).

Some males started dancing circularly in front of the Shamans. Others were either sitting or standing. A woman was possessed by the *debi.* She joined the dance. Her possession was over after the *debi* text and music known as *baju* 'play' or *baja* 'plays' were finished by the Shamans.

Then the Shamans started the *baju* of *narsin* or *narsing* (to be explained below.) It began with the story of *parlad.* The Shamans sang how *parlad* started uttering the name of *ram.* In a few minutes BH, who was seated in the audience, began to shake and scream. He got up and went to sit close to the Shamans near the bonfire. A young priest, who was BH's nephew, came out with a tray in his hand. The tray (Garhwali *thali*) contained rice, whole black beans (*urd*), one rupee and twenty-five naye paise, burning incense (Garhwali *dhup*) and cotton candles. The priest went in front of the possessed BH. Holy water of the Ganges was sprinkled over BH's head while the priest was reciting the *devi* hymn in Sanskrit that begins with the words *ya devi sarvabhutesu...*'the Goddess who in all beings....'

BH was, however, possessed by *narsing.* Thus it might seem odd that the brahmin (priest) chanted the *devi* hymn in Sanskrit while BH was passessed by *narsing.* But in this context BH was identified as the devotee of the mother (Garhwali *mayi*) which is *debi* herself. The Shamans in their songs associated *narsing* with many *nat* (Sanskrit *Natha*) gurus such as Goraknat (the famous Yogi Goraksanatha or Gorakhnath). Then after the Devi hymn BH (as *narsing*) asked for his ax (Garhwali *phauri*). The 'ax' is actually an iron cooking ladle, but here it symbolically represents an ax.) The ladle was brought to him. He put its round flat front part inside the burning ambers of the bonfire. BH signalled to Manjul (my son) who was escorted to him. He picked up some ashes from the bonfire in his fist which he moved over Manjul's head in a circular motion. Then Manjul was discharged. BH asked for the ladle but its front part was not red hot yet. So he waited. In the meantime he picked up burning ambers and chewed them and also swallowed some burning candles. Then he picked up the ladle whose front part by now had become red hot and he licked it several times over and over. Then he reheated it and held it by his teeth. Then he put it back in the fire again.

In the meantime BH had a discourse in Garhwali (with occasional bursts in Hindi) with the Shamans and also with a few members of the audience. Then BH made a signal to my wife, Sudha, who was busy taking pictures of him with her camera. She could not understand what the meaning of his gesture was. My father, who was in charge of recording the session, asked her to go to BH, for the signal was meant to bless her. She handed the camera over to me and sat in front of BH. He picked up the ladle by its handle from the bonfire and asked Sudha to stretch her palms in front of him. She did so without expecting what was to come. BH rubbed her palms with the red hot front part of the ladle. Sudha said later that at the first touch she was frightened to death but instantly she felt that the red hot ladle being rubbed over and over again on her palms was really cool. He told her that the (research) job we had undertaken would be successful. He showed no signs of pain or burns.

After some discourse with others, BH was out of his trance; the god was sent away propitiated by the priest, the Shamans, and the audience.

Now BH asked Sudha to show him her hands. There were two or three tiny scars on her palms, otherwise there was no indication of any pain or burns. BH told us that those tiny scars were there because Sudha was frightened, that it was due to initial lack of confidence in God's power. He also told us that this was his first experience of hot ladle licking. He had seen his older brother going through this experience several times. His brother had died nine years ago and since then no one in the village had ever had this experience.

We could not attend the religious ceremonies of the following night. But we were told that BH went into a trance again and licked the hot ladle again just like the night before.

The Garhwali myth of *narsing* is based on the Sanskritic *Narsimha avatara* or the 'Man-Lion incarnation' of Lord Visnu. Hiranyakasipu was a demon and was angry at his son Prahlada (Garhwali *parlad*) because he was Visnu's devotee. In the Garhwali myth Prahlada utters the name of Rama (Garhwali *ram*) which is Visnu's incarnated name. Hiranyakasipu finally decided to punish his son for this act. The Shamans were at this point of the story in their song text when BH was possessed by *narsing* (Nrsimha). They never finished the story, though the audience knew it anyway. The complete story is this : As a punishment, Prahlada was to be hung by a red hot iron pillar. No sooner had Prahlada come near the red hot pillar to be burnt, than the pillar was broken and the Lord appeared from it as Nrsimha. He saved Prahlada and killed Hiranyakasipu.

Theoretical Discussion

The central question is : How does a myth like this survive in a religion or culture ? Our answer is that a myth survives because its metaphoric level can be transferred to a literal level. All symbols have to be metaphorical. A symbol will not be part of a belief system if it cannot be related to concrete acts or performances. In the context of metaphor, Mammata's view—as given in his *kavyaprakasa*—is noteworthy. According to him, when the literal sense (*mukhyartha*) is blocked, another related sense pertaining to convention or purpose is invoked. The process that invokes this different meaning is known as *laksana* or metaphor, hence *laksyartha* or metaphorical sense. What I intend to say here is that for the continued existence of a symbol or metaphor, it must evolve to a literalness that is acceptable to the members of the community in question. (See Chandola, 1978; 1979 for more details on metaphor in social context.)

This idea is supported by Pavlov's experiments on conditioning. The bell in the famous experiment makes the dog salivate because the food is shortly to follow. Here the 'bell' is a symbol whose ringing is transferred to 'food production' for the dog. Thus 'food production' is the literal level. If the bell ringing is not followed by food, then the value of or the feeling for the bell as the symbol of 'food production' will be lost. Thus a symbol represents not only an object or concept but also the values associated with it. Tyler (1978) has rightly pointed out that "A symbol, then, is more than a means of representation; it is representation plus evaluation... Modern theories of symbolism fail because they focus exclusively on the representational function, forgetting that representation is only the minimal role of symbols. Symbols, and our understanding of the world, are always unities of fact and feeling."

Thus the literal or factual is evolved into a metaphor, hence a symbol, which then is evolved once again into a literal. This means, as I have shown elsewhere, that for non-linguistic acts we must have instructions available at the literal level. All the instructions are coloured by pre-syntactic or semantic decisions. Many researches have shown that prior semantic considerations are essential in our linguistic and non-linguistic acts (Austin, 1960; Searle, 1969; Klaiman, 1980; etc.) A non-linguistic act, then, must pre-suppose a literal linguistic act.

One of the popular miraculous parts of the Garhwali *narsing* myth is that a true devotee could not be burnt by red hot metallic stuff such as a pillar. The possessed person, such as BH, is the ideal example of a true devotee because he comes literally in contact with a red hot metalic ladle which, however, cannot harm him in any sense. The fire test is really symbolic of extreme hardship for the devotee and also of his unshakeable faith in the power of God. Indeed the good of the village is related to such religious performances. For example, if there are good rains the villagers associate such a natural act with such religious services in a cause-and-effect relationship. If someone sick in the family recovers his health after this ritual it reinforces faith in its performance. And so on.

Smarta symbolism is also evident in the reinterpretation or modification of the myth. The Shamanistic version of the myth varies from the puranic one. For example, the head Shaman (the *dhol* player) addressed the spirit of *narsing* as the devotee of Mother or *debi.* He also identified the spirit as the devotee of Nath gurus such as Gorakhnath (Garhwali *goraknat*). In the puranic version there Nrsimha has no such associations. But the Garhwali myth unites Vaishnavism (Nrsimha), Shaktism (*devi*), and Nath sectarianism (Goraksanatha) in one single story—a realistic representation of the popular Garhwali religion. The Shamanistic version poses no problems in such performances despite the fact that some members of the Garhwali community, e.g., my father, do not share those features which contradict the puranic version of the Visnu incarnation. In the separate Sanskritic puja of Nrsimha as practiced in the Garhwali region, there is no such association of Nrsimha with *devi* or Goraksanatha. In the exclusive Sanskritic puja, the brahmin priest follows the puranic version. In this puja the same shaman drummers play these drums without their version.

Conclusion

Thus in cultural performances mythical versions are not viewed as high or low but rather as mutually exclusive. They parallel with the 'caste roles' in such performances. For example, the shamans are from the *auji* caste of the silpkars, who are tailors also, whereas the priest is from a brahmin caste. Both have roles in these performances and no role is viewed as high or low. Such cultural performances cannot be successful if some caste members feel that their role is inferior. Hostile caste attitudes that do exist are ignored at this time. The castes from the *bit* (the Brahmins and Rajputs) and the *silpkar* groups dance together and any person, male or female from any caste can be possessed by one and the same 'god' (Garhwali *debta*) or 'goddess' (Garhwali *debi*).

There are, however, a few gods which are worshipped only in the home of a *bit* or a *silpkar*. For example, *nirankar* is such a god; he possesses only a *silpkar* member. There is no Sanskritic puja involved with *nirankar*. The element seems to have come to the silpkars from the Nath Panth or the sect of Gorakhnath (Goraksanatha). It must have appealed to the silpkars because admission to it was not based on caste. Eventually the symbol *nirankar* was associated with the symbols that were acceptable to the *bits*. This may be the reason why the drummers called *narsing* as the devotee of *goraknat* and other gurus of the Nath Sect. The *nirankar* ritual is performed entirely by the silpkars, except for the dance, in which both the *bit* and the silpkar members participate at the host silpkar's home. Thus, whether it is the *narsing* type or the *nirankar* type dance, all castes join it. This symbolizes equality in the presence of the divine spirit This dance, then, is the literalization of the symbolic value of equality.

These cultural performances are now on the decline because of changing social conditions and attitudes in Garhwali society. Such changes are in line with the modernization experienced in other parts of India (cf. Singer 1972). The old symbols will gradually lose their values because more efficient symbols are replacing them. The democratic set up provides these efficient symbols and they are indeed at work, where 'work' means literal conversion of symbolic values into actual performance. Thus, old terms such as *bit* and *dum* which symbolize negative values of hostility, inequality, etc. will become less functional as the positive values of modern democratic symbols are experienced by people in actual social interaction.

NOTES

1. I am grateful to Dr. M.H. Klaiman for her comments and corrections on the manuscript. However, I am fully responsible for any errors in the contents of this article.

2. This study was done in conjunction with my sabbatical project on the trance phenomenon in the Central Himalayas in 1979. My thanks are due to all the participants, especially my relatives, shamans, priests, doctors and to Mr. BH, whose case is given in this article.

3. The Garhwali language, like the neighbouring Kumauni, is a Central Pahari language of the New Indo-Aryan group, hence these etymologies.

4. The Sanskrit word *smarta* (from *smrit*) refers here to the traditions and rituals of the Sanskritic books known as Dharmasastras, e.g., Manusmrti 'The Laws of Manu'. The word *smrti* 'memory' is true to its metaphorical sense which is any 'memorable tradition'. Thus the Vedic as well as the non-Vedic beliefs of India are practiced by the Smarta Hindus. Any 'other' traditions or elements are accommodated in this Hinduism by linking it with the existing ones. Thus many 'other' folkloric and non-folkloric beliefs have found their way in the Garhwali *smarta* religion. However, it should be noted that all the Smartas do not share all the beliefs with each other.

5. The Garhwali *debi* corresponds to Sanskrit *debī* 'goddess'. In this context *debi* represents the Mother Goddess who in the Sanskritic tradition is also known by such names as Durga, Kali, Gauri, Parvati, Sakti, Candika, Bhavani, Siva (consort of Lord Siva), Mahamaya, Yogamaya, etc.

REFERENCES

1. Austin, J.L., 1960 *How to Do Things with Words*, Oxford.

2. Berreman, G.D., 1972 *Hindus of the Himalayas*, University of California Press, Berkeley and Los Angles.

3. Chandola, Anoop, 1977, *Folk Drumming in the Himalayas : A Linguistic Approach to Music*, AMS Press, New York.

4. Chandola, Anoop, 1978 "Sex and Language Abuse : Metaphoric Pressures from Social Privileges", paper presented at the Xth International Congress of Anthropological and Ethnological Sciences, New Delhi.

5. Chandola, Anoop, 1979 *Situation to Sentence : An Evolutionary Method for Descri-*

ptive Linguistics, AMS Press, New York.

6. Klaiman, M.H., 1980 Volitionaligy and Subject in Bengali : A Study of Semantic Parameters in Grammatical Processes, University of Chicago, Ph. D. dissertation in Linguistics, reproduced by Indian University Linguistics Club.
7. Searle, John R. 1969 *Speech Acts : An Essay in the Philosophy of Language*. Cambridge.
8. Singer, Milton 1972 *When a Great Tradition Modernizes : An Anthropological Approach to Indian Civilization*. Praeger Publishers, New York.
9. Tyler, Stephen, A. 1978 *The Said and the Unsaid*, Academic Press, New York

CHAPTER XIII

CHANGING MILIEU AND DEVELOPMENT STRATEGIES IN GARHWAL

M. M. DHASMANA

Garhwal deriving its name from the land of glens (*garh*= forts) is pauranically known as Kedar Khand. Its geographical boundaries underwent constant re-organisations under various administrations and rules. The area drained by the Alaknanda, the Bhagirathi and their immediate tributaries, can be called as Garhwal. Garhwal which consists of five districts today viz. Pauri, Chamoli, Tehri, Uttar Kashi and Dehradun alongwith three districts of Kumaon viz. Almora, Nainital and Pithoragarh i.e., the hill districts of Uttar Pradesh are also called as Uttarakhand or the 'Valley of Gods'. The regions of Garhwal and Kumaon belong to identical ecological pattern and depict similar socio-economic milieu. This paper is based on an extensive field study of the four hill districts of Garhwal region. However due to existence of similar conditions these problems and prospects are applicable to entire Uttarakhand region today.

This Himalayan tract due to its massive mountain ranges, magnificient peaks, nectarial rivers and kalieodoscopic flowers was a celestial abode and became famous as the Valley of Gods. From times immemorial its grandeur and mystery attracted millions of people from the Indian sub-continent for solace and salvation. There are over nine hundred sacred complexes in Uttarakhand out of which over five hundred and fifty worship centres are located in the Alaknanda and the Bhagirathi valleys. The riverine oriented pilgrimage to Uttarakhand though a seasonal affair, was one of the major sources of economy for the native population.

But today tranquility does not region in the Valley of Gods. Its salubriously sequestered forests and salutiferous vegetation is threatened with ecological imbalances. Denudation of trees have led to soil erosions, landslides, heavy silting of river beds, river blockages and catastrophic floods. Heat waves from the plains easily reach the snow line and the glaciers are receding at an alarming rate. The boons bestowed by nature are diminishing and the people of this region are faced with a critical shortage of fodder, fuel and manure. Wild life and medicinal plants are endangered with many nearly extinct due to unscrupulous over exploitation and poaching. Unregulated grazing of cattle and misuse of pastures have minimised the local animal husbandry production. It is beyond the scope of this paper to find the factors responsible for this upheavel or involve in any controversy about the forest policy or the stabilization of the eco-system. However it may be added that the age old difficulties of women catering for FFM[1] (fodder, fuel and manure) have menacingly increased. Due to opening of roads the confluences have been deserted. Faced with occupational transformations the local people move to plains in search of petty jobs.

The legacy of transhumance[2] from rural hill areas to urban industrial plain areas started with the arrival of the British administration in Garhwal. But in those days the money order economy and the return of majority of population after retirement kept the social system intact. Today the highland social system is crumbling. Its syneretic culture is disintegrating due to mass exodus of population. Factors like terrain, difficult communication, illiteracy, non-utilization of natural resources contributed for the backwardness, poor economy and difficult living conditions in the region. But these are not the only reasons.

In the preceding paragraphs an attempt has been made to pin point the root causes of the present day malaise in Uttarakhand, specially in the four hill districts of Garhwal region. An Anthropo-historic inquest will reveal how these factors transformed and shaped the development of this region, and now inspite of best efforts of the administration have paved the foundations of economic backwardness in the area.

The Migrant Syndrome

In the socio-cultural history of Uttarakhand, nothing could be more unfortunate than the migrant syndrome[3] characteristic of its population. From time immemorial it has been a typical characteristic of the people of Garhwal and Kumaon, specially of the elites. Whatever may be the reasons of origin of this characteristic pattern and without challenging its authenticity or questioning the loyality of its people for their land, it was clear that the inhabitants of Uttarakhand always claimed to be immigrants. It is difficult to ascertain the exact time of origin of this social phenomena but it can be alluded that this must have originated in 1516 when Raja Ajai Pal shifted his capital from Chandpur Garhi to Srinagar. Ever since sooner a person attained some status in socio-economic field, he claimed to have migrated from different parts of the country. This syndrome as a status symbol was in vogue for over four hundred years. During this period leading class of the Brahman and Rajput castes could list their claims to have migrated from different parts of the country and established a superior hierarchy over the remaining people. Early history writers highlighted exotic origin claim of the superior Brahman and Rajput castes (Raturi : 1980). The migrant claim was a race for social status and an attempt to sever links from the Trans-Himalayan culture. In this process the people living in their own area developed a sence of discontent for their culture and ethnic origin. It divided the population into various hierarchies, stratified social mobility, annulled the gains achieved by elites and hindered socio-economic progress.

With the arrival of the British administration the migrant syndrome underwent a diagonally opposed transformation. It changed its course. The people of Uttarakhand started trickling to plains for education and in search of livelihood. From the middle of nineteenth century to early fifties of this century it was a sort of transhumance—a seasonal migration of rural hill population to urban-industrial centres in plains. During winter people used to go to plains in search of jobs and return to hills for cultivating summer crops. Defence or other Government employees served in plains but kept their families in native villages. They returned after their retirement. The money order economy played a helping hand in the rural areas, and there was no threat to the drainage of population. But the Garhwalis who attained some success or economic status took their families with them and started settling down in urban cities where they worked. Not everyone of them revealed their origin. Some such settlers dropped their agnatic clan titles[4] and adopted the common prevalent caste titles in plains.

Since the early fifties of this century, the Garhwalis have fared considerably well in various fields and are in coveted posts in the country. They are not shy of their origin and are proud to call themselves as the Garhwalis. People who had dropped their agnatic clan titles have reverted to their usage. But this attitude has not been of any help to the origin of their region. After serving in plains a good number of the hill people is not returning to their place of origin. A new concept in the migrant syndrome has become the status symbol today.

This is the concept of being a Garhwali but settled outside Garhwal. There is a mass exodus of people from hills. Many of the Garhwalis who attain success or economic status, settle down in urban towns. Consequently the highland social system is crumbling. Its culture is disintegrating. Many of the new generation of Garhwali settlers have almost forgotten their language, rituals and social customs. They are scattered all over and sometimes facing the problems of finding suitable matrimonial alliances. A hill Garhwali girl married to Garhwali settler may cope up in her duties but a migrant Garhwali girl, may sometimes find it difficult to accept the rigorous life pattern of hill women.

Besides the socio-cultural malaise generated by the migration of the population, there has been an economic vacuum in Garhwal. There is a serious drain of intelligentsia from the area. Many of the Technicians or other craftsmen, who could have been of use of the local population, usually do not return to the area after retirement. The region is almost devoid of urban cosmopolitan population or a developed town. Inspite of such a large and luminous population the region could not develop a city which could be made a base for industrial, technical and educational centre. In this respect the Kumaon region has two or three better developed towns and have a slight edge over Garhwal. Even if fifty percent of the Garhwalis who have settled in UP, Punjab, Haryana, Delhi and Rajasthan would have returned and settled in one place a good township could have been built. It is true that unless basic civic amenities are not provided no one would like to settle down in a remote outgrown hill village. But unless some crusaders take initiative this vicious circle will continue. The future settlers should take example from the people of Manipur, Nagaland, Mizoram, Meghalaya, Tripura and Arunachal Pradesh where the elites after serving in all India services, return to their native towns and have tremendously helped in building modern townships in the North Eastern region. The towns of North East region during sixties were much primitive and isolated. But within a span of two decades because of local initiative and love for land the small towns like Kohima, Aizwal or Itanagar have become good developed cities providing many amenities.

Histo-Geographic Isolation

Geographical isolation[5] played a dominant role in the present day state of affairs in Pauri, Tehri, Chamoli, Uttarkashi and Pithoragarh districts of Uttarakhand. Turbulent rivers, difficult communications and dense foot hill forests made this mountainous region less accessible from the plains of Uttar Pradesh. A lock at the past history of the region will reveal that the kingdoms of Garhwal and Kumaon were torn with internal strife and factional clashes and rarely saw a stabilised powerful and peaceful era. In conditions of physical isolation and political instability the effectiveness and defacto control over the old kingdoms of Garhwal and Kumaon by their rulers is anybody's guess. The regions nearer to the capitals only derived the benefits. When Chandpur Garhi was the capital of Garhwal, people encircling the fortress were beneficiaries of the kingdom. Even when Raja Ajai Pal shifted his capital to Srinagar, the same coterie of Brahmans and Rajputs formed the administrative nucleus. The region was further plagued by a large number of battles. From the time of Ajai Pal (1500 A.D.)

to Pradyumn Shah (1804 A.D.) within a span of about three hundred years eighty five battles were fought by Garhwali kings (Dabral, 1971 : 515). Being forced to follow the whims and fancies of the warring kings of Kumaon and Garhwal, the people belonging to same origin and culture fought thirty five wars and suffered immensely. In the face of invading armies the people had to run to safe places leaving behind their rich and fertile lands. From 1790 to 1815 the land came under the Gorkhas and the people ran to jungle hideouts. According to Frazer (Dabral, 1973 : 295; Raturi, 1980 : 215) two lakhs Garhwalis were sold as slaves by the invaders at Hardwar.

The coming of the British administration in Garhwal saw its division into British and Foreign or native Garhwal. The British Garhwal was put under Kumaon commissionary. During the British period Almora and Nainital districts proposed better and became more advance than other districts. These districts were nearer to urban centres of UP. The Britishers made hill resorts in Ranikhet and Nainital, and they were developed. People came in close contact with the senior administrators and the creation of western educated local intelligentsia took place much earlier there than in Garhwal region. The elites in Kumaon got into administrative and all India services much earlier and this elite class always kept its links in developed cities of Almora or Nainital. The Garhwalis were not so lucky being away from the centre of power. This is evident from the example of their first six pioneers in the field of education.[6] None of them could be nominated to ICS or be given a sub deputy collector's post on graduation, which was quite a big land mark in those days. The story after the independence is different. The hill districts are tied with the plains of Uttar Pradesh. Part of an over populated state with more than fifty districts and a state capital situated more than five hundred kilometers away, the hill region in view of its histo-geopraphic past requires special attention. The Government is fully alive and abreast of the situation. The newly formed Hill Development Boards are doing Yeoman's service. In later stages establishment of Headquarters of similar development schemes in advance areas like Gopeshwar, Uttarkashi and Pithoragarh may help in development of these towns as well.

Benefactory Contrivances

The geographical seclusion, political instability in the past and distant located administrative centres in British days have been mainly responsible for not promoting opportunities to the upcoming generation of those days in Garhwal region. The natural impact was the absence of an intelligentsia class and a socio-economic and educational infrastructure which could foster or offer career avenues to the youth in early thirties to fifties of this century. Those who migrated outside are much better but the left behind require special attention. In view of their handicapped past conditions the provision of some incentives or benefactory contrivances[7] for the younger generations living in the far flunged interiors are mooted. The idea is not to plea allocation of reservation of seats in competitive examinations or fixing up of a quota system. Benefactory contrivances should be those socio-economic and educational plans in which young men belonging to lower economic strata from the deep interiors of hill districts could be given some safeguard or protection in face of their educationally and socio-economically advanced colleagues. A few examples will further elucidate this point. The students of Uttarakhand have the privilege of reserve seats in medical, engineering and other institutions. In allocation of these seats the students from lower economic strata and interior schools should get preference over affluent boys settled in Uttarakhand or Uttarakhand boys educated in advanced urban centres. Similar plans can be envisaged in giving contracts, labour and other petty employments.

Uttarakhand has a large potential in its mountains and high altitude vales. Occupations allied to mountaineering can be a rich source of revenue for the poor villagers living in the foot hills of the Nanda Devi, Kamet, Banderpunch and several other peaks. The example of Nepal is quite encouraging, where mountaineering after fifties became a rich source of economy and raised the living conditions of the Sherpa porters. In comparison the conditions in Uttarakhand require some benefactory contrivances as the expeditions here do not encourage the local porters. If we look at the history of mountaineering in the country and the national records, the people of Garhwal and Kumaon have done slpendidly well in the field of mountaineering including the Everest expeditions. When such excellent records exist there is no reason why the local villagers should not be given employment in planning an accent to their hill top. To skill them a cadre of local people may be trained in ice craft, skiing and high altitude living conditions so that they can serve as professional guides, helpers and load carriers to the trekking and mountaineering expeditions covering Uttarakhand region. This will significantly contribute to the regional economy.

Harnessing High Land Resources

Primarily Uttarakhand is a hilly tract. The term 'highland' under the present context has been mainly used for high altitude areas falling within the summer and winter snow lines and to some extent to medium altitude areas roughly between the elevation of 1500 meters to 2500 meters. The area below 2000 meters is over burdened. Overwhelming majority of the agro based villagers of Uttarakhand are located in this zone. Developmental schemes regarding irrigation facilities, horticulture plantations, provision of poultry and piggery farms and safeguarding FFM (fuel, fodder and manure) are already in operation at small scale or village or block levels. The schemes if extended and become successful, will definitely bring prosperity to the area. In comparison to lower areas the nature has bestowed more valuable resources to the high land areas. When the winter snow recedes thousands of medicinal, ornamental, edible and aromatic plants sprout abundantly in high land forests, vales, slopes and *bugyals*.[8] Till recent past these kaleidoscopic plants were only a galore and grandeur of nature or at best were used of local *vaidyacharyas*.[9] Of late the people and the administration have realised the value of these plants and are trying their best in promoting their use and sale. They are being extricated for pharmaceutical products on commercial basis. But before their full or optimum utilization the existence or thriving of these plants has been endangered due to pilferage, over exploitation, ruthless extrication and unregulated grazing.

Developing new strategies in harnessing the highland resources can only check pilferage, ruthless and unlawful extrication of valuable plants. The first step should be a ban on the possession and carriage of these plants. Small scale production centres at area level catering for pharmaceutical products, edible and non-edible oils, scents, insense, shampoos and soaps be opened. Processing of raw materials in finished, semi-finished or crude chemical form before taking it out of the region will be far more better. This will also open avenues for cottage industries and employment to the people. Areas under highly successful co-operatives are not free from the evils of pilferage and poaching by unlawful elements. In areas like Panwali the situation is quite alarming. Moreover once the plants have been commercialised their growth should not be left to nature only. Large scale plantation of medicinal, aromatic and indigenous plants by growing high altitude nursuries will not only save them from extinction but also grow sufficient numbers for production centres. The high altitude Plant Physiology Research Centre of Garhwal University has undertaken extensive scientific study of the high altitude plants in Tungnath region. Similar research centres can be extended to other places. The highland areas recommended for mass plantations of medicinal plants and setting up of production centres are Tarkeswar, Khirsu and Dudhatoli ranges in Pauri district, Nandakharak, Tungnath, Valley of Flowers in Chamoli district, Kushkalyan, Sahasra Tal and Panwali slopes in Tehri district, Dodital, Harsil, Neland and Bunderpunch in Uttarkashi district. The dense forests in these areas can be made wild life sanctuaries like the Nanda Devi or Kedarnath wild life sanctuary. Wild life sanctuaries will preserve near extinct wild life, encourage afforestation and help in stabilization of eco-system. Moreover it will attract visitors without disturbing the forest potentials, wild life and landscape. It also will encourage tourism and allied infrastructure. The *bugyals* in high altitude can be excellent skiing resorts during winters. If developed, the slopes of Bunderpunch, Panwali and Chandrashila can become skiing paradise. Provision of alpine huts for trekkers and ornithologists in wild life sanctuaries, high altitude vales and *bugyals* will serve as an added attraction. The medium altitude zones can be made centres of pastoral products and horticulture. The districts of Chamoli and Uttarkashi are becomed encouragingly by both pilgrims and fruits. Ironically their timing cycles are different and are unfavourable to visitors as well as local owners. A visit to Mandakini valley during summers of 1979 revealed unmeted demands from large number of pilgrims. Whereas during winters of 1981 surplus citreous fruits were seen marketless in abundance in the same area. Setting up of small scale canning, bottling and processing units at Guptakashi, Dharasu, Bhatwari and Harsil will be a boon to the local inhabitants.

Alternate to Riverine Oriented Pilgrimage

There is hardly any mountain or river in Uttarakhand which is notas sociated with celestial deities. Since ages the devotees thronged along the banks of the Ganges and its tributaries to have a glimpses of the divine abodes and in the process of invoking Gods, countless sacred complexes and temples were constructed in this region. There are more than five hundred and fifty sacred complexes and worship centres in Garhwal region.[10] These sacred complexes and temples can be classified into a three tier hierarchy. The major shrines of Badri, Kedar, Gangotri and Yamnotri were at apex and are still visited by pilgrims. The Panch Badris and the Panch Kedars were at the intermediary stage and their pilgrimage has decreased. The other temples though sacred and full of importance were subsidiaries to the four major pilgrimage routes, meandering along the Alaknanda, the Bhagirathi, the Mandakini, the Yamuna and the Ganga. The pilgrimage was a long drawn affair. A visit to any major shrine from Hardwar and back took a minimum period of one month.[11] Till late twenties of this century *yatra*[12] to four apex shrines took about three to four months. The conditions till middle of fifties were similar. Pilgrimage was an industry and a rich source of income for the people living in the valley of the Ganges and its tributaries. Not only the priests, shopkeepers and allied traders, horse and carriage keepers, guides, innkeepers and others were also getting enough clients. The sudden opening of roads within the last two decades have no doubt opened the communications in the region, but the transformation was so fast and unregulated that it had spurned the riverine tracks, mechanised the pilgrimage and thrown the old infrastructure out of gear.

The pedestrianised salvation mode has been transformed into a wheel-borne pilgrimage. With the advance of times this ritual may be ropeway or heliborne affair. Even today the metropolitan based travel agencies are more involved than the people living on the banks of the Ganges, and a part and parcel of retinue for the last few centuries. Evolution of dynamic strategies as alternative to the age old riverine oriented pilgrimage are imperative for restoration of employment opportunities, economic survival of the people and reblossoming of the deserted confluences. To attract people ten *prayags*[13] may be developed as centres of tourist attraction. Audio-visual media urging the tourists to see places and seek blessings of different gods be activated to maximum extent. Loans be given to local inhabitants to open motels and lodges, and package tours to Badri, Kedar, Gangotri and Yamnotri be so conducted that developed *prayags* are included in the itinerary. By opening floating hotels and restaurants, construction of alpine huts on river banks and confluences, promotion of aquadromes in safer zones, and organization of acquatics can only reactivate the banks of the Alaknanda and its tributaries and once again make them centres of mass attraction. And if Rajasthan can successfully sell its sanddunes and the swamps of Assam can be attractive. Uttar Pradesh tourism can never lag behind in obliging people to have aqueous entertainments with the blessings of the Mother Ganges.

Acknowledgement

I am grateful to Indian Council of Social Science Research for sponsoring the field study and the Centre for the study of Social Systems, Jawahar Lal Nehru University for affiliation of my project (Phase I) "The Brahmans and Rituals of the Sacred Complexes of Uttarakhand" during 1980.

NOTES

1. *FFM*. Fodder, Fuel and Manure. Collection of FFM is the responsibility of women folk in Uttarakhand. Availability and distance regulate the rigors of life and matrimonial prospects for future brides.

2. *Transhumance*. The term is mainly used for migration

of population from summer to winter pastures and vice versa. Here it hasb een used for similar conditions like migrating from hills to plains and back for occupational pursuits.

3. *Migrant Syndrome.* Denotes the psychological mentality of the elite class and how the migrant's claim has been a status symbol during different times.

4. *Agnatic clan titles.* The trans-Himalayan practice of deriving clan names from the place of settlement of forefathers.

5. *Histo-Geographic Isolation.* In addition to physical isolation the term has been used for political instability and constant warfare in the historical past.

6. The names of first *six graduates* from Garhwal region with date of graduation and initial professions are as follows :

(a) Sh. Keshava Nand Mamgain 1877—Retired as forest official in Tehri state.

The next five graduated in 1900 A.D.

(b) Sh. Gobind Prasad Ghildyal

(c) Sh. Hari Ram Dhasmana
Both started in education Dept. and entered civil service in later life.

(d) Sh. Chakra Dhar Juyal started as police officer and later became Dewan in Tehri

(e) Sh. Tara Datt Gairola, and

(f) Sh. Braj Mohan Chandola remained in legal profession.

7. *Benefactory Contrivances.* Planning of preferential safeguards for geographically isolated and economically backward people in terms of education and employment.

8. *Bugyals.* High altitude pastures which remain under snow during winter and blossom with grass, ornamental and medicinal plants during summer.

9. *Vaidyacharya.* Local medical practitioner who treat with indigenous herbs and plants.

10. *Sacred Complex.* The term has been used on the pattern of sacred complex in Hindu Gaya (Vidyarthi: 1978). The number of temples is from Atkinson (1973).

11. The four main pilgrimage routes started from Hardwar and their distances were in terms of days viz.

Hardwar—Gangotri	—20 days	ONE way
—Yamnotri	—17 days	
—Kedarnath	—14 days	
—Badrinath	—18 days	

(Uttarakhand Rahasya—Vaisnava, S 1926)

12. *Yatra*: Holy travel or pilgrimage.

13. *Prayag*: Confluence of two rivers and sacred place on it. There are numerous *prayags* in Garhwal. Prominent among them are :

Indra Prayag	Dev Prayag	Shiv Prayag
Rudra Prayag	Karna Prayag	Nand Prayag
Vishnu Prayag	Keshav Prayag	Son Prayag
Ganesh Prayag	Bhaskar Prayag	Hari Prayag
Gupta Prayag	Shyam Prayag	Shani Prayag

REFERENCES

Atkinson, E.T. 1973 *Himalayan Gazzetter*, Cosmo Publications, Delhi, (Reprint).

Bahuguna, S.P. 1950 *Virat Hridaya* (Hindi), Alaknanda Mandakini Prakashan, Lucknow.

Bhatt, B.K. 1961 *Kanak Vansh* (3 Volumes), Sanskrit with Hindi Commentary, Tehri.

Bhatt, C.P. 1980 *Eco-System of the Central Himalayas and Chipko Movement*, Dasholi Gram Swarajya Sangh, Gopeswar.

Barthwal, M.S. 1950 *Garhwal Main Kaun Kahan* (Hindi), Published by the author, Delhi.

Dabral, S.P. 1961 *Uttarakhand Yatra Darshan*, Vishal Karyalaya, Narayankoti, Chamoli.

Dabral, S.P. 1971 *Uttarakhand Ka Itihas*, Vol. IV, Veergatha Prakashan, Dogada.

Dabral, S.P. 1973 *Uttarakhand Ka Itihas*, Vol. V, Veergatha Prakashan, Dogada.

Dabral, S.P. 1975 *Uttarakhand Ka Itihas*, Vol. VI, Veergatha, Prakashan, Dogada.

Dabral, S.P. 1978 *Uttarakhand Ka Itihas*, Vol. VIII, Veergatha Prakashan, Dogada.

Dhasmana, H.R. 1954a *Sabhya Manav Ka Mool Sthan* (Hindi), Taran Taran Dhasmana Char Kothi, Lucknow.

Dhasmana, H.R. 1954b *Ved Mata* (Hindi), Taran Taran Dhasmana Char Kothi, Lucknow.

Dhasmana, H.R. 1954c *Rigvedic Itihas* (Hindi), Taran Taran Dhasmana Char Kothi, Lucknow.

Dhasmana, H.R. 1954d *Rigvedic Shiksha Vigyan* (Hindi), Taran Taran Dhasmana Char Kothi, Lucknow.

Dhasmana, M.M. 1979-80 The Brahmans and Rituals of Sacred Complexes of Uttarakhand —ICSSR Field Study Report (unpublished).

Dhasmana, M.M. 1981 Syncretic Polytheism in Central Himalayas—*Himalaya Man and Nature*, Vol. IV, No. 8, New Delhi.

Dhasmana, M.M. 1982a Transformations and Development in Central Himalayas—*Himalaya Man and Nature*, Vol. VI, No. 2, New Delhi.

Dhasmana, M.M. 1982b Himalayan Pilgrimage—*Journal of Social Research*, Vol. XXV, No. II, Ranchi.

Dhasmana, V.D. 1978 *Naitikata Aur Sagun Bhakti Sahitya*, (Hindi) Surya Prakashan, Delhi.

Pati Ram 1916 *Garhwal Ancient and Modern*, Army Press, Simla.

Rahul Ram 1970 *The Himalayan Border Land*, Delhi.

Sankrityayan Rahul 1918 *Himalaya Parichaya*, Vol. I, (Hindi) Lucknow.

Raturi, H.K. 1918 *Narendra Hindu Law* (Hindi), Lucknow.

Raturi, H.K. 1980 *Garhwal Ka Itihas* (Hindi), Bhagirathi Prakashan, Grih Tehri, (Reprint).

Vaishava, S. 1926 *Uttarakhand Rahasya*, Garhwali Press, Dehra Dun.

CHAPTER XIV

HINDU SECTS AND TRADITIONS OF THE CENTRAL HIMALAYAS

AN ANTHROPOLOGICAL PERSPECTIVE

MAKHAN JHA

The cultural boundary of the Central Himalayas, also known as Uttarakhand as referred to in the sacred texts of the land, more or less, coincides with the administrative boundary of the eight hill districts viz. Dehradun, Tehri Garhwal, Uttarkashi, Pauri Garhwal, Chamoli, Nainital, Almora and Pithoragarh of Uttar Pradesh. This part of the Himalayas is full of Hindu shrines belonging to various sects and traditions, which have been centres of pilgrimage since time immemorial. Here an attempt is made to throw light on some of these major Hindu shrines and sects of the Uttarakhand for understanding the integration of different Hindu sects and complexities of Hindu religion of the Himalayas, on one hand, and the nature and extent of absorption of the elements of "Great and Little Traditions", on the other.

Text al Dimensions of the Himalayan Shrines

The largest number of the sacred centres are located in the Central Himalayas. As already mentioned above the cultural boundary of the Central Himalayas coincides, more or less, with the Uttarakhand, which has been vividly mentioned in the Puranas. In various sacred texts Uttarakhand is also known as Brahmapura, Bhu-swarga, Swapna-Brahmpura etc. In the Rig Veda as well as in the Sathpatha Brahman, the word Gangotri occurs for the first time. In the Buddhist literatures specially in different Jatakas we find the word Uttarakhand as the place of pilgrimage. In the various Puranas like the Skanda Puran (specially the Shristhi Khand), the Shiva Puran etc., we get a vivid description of the Uttarakhand and its various sacred centres. In the Aswamedhaparva of the Mahabharat, Uttarakhand is described in detail when, Arjun conquered and defeated the inhabitants of the Uttarakhand viz. the Nadhot, the Prakashya, the Prashu, the Kulinda, the Partangana etc. In the works of Kalidas (4th century A.D.) we find a detailed description of the places of Uttarakhand specially in Raghubansham, Kumar Sambhavam, Meghdootam etc., which reveal as to how Himalayas attracted the attentions of writers, poets, saints and sages even during those days when there was lack of developed means of communications.

Adi Shankar (788-820 A.D.) visited the Himalayan shrines around 814 A.D. and lived there for 6 years till he died in 820 at Kedarnath. We are further told that each year during summer he used to stay for six months in the *vyasgupha* near Mana village in Badridham and six months during winter at Kartikeypur (now modern Joshimath). It was he who established the idols of Badrivishal at Badridham after taking them out from the Narad *kund.*

Through historical documents we have come to know that during ancient period of Indian history there were many ancient kingdoms viz. Rinida, Yodhem etc., whose cultural patronages are still there. Shiva Prasad Dabral, a local historian, has deciphered and described the various coins, written in the Kharosthi and Brahmi scripts of these Himalayan kingdoms of ancient India. Again, during the mediaeval period there were many kingdoms, among them special mention may be made of Kulindanagar, Kartikeypur, Chandragarhi, Devalgarh, Champabat etc.

During our last visit to Badrinath in May 1980 we were shown two pieces of *shilalekh* (stone-engraving) by the Magistrate-In-Charge of the Badrinath Trust, which were of 9th century A.D., and belonged to the Sena dynasty of Bengal who had donated land and villages for the maintenance of Lord Badrinath.

Some of these textual and historical evidences, mentioned above, reveal that these Himalayan shrines and other centres of interests have a great historical depth, which have not been studied in detail from the anthropological point of view as yet. Some of these Himalayan shrines, as referred to in the texts, are now examined here from the contextual and sectarian points of view to understand the complexities of Hindu religion in particular, and the integration of diverse cultural traditions into a common bond of Indian civilization, in general.

Hindu Shrines of the Central Himalayas

E.T. Atkinson made a preliminary survey of the Himalayan shrines about one hundred years ago, when he was the Commissioner of Kumaon in 1882-84. He has noted that there were 350 temples of ancient antiquity in Kumaon and 550 temples in the Garhwal area, besides more than a hundred temples in Dehradun and Jaunsar Bawar area. Thus, in the Uttarakhand there are more than one thousand temples of ancient antiquity belonging to various sects viz. Shaiva, Vaishnava, Shakti, etc. Besides these major dominating sects there are also some shrines dedicated to Surya, Ganesh and other minor deities.

However, the importance of the Central Himalayas, what our Purans call to the Uttarakhand, in the history of religion in India is mainly due to the existence therein of the great shrines of Badrinath and Kedarnath, containing the forms of Vishnu and Shiva, which still hold a foremost position in the beliefs of the people of the Hindu universe. To them the Uttarakhand is the home of the great gods or the gate way to final liberation of soul i.e. *moksha.* This is a living belief and, therefore, thousands of pilgrims have been visiting these shrines even when there was lack of communications.

The chief priest, both at Kedar and Badri, who comes from the Nambudri Brahmin of Kerala, is called *rawal.* A host of other priests and *pandits*, who have developed *jajmanika* relationship with the people of India, reside at Devaprayag. Again, the Madhameshwar temple is served by the Jangams from Chitrakali in Mysore. The Rudranath and Kapileshwar temples are served by the Dasnamis Gossains and the Tunganath by the Khasiya Brahmins. All these groups come from south viz. the Nambudris from Malawar, the Jangams are pure Lingayats and the Dasnamis were founded the Adi Shankar.

Again, we are further told that at Badrinath about two hundred years ago Dandi Paramhansas from south were conducting the main *puja* but later on they handed over the charge to the Dakshni Brahmins from Malawar, who are presently conducting the *puja* at Badrinath. However, at Badrinath the Brahmins from Devaprayag officiate at the Tapta-kund; Kotyal and Hatwal Brahmins at Brahma-kapal; Dimri Brahmins at the temple of Lakshmi; and the Mailiya Brahmins of Tangami at a few Shiva shrines. The attendant priests at the Yog-Badri are the Bhatts from south; at the Gyan-Badri are the Dimris and at the Bridh-Badri and Adi-Badri are the Brahmins from the south. As a rule, the Bairagis serve the other Vaishnava shrines in the Garhwal and Kumaon areas.

From the above descriptions it appears that in most of the shrines of the Central Himalayas, the chief priests and some of their associates come from different parts of south India. Thus, the sacred centres, location in the deep Himalayas even at Kathmandu in Nepal, are served by the priests of deep south and between them live their *jajmans*. It, therefore, establishes a cultural continuity, and the elements of 'great tradition' are transmitted to the masses through their net-works. Here it may also be pointed out that the ecological obstacles and the language barriers do not come in the way of cultural communications from one corner of the country to another. Such a fascinating study of the Himalayan shrines has not been attempted to in detail and, therefore, it required to be done on an urgent basis.

In addition to the panch-kedar and the panch-badri, about which mentions have already been made earlier, there are panch-prayags viz. Devaprayag, Rudraprayag, Karnaprayag, Nandaprayag and Vishnuprayag, besides a large number of shrines belonging to the Shakti cult. Except the Rudraprayag, where the myths and shrines are mostly associated with Shiva, all the different shrines at different *prayags*, which fall on the route of Badrinath, are associated with the Vaishnava cult.

So far as the shrines of the Shakti cult are concerned, there are many shrines in the Central Himalayas dedicated to the various forms of Uma, Parvati, Nanda, Ambika, Gauri, Durga, Kali, Mahishamardini, Tripur-sundri, Chamunda, Chandika, Matris, Haimavati etc. Thus, there are different forms of Shakti, which are worshipped in the Central Himalayas. These deities have different shrines located in various parts of the Himalayas. For instance goddess Nanda who is most popular as the Rudra form of Shakti in the Kumaon Himalaya, is worthly represented by the lofty peak of Nanda Devi, the daughter of Himachal and many temples are dedicated to her exclusive worship. There are well known temples of this goddess at Semli Ming and Talli Dhura in the Pindar *pattis* at Nauti in Taili Chandpur and at Gair in Lobha. The worshippers at all of them unite to celebrate the marriage of Shiva and Parvati on the *nandashtmi*. A procession is formed at Nauti, which, accompanied by the goddess in her palanquin (*doli*), proceeds to the Baiduni-kund at the foot of the Trishuli peak, where she is worshipped with great reverence and rejoicing. A great festival also takes place every twelfth year when, accompanied by her attendant Latu, who also has a temple at Nauli in Dasauli, the goddess is carried into the snow as fat as the people can go beyond the Baiduni-kund and worship there in the form of two great stones slittering with mica and strongly refleeting the rays of the sun. The local legend says that on these great occasions, a four-horned goat is invariably born in Chandur and dedicated to the goddess, accompanies the pilgrims. When unloosed on the mountain, the sacred goat suddenly disappears and as suddenly returns without its head and, thus, furnishes consecrated food for the party.

There are also some temples to Nanda at Almora, at Ranchula in Katyur and at Bhagar in Malla Danpur in Kumaon. Another popular name for Nanda, amongst the lower classes, is *upharni* (or *u-parni*), under which name she is represented at Nauti and elsewhere where no temples are erected to her beyond a heap of stone on a peak. At Nauti she has a regular establishment of priests, called from the place, Nautyal and who were, in former times, the favourite *purohits* of some of the petty Rajas of Garhwal. There is a local *Upapuran* devoted to the worship of Nanda and a description of the places sacred to her in the Central Himalayas.

Similarly there are many temples in the Central Himalayas dedicated to Ambika, Gauri, Durga, Mahishamardini, Raktavirja, Tripur-sundri, Kali, Chamunda, Chandika, Sitla and others. For instance, while Tripur-sundri has temples at Almora and Bininag in Patti Barun as well as at Joshimath, there are numerous temples of Kali at Bhadoi, Naini, Kota, Gangoli, Askot etc. Again, Chandika or Chandi has nine temples in Garhwal and two in Kumaon, specially at Kamaltiya in Gangoli and Jageswar. Sitla, the goddess of small-pox has temples at Almora, Srinagar, Jageswar, Nati in Bel, Dola in Mahar as well as at Dwara and Ajpur in Dehradun. In this way we find that the shrines of the deities of Shakti cult are found in large number, which are located in different parts of the Central Himalayas.

A few shrines dedicated to purely local deities viz. Gurail, Bhutni, Ghantakarn, Ghatotkacha etc., are also found, which have been patronised by the local people without any descrimination from the great traditional or the textual deities, as referred to above. Thus, we find that in the Central Himalayas the deities of the *shastrik* and the *laukik* traditions are patronised. It further reveals that the places of Himalayas have been the centres of religious interactions between various sects and traditions, which needs to be studied intensively for understanding the configuration of different sects and traditions in the Central Himalayas. However, on the basis of our preliminary study I propose below a broad typology of the sacred centres, dedicated to various sects of the Central Himalayas, which may be helpful for further deep anthropological analysis.

A Broad Typology of the Sacred Centres of Central Himalayas

Firstly, there may be various important sacred centres of the *shastrik* (textual) importance which may be classified under *panch-asthali* viz. there are five *prayags*: Deva-prayag, Rudra-prayag, Karna-prayag, Nanda-prayag and Vishnu-prayag; *panch-badri* viz. Vishal-Badri, Yog-Badri, Bhavishya-Badri, Bridh-Badri and the Adi-Badri; and *panch-kedar* viz.

Kedarnath, Pashupatinath (not of Kathmandu), Rudranath, Madhameshwarnath and Kapleshwarnath.

Secondly, some of the river shrines of the Central Himalayas such as Gangotri, Jamnotri, Saraswati, Malini, Mandakini, Alaknanda etc., may be classified together.

Thirdly, some of the local and village deities, besides the major Hindu deities of dominant Hindu sects, as referred to above, of the inhabitants of the Himalayas such as Ghantakarn, Ghatotkach, Bhairab of different types and importance, Ganganath (of the Doms), Masan or Khabish, Goril, Kshetrapal or Bhuinya, Airi, Kalbistha, Chaumu, Badan, etc., may be classified together to understand them in terms of local cultural traditions. At certain places some *shanskritic* deities have been transformed and assimilated into the local fold of deities and this transformation may be examined under ecological basis of religious transformation. Thus, the Hindu sects and traditions of the Central Himalayas, which have flourished under different ecological set up since time immemorial, are based on the *shastrik* and the *laukik* traditions as prevalent in the plain land. However, their transformations have taken place due to their location at the varying altitudes of the Himalayas, which have not been studied in detail by the anthropologists. Therefore, with a view to examine the different dimensions of Indian civilization (Jha : 1979), the "net works and centres" (Cohn & Marriott: 1958) of the Himalayan shrines should be studied on priority basis so that the "cultural types" (Vidyarthi & Jha: 1982) and the "level of socio-cultural integration" (Ibid) may also be revealed.

RFFERENCES

Atkinson, E.T. 1976: *Religion in the Himalayas*; Cosmo Publication, New Delhi.

Berreman, G.D. 1978 Ecology, Demography, and Domestic Strategies in the Western Himalayas: a case study; *Journal of Anthropological Research*, Vol. 34.

Bernard, S. Cohn, & Mc Kim Marriott 1958 Networks and Centres in the Integration of Indian Civilization; *Journal of Social Research* Vol. 1, No. 1.

Jha, Makhan 1979 Studies on Sacred Complex: A Methodological Approach to Study Indian Civilization; *in Anthropology in Bihar*; edited by L.P. Vidyarthi & M. Jha, Classical Publishers, New Delhi.

— 1979 *Dimensions of Indian Civilizations*; Classical Publishers, New Delhi.

Vidyarthi, L.P. & M. Jha (Ed.) 1982 *Transactions of the Centre of Himalayan Studies*; Council of Social and Cultural Research, Bihar and the U.G.C. Department of Special Assistance, Ranchi University, Ranchi.

CHAPTER XV

BADRINATH: A STUDY IN SITE CHARACTER, PILGRIM PATTERNS AND PROCESS OF MODERNISATION

JAGDISH KAUR

Badrinath is Hindu's super-pilgrimage resort (*dhama*), located in the higher Himalayan region of Chamoli (Garhwal-Himalaya). Amongst the four most sacred pilgrim destinations of the Hindus, Badrinath singly represents the Himalayan majesty; the rest three (Dwarka, Jagannath Puri and Rameshwaram) look towards the Arabian sea, the Indian Ocean and the Bay of Bengal, respectively. Spectacular land-scape, superb ecological features, sanctity and religiosity must have been some of the site attribute in the establishment of this highly revered and most ancient of the *dhamas*[1] that now attracts about two hundred thousand pilgrims/tourists every year from far off Indian States and territories, despite strenuous hill journey of 301 km from Rishikesh rail head. The challenge of the pilgrimage (*yatra*) was far more formidable when rail road network left Himalaya inaccessible.

Badrinathpuri is a small township with ribbon settlement along the bank of the turbulent Alaknanda that flows southwards, embracing the Rishiganga to the south of the township. It runs longitudinally into a spacious valley (4.5 km long and 1.5 km wide), opening up northwards to the Bhotia village of Mana—the last human settlement of this region. In elevation, it is 3122 m (10244′) above the mean sea level.

Badrinath landscape is undulating, with encircling high black mountains superposed by snow-clad ranges and lofty peaks. The mount Narain in the west, slopes down abruptly eastwards into the Alaknanda whereas the Mount Nar, eastwards, leaves adequate space for human settlement. The two mountain ranges embody in them Hindu mythological belief and breathe Puranic faith.[2] The Nilkant peak mysteriously lonely, peeps out majestically from the west; where the Rishiganga has her source. The Badrinath surroundings with adjoining meadow, and the Vasudhara fall are no less enchanting. In fact the Badrinath township should not be studied in isolation. It is a religious belt[3] spreading from Kanav Ashram[4] to Satopanth—23 km north of present Badrinath which is considered highly sacrosanct for religious persuits where sages and saints devoted major part of their lives. This religious belt has often been alluded as Badrivan or *badri-ka-mandal* in puranic literature. According to Singh, 'Hindu missionaries had a purposeful design in assigning pilgrims itinerary along the sacred Alaknanda in the Badrinath circuit, having the sublimest mountain scenery and the noblest river aspects, particularly river junctions (*prayags*), the five (*panch*) *badrees* and the five *kedaras*' (1975: 15). A sacred journey to Badrinath is invariably linked up with Kedarnath and its adjuncts. Considering outstanding religious cum scenic resources of this belt, the Hindu expertise seems at its best in *tirtha* planning and in placing pilgrim centres, in heirarchical order, climaxing in Badrinath. At present road system has altered the prescribed pilgrim scheme and has interfered with traditional itinerary. None was indeed, allowed to visit Badrinath at the first instance. This is not so now.

The Himalayan pilgrimages in Garhwal were ordained to be performed from west to east[5], viz., Yamnotri, Kedarnath and Badrinath, after completing visits to their satellites on a definite time scale. All these pilgrim centres had unusual physical background though difficult to access which perhaps lent them more enchantment. Puranic references support the fact that selection of *badri-ka-ashram* was no accident. The hectic efforts of Dharm's[6] progeny for the choice of an ideal religious space, led to the establishment of the five *badrees* in the *gandhmadan* region,[7] Raj Badree (present Badrinath) having the crowning glory.

Badrinath acquired fame during Mahabharata time for its environmental values, and for being the 'hermitage of the perfect'. Sages and saints, priests and *pundits*, scholars and savants, all flocked to the Hindu Elysium; braving the hazards of the journey (Kaur, 1982: 117). Popular belief, anecdotal myths and some oral history make believe that Puranas were composed in this *Gandhmandan*[8] environment. There are references to the effect that many founders of the Hindu schools of philosophy received inspiration in this divine wilderness.

Lord Narain, over time, acquired big following in the work-a-day people of mundane existence, who found necessary to move to this beautiful Himalayas, both for religious merit and for change from humdrum life and living. Religious benediction bestowed upon the laity, led a movement of pilgrimage—a *yatra* tradition. This movement of people of the Garhwal Himalaya suffered a severe setback when Buddhism had its sway in this region and a queer mix of cults—Tantricism, Shaktism, Saivaism and animism began to be practised. This was a period of decadence when the iconoclastic activity reached its acme. The image of Lord Vishnu was thrown into the Alaknanda and the temple was demolished.[9]

It was around the eighth century that a young Brahmin philosopher, Shankaracharya, who installed the image in the Garur Gufa (near Tapt Kund), having found it in Naradkund. Later, tradition has it, it was removed to the present site by the ruler of Garhwal. The gold canopy of the temple is said to be the gift of queen Ahilyabai. This marks the period of renaissance in Badrinath pilgrimage, when the temple was dedicated to Vishnu, Shiva, Surya, Shakti and Ganesh to integrate Hinduism and to restrict worship of unauthorised gods, a practice which had come into vogue.

The temple is situated on the right bank of the Alaknanda, standing over 15m high from the base, built in the form of a cone with small cupola on the top of which is a gilt ball and spine. The main body is made of flat blocks of stone and plastered with cement that belies its antiquity.

Architecturally, the temple has taken after the early *nagar* style[10] with a definite hill stamps. Divided into three parts (a) *garbhgrah* (the sanctum sanctorum), (b) *darshan mandap* (rectangular shaped where *puja* is performed) and (c) *sabha mandap* (outer hall where devotees stand for *darshan*), it has square plan with number of graduated projections in the middle of each side that lend it a cruciform shape. Much of its form has suffered from a change on renovator's hand as it often fell to the invasion of avalanches and men. The colourful entrance gate has put on a Turkish cap, camouflaging the traditional exterior.[11]

The temple stands high on "Puri's" dense religious core with little space around for extension or development. The shrine with its attendant services occupies an area of 0.39 acres which being the 1.18 per cent of the developed area—the planners' predicament.

Religious Cum Recreation Resources

Essentially a religious destination, Badrinath attracts both religious and secular visitors, the latter are steadily on the increase. With the process of modernisation and better facilities in transport and accommodation, Badrinath, with its multiple outdoor recreation resource endowment, promises an upcoming tourist destination. In fact, the Badrinath *yatra* has been responsible in opening up this area for tourism. The Badrinath recreational cum religious resource may well be studied in two parts, the one which exists within the township and immediate surroundings and the other that may be developed on a tourist complex planning base on a time scale. It is pertinent to discuss the first one here for inclusion in tourist itinerary.

In the vicinity of the temple are hot and cold cistern (*kunds*), *ghats*, engraved boulders and geologic forms. Of these, *Taptkund*,[12] a hot spring having a temperature of 130°F, and closely *Suryakund* are user-based resources, associated with *panch-tirth* sacrament.[13]

Five giant formations known as the Panch-Shilas[14] are linked up with religious myth and puranic legends. There are huge sized boulders that are worshipped and enjoyed as 'sites' by the visitors.

The Ganga Ghat where Mahatma Gandhi's ashes were

consigned to the holy waters of the Alaknanda, is another point of visitors' attraction. This is located midway between Brahma Kapal and Taptkund.

Away from the temple (1.6 km) is Shesh Netra, a boulder having engraving of a legendary snake's eyes is a geological fossil phenomenon.

The Nilkantha is a pyramidal snowy peak (21,650′) which towers above Badrinath and presents a most enchanting sight, best enjoyed from the left bank of the Alaknanda.

The Charan Paduka is a beautiful meadow, about three km. west of Badrinath, towards the foothills of Nilkantha peak. In this emerald green environment are found the foot-prints of the Lord. As July approaches, this beautiful meadow is carpeted with flowers.

The Mana valley has many potential touristic attractions, viz., the Vyas Gupha—a rock-cave where sage Vyas is said to have complied Puranas; the Keshav Prayaga the confluence of the Alaknanda and the Saraswati and the natural bridge, Bhimpul. The Mana valley with the Bhotia settlement and with their unique lifestyle is itself a source of attractions.[16]

The Vasudhara is an enchanting site of a water fall at an elevation of 3658 m from where the water jumps from a height of 111 m in a trans-inducing manner. It is situated about 5 km from Mana.

The Alkapuri which is about 8 km further north of the Vasudhara is the source of the Alaknanda, from where the river gushes out from the glacier snout of the Bhagirath-Kharak and the Satopantha, much like the Gaumukha, the source of the Bhagirathi. The Satopanth lake, with its serene water, is a potential tourism resource for trekkers and trailors. Poet Kalidas presumably alludes to this point in his famous play Meghdoot.

Pilgrim Traffic and Patterns

The Badrinath pilgrimage lasts for six months, mostly in summers and rains (May-November). May-June being the drier months the majority (35.0 per cent) takes to pilgrimage during this period to safeguard against inclemency of weather and road breaches. On an average, over 1000 pilgrims visit Badrinath per day. However, peak is touched in June when 2000 to 3000 visitors may come in a single day. August, normally, has a low profile when rains threaten landslides and slope failures are not uncommon on the mountain roads. September picks up again when weather is fairer, sky is clearer, hills are greener and journey is more rewarding. The traffic flows during November begin to fade out with the onset of snows. Finally, doors of Badrinath are closed and the chief priest moves to Joshimath—the winter seat of Badri Narain.

Badrinath attracts pilgrims/visitors from all over the country and a few tourists from overseas. Results of 1803 interviews, conducted by the Institute of Himalayan Studies and Regional Development, Srinagar, show that the largest number of visitors originated from West Bengal (560), Uttar Pradesh (310) and Gujarat (220), followed by Andhra Pradesh (120) and Rajasthan (117). Only a few came from Kashmir (2), Assam (2) and Meghalaya (2). Of the 108 foreigners interviewed at the Tourist Rest House, Srinagar, the largest number was of the Australians (28), followed by the Japanese (13), Britishers (13), West Germans (7), Americans (6), French (6), Dutch (4) and the Belgians (2). However, the Nepalese were 29. A few of these foreign visitors entered have the purpose of their visit as 'pilgrimage' and styled themselves as *yatrees.* Many were expenditionists, or field scientists.

Another study, conducted by the U.P. Town Country Planning Unit of Srinagar[16] in 1979 revealed that 11.3 per cent of Badrinath's total visitors originated from Garhwal region, 17.5 per cent came from Uttar Pradesh (outside Garhwal) and 71.2 per cent came from other states (outside Uttar Pradesh). Majority of them (74.0 per cent) belonged to 30-60 age group. About 78.0 per cent of the total visitors in 1979 had motivation for Badrinath as destination, whereas 22.0 per cent of them had Kedarnath, Gangotri, Yamonotri, the Valley of Flowers and Hemkund as their destinations.

Surveys conducted by the Town Planning Unit of Srinagar reveal that the visitors' income group varies considerably though a good number of them falls into lower and lower-middle class. (15.5 per cent belonged to the income group of Rs. 801 to 1000). 4.1 per cent of the visitors belong to students' category.

While the Himalayan pilgrimages have gateways in Kotdwar and Rishikesh, almost 91.0 per cent visitors prefer entry from Rishikesh, both for transit facilities and en-route attractions, particularly for Devprayag. The 310 km long journey is completed in one halt at Joshimath on the onward and Srinagar on the backward journey. Both the stopovers have developed adequate accommodation facility. Average two-day stay at Badrinath has been registered. However, Badrinath Master Plan Report reveals that of the total visitors to Badrinath, 18.5 per cent stayed at Badrinath only for one day, 58.5 per cent stayed for two days; 19.9 per cent for 3 days and 3.1 per cent stayed for 4 days (1979 : 21). It may be observed that length of stay is directly proportional to recreation, resource attraction, facilities, hospitality and travel costs. Badrinath being mainly a religious destination, would take sometime to cater to the tourist needs, though the trends have set in.

Visitors' influx to Badrinath shot up after 1968 when metalled road reached Badrinath for the first time.

Table 1
Badrinath Visitors 1976-1979

Year	*Visitors*	*Percentage growth*
1976	174,000	—
1977	196,000	+12.6
1978	144,000	−26.5
1979	180,000	+25.2

Source : Badrinath Temple Committee

The Badrinath road provides fresh opportunities for opening up new areas for tourism promotion. The Valley of Flowers, accessible enroute, has caught up the market and developed an independent destination in its own right. Many other micro regions are receiving the attention of the developers, particularly The Garhwal Regional Development Corporation and the U.P. Tourism. The problem of right kind of facilities is the foremost.

The Hosting Town

Badrinath faces many constrains in meeting market demands. The major problem is geographical in nature. A town goes lives only for six months, May to November, and the rest is the sway of snows. This hard seasonality of character is further accentuated by limited land-use adequacy. Man power resource is another limiting factor for taking up any enterprise which may confer benefits locally or regionally. A hosting town shall reveal enormity of the situation.

Badrinath has a resident population of 1398 people, dwelling in three Mohallas of Badrinathpuri (883), Bamni village (223) and Nar Parbat (292) constituting 278 families.[17] Badrinathpuri being the oldest settlement forms the core where the shrine has cluster of *panda* population and services. Here, practically every inch of ground has been used for religious purpose. Of the 225 houses, about 140 are in this Mohalla. As a whole, township has only 140 shops.[18] Of them, 33.3 per cent shops are devoted to hoteliering, eating and sweets stores, and 31.0 per cent sell cloth, medicine or religious souvenirs.

In terms of civic services, such as water supply, electricity, hospital and toilets, Bamni is poorly served. Leaving Bamni, tap water and electricity is supplied to the rest of the town. Bamni receives 100.0 per cent water supply from the river Rishiganga. The following table provides classified information on water supply :

Table 2

Water Supply in Badrinath (1979)

Moh/Village	*Total Families*	*Percentage*		
		River	*Private*	*Public*
Badrinathpuri	185	29.7	2.2	68.1
Bamni village	46	100.0	—	—
Nar Parbat	47	4.2	20.8	75.0
Total	278	18.6	23.2	58.2

Source : Badrinath Master Plan (1979) p. 11.

Struck by avalanches, Bamni has been deprived of electric lights; Puri and Nar have 46.6 per cent and 25.5 per cent electric supply respectively. Street lights are available to 49.7 per cent of the Puri families. Considered as a whole 35.0 per cent families have street lights.

Badrinath has only two public toilets; one near the bus stand and the other in Puri. Use of septic tanks has been introduced and the Jal Sansthan has started laying sewerage lines in the town.

Badrinath has only two public hospitals—one allopathic and the other ayurvedic. Together they can attend 60 patients, per day. The town has one Post Office, one Telephone Exchange, one Police Station and one Information Centre.

These facilities however modest, look pretty impressive for a semi mobile township of 278 families that stay hardly for seven months. But considering the vast floating population of about two hundred thousand pilgrims/tourists and their heterogenous needs, these services are all too meager, besides being wanting in grade. The town fails short miserably in accommodation, the foremost destination facility.

Accommodation Facility

Badrinath accommodated 53,290 visitors in its 36 accommodational units[19] having 525 rooms during 1979 (upto August). A large number of these units came up after 1960 when road to Badrinath began to be constructed.[20] The Parmarth Niketan has the largest capacity (40 rooms) providing 7.6 per cent of total accommodation, followed by the Bhajan Ashram (35), the Manav Kalyan (25), Sant Nivas (23), Ashtakshri (23), Devlok Tourist Rest House (22), Jalan Tourist (22) and Shankracharya (20). Many of them do not have basic facilities such as bath, toilet, kitchen and electric light.[21] Nevertheless a few of them have standard facilities and obviously they are quite expensive.[22] On the contrary there are many expensive stay places with the *pandas* who look after their clients on a traditional style,[23] and charge exorbitantly though at the 'sweet pleasures' of their clients.

Since many stay places are without bath, toilets and other basic facilities, and that Badrinath township has only two public toilets, the environment suffers the worst from litter and wastes, responsible for health hazards and infection that inflict the visiting community who helplessly carry it to other places.

Most agonising feature of the Badrinath pilgrimage is the difficulty in getting a chance to have a look or *darshan* at the deity. The premises of the temple is too small to accommodate even 200 pilgrims at a time. Pilgrims wait in endless queue from the small hours of the morning till afternoon.[24] In fact, the township faces serious challenges for the development of an adequate pilgrim-cum-tourist service system, particularly the constraint of limited landuse at the Narain, close to the temple, to which are tied up superstition and attachment of the local people. Across the Alaknanda beneath the mount Nar, there is adequate space for the organisation providing an opportunity that the town plans have seized upon. It needs some discussion here as the new structures are coming up, giving a modernised look to a far Himalayan shrine resorts, deep in tradition and religious history of the country.

The Master Plan

Physical land surveys completed by the Town Planners reveal that the township between the Nar and the Narain has only 125.90 acres of land available of which about 92.82 acres are 'undeveloped' and 33.08 acres suitable for development. The latter should include residents 'zone, visitors' housing, commercial and official zones, transport and community services, besides the religious zone of the temple. The following table provides details of the land use:

Table 3

Badrinath Master Plan Land-Use 1979

Undeveloped land use	*Area*	*Percentage*	*Developed land use*	*Area*	*Percentage*
Agriculture	34.14	36.8	Resident's Housing	9.02	27.3
Open Space	32.40	34.9	Visitor's Housing	6.60	19.9

Undeveloped land use	*Area*	*Percentage*	*Developed land use*	*Area*	*Percentage*
Low Land	07.18	7.7	Commercial	2.12	6.4
			Govt. offices	3.12	9.4
River Sides	19.10	20.6	D.G.B.R. area	2.52	7.6
			Community services	0.75	2.3
			Transport zone	8.56	25.9
			The Temple	0.39	1.2
	92.82 (73.72) per cent	100.00		33.08 (26.28) per cent	100.00

Source : Badrinath Master Plan 1979, p. 25.

While pilgrim zone has been created mainly to the right bank of the Alaknanda, the new township with pronounced Tourist Zone is emerging on the eastern side beneath the mount of Nar. A separate commercial zone has been created here. Proposed area along the Nar has been divided into three sectors:

(i) *Northern Sector* : It extends from northern boundary to Hotel Devlok, purporting to be a Regional Commercial Centre.

(ii) *Middle Sector* : It is to serve as CBD, rendering town and regional services. This extends from Hotel Devlok to the Hospital.

(iii) *Southern Sector* : Having a regional outlook it will have bus stand, petrol station and the like.

The best land has been reserved to the south of Joshimath Mana road for tourist accommodation and services. This would also be close to the transport zone. Optimal connectivity with tourist service zone and community service centres has been planned. The Master plan envisages development of all important activities on a horizontal axis, keeping off the Bus Stand to the southern outskirts to screen of noise and congestion.

The Joshimath-Mana highway (66′ wide) will pass through the middle of the new town with links to various zones. The only other motor road will link the PWD rest house to the Manav Kalyan Ashram. There would be recreation parks, social/cultural centres and Green Belts on the skirts.

Much of the town has come up after the Plan and it gives an impressive look seeing a space organised to meet the needs of a modernised society. The town planners can layout the street patterns and delimit the zones, they cannot ensure continuum of culture or preservation of the heritage nor can they dictate terms to the architects who give form and shape to the buildings. Incidentally the structures that are coming up are in some cases refuse to harmonise with the mountain milieu. This should be the role of the Departments of Environment, Culture and Tourism to see that the town does not shed its 'genius' and 'character' altogether. Conscious efforts in this direction have to be commissioned so that Badrinath keeps up its personality of a *dhama*, a super pilgrimage resort on the Himalayas. Modernisation of facilities is very much desired and should be welcomed, too, but the abruptness with which it is altering the age-old tradition raises eye-brows.

NOTES

1. Of the four *dhamas,* Badrinath is supposed to be established earlier than Dwarka and Rameshwaram (Vishnu Puranas, 5.24.6).

2. Indian scriptures, particularly the Mahabharat and the Vishnu Purana have the parables that how Arjuna and Lord Krishna, in the disguise of a recluse—Nar and Narain, performed, penances over these ranges, given the name of the Gandhmadan.

3. This region has been given the name Vaishnav-Ka-Kshetra, which according to Atkinson comprised a dozen micro-regions (*kshetras*) of which Badri-Kshetra was supposed to be most holy (Atkinson, 1973: III: 24)

4. There is a controversy about the location of 'Kanav Ashram'. Govind Prasad Nautiyal and others locate it near

Nandprayaga while others place it near Kotdwara where the rivulet Malini flows by: the latter has also been recognised by the Department of Tourism, U.P., and a forest has been reserved as sanctuary.

5. Hindu *tirtha* itinerary followed a circulatory mechanism in clockwise order (Bharadwaj, 1973: 43).

6. According to Vishnu Purana, Dharma had two sons, Nar and Narain who were divinely inspired to set up *ashramas* in the Gandhmadan where ultimately they chose their abode. Since they desired to spread their religious activities on a larger scale they needed spacious valley in this part of the higher Himalayas. In their search for an ideal, they set up *ashramas* at different places of natural beauty, viz., Vridh Badree, Yog Badree, Dhyan Badree and Bhavish Badree. Conclusively, they found the present Badrinath more suitable for having hot and cold springs besides the Alaknanda waters. In time, their devotees gave form to the settlement.

7. Yet another tradition has it that Lord Vishnu along-with espouse Laxmi left Thuling as the place got corrupted by meat eating monks and licentious priests. He set up his *ashrama* 4 km south of the village Mana, beside the Alaknanda. Laxmi, finding her husband exposed to clemency of weather assumed the form of Badree tree (Jujubi) protecting him with her foliage. Having been pleased with her devotion, Lord Vishnu named the place Badri-Ka-Ashram. Atkinson holds that these used to be jujubi forests (*badree van*) here, but they are not to be found now. (Atkinson, 1973: III:23)

8. Expert opinions find the Gandhmadan area in the higher Chamoli close to Badrinath environs. Atkinson associates Badrinath group of peaks with the Gandhmadan (op. cit.: 283). Ali does not seem to be sure of the exact location but finds support in Vayupurana and Matsyapurana where Gandhmadan is placed on the west and south of Mount Meru respectively (1966: 58). However, Bharadwaj puts it in proximity to Badrinath (1973: 72).

9. The temple structure must have also suffered the ravages of avalanches and earthquakes which are not uncommon in this area.

10. Nagar style of temple architecture exhibits distinct

varieties and ramification in different localities and geographical regions, conditioned by different lines of evolution and elaboration that each locality/region chose for itself. The cruciform plan and crucilinear tower are common to every medieval temple.

11. Recently business magnet Birla's efforts for temple renovation invited severe comments, and had to be stopped.

12. Dr. Heim discovered it to be a ferruginous calcareous water containing very little sulphur and having a temperature of 130°F the volume of the flow is about one gallon per second.

13. *Panch tirth* include (i) Tapt Kund (Bahri Tirth); (ii) Prahlad Kund (Lukewarm Dhara near Tapt Kund), (iii) Narad Kund (a recess in the bed of the Alaknanda forming a pool, close to Tapt Kund), (iv) Kurma Dhara (a cold water stream associated with tortoise legend) and (v) The Rishiganga, cascading down the Nilkantha and meeting the Alaknanda at Badrinathpuri.

14. *Panch-Shilas* in Badrinath are (i) Narad Shila (after the sage Narad), (ii) Varha Shila is a huge boulder amidst the Alaknanda waters that commemorates the return of Varha to Badrinath after killing Hiranyakshipa, (iii) Garur Shila—in a rock dedicated to bird-god (Garur who became the vehicle of Narain), (iv) Markandeya Shila—is after the sage Markandeya who is said to have performed austerities here, (v) Narasimha Shila—after the Lord Narasimha who resorted to Badriban after slaying Hiranyakshipa.

15. Recently it has again been declared as restricted area being the border area. Mana, the last village of the region, has road and is very rich in Bhotia culture.

16. The author also participated in this Survey team.

17. 273 households are of Garhwalis, 4 of Uttar Pradesh and one outside U.P. 86.6 per cent of the population are engaged in tartiary sector, of them 40 per cent are engaged in *panda* services.

18. Imagine these handful of shops serving over 20,000 people. During peaks, essential service centres face crisis.

19. 12 *dharamshalas* are owned by the temple committee, 2 by Garhwal Mandal Development Corporation and 17 are owned by Tourist or private agencies.

20. 5 *dharamshalas* were constructed up to 1947, 7 from 1948 to 1960, and 17 from 1961 to 1970 and 7 from 1971 to 1978.

21. Kali Kamli, Sant Niwas, Nepali Jaipuriya, Bhurimai.

22. One has to pay Rs. 120 per day per room in Alwasia Dharamshala.

23. On the face, the *pandas* do not charge for their all-inclusive services, except, the tip or *dan* that his 'Jigman' or client would like to offer in the name of Vishnu. A *panda* problem is found universally on all Hindu places of pilgrimage, only with a difference of degree.

24. *Darshan* is facilitated on a promise of offering "Chhota Darshan" or "Bara Darshan".

REFERENCES

Ali, M. 1966 *The Geography of the Puranas*, Peoples Publishing House, New Delhi.

Atkinson, E.T. 1973 *The Himalayan Gazetteer*, Vols. I, II, III, Cosmo Publication, Delhi.

Bharadwaj, S.M. 1973 *Hindu Places of Pilgrimage in India: A Study in Cultural Geography*, University of California Press, Berkley.

Govt. of Uttar Pradesh 1979 Badrinath Master Plan

Kaur, Jagadish 1982 "Pilgrims" Progress to Himalayan Shrines: Studying the Religious phenomenon". In Singh T.V., Kaur, J. and Singh, D.P. (eds.) *Studies in Tourism, Wildlife Parks and Conservation*, Metropolitan; Delhi.

Singh, Tejvir 1975 Badrinath: A study in Himalayan Pilgrimages in *Tourism and Tourist Industry in U.P. (India)*, New Heights.

CHAPTER XVI

THE CHIPKO

A PEOPLE'S MOVEMENT

SUNDERLAL BAHUGUNA

Chipko, the movement to protect the forest and conserve the environment, gained immense popularity within ten years of its birth. The protest of the people of a small village—Mandal in Chamoli district of U.P.—in March 1973 against the allotment of ash trees to a sports goods company and the demand for a tree for agricultural implements from the reserve forest, grew into a big movement, challenging not only the age long forestry management, but also the present pattern of development. But how ? The reply comes from the teachings of Indian philosophy to show reverence to Nature. Our culture as Tagore has stated, had its origin in *aranyas* (forests). The sages, saints and the great teachers of India lived in their *ashrams* in the forests, meditated on the problem of mankind there and presented the essence of their research to the society in the form of Vedas and Upanishads. One of the main gifts of Indian culture is to see God in Nature—in rivers, mountains, forests and in all forms of life. It is a sacred duty to protect these (Bahuguna, 1981 : 15). This tradition was kept alive by our great teachers and saints, through their preachings. Lord Buddha described forests as "a peculiar organism of unlimited kindness and benevolence that makes no demands for its substenance and extends protection to all beings offering shade even to the man with the axe who destroys it."

People resisted against tree felling since long. During the excavation of the historical township of Patan in Gujarat, a stone carving was found depicting a woman hugging a tree and an axeman standing nearby to fell the tree. But it actually happened on tenth full moon-day of September 1730 in Khejadli village of Jodhpur in Rajasthan, when Amrita Devi led 362 men, women and children to be axed to death while protecting the Khejadli trees from the axemen of Maharaja of Jodhpur. The inspiration for this great *saka* (sacrifice) came from the teachings of Cowherd Saint Zambhoji—the founder of the Vishnoi cult. The main tenets of this cult are not to fell green trees and not to kill wild animals. Amrita Devi offered her head to protect the trees (Baker, 1983 : 1-3).

This old spirit of love for nature received a set back when the British rulers needed large quantity of teak from India to meet the ever increasing demand of wood for ship building and railways as supplies of first class oak timber became short in England. They needed ships to expand their trade and railways to administer a revolting country. They took over the control of the forests from the village communities. This process started in the beginning of last century. But the forest dwellers, who regarded forests as their own, revolted against this. In Uttarakhand (the hill region of U.P.) there were mass movements against the Government control and the commercialization of forests, which culminated into an open revolt in the Yamuna valley of the erstwhile Tehri-Garhwal State (now Uttarkashi district). The people established an independent government of their won in May 1930. The revolt was suppressed by the Army killing 17 persons and arresting and imprisoning 80 others on May 30th, 1930 at Tilari on the banks of the Yamuna near Barkot village. But later the two disciples of Mahatma Gandhi—Mira Behn and Sarala Behn, brought a new conception about the importance of hill forests and laid foundations of a peaceful peoples' movement. Mira Behn after seeing the devastating Ganges floods as early as 1946, felt that something was redically wrong in the Himalaya and that something

> "is without doubt connected with the forests. It is not I believe, just a matter of change of species... I have become

painfully aware of a vital change in species of trees which is creeping up and up the southern slopes—those very slopes which let down the flood waters on the plains below. This deadly change over is from Banj (Himalayan oak) to *chir* pine" (Behn, 1982 : 5).

Sarala Behn who had taken active part in 'Quit India' movement in the Kumaon hills, had seen the strength of hill women. They did not mind their husband being in the Jails. It was the impact of her devoted life that a band of woman social workers came upon the scene. Her disciples were responsible for bringing unprecedented awakening among the hill people, specially women (Bahuguna, n.d. : 2).

The small group of Sarvodaya activitists, who had successfully organised and launched prohibition movement with ladies on the forefront, took up the forest problems. The Martyrs' memorial at Tilari (of 1930 forest movement) became the source of inspiration to the new movement. The pledge to re-establish the harmonious relationship between the forests and the people taken in front of this memorial, was repeated by people in several villages on May 30th, 1969 and onwards. They demanded that the exploitation of forests by contractor should be ended and replaced by the forest labourers' co-operatives, raw material should be made available to local small scale forest based industries and the revision of the rights and concessions of the people.

Demonstrations and meetings in support of these demands started in December 1972 and finally in March 1973 when the villagers of Mandal declared their determination to hug the trees (*chipko*). The movement spread from Mandal to the Kedarnath valley in the same district, where some sports goods company was reallotted ash trees. Later in 1974, the people of Roni in the upper catchment of the Alaknanda under Joshimath tehsil drove away the axemen of a contractor from the forest. They had seen the devastating Alaknanda floods in 1970. The state Government took a sympathetic view of their demand, appointed a committee and finally stopped tree felling in that area. Certain economic demands like end of contractor system, increased wages to forest labourers and assured supply of raw materials to local small scale forest based industries were also conceded (Govt. of U.P. 1974). This was the first victory and recognition to the movement.

Chipko soon became the catchword with the hill villagers, who had century old grievances against the commercial management of the forests. Their water sources had dried up. Fuel and fodder had become scarce. Top soil had eroded and turned acidic. This was mainly due to the mono-culture of *chir* pine. Huge landslides had threatened their very survival. They had seen the fury of the Alaknanda floods in 1970, floods and landslides in other valleys during the subsequent years. The acceptance of a few economic demands was not the solution to these problems. Popular folksingers, like Ghanshyam Sailani, came out with their songs, giving a call for mass movement:

> Come on Brothers and Sisters! Let us unite
> Protect our forests from contractors' exploitation
> Both—the Govt. and the contractors are chopping trees,
> With no care to plant new saplings
> Hug the trees, do not allow anybody to fell,
> Stop the plunder of the wealth of the hills (Sailani, 1973)

Padyatras (foot-march) were undertaken to take the message to remote villages. Young students walked with the message from Askot to Arakot (in May-July 1974), Srinagar (Garhwal) to Simla (September 1975), Srinagar to Pithoragarh and to several other places. Protection of the dying Himalayas became their mission. Lady disciples of Sarala Behn walked from Uttarkashi to Pithoragarh and Kausani. Thus between 1973 and 1976, the whole region became conscious about their forests.

But initially *chipko* was an economic movement. The activities planned with great enthusiasm various economic programms like setting up of small saw mills, working with forest labour co-operatives to fell the trees and extract resin from pine trees etc. But these are what men thought. The women's thinking was different. The hill women were involved in the actual struggle of life. Most of the able bodied men from the hills remained away from their home to earn money in the plains.

And so the women had to shoulder the whole burden of managing the family. For the whole day they had to keep themselves busy in collecting fuel to cook and fodder for the cattle, in fetching water and in working in the fields. They knew the reality, they knew the actual meaning of the struggle for existence. They knew the value of the forest because from forest they got fuel, fodder, roots and fruits, their basic needs. They knew these and still know these through generations' experiences. But men thought differently; they thought forests—a source of their employment through tree felling and resin tapping till December 5th, 1977 when the women of Henwalghati in Tehri Garhwal put sacred ribbon (*rakhi*) round the trees marked and auctioned for felling by the Forest Department. In Bhagwat Katha (all the organisation and people's education for *satyagrah* was done in Bhagwat Kathas—the story of Lord Krishna in the forests) they declared their firm determination to save these trees from contractors' axes at the cost of their lives. These became an eye-opener for the malefolk of the hill region who then started realising the actual value of the forest.

News of this incident reached New Delhi, where administrators, forests and social workers had gathered in a seminar on People and Forests in the Himalayas inaugurated by the then Prime Minister. But as usual, the high sounding deliberations of the seminar, presentation of papers by the experts and finally the recommendations had nothing to do with these village women. A forest officer was deputed to dissuade them. He was welcomed with lit lanterns in the broad daylight to show that when trees were fallen what havoc could be created. He explained to them the necessity of the scientific exploitation of forests to meet the requirement of raw materials of industries, timber and earn foreign exchange. He ended by saying in rythmic tone:

Kya hain jungle ke upkar ? (What do the forests bear ?)
Lissa, lakri aur vyapar (Resin, timber and trade)

And instantly the reply came from the gathering of simple village women in the same tone :

Kya hain jungle ke upkar (What do the forest bear ?)

Mitti, pani aur bayar (Soil, water and pure air.)
Mitti, pani aur bayar (Soil, water and pure air.)
Zinda rakhne ke aadhar (Are the basis of life) (Bahuguna, 1978)

This simple but remarkable scientific truth was difficult to digest by those who had been traditionally managing the forests. The State Government of Uttar Pradesh instead of conceding to people's demand to spare the few trees from the axes, which they needed for their survival, sent a well-equipped armed police force on February 1st, 1978 to terrorize the villagers and suppress the movement for ever. They had already suppressed the young students' movement of Nainital, who had opposed the auctioning of forests two months back. But now hundreds of women hugged the trees in Advani forest. The bayonets proved futile. A few days later, the women staged *dharana* at Narendranagar, where the forests were being auctioned. They were arrested and sent to the jail. This struggle of Henwalghati brought a basic change into the *chipko* movement. Now it is an ecological movement.

There were the Bhagirathi blocade in Uttarkashi district in August 1978, huge landslides in Chamoli and Pithoragarh districts next year and again the same in Uttarkashi district. But all these were not enough to move the policy makers. The struggle to save forests continued till 1980. At places like Kangar Badiyargad and Lhashi, there were mass upsurges in 1979 and everywhere people succeeded in driving away the axeman inspite of police terror. The non-violent force of women and children was on the forefront. Before 1980 Parliamentary elections an appeal was issued to all the political parties by leading conservationists and elders like Dada Dharmadhikari, Dr Salim Ali, Sarala Behn, Acharya Banarasi Das Chaturvedi to save the Himalayan forests. This had the desired effect as all major political parties included protection of environment in their election manifestos. When the elections were over, Mrs. Indira Gandhi invited the *chipko* activities in a meeting of environmentalists and hereafter the Centre started taking active interest in the *chipko* demands. In April 1981, the U.P. Government under instructions from the Deptt. of Environment of

Govt. of India, clamped a temporary ban on the felling of green trees for commercial purposes in hill areas above 1000 metres altitude and slopes above 30° gradient, pending the report of a Committee on issues raised by the *chipko* movement. The *chipko* activists however, boycotted the Committee as it was dominated by those who had been mainly responsible for the destruction of the forests. The Committee is said to have recommended resumption of tree felling, but the report has been studied by the Department of Environment, and it is learnt that the Govt. of India has suggested ban on tree felling for commercial purposes in the hill areas right from the Shivalik hills for 15 years.

The ban on felling of green trees has given a breathing time to the *chipko* activities after eight years of continuous struggle. After all they have their own dreams for healing up the wounds of the Himalayas and the welfare of the miserable highlanders. In some areas specially in the upper catchments of the Alaknanda where tree felling had been stopped in 1974, plantation programmes in the denuded watersheds have been intensified. Eco-development camps to educate the masses are being held. An organisation has taken up the work of popularising improved *chulhas* (stoves) to minimise the consumption of firewood.

But meanwhile what has happened at Henwalghati? Recently (March 5th to 7th) a women's camp and a conference are attended by delegates from far away villages; there they have declared, "Any attempt to revive the commercial exploitation of forests will be opposed tooth and nail. We need natural forests for soil and water, for fuel and fodder. We stand for a new socio-economic order free from the exploitation of human beings and Nature alike."

The *chipko* movement is the first movement in the hill regions of Uttar Pradesh which has stirred more people than many other movements in different parts of India. In the beginning it was rediculed by the elites and those who decide the destinies of the common people while sitting at the citadel of power. But later it has completely smashed the 'modern' thinking of the urban elites, the laboratory scientists and of the professional political agitators that whatever they think is right and rural ignorant mass has neither power, nor capacity to think about the basic problems of the area they inhabit. On the contrary, it has established that the clique of a few elites supported by short-sighted politicians, is responsible for the woes and miseries of the masses. This clique is the exploitation of Nature for short term economic ends blurring the future posterity.

In the Uttarakhand this movement has created tree-consciousness. The common people have rejected the prevailing notion that tree means timber; they have now realised that trees are for their survival. They need trees to protect themselves against avalanches and landslides, which have become so common in the hills. Then they require trees to save their land from soil-erosion and of course, trees are essential for soil-building and soil-improvement. This consciousness has been reflected in their opposition to the mass plantation of soil-depleter and water-sucker pines. Unfortunately, in the plains areas where people are not much conscious about soil and water, mass plantations of eucalyptus is going on abated. This has impact on Government policies also. A massive programme of tree plantation under social forestry has been taken up. Nurseries of fodder tree species have also been nurtured. Some plantations have been raised.

But a peoples' movement always explores new areas of action. The *chipko* activists in the Alaknanda valley have achieved success in growing tree plantation, a peoples' programme. In Himdarshan Kutir, Pithoragarh district, where Sarala Behn worked till the last moment to awaken people, a nursery of 2 lakh walnut, chestnut and fodder trees is being raised independently without any official aid. Some other institutions doing constructive work, are also following this example by raising small nurseries in their respective areas.

Another very remarkable achievement of the *chipko* movement is to bring women in the mainstream of public life. Though this started with the Prohibition movement which preceeded the *chipko* movement (1965-1971), yet the *chipko* movement provided them with an action programme—a programme to protect forests and to plant trees. They challenged the urban based planning by saying :

First priority to fodder, fuel and water
other things may come later.

Further they say:

fodder, fuel, soil and water
Are the basis of our prosperity

Everywhere in the hills, women are the backbone of economic and social life. Their active participation in the public life will go a long way in establishing a sane society which is free from exploitation—both from the exploitation of man and the exploitation of Mother Earth.

Chipko's Goal

Chipko was born in a region, where forest plays an important role in the lives of the hill people, so the movement has given a clear out view about the forest policy in the following statement adopted by Uttarakhand Sarvodaya Parivar (Family) under the leadership of late Sarala Behn :

"We must remember that the main role of the hill forests should not be to yield revenue, but to maintain a balance in the climatic condition of the whole of northern India, and the fertility of the Gangetic plain. If we ignore their ecological importance in favour of their short time economic utility, it will be prejudicial to the climate of Northern India and will dangerously enhance the cycle, recurring and alternating floods and droughts...Every green tree standing on the hills is a sentry against the invasion of flood and famine. Felling it on any pretext is an encouragement to flood. Moreover, owing to the increasing pressure of population of people and cattle, we are faced with a critical shortage of fuel and fodder" (Devi, 1980 : 3-4).

This instils in us to a new conception of development. The conventional model for development encourages us to work towards a life style of affluence. The technological advancement has taught the present day material society to exploit more and more the centuries old stores, the Nature. And as a result most of the non-renewable resources are on the verge of extinction. This will ultimately affect the hungry millions, who need food first. Every living being has a birthright to fulfil his basic need from the Mother Earth. Every one needs oxygen first, then water, food, clothing and shelter. This is possible to get all those if we give top priority to the plantation of five 'F'—Food (nuts, edible seeds, oil seeds, honey), fodder, fuel, fertiliser and fibre-trees. These trees, of course, should be good soil builders and soil improvers with greater capacity to conserve water, as soil and water are the two basic capital resources of mankind. This will re-establish the harmonious relationship between Man and Nature—the relationship of Child with the Mother.

The *chipko* is a revolt against the butchery of Nature. It is an attempt to re-establish the values of *aranya* (forest) culture by making spirituality the guide of science and technology for the well-being of all living beings. We have been saying :

The whole Earth can be made our family. This can be achieved if we ponder over the words (*mantra*) of Mahatma Gandhi—the greatest humanist of this century. He said, "The Earth has enough for everybody's need but not for everybody's greed."

REFERENCES

Bahuguna, S,	1978	*Himalaya Bachao* (in Hindi) Parbatiya Nawajeevan Mandal, Silyara. Also lecture given in Himalaya Club Golden Jubilee Celebrations, New Delhi on Feb. 19, 1978.
	1981	Ecological Development and N.S.S. Lucknow University, Lucknow.
	nd.	Gandhi 'Betis' in save Himalaya.
Baker, R. St. Barbe	1983	Chipko—Hug to the Tree People, in *Chipko*, Chipko Information Centre, Silyara, U.P.

Behn, Mira	1982	Something Wrong in the Himalayas. *Hindustan Times* (Aug. 1982) and also in *Save Himalaya*, Chipko Information Centre, Silyara, U.P.
Devi, Sarala	1980	*A Blue-print for survival of the Hills*, Parbatiya Paryavaran Sanrakshan Samiti Kausani, U.P.
Forest Research Institute	n.d.	*Hundred Years of Indian Forestry—Forests of India : History.*
Govt. of Uttar Pradesh	1974	Proceedings of the Meetings of the Chipko Activists with U.P. Chief Minister in Nov. 1974.
Saileni, G.	1973	*Chipko Geet.*

CHAPTER XVII

THE CHIPKO MOVEMENT

STRATEGIES, ACHIEVEMENTS AND IMPACTS*

CHANDI PRASAD BHATT

In the first half of the seventh and eighth decades of this century, the policy of alienating the people of the Uttarakhand region from their age-old right over the natural resources in the fragile catchment area of the Alaknanda, the main tributary of the Ganga, and the unabated spate of a callous exploitation of the jungles, have amounted to a threatening disbalance of the Himalayan eco-system. This hastened the people of the region to take up the road to revolution. *Chipko* (to cling to the trees in order to save them from felling) emerged as a humble, non-violent protest of the inhabitants of Garhwal against the atrocities launched by a distant 'bureaucratic set-up' at the life-giving trees.

The Uttarakhand region is constituted of eight hill districts of Uttar Pradesh namely-Chamoli, Uttarkashi, Pithoragarh, Almora, Nainital, Dehra Dun, Tehri and Pauri. The mountains are very strikingly in height ranging from 1000 ft. to 25,000 ft. above the mean sea level, and the plain stretches are hardly visible in this region. A host of species of trees and plants grow in whatever and wherever soil remained amid the winding, rising

*Rendered into English by R.K. Kala of the University of Garhwal, Srinagar, U.P.

hills, and the region arose as a conspicuous forest-land in the course of time.

Plenteous forest area and suitable climatic conditions attracted the people who finally settled in the region, humbly limiting their needs according to whatever had been afforded to them by the kindly Nature and living in symbiosis with the lush flora and fauna. But with the passing of time, the nonchalant bureaucratic system, with its base elsewhere, touched the region and finally took control over the forests. The new system regarded the trees as means of extracting quick revenue, introducing into the region commercialised approach towards Nature's gifts. The new phenomenon worked in close design with the ever-increasing needs of the thriving communities in the region and inevitably put an end to the age-old harmony between man and Nature. The multiple effects of this double-forked attack were witnessed clearly in the first half of the seventh decade when, owing to strategical consideration, the three border districts of Garhwal and Kumaon, namely—Uttarkashi, Chamoli and Pithoragarh, were given the status of full-fledged districts with a view to their all-round development. The developmental activities in these districts were comprised of massive road-building on war-footing. A dozen of new departments were established and the region came under unprecedented stress of population influx. The density of population, which was earlier one person per square kilometre in the upper Himalayas, quickly rose to its double. Naturally enough, the forests were then looked upon as the only way to feed the needs of the encroaching influxes.

The construction of a vast net-work of roads in the name of development, proved to be a threat to the forests and the people of the region. The jungles were removed farther and farther away from the human settlements, as the motor roads facilitated the extraction of timber wealth out of the region; this also happened because the overincreasing requirements of the swollen population had also to be catered for. And thus began the endless exploitation of the forests largely due to the untutered attitude of the so-called 'system'. The unscientific clearing of the innumerable trees in a small region heavily bruised the crust of the forest-land and the ramping of rain water mixed with stones, pebbles etc. got increased to a tremendous extent. All this boosted the process of soil erosion, landslides, and floods in the region. The Alaknanda's catchment area is a living example of the fact. Here, under the working plan, logging was done on big scale, rendering the catchment of the Mandakini, the Birhi, the Garurganga, the Patalganga and the Helang most vulnerable to natural disasters. The table below indicates to the massive deforestation in the catchment of the Alaknanda :

Table 1: Rate of Deforestation in years

Sl. No.	*Year of Felling*	*Block No.*		*Area in Acres Gross*
1.	1959-60	Dasholi	VIII-IX	6508
2.	1960-61	Mandakini	I	498
3.	1961-62	,,	I	1659
4.	1962-63	,,	I	1068
5.	1965-66	Dasholi	V	1872
6.	1966-67	,,	VI	1500
7.	1967-68	,,	VII	1421
8.	1968-69	,,	VI	973
9.	1968-69	,,	V	583

In this way, tree felling was done mercilessly in a total area of 16,082 acres of forest-land. Ironically enough, the geologists regard the entire area as seismically very sensitive. The landslides have also remained a common feature here. Apart from this unscrupulous tree felling, a fire was also set in the jungles of this region during April-May 1970. Needless to say that all such human activities resulted in the nerve-shattering drama of July, 20, 1970, when the tributaries of the Alaknanda lost their usual temper and eversweeping their bounds left a trail of unprecedented horrors behind :

In the upper catchment zone of the Alaknanda, 6 motor and 16 pedestrian bridges and 25 motor-buses were destroyed; 55 human and 142 cattle lives were wiped off; about 604 houses, 47 watermills, 27 cowsheds, 4 lift-agricultural machines, and 500 acres of standing paddy crops in 101 villages were marooned. Large cracks developed in the land and houses of about a dozen of villages. Moreover, about 100 kms away from the main source of the flood, in Srinagar (Garhwal), the I.T.I. building came under knee-deep water. And when the water level of the swollen river was reduced, 6 ft. thick layer of silt was left behind as a token of annoyance of the river.

The same day, in the catchment areas of the Birhi and the Patalganga, two artificial lakes, which had been formed in the past, got stuffed with silt. Infact, the Alaknanda disaster of 1970 would have been indescribably unparalleled, had these two lakes not hidden in their depth a considerable part of the disaster; they had actually thrown cut only a token-terror-merely the trailor of a breathtaking drama. These lakes, by way of destroying themselves, sacrificed their existence to save a large part of the fertile plain-stretch of the Ganga. Yet, they could not help the effects of the havoc reaching 300 kms away in Haridwar where a 10 km long and 3 metre thick layer of silt choked the Ganga-canal. This devoided about 9,50,000 acres of agricultural land from irrigation for about six months. It took a crore of rupees to help clear the deluge of silt from the canal. In short, after the flood, the vulnerability of the region to similar havocs in future can not be denied.

Now, it is a scientific fact that the trees act machine-like to protect the scil and water. Their leaves bear the onslaught of rain water falling from above, thus reducing its effect to a bare minimum. Penetrating deeply inside, their roots tightly take the earth in their protective grip and help it fight against any kind of disintegration. The trees also help the earth in storing the water and in controlling the rains by centralising the clouds. On the contrary, the denuded lands increase the ramp power of the speedy raindrops, multiplying the horrors of floods to a large extent. Such lands also lose the capacity of absorbing the water which, by slipping over the outer layer of the land and into the rivers, result in floods. Moreover, the naked lands can not help in storing the water. Thus, when the rainy season ends, the natural resources dry up causing serious water-crisis in denuded areas. Because of all these factors stated above, the social, economic, and cultural milieu of this region has remained largely depended on the forest which form the main pivot of existence here. The forest has been chiefly catering for the needs of fuel, foods and fodder of the local people. But the increasing trend of uncontrolled exploitation of the forest resources has culminated in the loss of the traditional rights of the local folk over the forest wealth, and they had to escape the other regions in order to struggle for survival. This also amounted to a serious dearth of manpower in the region as the local talents left the region to buy their skills elsewhere. They left behind them a humbler, innocent lot of people who were not exploited along-with their magnificent flora on a comparatively larger scale. The hardships of life and the rising trend of the natural catastrophies ultimately compelled the people to think seriously for their safety and security, finally marking the birth of *chipko*, a movement connotative of personal, regional, national and human interest. The year 1973 witnessed the dawn of the movement when a firm of Allahabad was allotted some ash trees from the Mandal forest in Gopeshwar which is the seat of district headquarters of Chamoli. The local people had been customarily using this species for making *juva*—a traditional agricultural implement. Hence, the auction meant more than a blow to the very nexus of their living. So, fortified with the genuine demand of claiming these trees as their birth-right, the *chipko* soldiers in 1973 took to the task of clinging to the marked trees in the Mandal forest, and later in Phata-Rampur repeated this action. They had struck gold and rejoiced as the trees were thus saved from the greed of the commercialised axes.

Further in 1974 a large portion of the most sensitive Reni catchment area of the Rishiganga—a tributary of the Alaknanda which had already tasted the bitter bites of the flood of 1970, was saved from any further disintegration in the climatic *chipko* drive. Following this epoch making event, there were the other clings at Gopeshwar (1975), Bhundar (1978), Dungri-Pantuli (1980), and Khalla-Kotesher (1982), resulting in the total ban on logging in these areas. The *chipko* people appeared to have been clamouring for the following demands :

1. Any kind of tree-felling in the sensitive catchment of the rivers must be banned; plantation should be done thickly in such areas. The trees must not be cut for other construction.

purposes unless it is ascertained that it would have no adverse bearing on the eco-system. In such areas, the forest conservation system ought to aim at protecting the soil-fence of the forest land and the water resources as well as balancing the climatic features.

2. The contractual-system in the forest should immediately be stopped, and rural organisations and labour co-operative societies should be established to replace the contractual-system. With active involvement and consultation with the local hill-folks, the entire forest work should be done through such organisation and societies only. The native must also be provided with relevant training and guidelines to fulfil the objective.

3. The daily needs of the forest-dwellers in the region should be duly evaluated and accordingly reasonable rights should be given to them over the forest resources. Forests must be surveyed properly in order to know their exact condition as well as to evaluate the rights of the native in proper perspectives.

4. Rural industrial ventures, based on the forest resources in the region, involving the local labours, industrial workers and villagers, should be given all incentives. For this, assistance must be provided to them in obtaining the sufficient raw materials, finance, and technical know-how.

5. The denuded hills must be regreened through afforestation drives on war-footing. Again, the local people must be involved in and encouraged towards forest-farming. Efforts should be made to germinate love and affection among the locals towards tree and plants.

6. A detailed geological, ecological, and botanical survey of the hills should be done before any heavy construction or forest Department's working plans are hatched in the region.

The demands, stated above, are no bellow boasts but are based on the personal experiences of the *chipko* representatives. It is indeed surprising to note that *chipko* has germinated a tremendous environmental awareness among the people and has attracted the entire national and global attention to its genuine demands. Soon after the all out *chipko* action at Reni in 1974, the U.P. Government formed a committee, under the chairmanship of Dr. Virendra Kumar—a renowned botanist from Delhi, which included a host of experts from the relevant disciplines alongwith the *chipko* representatives to review the local peoples' resentmant against man-made encroachments and resulting outcome of the natural disasters in Reni; a detailed study of the area was done by the committee and it strongly recommended a total ban on logging in the Alaknanda catchment of the Mandakini, the Birhi, the Garurganga, the Patalganga, and the Rishiganga, covering an area about 1200 sq km. Finally, the U.P. Government released orders prohibiting any kind of tree-felling in this area as per the committee's recommendations the details of which are given below:

(A) Areas in which felling has been suspended, based on the report of Reni Van Katan Samiti approved Vide G.O.No. 3055/14-2-585/77 dated 19-5-1977. Govt. of U.P.

Name of Forest Division	*Year of Felling prescribed in working plan*			*Area in Hectares in which felling has been suspended*
1	2			3
Badrinath	1974-75	Dasholi	VII	1319.0
	1975-76	,,	VII-VI	1247.7
	1976-77	,,	VII	1679.3
	1977-78	,,	VI	1501.2
	1978-79	,,	V	2350.6
	1979-80	,,	IX-VIII	2374.3
	1980-81	Mandakini	I	1969.2
	1981-82	,,	I	757.9
	1982-83	,,	I	118.5
Total				13317.7

(B) Area in which felling has been suspended as these areas are susceptible to soil erosion.

1	2			3
Badrinath	1978-79	Pinderpar	III	200.7
	,,	Kandai Block		95.5

1		2		3
Badrinath	1979-80	Pindarpar	IV	122.6
	1979-80	Dasmoli	IV	26.3
Kedarnath	1976-77	Bamsu	1-2	594.8
	1978-79	Churani Danda	1-4-5	129.0
	1979-80	Dhanpur	II	285.36
	1977-78	Ukhimath	II-I,2-3	575.15
	1978-79	,,	II-3	281.35
	1979-80	,,	II-5	272.25
				2583.01
Total of categories— (A) and (B) areas				15900.71

In the similar way, the proposed tree-felling to fulfil the fuel-supply to Badrinath town was also checked with the *chipko* drive enacted at Bhundar. The details of the resulting ban in this area are as under :

Badrinath	—	1977-78	Pankhanda —	10-0	hectares
,,		1978-79	,,	10-0	,,
,,		1979-80	,,	10-0	,,
.		1980-81	,.	10-0	,,
,,		1981-82	,,	10.0	,,
,,		1982-83	,,	10-0	,,
		Total		60-0	

Further, the felling of the oak trees at Dungri-Pantali in the catchment of the Pinder valley was banned as per the recommendations of a high official committee which also consisted of the members of the *chipko* movement. This saved the life of thousands of lush oak, rhododendron, and Mehal trees, spreading in an area of about 90 acres.

The broad-leaved oak and rhododendron are the chief peculiarity of the region where grows an exquisite abundance of these species. These species are not only regarded here as *kalpavriksha* (a mythical species of tree of perpetual), but also serve as shelter to numerous water resources apart from contributing in the preservation of the soil to a mighty great extent. Hence, the protection of these trees is a foremost necessity and priority. The issue was raised by the *chipko*, resulting in another great achievement as the Uttar Pradesh Government passed orders of banning these life-giving trees from felling on the 25th of May, 1974.

In February 1980, the U.P. Forest Department also sent directives to revise its working plans with a view to harmonize them with the notion of 'sensitivity' of these areas. They, however, defined 'sensitivity' in their own why which does not tally with the definition of 'sensitivity' offered by the *chipko* members. The official definition includes: (a) All such areas which are on an altitude of more than 2750 metres; (b) All such areas as are sensitive to landslides because of certain geological reasons; (c) All such areas as are generally situated on a slanting position at an angle of more than 45°.

But the *chipko* interpretation of 'sensitivity' does not apply any yardstick of slant and height; they regard the entire high Himalayas and mid Himalayas, as put in two broad categories by the geologists, highly sensitive to any kind of provocation. That is why, they resent strongly against commercialised tree-felling in the area.

Fortunately, in 1975, the Alaknanda Soil conservation of the Forest Department came into existence in Chamoli in order tounder take the Himalayan task of rejuvenating the naked forestland in the region. The next five years witnessed the Civil Soyam Forest Department functioning in the entire Garhwal and Kumaon Divisions. To intensify such steps in Chamoli, the upper Ganga catchment of the Forest Department has also been established which will make plan for the security and safety of the small rivers and rivulets affected by soil-erosion and landslides besides engaging itself in afforestation drives in the region.

Although the *chipko's* demand to abolish the contractual system in the forest management has also been accepted in principle by the Government, yet the schism between policy and practice still exists. The establishment of the Forest Corporation is a living example to illustrate the unhealthy dichotomy.

The Corporation was established so as to fulfil the long-cherished *chipko* demand of providing respectable job opportunities to the local people of the region derived out of the forest resources and to put a final end to the contractual system. But instead of giving straight employment to the rural folk, it has been functioning by employment the petty contractors. So the situation is more or less back to square 'A'. The idea behind the Corporation should have been to form a strong, effective organisation of workers who would fell trees, wherever necessary, and work simultaneously for forest conservation and enhancement so as to maintain a tectical harmony. Far from this, the Forest Corporation is given to 'small scale contracts' for a 'large scale logging' and has kept its hands off the responsibility of forest conservation.

The official definition of 'forest work' also varies from that of *chipko*. The former regards it as denotative to tree-felling alone, and the latter treating it as connotative of the collection of minor forest-produce and seeds for nurseries, wall-fencing for the safety of new plantations, and digging of pits for afforestation.

It is a pity that the Government has remained apathetic to the labour co-operative societies in the region which have so far been ineffective due to official victimization and malfeasance. Moreover, in the vital issue of encouraging and providing raw material to rural industrial ventures, the Government's attitude is a total violation of its socialistic rhetoric. Consequently, new entrepreneurs fear to take up such ventures based on minor-forest-produce. The growing resentment among the youth of the region is a direct result of this lackadaisical tendency of the Government.

Moreover, the rural areas are being least benefited by repeated assurances of the Government to compensate the increased result of the daily needs of the thriving communities in the region. This has, time to time, compelled the hill-folks to take indiscreet measures which badly affect the forest wealth of the region. Unfortunately, only a crafty set of the go-betweens is taking undue advantage of the Governmental plans in the name of minor demands of the local people. This has further speeded up the process of exploitation of the forests and the innocent forest-dwellers. Furthermore, even the previously inaccessible mountains are exposed to greedy eyes as the entire region lay criss-crossed with roads which are being used to transport the fuel wood to the numerous upcoming towns of the region on massive scale. Thus, an all-out offensive against the forests seems to be imminent. The forests have already been removed farther and farther away from the reach of the local people, and their hearths have to have a long wait before they are lit up for cooking, and that, too, by the tired, exhausted bodies.

The process of extracting pine sap has also rendered the trees vulnerable to any slight provocation by the wind and the storm. In 1974, *chipko* protested against this unscientific process, but even then it has gone unabated in some areas despite Government's assurance in principle not to employ it in the region.

According to geologists, the Himalayan region is till in a growing state. It is seismically very sensitive and its rocks are far from being stable. Paying no heed to this, the man-made encroachments here in the last two decades in the form of heavy road-building, tunnel-construction, mineral extraction, hectic tree-felling, and uncontrolled grazing have amounted to repeated landslides and large cracks which are visible all around. If the man-made forces of destruction are not checked, the consequences in future will be unparalleled. In Chamoli district alone the existence of numerous fields, houses, and jungles of about 400 villages is in serious danger. Not only this, the motor-roads and various irrigation drinking water and hydro-electrical projects are regularly being affected. Doubtlessly, the flood of the Alaknanda and the alarming instability of Joshimath, Kontha, Karnprayag, Sera Malkoti, Harishankar, Satiyana, Nautha, Kaleshwar, Gandhi Nagar, Garurganga, Tangni etc. are largely due to man's increasing activities in the region. Inspite of all this the process continues. The unscientific projects and plans in the sensitive areas of the Birahi, the Patalganga, Tangni and Joshimath clearly indicates to the possibility of a would be drama of unprecedented tragedies. And yet, the geologists are remembered only when the havocs culminate in actual and serious losses, overlooking completely that their predictions are warning. The time has arrived when a detailed survey of the geographical, geological, and weather conditions of the entire inner catchment zone of the Ganga must be done with all cares so as to ascertain the validity of the tremendous uproar caused by the construction of the gigantic hydro-electric projects and dams in the region.

Against the background of this turbulent scenario, *chipko* has been vehemently emphasizing the necessity of imparting more and more vigils to the threatened Himalayas in the form of trees who alone can stand inlocoparentis to the mother Earth. This cannot be done unless the local people are involved in the onerous task of regreening the naked Himalayas. The damages done by man's axes and pocket-matches, and by his herd of animals, are to be repaired by man only. Ever since *chipko* has been geered into action to draw the local masses' attention to this vital point. On the other hand the Government has failed to associate and link local people's support with its afforestation drives. Except for making ludicrous proposals on social forestry which included the construction of pits and walls for plantation alone through the contractual system, the Government has nothing to say on the local involvement. Hence, the unhealthy factors of uncontrolled grazing and man-made fires in the jungles are still persisting. In spite of heavy expenses, the much needed species of trees, other than the fast growing conifers and the ornamental Eucalyptus and Populus, are few in number because the local people have not been consulated; they alone know what can grow on their land and what species are useful to them. In some areas, the afforestation done by the Government, is no more than a heap of dry stone.

We have examined these Himalayan plantations in Badrinath, Kedarnath and Garhwal divisions of Uttar Pradesh. In the Badrinath Division the percentage survival of the plantation in quite low ranging from 7.6 to 25.8 per cent with an average of 14.2 per cent, and that in Garhwal is a little better, ranging from 10.4 to 35.1 per cent with an average of 21.5 per cent. The survival rate in the Kedarnath Division ranges from 0.0 to 90.0 per cent with an average of around 20.0 per cent. The Government officials never, cared to think that mere afforestation is not social forestry. Actually, it is an efficient means of forest conservation and enhancement of the villages' live. It is almost impossible to work towards these objectives without involving those who live in the forests. Social forestry would remain a fanciful idea only unless the economic interests of the local people are tied with every tree which grows in these forests. Hence, *chipko* considers it of paramount importance to involve the local mass in forest conservation and enhancement of the rural life. And for this, it is of vital significance to distribute among the natives vacant forest lands in these areas as well as those nudging their agricultural fields. The right of growing the fuel, fodder and fruit trees must be handed over to the locals. In making wall-fence and pits for plantation, the collection of seeds, the folks should be linked straightaway with the task.

The Dasholi Gram Swarajya Sangh (D.G.S.S.)—the parental body of *chipko* has been endlessly working with the support of the local people to achieve the high goals of agro-forestry and social forestry for the last five years in 25 villages of the Garurganga area. The national rural employment plan has further speeded up the Sangh's activities. Every year the D.G.S.S. organised eco-development camps in this area to aim at high public-education and germination of environment awareness among the people. Even the coy women have come out to join hands and have given enthusiastic participation in the Sangh's activities. This has indeed paid rich dividends.

The success of these plantations with real participation by people has been good: with survival exceeding 70 to 90 per cent as compared to 20 to 50 per cent in Government plantation in the region.

Infact, the D.G.S.S. upholds the view of a 'development without destruction' and by creating a right atmosphere through public teaching and actual work for decording the naked lands with the green garment of trees, it is engaged sincerely to nurse the Himalaya back to health. Unless the Government follow suit, *chipko* will continue.

Chipko will go on claiming for a new forest policy and a pragmatic approach toward forests in the region so that the life of the forest-dwellers of the region alongwith the flora and fauna is truely recuperated.

Chipko, in its conception and execution, has remained a

rural-mass movement. Practical and personal, not hypothetical, experiences have given rise to *chipko*. This was precisely the reason why a large multitude of Gopeshwar and the neighbouring villages demonstrated for the overhauling of the hackneyed forest policy for the first time in the history of the region on December, 1972. It was frankly an unprecedented sight to see the men and women dressed in traditional costumes, their crude musical instrument such as *dhol, dharmau* etc. making a loud uproar and echoing the entire sky with exciting beats which further added to the fury of the slogan-raising lot. It is curious to note that such instruments are used in the religious ceremonies alone and their use in such demonstrations significantly refers to the hill people's belief in the sanctity of the *chipko* demands. Needless to say, *chipko* is now a part of their unconscious mind. And that is why the people of Phata-Rampur in their drive to save the *angu* trees, used traditionally here for making agricultural tools, themselves took to the *chipko* task with a negligible number of the *chipko* representatives helping them. The tree fellers had to return empty-handed as all the marked *angu* trees were in the protective embrace of a vast multitude of people. They were inspired by the realisation that the species will be near extinction since it has to bear a two-forked onslaught, that of the commercial axe and the traditional use.

Another striking feature of the *chipko* movement has been that instead of being led by the professional leaders and demagogues, it is guided by the common rural folk. It has also attracted the students of the region who went on demonstrating continuously for two days against the arrival of the tree-fellers in the most sensitive area of Reni which finally resulted in the climatic victory of the movement. Infact, the menfolk of the area was absent that day as they had gone to Gopeshwar to collect the money as compensation for their lands. Even the *chipko* representatives were not there as they had also been called at Gopeshwar for consultation. Only the women remained in the village 27 frail bodies against a lot of sturdy, professional axe-men. Not caring for the odds against them, these women rushed to the forests and clung to the marked trees with angry tree-fellers threatening them with glistening axes. On the second day, their number increased as the men and women of about one dozen villages above Joshimath area reached on the spot to take to the holy cling in the Reni forest. The *chipko* vigil continued until finally in 1977, the Reni Survey Committee recommended the total ban on logging in this area. In this epic struggle, not only the border folks of Reni took part but the entire hill-lot of the region participated with unrivalled patience and courage.

Later, the Bhyundar valley, situated in the lower parts of the celebrated Valley of Flowers, followed suit when the local women, despite heavy snowfall, saved the trees which were being felled by the professional loggers. In February 1980, another village Dungri Pantuli in Chamoli District, took to the *chipko* task against the felling of trees which the government was to use for building a garden. The women were so much inspired that they even disobeyed the male members of their own village, and remained firm to register dissent. In deep anguish the village Pradhan served the *chipko* representatives a notice on 18-12-1980, stating that they had illegally misguided the women folk of the village, so much so that the latter had even started disobeying their own male relatives and had created serious impediments in the way of the official plans for the betterment of the village. He further warned the *chipko* representatives not to enter the village failing which they would have to bear grave consequences. One would have marvelled the courage of the women of the village when they asked the officials sarcastically why they had not been consulted prior to any tree-felling since they alone are most attached to the jungles (significant to note that the daily collection of fire wood and fodder from the jungles is done by the women in the region). Mocking bitterly at the so called slogan of the equal rights to men and women, they pointed out that men only were to listen such matters.

In this way *chipko* not only endeavours to grapple with the issue of the safety of trees, it clings to the manifold aspects of life in the region. *Chipko* has brought about a definite change in the mentality of the common man of the region. He now treats jungles as closely intertwined with his very existence. Today, he is bound to regard the various construction activities and proposed projects in the region as a credit-card to yield ugly payments.

It is indeed miraculous that the *chipko* movement, which originated from Chamoli District of Garhwal, now spread over the entire Uttarakhand region which comprises of the Garhwal and Kumaun Divisions. The Chancharidhar drive of Almora District in Kumaon in December 1977 and January 1978, added fresh laurels of victory to the *chipko* movements as the people succeeded in saving the life of 1000 trees. And today, the Forest Department has to think twice before they declare any forest for auction in the region. In this context, the Khalla and Kotseer (Chamóli) episode of October 1982 is worth mentioning. Despite repeated official declarations, the Forest Department with the help of the Uttar Pradesh Forest Corporation conspired to clean shave more than 300 young, green trees off the forests of Khalla and Kotseer. But the watchful villagers immediately informed the *chipko* representatives; and although the life of 19 trees was mercilessly wipped off, the *chipko* soldiers compelled the Government to cancel the felling of the rest of the trees.

One would go on recounting the *chipko* endeavours and yet would come to no end. Infact, the greatness of *chipko* lies in the fact that it has stimulated the people of the region to save the forests though the device of humble resistence without any professional leadership. This is due to the incessant *chipko* efforts for public teaching on the importance and safety of the forests. The *chipko* teachings effectively aim at linking the human emotions with the natural, economic and social significance of the trees. *Chipko* bears a direct relevance to the daily life of the local people and hence, it has hit the centre of their emotions. *Chipko* has germinated a devotional attitude among them towards the trees which stand sentinal over the troubled Nature. Today, *chipko* has ceased to be a movement and has become the very incarnation of bliss and benediction which affords respectability and prosperity to the woodlands and woodlanders of the region.

REFERENCES

Bhatt, C.P.	1980	*Eco-System of Central Himalayas* Dasholi Gram Swarajya Mandal, Gopeswar, Chamoli.
Dinman	1980	Pahele Auroton se poochou, 30th March to 5 April.
Gadgil M., Prasad S.N. and Ali Rauf	1982	Forest management in India : A Critical Review, Centre for Monitoring Indian Economy, Vol. 54, Bombay.
Joshi V.D., Khanduri H.C. and Doval G.P.	n.d.	Four Itinerary and Rout-map for inspection in Chamoli District by the Committee formed by the Govt. of India to Recommend Development of Forestry Extension Services.
Lohari	1974	Working Plan for the North and South Garhwal Forest Divisions and Kumaon Circle, U.P., 1958-59 to 1972-73 (Volume I).
Negi, N.S.	n.d.	Kedarnath Van Prabhag-Garhwal Vrit Uttar Pradesh Ki Karyayojana, (1982-83 to...) Karyayojana Vrit (Second, U.P. Nainital.)

CHAPTER XVIII

UTTARAKHAND AND CHIPKO

REGIONALISM AND ENVIRONMENTALISM IN THE CENTRAL HIMALAYAS

GERALD D. BERREMAN

Introduction

Over a period of 25 years, my research in the Central Himalayas of Uttar Pradesh has made me actually aware of the increasing hardship their residents have borne, and the cumulative resentment they have harbored, as a result of the rapid destruction of their environment resulting from the manner of its governance and resource exploitation (Berreman, 1963; 1972; 1979; 1982).

During 1981-82, a bitterly contested and heavily publicized parliamentary election took place in Garhwal, the heartland of the region, bringing to the fore conflicting expressions of regional identity and interests. At the same time there was increased regional participation in a ten year old indigenous movement to save the Himalayan environment through saving the forests upon which the indigenous people depend for their livelihoods as subsistence farmers. Militant, non-violent action to save the forests was mobilized under the rallying cry the movement has made nationally and internationally famous, *chipko*, the "hug the trees" movement. These two responses in the region to its situation might also be described, respectively, as "elite politics", i.e., the politics of power, and as "grass-roots politics", i.e., the politics of survival.

Although the election was confined to the tiny Garhwal Lok Sabha (parliamentary) Constituency, it became an issue of overriding importancc throughout 'Uttarakhand' and beyond. Similarly, although the activities of the *chipko* movement took place primarily in two subregions (that of Pauri Garhwal and Chamoli districts, and that of Tehri Garhwal and Uttarkashi districts), its goals, methods and accomplishments became watch-words throughout 'Uttarakhand' and beyond.

The Uttarakhand comprises a rectangle of about 300 by 150 kilometres, encompassing all of the Himalayas between the state of Himachal Pradesh on the west, Nepal on the east, Tibet on the north, and the plains districts of Uttar Pradesh on the south. It is made up of the eight Himalayan districts of Uttar Pradesh; : Dehra Dun, Tehri Garhwal, Uttar-kashi, Garhwal (often called Pauri Garhwal), Chamoli, Naini Tal, Almora, and Pithoragarh. They constitute a lightly populated, topographically rugged, relatively inaccessible mountainous appendage to the state of Uttar Pradesh. Its capital, Lucknow, lies about 500 kilometers away in the midst of the immense, flat, Gangetic plain, the western half of which makes up the bulk of the state. The people of the mountain region are predominantly Hindus (with a scattering of Muslims), and along the northern, high-altitude fringe, some Bhotiyas. The Hindu population includes two closely allied, land-owing high castes, the Brahmin farmers and priests, and the Rajput farmers, comprising about 8 per cent and 68 per cent of the population respectively. Various artisan and service castes make up the remaining 24 per cent of the population. Before India's independence they did not own land, they were collectively known as the Dom in most areas, and were regarded as "untouchable" (for which the euphemism "Harijan" is now widely substituted).

The entire population except the Bhotiyas speaks what Grierson in his classic Linguistic Survey of India (1910) called the "Central Pahari" branch of the Pahari ("of or belonging to the mountains") language group which is of Indo-Aryan stock and is spoken throughout the lower Himalayas from western Kashmir across to eastern Nepal. Those who speak these languages are known conventionally and collectively as the Pahari people, and generally so designate and identify themselves, for they share many features which identify them to themselves and others as distinct and related—in short, as an ethnic group. Their languages, while mutually intelligible, are not easily understood by people of the plains. Similarly, their marriage networks overlap throughout the hills, but overlap scarcely at all with those of plainsmen. Their culture is thus bounded and readily distinguishable from that of the plains, but is not entirely unique or divorced from it or from that of the rest of North India from whence some, and perhaps ultimately all, of their ancestors came. They share common origins (Berreman, 1960).

Regardless of stereotypes, however, it must be understood that the Paharis are not tribal people in any conventional or anthropological sense of the term. Rather, they are hill-dwelling, Indo-Aryan-speaking, caste-organized, agricultural Hindus who share much of the tradition of North Indian culture and society and are well within the range of variation found in village culture and society elsewhere in North India.

The degree of cultural sharing or commonality is greater within the Pahari area than between it and the plains. Theirs is not, however, a homogeneous culture throughout the region. Geographic, environmental, social and political barriers of long standing have limited interaction between people, and this largely accounts for their contemporary diversity. This diversity is most conspicuous at the sub-regional and local levels where differences occur in precisely the features shared at the broader levels : speech, ceremonial forms, deities worshipped, architecture, dress, ornament, folklore, technology, organization of family and caste, marriage rules, and the like. Within the Himalayas, and within each of their major regions, and again within their constituent sub-regions, down to particular watersheds, valleys, hillsides and localities, are social, cultural and linguistic territories of varying degrees of difference and inclusiveness which are recognized and acted upon, especially to the extent that they comprise network of intermarriage. Social interaction and cultural commonality within these area translate easily and naturally into fellow-feeling and ethnic identification under circumstances of confrontation with people of contrasting characteristics and interests (cf. Berreman, 1960; 1963 : 295-299;

1982). There is, in effect, a system of regional or segmental ethnic identification analogous to the system of segmental lineage organization found within each caste (*jati*) of the region and of India, and well-known elsewhere through the literature of social anthropology (cf. Evans-Pritchard, 1940).

Just as the shared and distinctive characteristics of Pahari culture may obscure its subregional and local variety to the outsider, so its subregional cultural and social differences may obscure the common culture to the people themselves. This is no doubt a feature of all ethnic identity.

Issues

A look at any contemporary political map of South Asia will reveal an important feature of the political context for regionalism in the Central Himalayas.

Most sectors of the Himalayas have attained a degree of self-governance, a reflection of the topographic and ecological distinctiveness of the environment, the socio-cultural distinctiveness of the population, and the assertiveness of the mountain peoples. The socio-cultural distinctiveness has been the basis for ethnic consciousness among mountain peoples, while the distinctive environment has provided the material conditions upon which the common interests of the mountain populations are based, recognized and asserted. Together, these facts have focused the attentions and energies of the Himalayan peoples towards improving their situation through self-governance.

Regionalism

The politics of the Uttarakhand reflect the minority status of its people, comprising as they do but 4 per cent of a population of 110,000,000 in Uttar Pradesh, a large number of population not much aware of the culture and environment of the mountain region. The politics of the Uttarakhand also reflect the fact that it constitutes of precipitous, fragile mountain land, rich in forest, mineral and hydro-electric resources in a state of 300000 sq. km. of alluvial land.

The desire in the Himalayas for regional self-determination and the desire in the plains for the Himalayan resources, with the added fear of separatism and fission, create a mutually reinforcing system of contradiction, friction and provocation.

Resource Exploitation

When an extensive network of roads was built throughout 'Uttarakhand' following the Indian-Chinese border conflict of 1962, the motive was clearly strategic, but a major consequence was the opening of this formerly largely impenetrable area, rich in resources, to traffic of all kinds. Timber and other forest products ranging from resin to medicinal herbs, and minerals ranging from limestone (of which the outer ranges are largely composed and which, as cement, is the major building material of India) to potassium and rare metals, suddenly became accessible to contractors and other entrepreneurs. The blasting of mountain sides, the hundreds of vehicles and the thousands of laborers used in road-building, were soon replaced by those used in extracting resources. The overall environmental degradation wrought by road construction—the massive erosion and landslides caused by the road cuts and blast-shocks, the resulting loss of soil, forests and water sources, and the decimation of firewood and other forest products by labour crews and others together with the social and economic dislocation those brought to the local populace—was quickly dwarfed by the same phenomena on a magnified scale as a result of the extractive industries' activities.

Hydro-electric sites along the Ganga and the Yamuna rivers and their tributaries were promptly exploited with similar consequences. Now, for example, the Tehri Dam, Asia's largest, is being built on the Bhagarathi where it will submerge historic Tehri City and many villages (cf. *Indian Express*, 1981; V. Verghese, 1982).

In addition, when the roads came, land previously cultivated by the local farmers for their subsistence crops or devoted to pasturage, suddenly also became of interest to entrepreneurs for the cultivation of cold-climate luxury crops, such as apples and apricots, and other commercially valuable crops suited to the environment such as potatoes, ginger and (illegally) opium. Accordingly, industrial giants vied with lesser capitalists in buying up and exploiting the new found agricultural bonanza at the expense of local people.

The Himalayan shrines of Badrinath, Kedarnath, Gangotri, Yamnotri and other places sacred to Hindus became accessible to pilgrims and tourists by bus and taxi in a day or two of travel rather than the weeks or months of trekking formerly required. This new form of mass tourism taxed the capacity of the Himalayan environment heavily as it populated the pilgrimage routes with hotels, restaurants, shops and other impediments of the industry. At the same time, and on many of the same routes secular tourism flourished, attracting plainsmen and foreigners alike to the vacation spots featuring snow-views and wildflowers, touring, trekking, hunting fishing and mountain climbing. Tens of thousands annually take advantage of these attractions with little or no attention paid to their impact on the environment of the mountain people.

The major beneficiaries of these kinds of development are outside entrepreneurs, their customers and their patrons. Most of them are absentee owners from the plains, a few are expatriate mountain people, and a very few indeed are elite, educated, wealthy, plains-oriented (and usually plains-returned) residents of the mountains. On the whole, local people are not properly employed in the enterprises which the opening and "development" of the mountain regions has brought.

The usual impact of some of these development activities has partially been to deplete the forests, erode the soil, dry up the water sources, pre-empt the firewood, fodder and building materials, co-opt or distroy some of the viable agricultural land and pasturage, leaving many of the mountain people unable to make an adequate living. As a result of this and other reasons, in the past 20 years, there has been accelerated emigration of men to the plains in seek of work, most of whom become part of the oversupply of urban unskilled, underemployed. This has resulted in Uttarakhand villages which have been described by some observers as "maleless," where, as in one described by Rawat, cited by Rao: "most of the adult and able males have emigrated leaving behind their wives, children and old parents" (Rao, 1980: 2). These people are left trying to run farms with broken families, partially depleted soil, reduced forests, receding sources of firewood and fodder such that required daily supplies are up to half a day's walk from the villages, and diminishing streams and springs such that water must be carried for up to an hour several times a day. The effect on Uttarakhand is not lost on observers of the Himalayan scene. Dhasmana, in a paper on "Transformation and Development in Uttarakhand," observes that.

> "By the grace of holy Ganges the hill districts of Uttarakhand are tied with the plains of Uttar Pradesh. Part of an over populated state with more than fifty districts and a state capital situated more than five hundred kilometers (away), the hill region view of its histo-geographic past requires special attention" (Dhasmana, 1982: 11)

One of the most noted foreign experts on the Himalayas, German economist Hans Rieger, concluded a recent paper which detailed the decimation of the Himalayas with these remarks:

> "If this pace of progress goes unchecked and unplanned there is every danger that the every existence of life dependent on them, directly or indirectly, may be in jeopardy. It is now high time that the Himalayan states may form a consortium for the protection, preservation and conservation of the natural resources of the Himalaya" (Rieger, 1980: 9).

Regional Identity : The Definition of the Situation

Bharati has observed that "Himalaya is a state of mind," that they "tend to be ascriptive rather than actual mountains." He goes on to quote T.V.R. Murti, noted Hindu philosopher: "Existentialism says that potentiality is more important than actuality. This is true: the Himalayas of the rishis and the yogis is more important as an ideal to us than are the actual rocks and the miserable huts of the people there" (Bharati, 1971:78).

The relevance of those statements in this context is that the Himalayas, and particularly that portion called Uttarakhand, constitute the Holy Land of Hinduism—in a sense, heaven itself. Like all holy lands and heavens, they are idealized. They are the abode of the gods, the place of celestial beauty and perfection. Fonia says, in his book, *Uttarakhand : Garhwal Himalayas* (1977 :4), "Perfection is the other name for this holiest of the Holy Land." The Hindu scriptures repeatedly praise the glory of the Himalayas: "In a hundred ages of the Gods I could not tell thee of the glories of Himachal. As the dew is dried up by the morning sun, so are the sins of mankind by the sight of Himachal" (*Skanda Purana*).

But unlike many holy lands and most heavens, the Himalayas have a solid, tangible reality, and flesh and blood people make their living there through the dint of very real sweat, employing easily observable customs, traditions and practices, according to ideologies which they can readily articulate, and under eminently tangible material, political and historical circumstances. When outsiders and idealists are confronted with the disparities between the ideal and the actual Himalayas, and especially between ideal and actual Himalayan peoples and cultures, the result is likely to be traumatic. For the people turn out to be hard-working farmers, herdsmen and artisans, rather than saints, rishis or yogis, much less gods. Their culture turns out to be pragmatic and mundane rather than other-worldly and idyllic. Their beliefs and customs prove to represent simply another in the wide range of sincere but variable interpretations of the traditions that comprise the whole of Hinduism, rather than meeting the strictures of the most demanding Sanskritic texts and the most pious of Brahmanic advocates.

Bharati observes (1978:79):

> "There is the pervasive feeling among the learned in the Hindu tradition, that ideologically important concepts cannot be expressed except in elegant or at least standard grammatical Sanskrit. Meat eating, irregular bathing, unpredictable sex habits, and bad or no Sanskrit in religious matters form a quartet in the Brahmin's mind... a 'noxious fusion'...."

Yet mountain people exhibit these very characteristics, unholy in the eyes of some plainsmen, while they occupy the holiest of environments.

If outside advocates of orthodox Brahmanism are alarmed

at these revelations, a section of the educated elites of the mountains themselves, and especially those who are expatriates, are embarassed as well as alarmed, for they are anxious to be identified with the ideal rather than the actual Himalayan culture. They are likely to be people who have denied, repressed, forgotten, or concealed the actual in favour of the ideal, in confidence that the later—and the cultural mobility it represents —is the avenue to the social, economic, and political mobility (and often spatial mobility as well) they have sought. I have elsewhere described this as "plainsward mobility," or "plains emulation" (Berreman, 1963:128-29, 395).

Another quotation from Dhasmana will help to define the situation. He identifies what he calls the "migrant syndrome" in Uttarakhand, as:

> "The psychological mentality of the elite class [wherein] migrant claim has been a status symbol during different times" (Dhasmana, 1982:21).

He continues, describing it in these words:

> Whatever may be the reasons of origin of this characteristic pattern and without challenging its authenticity or questioning the loyalty of its people for their land, it was clear that the inhabitants of Uttarakhand always claimed to be immigrants... This syndrome as a status symbol was in vogue for over four hundred years. During this period leading class of Brahmans and Rajput castes could list their claims to have migrated for different parts of the country and established a superior hierarchy over the remaining people... The migrant claim was a race for social status and an attempt to sever links from the Trans-Himalayan culture. In the process, the people living in their own area developed contempt for their culture and ethnic origin. It divided the population into various hierarchies, stratified social mobility... and hindered socio-economic progress" (*Ibid*: 4-6).

He goes on to report that under British rule, from the mid-nineteenth century, "The people of Uttarakhand started trickling to plains for education and in search of livelihood," (*Ibid*: 6), returning seasonally, or at retirement, or not at all, depending upon their experiences outside.

> "But the Garhwalis who attained some success or economic status took their families with them and started settling down in urban cities where they worked. Very few of them revealed their origin. A great number of such settlers dropped their [Garhwali] clan titles and adopted the common prevalent caste titles in plains" (*Ibid*: 6).

But in the past 30 years, another change has occurred, he notes. Many emigres have fared well in the cities of the plains.

> "They are not shy of their origin and are proud to call themselves Garhwalis. People who had dropped their (Garhwali) clan titles have reverted to their usage. But this attitude has not been of any help to the region of their origin. After serving in plains the majority of the hill people are not returning to their place of origin. A new concept in the migrant syndrome has become the status symbol today.
> This is the concept of being a Garhwali but settled outside Garhwal... Ninety-nine per cent of the Garhwalis who attain success or economic status settle down in urban towns. Consequently the high-land social system is crumbling. Its culture is disintegrating. The new generation of Garhwali settlers are devoid of their language, rituals and social customs" (*Ibid*: 7).

The "actual" Himalayan culture becomes an embarrasment to those who aspire to the definitions of respectability demanded by the Brahmanic plains culture, for they have adopted plains standards as their own, in a typical instance of adoption of an alien reference group (Merton, 1957: 225-386; cf. Newcomb, 1950: 225; Berreman, 1964). Plainsmen for them have become that type of reference group that (Turner, 1956: 328) has termed an "identification group", "the source of the individual's major perspectives and values," whether or not one is recognized by others, or even by oneself, as being a member of the group. The culture of one's membership group may be more than an embarassment when (and to the extent that) it deviates from that of the identification group, for it becomes an obstacle to mobility and the advantages that promises.

The response by those who take offence at the actualities of mountain society and culture is varied, but all to one end to disassociate themselves from these attributes and from any hint of legitimizing them. To do so, they must also disassociate their compatriots, their caste and their religion from the compromising attributes. Therefore, they simply deny that mountain people of their own ethnicity and region are less than paragons of Sanskritic, Brahmanic plains-style orthodoxy in culture, social organization and even language.

The vehemence of the disassociation from actual Himalayan culture, and the eagerness to identify with an idealized one, is indicative of the emotional charge associated with the issue. Certain tactics are recurrently employed by those faced with reports of customs, beliefs, practices, norms and social organizational features contrary to those envisioned as embodying the ideal Himalayan culture. Among them are the following:

(1) Reports contrary to the ideal are sometimes branded as false, and often as defamatory as well. They are attributed to gullibility, misinformation, misinterpretation or deliberate misrepresentation.

(2) If this is not plausible or palatable, then it is likely to be asserted that the reports were in fact derived from regions, peoples, or ethnic groups other than the one reported or other than the one with which the respondent identifies. That is, it is charged that the characteristics reported were infact observed not among Hindus, but among "tribals", or not among "caste" Hindus but among untouchables, or not among people of Uttarakhand (e.g. Garhwalis or Kumaonis) but among people of neighbouring and suspect regions (e.g. among people of Jaunsar Bawar, or Jaunpur, or Himachal Pradesh), or not among genuine (*pakka*) Garhwalis (e.g., if the speaker is from Pauri,

then the observations were not made there, not in the Alaknanda river drainage, not in what is often called "trans-Ganga" Garhwal), but instead they must have been made among doubtful (*kachcha*), peripheral Garhwalis (e.g., in the same case, the observations were perhaps made in Tehri, in the Bhagirathi river drainage, in what is often called "cis-Ganga" Garhwal). In short, the reported observations, if true, were made not among "us," but among "them".

(3) Resort to the categorical local designation "tribal" is a particularly widely and effectively employed defence in these circumstances, useful because it has little explicit, substantive meaning. It is simply a category used to distance, exempt or exclude any group at all which manifests "actual" Himalayan culture from those claiming to manifest the "ideal" version, or to exclude any socio-cultural feature regarded as backward, exotic, alien or simply different. It is condescending but it can be used to imply sympathetic concern for the well-being of the group in question by suggesting that its improvement be undertaken while at the same time some distance is being placed between that group and ones own.

The "tribal" designation thus separates and exempts exactly where the term "Pahari" unifies and includes. There is no limit on the application of "tribal" to exclude those who do not make one's own claims, or who do not believe or behave as one thinks they should. Complementarily, there is no escape from applicability of "Pahari" among those who live or hail from the mountains. Doubtless this explains why some mountain elites and expartriates resent and deny the designation "Pahari". It prevents them from disassociating themselves from the actual world of their country, cousins, neighbours. This is the source of the vehemence of their objection to the term: as a collective description of all Himalayan Hindus, it ignores the very distinctions upon which their claims to ethnic superiority are based—distinctions of sub-region, sub-culture and caste.

The techniques of exemption, exclusion and self-elevation described above, are limited almost entirely to some elites in defence of their claims to superior socio-cultural identity. Rural village folk continue to value their "actual" culture and social organization as they pursue their livelihoods according to the traditions and distinctions to which they are heir, as those traditions have been handed down and modified over the generations, serving them well in their unique and challenging environment. They honour their traditions and practise them with pride. They do so, that is, unless and until they are resocialized by outside residence and schooling, or they migrate leaving their land and livelihood so that they are unable to continue to survive according to the traditional ways (cf. Berreman, 1963; 1978; 1979; Dhasmana, 1982). Then do they accept to the definition of progress implemented by plainsmen and elites (cf. Bodley, 1982: 13-22).

Those who are forced or enticed into changing—into giving up their traditional ways to become part of "modern" plains-oriented society and of the dominant political and economic systems of the state and nation—often in that process give up not only their traditional ways of life and their means of livelihood, but sometimes their homeland too.

Thus there has emerged a split in the identity of the people of the Uttarakhand, corresponding to ideal and actual definitions of their socio-cultural situation. The ideal identity is that claimed and imposed by some alienated, urban and expatriate elites, reflecting their aspirations and interests. The actual identity of the mass of indigenous, rural people reflects their experience and interests as traditional mountain farmers, herdsmen and artisans. This split is manifest in the contrasting interests those exemplifying these disparate identities pursue. It is expressed vividly in contemporary political and socio-economic movements and actions in the region, which I think encapasulate and highlight regional socio-cultural dynamics. The remainder of this paper deals directly with these.

Uttarakhand: Electoral Politics

Electoral party politics are basically the politics of ethnic regionalism. The key to understanding them in relationship to the people of the region is the fact that are elite politics—the politics—of the advantaged, of the privileged and powerful. Grass-roots involvement is minimal. Yet the masses are inevitably involved, for they are the voters.

The parliamentary by-election in the Garhwal Lok Sabha Constituency in 1981-82 pitted the dominant, national party, the Congress (I), and its candidates, C. M. Negi, against the challenge of the newly formed Democratic Socialist Party under the leadership of its founder and candidate, H. N. Bahuguna, an apostate Congress (I) notable. With both candidates being native sons of the region, both promising regional benefits and development, the election focused nationwide attention in an unprecedented way on the region, its people and their interests.

Bahuguna brought about the Garhwal by-election by resigning from the Congress (I) and from his seat in parliament, after a distinguished, varied and stormy career as a party stalwart for over 40 years including the Chief Ministership of Uttar Pradesh (1973-75) and successive cabinet ministerships under Mrs. Gandhi and (during the 1977-79 interregnum in her rule) under two opposition Prime Ministers, after which he had rejoined the Congress (I) as the party's Secretary-General. His resignation, on May 19, 1980 coincided with his founding of the opposition Democratic Socialist Party. The surprising feature of his resignation was not that he changed his party affiliation, but that he resigned his seat in parliament in order to give voters a chance to vote him up or down under his new banner. The election for the vacant seat took place after more than a year, and after a vehement, controversy-ridden campaign involving personal electioneering by the Prime Minister Mrs. Gandhi, unprecedented in the remote mountain province where the Garhwal constituency (with the exception of Dehra Dun city) is located. The campaign was accompanied by some of the most flamboyant charges, counter-charges and propaganda on record. But before the ballots could be counted, the election was challenged by Bahuguna on a variety of charges. The Election Commissioner of India declared the election void. The ballots were destroyed without being counted, and a repoll was ordered. These events, and many of those of the next few months, have been carefully researched and reported by the fact-finding committee of Citizens for Democracy (Ahmed, et. al., 1981: cf. Verghese, 1982).

Thereafter the repoll was delayed and rescheduled for various reasons, until finally, it was scheduled for May 19, 1982.

—two years to the day after Bahuguna's resignation. It was scheduled so as to occur simultaneously with major state-wide Assembly elections in four other states.

The campaign was fought on several issues and at several levels. First, of course, it was fought on the issue of party loyalty and regional and national patriotism; Congress (I) announced that a vote for Congress (I) was a vote for the nation, and therefore for the region, and it opposed statehood for the Uttarakhand. Bahuguna, while he did not advocate Uttarakhand, did not oppose it, and he did take a mildly stated position advocating the interests of his constituency, implying that what is good for the region is therefore good for the nation. Second, the election was fought on the basis of personalities; Bahuguna, son of Garhwal versus C.M. Negi, also Garhwali. Third, the election was fought on the basis of promises and accomplishments toward the "development" of Garhwal and the region, Negi had been Minister for Hill Development in the state, but Bahuguna had founded that Ministry and created its unique budget, separate from that of the state at large, while he was Chief Minister of the state. The primary promise of Congress (I) was industrialization of the region. So far as accomplishments were concerned, however, Bahuguna outshone his opposition with his record of having founded not only the Hill Development Ministry, but the village water scheme, the Garhwal University, and other regional projects, as well as putting his constituency "on the map" politically.

It would seem that Bahuguna won primarily on a combination of personal charisma, long-standing identification with Garhwal, a record of attention to issues of concern in the region and a record of political power.

Although Bahuguna was elected, and his candidacy and its Congress (I) opposition dominated the media, it must not be overlooked that he and Negi were not alone in the election—campaign almost, but not quite alone.

The Uttarakhand Revolutionary Party (Uttarakhand Kranti Dal, or UKD), was a presence in the Garhwal by-election although it did not run a candidate. Its platform was much milder than the party's name might suggest, but it was of special interest because it advocated that Uttarakhand be constituted as a state within the Indian republic. Aside from that, it advocated that in this way the deficiencies, problems and evils of the region and its culture in the relation to neighbouring regions could be corrected, the outflow of its resources stopped, and the region developed quickly to bring it to a par with other regions. The party has little popular support beyond the small group of intellectuals and professionals who are its spokesmen and leaders, and it receives little public attention.

One Independent candidate did enter the fray, whose platform was nearly identical to that of the UKD, but he received only three tenths of one per cent of the vote. Three other Independents received comparable votes. In general, neither the campaign statements nor the votes received by Independent candidates were reported in the press. It was therefore virtually a two candidate election.

Finally, there was also a Communist Party (India) presence reported as well—more prominent in the news than the UKD or the Independents, but with no candidates espousing its position. Its principle manifestation was in the form of graffiti attributed to it, and the reported existence of some students, organized labour and labour organizers advocating its programms, especially around major construction sites in the region such as that of the Tehri Dam.

The appeal of the Communist Party in Garhwal is reported to be primarily to students and labourers. On the other hand, people associated with it have been represented activily among such rural, grass-roots activities as social work, organization of labour and co-operatives, and environmental preservation efforts. This is the only political party in Uttarakhand, that I know of, which explicitly participates in such activities.

In sum, party politics as exemplified in this election constitute an overwhelmingly elite process. Some of its candidates, proponents and active participants are elites (educated, plainswardly mobile, often exemplars of the "migrant syndrome"). Some of its methods are those which reach elites (pamphleteering, press conference, speech-making—all focused especially on literate urban-dwellers). Some of its programs are those which appeal to elites (industrialization, promotion of tourism, modernization, socio-cultural "reform" and alleviation of "backwardness"). Some of its claimed achievements are those which gratify and benefit elites (encouragement of research concerning literary and cultural achievements of the region's elites, radio programming in Sanskritized Garhwali language, promotion of entrepreneurship in the Uttarakhand, of industrialization, of cash-cropping, mining, timber extraction, hydro-electric development, tourism development, airports, heliports, aerial ropeways, etc.). All of these benefit massively the very few people of the region already involved in the national economic and political arena in a profitable way. Politics is by definition power brokerage, and party politics is power brokerage on a regional and national scale that goes far beyond the mountains.

The socio-cultural impact is equally oriented to the benefit of elites. Party politics seeks to identify the regional culture and society according to the elite, idealized view of those who participate in the benefit from those politics. It promotes a view of the mountain people and their culture as one of unique Hindu orthodoxy and purity; as Sanskritized, as Brahmanical and puritanical. The situation and its effects are remarkably similar to those described by Brass, for the Maithili movement in the plains of Bihar.

> "...The elite Maithil castes have been ineffective in transmitting their sense of regional identity to the mass of the Maithili-speaking people (because) their orientation toward the distinctiveness of Maithili culture has placed less emphasis on the separateness of Maithili culture from other cultures in India than on its distinctive purity and devotion to all-India culture, particularly to Sanskrit education and orthodox Hinduism. Second, and partly for this very reason, the culture gap between the elite... and the rest of the population of Mithila has been very sharp" (Brass, 1974: 114-115).

The elite political assertion amounts to an accusation and, indirectly a confession, of cultural inferiority, confirmed by the call for reform in many of the very elements of the culture and society of Uttarakhand which give it its distinctiveness and give its participants a sense of pride. It therefore engenders feeling of inferiority and vulnerability among those whom it seeks to change. It would betray their distinctive socio-cultural traditions and the unique interests which accompany them. From the point of view of the rural people of Uttarakhand, the political aim should be an instrument toward the socio-cultural goal of a viable life in their homeland. Evidently from the point of view of some of the politicized elites, the political aim of autonomy would be achieved through the instrument of socio-cultural assimilation, to be derived from the larger society. Here, "migrant syndrome" rears its head in yet another guise.

Party politics has not simply passively bypassed the people of Uttarakhand. On the contrary, the occasional emphasis on elite society and culture may be an actively divisive force among them. It may separate the educated urbanites from rural farm folk, the rich from the poor, the privileged and powerful from the deprived and vulnerable, the leaders and decision makers from the followers. The technique of calling traditional culture backward, or uncivilized, map further fractionate the populace, leading to mutual disparagement, competition and alienation. Animosities may arise as to who is Garhwali and who is not; whether a resident of the northwestern area called Jaunpur is a Garhwali or not; and what the relative status is as between being Garhwali or merely tribal; and what the relative status is as between being Garhwali or Kumaoni. This divisiveness may take on profound political significance when one recognizes the ethnographic fact that the Kumaoni, Garhwali, Jaunpuri, etc., are all terms for the indigenous people of various regions within Uttarakhand, representing a continuum of social, cultural, linguistic variation in a single tradition. If such invidious distinctions are employed socio-culturally or politically, then the people of the region have been set at odds with one another.

It is sometimes used to manipulate class differences (elite versus mass; urban versus rural, etc.), regional differences (as described above), ethnic differences (Hindu versus non-Hindu; Bhotiya versus Pahari), caste differences (Brahmin versus Rajput; high versus low caste), and almost any other potential cleavage one might be able to think of. Ethnic identity was perfectly openly employed as a political weapon in the Garhwal by-election, for example. More precisely, caste (*jati*) was so employed, and of course castes can be defined as birth-ascribed ethnic groups (Berreman, 1972; cf. Berreman, 1981). It is possible that the Congress (I) chose its candidate with an eye to capturing the vote of the caste constituency its leaders thought existed in the area, for Congress (I) candidate is a Rajput whose caste-fellows constitute 68 per cent of the rural population, whereas the DSP candidate is a Brahmin whose caste is only 8 per cent of the population (the remainder being artisan castes and untouchables). But the appeal to presumed caste loyalties profited the Congress (I) nothing for, as those familiar with the Pahari social organization know, Brahmanical aspirations to the contrary notwithstanding, Rajputs and Brahmins are closely allied castes in the region, who do not regard their interests as conflicting significantly and who join forces far more often than they compete. In any case, Bahuguna won by a percentage of about 55 per cent of the total of about 270,000 votes, and 60 per cent of the 210,000 rural votes (i.e., excluding the 60,000 urban votes of Dehra Dun, majority of which are non-Pahari votes).

That high caste, Brahmin/Rajput divisions were not successfully exploited by the Congress (I), does not mean that caste as such has not been significant in this or other elections in Uttarakhand. The low castes are largely excluded from effective participation in the political process there.

Although there were no low-caste candidates in the Garhwal by-election, there were, for the first time, quite a few in the local village council elections held at approximately the same time in various parts of Uttarakhand. In one area, for example, there were reportedly 25,000 "Harijans" ("untouchables") out of population of 75,000, yet not one was among the 65 village council presidents. On March 30, 1982, the *Himachal Times* reported that :

> "The most significant aspect of the (village council) elections...is that for the first time since the dawn of independent India, harijans have filed nomination papers for being elected as 'gram pradhan' (council president)" (Himachal Times, March 30, 1982).

But the outcome was predictable. The same newspaper followed up with a report that the region,

> "...has once again sustained its dubious reputation by defeating all eleven harijan candidates...A large number of harijan candidates were forced to withdraw from the husting..." (Himachal Times, July 9, 1982).

Thus, sometimes electoral politics becomes overwhelmingly the provenience of the high castes, some of whom, because they are the elites, are in a position to manipulate ethnic and class differences to their advantage and that of their patrons. The very existence of party politics sometimes and in some cases, magnifies and exacerbates the disparities in power and privilege. The existence of such cleavages as those discussed here, gives the some interested elites leverage for their continued domination of politics as well as of the economy and of society at large.

Chipko : Movement for Environmental Preservation

If party politics are remote from the experience and interests of village people in Uttarakhand, dealing as they do with the interests of those in distant seats of power, according to unfamiliar rules and in response to remote pressures, the environment is something which they understand well for it is close to their daily experience and interests. Accordingly, people in Uttarakhand have organized themselves to preserve their environment in a way that constitutes a significant contrast to the politics described above. The contrast is to be seen in almost every particular of the organization and impact of the political and environmental movements.

It is difficult to manipulate or mislead subsistence farmers and artisans about their environment. They are ready to protect and sustain it because its relationship to their well-being and survival is obvious to them. Power, which was a key issue in the discussion of electoral politics, is here an issue primarily in the immediate context of gaining and maintaining access to the environment and mitigating its misuse. On the village level it is also an issue in maintaining privileged access to it—a matter of class, and above all, of high castes versus low castes. This is an endemic and serious problem which must not be denied or overlooked, and one which is not unique to this region. It is universal in India and widespread in the world. But for the present I will attend to the problem of the Uttarakhand region wherein the people, whether land owners or service people, high caste or low, patrons or clients, all depend for survival on access to the environment and its resources, directly or indirectly, and therefore all depend on the continued viability of that environment.

Conflict between Uttarakhand villagers and the Government's Forest Department, including repeated violent incidents, goes back in history to the Trial Forest Settlement in Kumaon, 1821, by the British Government in India. This culminated 150 years later in *chipko*, a militant, non-violent movement to save the forests from the devastation wrought by timber merchants under contract with the Forest Department of the Government (cf. Banerjee, 1982).

The issue throughout this time-span has been exploitation of the forests by outside entrepreuners, with governmental sanction, at the expense of the mountain people whose livelihoods depend upon the forests—for the fuel, fodder, building materials and wood for implements which it provides—and upon the soil and water which the forests protect. Such exploitation has been accompanied by governmental denial or severe curtailment (or, in earlier days, heavy taxation) of utilization of the trees by the villagers who traditionally depended upon them. These were policies rationalized by the long-standing claim that deforestation results from misuse and over-use of the trees by indigenous agricultural villagers or transhumant herdsmen, or both (cf. Mathur, 1978; Dogra, 1980 : 40-42). In fact, villagers and herdsmen in the Himalayas usually do not cut trees for firewood (they usually use dead and fallen branches and trees), or for fodder (they lop branches instead). They fell trees only for their minimal needs in construction of houses (made mostly of stone) and manufacture of implements. Therefore, and especially in light of the devastation wrought by timber and charcoal contractors, to blame the local people for forest destruction is an egregious example of "blaming the victim."

The somewhat more moderate claim that, whatever the cause, forests are now too depleted to allow their further use by local people (Ashish, 1979), is a case of what might be called "further victimizing the victims." For the Government to have permitted non-Garhwalis to largely devastate the mountain environment and then, in a belated attempt to preserve it, to prohibit the indigenous people from using it at all, is quizzical at best—especially when some timber merchants, continue their destruction for profit.

In the early 1960's, local labour co-operatives and small-scale producers' cooperatives were established by villagers in each of the Himalayan districts of Uttarpradesh with the help of volunteer Gandhian social workers called "*Sarvodaya*" workers ("those building a just society"). Their aim was to bring to local people whatever benefits might be salvaged from the road building and other development activities. These co-operatives organized village people as labourers and craftsmen to secure contracts for labour and goods which at the time were going only to outsiders via private labour contractors and wholesalers.

In a series of incidents beginning in 1972, villagers and Sarvodaya workers confronted timber contractors, their employees, and the Government's forestry personnel who awarded and oversaw the contract-felling of trees, to stop the felling. The first, now famous, incident grew out of the fact that near Gopeshwar, headquarters of Chamoli district, the local co-operative had been denied permission to cut its usual small annual allotment of ash trees (12 in this instance) for use in construction and tools, whereupon it was discovered that the very same trees had been sold by the Government to a sporting goods manufacturer in the plains, to be made into cricket bats and tennis rackets. Resentful, and unsuccessful in arguing their case, the villagers and Sarvodaya workers hit upon the idea of employing Gandhian non-violent resistance by embracing the trees with their bodies to stop the axemen. This they did, to the amazement of their opponents, and so successfully that ultimately, in early 1973, the permit was cancelled and the trees saved. Thus the movement called after their technique *chipko* (in Hindi, "to stick"), and in English often called as "hug the trees" movement, was born.

The Sarvodaya worker in Gopeshwar who had organized the co-operatives there is generally credited with the idea of *chipko* and the founding of the movement. He is a native of Uttarakhand, a former ticket clerk in a transport company in Gopeshwar, named Chandi Prasad Bhatt. Another long-time Sarvodaya worker, in Tehri Garhwal and Uttarkashi, also credited with a role in founding the movement, also a native of the region, is Sunderlal Bahuguna (no relation to H. N. Bahuguna, the politician) (cf. Mishra and Tripathi, 1978: 1-2, 5, 7-12; Dogra, 1980 : 46-47, 50-51).

There followed some 12 major (and many minor) incidents of *chipko* confrontation with contractors over the next seven years, each adhering to the non-violent method and each impressively effective. The successes led to increasing national and international publicity and recognition. Whereas the first *chipko* action saved 12 trees, the third saved 2500 and subsequent ones saved even more. The *chipko* activists—villagers, Sarvodaya workers, high school and university students and teachers—prepared for their confrontations by going from village to village, informing the people and encouraging their support and participation. Workshop and training sessions were accompanied by rallies including informational and inspirational speeches, music, topical songs (cf. Shailani, 1979), and the like. In addition to confrontations in the forests, auctions of trees held in the towns and cities by the Forest Department were picketed and immobilized by the *chipko* activists. Symbolic marches throughout the Himalayas were undertaken to spread the word and gain support. Activists participated in research and publication on issues of forest, mineral, soil and water conservation. Reforestation and afforestation were undertaken as well, and in the past two years have overshadowed the confrontational activities, largely because the confrontations have been so successful that they are no longer as often necessary as formerly (for example, an interim ban on the felling of green trees above 1000 feet altitude above sea level in Garhwal and Kumaon, was declared in March, 1981, and was still in force at the time of this writing).

Articles in the popular press, and in journals of scholarship and advocacy, appeared widely in India and abroad, followed by several books and a BBC television special devoted to the movement (e.g., S. Bahuguna, 1980, 1981; Barthelemy, 1982; Bhatt, 1980; Berreman, 1979, 1980; Dogra, 1980; Gupta, 1977-83; Iliste and Goranson, 1980; Kunwar, 1982; Shepard, 1981). In 1981, Bahuguna received the Padma Shree award of the Government of India, and in 1982, C. P. Bhatt was awarded in Manila the Magsaysay award for public service to Asia.

At the same time, the movement itself gradually became divided and is now largely split between the followers of C. P. Bhatt and those of S. Bahuguna. Bhatt's group pursues a strategy of pragmatic conservationism with emphasis on ecologically sound use of forests by local people to meet local needs. Their activities include small-scale, local saw mills and other forest industries as part of the program of local cooperatives. S. Bahuguna's group has advocated a policy that no trees shall be cut, and therefore deplores Bhatt's saw mills. They have practised a more symbolic approach employing fasts, symbolic marches (called "*padyatras*", evoking the image of pilgrimages), and national and international publicity promoting environmental conservation. Whereas Bahuguna publishes often in newspapers, magazines, frequently in English, Bhatt writes relatively little about his work, and most of that in local publications in Hindi. While Bahuguna frequents the offices of newspapers and other media in India and is a participant in numerous international meetings and symposia, Bhatt is a relative stranger to both. Thus, the differences are those of style as well as of substance.

Bhatt and his followers view Government at the highest levels as primarily responsible for forest destruction who, beholden to timber merchants who profit from cutting, sell off the forests with promiscuous abandon and with devastating effect of the timber interests, thereby leaving the mountain people without their forests, their water and their soil. The Forest Department is in their view simply the instrument of these policies, and perhaps even a reluctant one. It is therefore a potential ally in conservation efforts.

S. Bahuguna and his followers tend to view the Forest Department as primarily responsible in the matter. It sells the trees to the contractors who then destroy the forests under their license. This view regards higher levels of Government as well-intentioned potential allies in conservation, but betrayed by the Forest Department.

The split can be seen in responses to the Forest Department's (and others') contention that villagers' use of the trees constitutes a major threat to the forests and must be stopped. Bhatt's followers dispute this claim in favour of careful use to the forests by villagers. Bahuguna's people accept it as part of their effort to ban all tree felling.

The division was also revealed in the response to S. Bahuguna's Padma Shree award. Congratulated by most of his followers, he was also criticized by some, who felt that he had compromised the *chipko* movement by accepting an honor from the Government, the very agency whose policies *chipko* is combating and attempting to change.

Every published account of *chipko* has used primarily one or the other, but not both, of these leaders as the primary source and model for the movement and its accomplishments. Only Dogra's book (1980) gives substantial weighting to both viewpoints, and even it clearly leans toward S. Bahuguna camp. The split threatens the movement seriously, delights its opponents, and saddens many of its supporters including perhaps especially the Himalaya Seva Sangh (Himalayan Service Society), with headquarters in Delhi and supporters throughout the world (cf. Gupta, 1977-83).

Yet, on the whole, the *chipko* movement is characterized by dedicated co-operative, energetic people of the Uttarakhand, determined to save the mountain environment for its people and the nation. Even those who disagree with one another, including C.P. Bhatt and S. Bahuguna themselves, share this determination and good will. The heart and soul of the movement are in its grass-roots participants, the villagers of the regions where it is active: mainly in the vicinity of Bhatt's headquarters in Gopeshwar and the surrounding area of Chamoli and Pauri Garhwal districts, and S. Bahuguna's headquarters in Tehri Garhwal and nearby Uttarkashi districts, with a significant presence also in the east in Almora and Naini Tal districts near the towns of those names, and with some impact throughout Uttarakhand and beyond.

By its very nature as a grass-roots people's movement. *chipko* endorses and enhances the distinctive culture and society of the mountain people and asserts its legitimacy by advocating and working toward the fulfilment of their requirements in order to survive and prosper in their accustomed environment, in the traditional ways. It, thus, reinforces rather than reforms the Pahari culture and society. Where it does call for reform, it is for reform of the negative consequences of infringements upon that culture rather than of its indigenous features. For example, excessive consumption of liquor is deplored by the movement, but this is recognized to be a response to—an escape from—economic hardship, environmental desolation and socio-cultural disruption occasioned by exploitation. These are defined as the causes to be remedied in order to restore the viability of the culture and economy of the region and thereby combat the appeal of escape through alcohol. This contrasts fundamentally with the political parties' position that alcohol consumption is a reprehensible feature (among many others) of the Pahari culture —that it constitutes a causal factor in the region's problems and must therefore be banished at once.

The *chipko* movement thus engenders pride in the region and its culture—pride in its distinctiveness, in the actualities of the Himalayan lifeways—and simultaneously astute analyses and genuine responsiveness to its needs and the threats that confront it. This is in stark contrast tó some party politicians who advocate assimilation to alien ways in pursuit of the unrealistic ideal version of the Himalayan culture.

An impressive feature of the grass-roots support which *chipko* has achieved is its integrative social impact in Uttarakhand. It cuts across social and cultural cleavages which might have been expected to divide it and which some politicians have attempted to capitalize upon. It unites people on the basis of their shared interests who differ by sex, age, religion, ethnicity, caste, class and region. This is an accomplishment rare indeed in post-Gandhian India.

Chipko has become famous, for example, as a movement wherein women have been prominent as leaders and participants (not that men are not involved too—but women are involved to an extent that is unusual, impressive and heartening). Sevreal of the heroes of the movement are women. In fact, it has been described as a women's movement by some commentators (cf. V. Bahuguna, 1975; Bhatt and Kunwar, 1982; Jain, 1983; Mishra and Tripathi, 1978). How has this come about? A combination of factors is no doubt responsible, prominent among them these: (1) Women have unusually high status throughout the Pahari society, with unusual freedom of action and movement which accompanies their heavy contribution to the agricultural economy—a contribution at least as great as that of men. (2) Because many men are away from their families and villages, seeking employment in the plains (a response to the decimation of the hills and the consequent need for supplementary or alternative sources of income), women—along with the old, the children and the infirm—are left to care for the villages. They are thus accustomed to responsibility and leadership and to the requirements for community survival in their environment. (3) Even when men are present, it is women who do most of the work which entails direct, daily use of the forests and who, therefore, feel most immediately and acutely the impact of its devastation. Therefore, women are alert to the changes, are inconvenienced and jeopardized by them, and respond readily to the need to protect against them.

Similarly, and for similar reasons, young and old are more heavily involved in *chipko* than might be expected. They share in the women's work as well as the men's, and they have shared in the efforts to protect the environment through militant action. Moreover, students in high schools and universities, including urban as well as village youth, and including students from plains as well as Uttarakhand, have been among the most active *chipko* workers, thus bridging an often difficult gap of age, class, region and social experience as they join their elders and other villagers in a common cause.

But the integrative nature of the *chipko* involvement goes further still. It also cuts across ancient and powerful ethnic barriers. The Bhotias and the Paharis occupy different territories determined primarily by altitude and environment, and therefore usually have little to do with one another even when they are not far apart. But in some of the *chipko* confrontations, they have joined forces to protect their common forests, and throughout Uttarakhand they have recurrently joined in support of the *chipko* cause. Perhaps the most famous of all *chipko* actions was that in the Reni Forest of Chamoli district in 1974, when Gauri Devi, Bhotia woman, became the most celebrated of *chipko's* heroes by saving 2500 trees that had been sold on contract from the local forest. The village and Sarvodaya men had been lured away on plausible pretexts by the contractors and Forest officials after long and frustrating negotiations on the fate of the trees had been unsuccessful. During their absence, Gauri Devi saw the contractor's axemen skirting the village in hope of avoiding detection en route to cutting the trees. She promptly mobilized the village women, who courageously confronted them and succeeded in completely stopping them, and even converting some to the *chipko* cause—an event immortalized in tales and songs of the movement (Mishra and Tripathi, 1978: 26-30; Dogra, 1980: 48-49).

Chipko has integrated regions within Uttarakhand as well as ethnic groups, for it has spread from easternmost to westernmost Uttarakhand, into areas whose people knew little of one another beyond casual (and often negative) stereotypes before its coming with its co-operative activities. *Chipko* workers and village and student participants have trekked from one end of the Indian Himalayas to the other as participants in S. Bahuguna's *chipko* pilgrimages (*padyatras*). People of the various regions of Uttarakhand have thus met one another on equal footing, working together in the common cause of the Himalayan conservation and survival.

Apparently low castes have been relatively little involved in *chipko*. But even they have not been without involvement, for their participation has been documented in some instances as they have recognized the importance of the forests to their well-being as the Himalayan villagers, despite the inequities and inequities of caste in the region.

The point, here, is that *chipko* is a grass-roots movement responding to the needs of the 99 per cent of the population of Uttarakhand who live in villages, drawing them together across cleavages that in social, political, religious and economic contexts have heretofore divided them, and which some politicians have attempted to exacerbate and employ in their own pursuit of power.

Uttarakhand and Chipko: A Contrast

An intriguing and fateful fact is associated with *chipko* in relation to the Uttarakhand movement and in relation to regional party politics wherein the issue of whether or not Uttarakhand, is disputed. Namely, that *chipko* despite its popularity, its wide dispersion, and its prominence in the region of Uttarakhand, did not figure in the Garhwal by-election, nor does it in the political platforms and statements of parties active in the region—not in that of the UKD whose platform is statehood for Uttarakhand; not in that of the Congress (I) which firmly opposes such statehood; not in that of the DSP candidate who is self-proclaimed champion of the people and interests of the Himalayan hills. It was not even mentioned in the maneuvering, posturing, organizing, agonizing, courting or accusing that were rife in the politics of the election. I have never seen it mentioned in any statement of any sort promulgated by any party save some mention in the tiny, sporadic voice of the Communist spokesmen.

Why?

In part, perhaps, because *chipko* is not political in the conventional sense. It is a village, grass-roots, non-elite movement which appeals to people who live close to the soil, the forests and the water of the Himalayas and who know them well because they wrest their living directly from them—they know well what threatens them, what could preserve them, and how crucial they are to human well-being. If one doubts that this is the case, evidence can be cited in the form of two quotations aptly juxtaposed by Dogra (1980:1). He first quotes a senior Forestry Department official in Almora, in 1977: "What do these villagers know about ecology? What do they know of forestry? They only know how to destroy trees."

He follows this with a quotation from Gauri Devi, hero of Reni village, speaking in remonstrance to the labourers come to fell the forest upon which her people depend: "Brother, this forest is our home. From it we satisfy so many of our needs. Do not axe it. If you do, landslides, will ruin our homes and fields".

So, villagers do recognize their interests where their environment and livelihood are concerned. Urban sophisticates, emigres, expatriates and outsiders are unlikely to see the relationship so clearly, if at all.

This may account in part for their silence on *chipko*.

But there is more to it than that. The other reason for their silence, I think, is that *chipko* is too hot to handle politically. It is too important to confront directly. It is too obvious in its intent and too effective in its actions to be subject to the sly words and ambiguous doublespeak.

It can be put very simply: *Chipko* is too popular with the voters of Uttarakhand—too vital to their interests—for the politicians to risk criticizing or opposing it. The voters' support for it is too unified, too broad based, too deep seated, to enable politicians to play off one element of Uttarakhand against another on the issue.

Then why do the politicians not support it?

Because *chipko* is too threatening to the moneyed interest. Therefore, *chipko* catches politicians and administrators on the horns of a dilemma: the dilemma posed by the fact that the voters favour it and the moneyed interests oppose it. Some of the politicians need both, fear both, will offend neither. They simply avoid mention of *chipko* altogether.

So, *chipko* goes it alone, politically non-aligned and self-determined. Probably that is in its best interests, for to be politicized would be to be beholden to outside interests and this would likely be destructive of the movement and its freedom of action. Politics is a power game, and power corrupts; surely politics corrupts. *Chipko* has remained largely uncorrupted and uncorruptable despite its internal disagreements. It has remained responsive to the needs of the people of Uttarakhand and immune to the demands of profiteers, politicians and administrators. That, I believe, is the hope that *chipko* holds for the people of Uttarakhand and as a model for the people of India. It is not a new model. Mahatma Gandhi held up such a model in the Independence movement. Vinoba Bhave tried to carry it on in the "land gift" movement. Now *chipko* seems to be the most viable manifestation in India of the Gandhian tradition—of the model of a grass-roots, people-oriented movement consistent with the small-scale development, appropriate technology, labour intensive, environmentally conservationist, co-operative, anti-colonial, egalitarian secular, locally self-sufficient and self-determinant kind of ideology with which the origin of the Indian republic is identified.

The expression of regional ethnicity and pursuit of regional interests found in the *chipko* movement is not a threat to national unity; quite the contrary, it is the best hope for it. As Zaman warns:

> "Any national political system which ignores the realities of ethnicity or denies wider participation for all ethnic groups may result in the subordination of weaker groups by more powerful ones and thus may generate ethnic disintegration and eventual national fragmentation" (Zaman, 1982:75).

"In the end," Erik Eckholm says, "the greatest challenge of all may be convincing the people of the plains that the future of the mountains cannot be isolated from their own" (Eckholm, 1976:100). This is a challenge that must be met in India.

REFERENCES CITED

Ahmed, Bashiruddin, Ajit Bhattacharjee, and B.G. Verghese. 1981. *The Garhwal By-election: Report of a Fact-Finding Committee.* New Delhi: Citizens for Democracy.

Ashish, Madhava. 1979. Agricultural Economy of Kumaon Hills: Threat of Ecological Disaster. *Economic and Political Weekly.* (June 23, 1979) 14:1058-1064.

Bahuguna, Sunderlal. 1980 and 1981. *Chipko: A Novel Movement for Establishment of Cordial Relationship Between Man and Nature.* (2 vols.) Silyara, Tehri Garhwal: Chipko Information Centre.

Bahuguna, Sunderlal. 1982. Let the Himalayan Forests Live *Science Today.* (March 1982): 41-46.

Bahuguna, Vimla. 1975. Contribution of Women to Chipko Movement. *Indian Farming*. 25:69-71.

Banerjee, Sumanta. 1982. A Critique of the Forest Policy. *Philosophy and Social Action*. 8 (2): 41-72.

Barthelemy, Guy. 1982. *Chipko: Sauver les Forets de l'Himalaya*. Paris: Editions L'Harmattan.

Berreman, Gerald D. 1960. Cultural Variability and Drift in the Himalayan Hills. *American Anthropologist*. 62: 774-794.

Berreman, Gerald D. 1963. *Hindus of the Himalayas*. Berkeley: University of California Press. (2nd ed., 1972).

Berreman, Gerald D. 1964. Aleut Reference Group Alienation, Mobility, and Acculturation. *American Anthropologist*. 66: 231-250.

Berreman, Gerald D. 1972. Race, Caste, and Other Invidious Distinctions in Social Stratification. *Race*. 13:385-414.

Berreman, Gerald D. 1978. Ecology, Demography and Domestic Strategies in the Western Himalayas. *Journal of Anthropological Research*. 34: 326-368.

Berreman, Gerald D. 1979. *Himachal: Science, People and "Progress."* (IWGIA Document 36) Copenhagen: International Work Group on Indigenous Affairs.

Berreman, Gerald D. 1980. The "Chipko" Movement in the Indian Himalayas. *Nepal Studies Association Bulletin*. No. 21: 21-23.

Berreman, Gerald D. 1982. The U.P. Himalaya: Culture, Cultures and Regionalism. In *The Himalaya: Nature, Man and Culture* (eds) O.P. Singh, R.K. Pandey *et al.* New Delhi: Rajesh Publications. pp. 227-265.

Berreman, Gerald D. 1984. *Chipko*: An Indigenous Movement to Save the Himalayan Environment. *The Global Reporter* (Boston: Anthropology Resource Centre) No. 4 (February) In Press.

Bharati, Agehananda. 1978. Actual and Ideal Himalayas: Hindu Views of the Mountains. In *Himalayan Anthropology: the Indo-Tibetan Interface*. (ed.) James F. Fisher. The Hague: Mouton. pp. 77-82.

Bhatt, Chandi Prasad. 1980. *Eco-System of the Central Himalayas and Chipko Development*. Gopeshwar, Chamoli: Dasholi Gram Swarajya Sangh.

Bhatt, Chandi Prasad and S.S. Kunwar. 1982. Hill women and their Involvement in Forestry. In *Hugging the Himalayas: The Chipko Experience*. (ed) S.S. Kunwar. Gopeshwar, Chamoli: Dasholi Gram Swarajya Mandal. pp. 84-89.

Bodley, John H. 1982. *Victims of Progress*. Palo Alto: Mayfield. (1st ed., 1975).

Brass, Paul R. 1974. *Language, Religion and Politics in North India*. London: Cambridge University Press.

Dhasmana, M.M. 1982. Transformations and Development in Uttarakhand. Unpubl. paper presented at the Seminar on Uttarakhand: Socio-Economic, Cultural and Ecological Environment. Srinagar, Garhwal: Garhwal University. March 25-27, 1982.

Dogra, Bharat. 1980. *Forests and People: The Efforts in Western Himalayas to Re-Establish a Long-Lost Relationship*. Rishikesh: Himalayan Darshan Prakashan Samiti.

Eckholm, Erik P. 1976. *Losing Ground: Environmental Stress and World Food Prospects*. New York: W.W. Norton.

Evans-Pritchard, *The Nuer*. 1978. Oxford: Clarendon Press.

Fonia, K.S. 1977. *Uttarakhand, Garhwal Himalayas*. Dehra Dun: Asian Journals.

Grierson, George A. 1916. *Linguistic Survey of India*. (Vol. 9, part 4) Calcutta: Superintendent of Government Printing.

Gupta, Krishna Murti (editor). 1977-83. *Himalaya: Man and Nature*. (A journal "devoted to the cause of people, forests and environment"). New Delhi: Himalaya Seva Sangh. (Subsequent vols. forthcoming).

Himachal Times (Dehru Dun). March 20, 1982. "No Harijan Gram Pradhan for 25,000 Kolta."

Himachal Times March 30, 1982. "Panchayat Elections: Harijan Candidates Evinced."

Himachal Times July 9, 1982. "All Kolta Tribals 'Defeated' In Gram Sabha Elections."

Iliste, Ivo and Birgitta Goransan. 1980. Crisis in the Himalayas, *Inside-Outside* (India) March 1980. Pp. 37-51.

Indian Express (Delhi). August 30, 1981. "Time Up For Tehri."

Jain, Shobhita. 1983. "Women and People's Ecological Movement: A Case Study of Women's Role in Chipko Movement in the Garhwal Region of Uttar Pradesh, India."

Unpublished paper delivered at the XI International Congress of Anthropological and Ethnological Sciences. Vancouver, British Columbia (Canada). August 23, 1983.

Kunwar, Shishupal Singh (ed.), 1982. *Hugging the Himalayas: The Chipko Experience.* Gopeshwar, Chamoli: Dasholi Gram Swarajya Mandal.

Mathur, H.N. 1978. Chipko Needs a New Direction. *Himalaya: Man and Nature.* 2 (5): 1-7.

Merton, Robert K. 1957. *Social Theory and Social Structure.* Glencoe: The Free Press.

Mishra, Anupam. 1978. *Chipko Andolan.* New Delhi: Gandhi Museum. (In Hindi).

Mishra, Anupam and S. Tripathi. 1978. *Chipko Movement: Uttarakhand Women's Bid to Save Forest Wealth.* New Delhi: People's Action for Peace and Justice.

Newcomb, Theodore M. 1950. *Social Psychology.* New York: The Dryden Press.

Parvatiya Navjeevan Andolan. 1977. *Save Himalaya.* Silyara, Tehri Garhwal: Parvatiya Navjeevan Mandal (Chipko Andolan).

Parvatiya Navjeevan Andolan. 1982. *The Chipko March.* Silyara, Tehri Garhwal: Parvatiya Navjeevan Mandal (Chipko Andolan).

Rao, M.S.A. 1980. "Some Aspects of Sociology of Migration: A Working Paper" Unpubl. paper presented to the Sub-Panel on Migration, 15th All India Sociological Conference. Meerut, U.P. April 2, 1980.

Rieger, Hans C. 1980. Whose Himalaya: A Study in Geopiety. In *Studies in Himalayan Ecology and Development Strategies* (ed) Tejvir Singh. New Delhi: The English Book Store pp. 1-9.

Shailani, G. 1979. *Chipko Songs.* Silyari, Tehri Garhwal: Parvatiya Navjeevan Mandal. (In Hindi).

Shepard, Mark. 1981. Chipko: North India's Tree Huggers. *The Co-Evolution Quarterly.* (Fall, 1981): 62-70.

Turner, Ralph. 1956. Role-taking, Role Standpoint, and Reference-group Behaviour. *American Journal of Sociology.* 61: 316-328.

Verghese, B.G. 1982. The Will of the People. *Express Magazine* (*Indian Express*) Delhi. Jan. 3, 1982: Pp. 1 and 6.

Verghese, Vijay. 1982. Dam that Generates Controversy. *The Times of India.* March 5, 1982.

Zaman, M.Q. 1982. Crisis in Chittagong Hill Tracts: Ethnicity and Integration. *Economic and Political Weekly.* (January 16, 1982) 17: 75-80.

CHAPTER XIX

SOCIOLOGY OF CHIPKO

A STUDY OF THE BADYARGARH ANDOLAN, 1979

RAMACHANDRA GUHA

Introduction

The ecological crisis caused by deforestation in the Garhwal Himalayas has been much discussed in recent years (Gupta, 1980; Ashish, 1979: 1058-1064). This was recognized by the newly created Department of Environment as the most pressing ecological problem facing the country (Indian Express, 7-5-1981). Simultaneously, the people movement against deforestation, the *chipko andolan,* has been widely reported in the national press (see, *inter alia,* India Today 1982: Bahuguna 1981). *Chipko* has gripped the public imagination on account of its spectacular technique and the initiative displayed by the women who form the backbone of the movement.

Indeed, the experience of Garhwal has been replicated elsewhere—*albeit* with variations—most notably in the tribal forest areas of peninsular India. Here, too, commercial exploitation of forests has been juxtaposed with growing militancy on the part of the local population adversely affected by state forestry practices. Thus, in recent years, there has been a spate of movements in tribal areas centred around the question of state intervention in the forests (see for a general review, PUDR 1982). These movements have initiated a re-examination of the forest policies followed by successive Governments (Gadgil *et al* 1982), while the *chipko andolan* has contributed significantly to the ongoing debate on the ecological problems facing the less developed countries. Movements like *chipko* have led to a heightened awareness of these problems, some distinctive and other a result of replicating western patterns of development (Guha, 1982a; Guha, 1982b: 2093-2098).

While journalistic literature on *chipko* abounds, there has not been any systematic study of the movement from a historical and sociological point of view. In this article, we shall analyse one particular *chipko* agitation that occurred in the Badyargarh Patti of Tehri Garhwal district in the winter of 1978-79, based largely on field work conducted in early 1983. Our basic endeavour will be to conduct an internal analysis of the movement, i.e. its patterns of mobilization and type of organization, the participation of different social groups, its ideology and methods, and the relationship between the leadership and the rank and file. This analysis would bring out the fundamental characteristics of *chipko*, as the movement is conceived by its participants, and the concommitant implications for social change.

Forestry in Tehri Garhwal

It is clear from the writings of early British administrators that under the native rulers the villagers were free to treat the forests as their own (Pauw, 1896). India's forests acquired strategic importance for the colonial rulers after the period of railway expansion from 1860 onwards (Stebbing, 1925), which was partly made possible through exploitation of the deodar forests of Tehri Garhwal (Hearle, 1888). Tracts of valuable forests were leased to the British by the Raja, divested of any existing right of user of part of the surrounding villages, and worked from 1865 to 1925. The enormous value of the forests being evidenced by the average annual profit of over Rs. 1.6 lakhs in the period 1910-25, the Raja did not renew the lease in 1925 and henceforth worked the forests, with professional help from the colonial Forest Department (FD), exclusively for his own profit.

The greatly expanded nature of industrialization since 1947 has led to an increased cut from the country's forests to feed the growing forest industries sector. This is particularly true of the Himalayan coniferous forests, used in bulk for railway sleepers, pulp and paper, and resin and turpentine manufacture. To facilitate increased exploitation, the building of roads into hitherto inaccessible forests became necessary. In the period 1948-78, the out-turn of the important conifers in the eight hill districts of Uttar Pradesh (UP)—deodar, fir, spruce, and the blue and *chir* pines increased from 72000 to 418000 cubic metres. Resin out-turn, after reaching a peak of 4.18 lakh quintals in 1974-75, averaged 1.3 lakh quintals in the year 1978-79, when the UP Forest Department extracted a net profit of Rs. 108 million from the hill forests alone (all figures from UP FD n.d.)

Discontent among the hill people on the issue of curtailment of forest rights has been evident from the initial stages of commercial forestry (Nelson, 1916). In Tehri Garhwal there have been sporadic *dhandaks* (Protest movements) since the early years of this century. In 1906, the Conservator of Forests was surrounded and his forehead was branded with a cattle iron (Panwar, 1982). In the following years, there occurred forest movements in 1916 and 1921, the latter one engulfing areas of British Garhwal and Tehri Garhwal (Brahmawar, 1932; Mobbs, 1926). And in May 1930, peasants protesting forest settlement operations in the Rawain Pargana of Tehri Garhwal were fired upon in an incident that soon passed into legend (Dabral, n.d.: 310 ff).

Badyargarh: The Setting

The *patti* of Badyargarh[1] is situated between the Bhagirathi and the Alaknanda rivers, about 130 km northeast of Rishikesh (by road). The social structure of this village, in conformity with the rest of Garhwal, is built around relatively homogenous and cohesive village communities. The strength of the Garhwal village community (single caste villages are not uncommon) has traditionally fostered a strong sense of clanship amongst its members, who are mostly peasant proprietors with a vested interest in land. There are no sharp inequalities in land ownership or ritual status within this body of cultivating peasants, though there does exist a small class of so-called "untouchables" performing artisanal and other functions (including, occasionally, bonded labour). In Tehri Garhwal the village panchayats have traditionally dealt with disputes, social matters, arrangements for festivities etc. with every adult members having a voice in its affairs (Joshi, 1929:35, 194-199).

For the past few decades, however, grain production in the hills has been inadequate to sustain the population. It is on the remittances sent by the male migrants who have obtained work in the plains, that the resident population manages to survive. The hills have been aptly characterized as 'money order economy'. The women labour hard in adverse conditions to perform the household and agricultural tasks.

Badyargarh is a relatively prosperous *patti*, containing a large number of retired and serving army personal. The opportunities offered to individuals by commercialization, education, Government employment, etc. has definitely contributed to the erosion of the community co-operative spirit. The possibility of individual social mobility that the outside world offers, is reflected in the village by the return of successful individuals to build cement structures. Although the community spirit is still present (as shown by *chipko*), there is, simultaneously, a slowly growing differentiation within the village due to the impact of commercialization. There is, too, a sense of disruptions of the traditional social fabric that the opening out of Garhwal has brought, as well as anger at the comparative underdevelopment of the hills.

Commercial forestry in the region started only around 1965 with the building of a motor road into Badyargarh. In the following years, the extraction of resin and turpentine was commenced, alongside the felling of *chir* trees. In 1979 the Van Nigam (forest cooperation)[2] gave out a big contract for the felling of *chir* pine in the Badyargarh area. The felling, which went on for several months, was according to villagers, very destructive, with young regeneration being removed apart from the logged trees. Several dozen trucks came and went daily taking away all the wood, including branches. As people later reminished, the contractor replied to early signs of protest by remarking that he would not leave any part of the tree behin ("Hum Ped Ka Koi hissa nahin choddenge").

The Andolan

Following upon this activity and just prior to the proposed logging in the Malgaddi forest, Sarvodaya workers, trusted associates of the *chipko* leader Sunderlal Bahuguna, came to Badyargarh to enquire into the people's grievances These workers, Dhum Singh Negi, Kunwar Prasun, Pratap Shikhor, and Vijay Jardari, among others, went from village to village informing people of the proposed felling and its harmful ecological consequences. At the same time, Bahuguna's wife, Vimla, and other ladies mobilized the village women on the issue.

The *andolan* started on 25-12-78, but acquired momentum only after Bahuguna went on a hunger fast from 9-1-79. Conducted in a disused shepherd's hut in the forest, and in the midst of winter, the fast was a rallying point for the people of the surrounding villages. Thus, over three thousand men, women and children participated, "one for every *chir* tree in the forest". An attempt at cutting by night was foiled by villagers taking night duty by turns. Classic non-cooperation tactics were adopted, there being no question of any violence. ("himsa ka koi saval nahin tha"). Bahuguna was carried away by the police on the night of 22nd January, and interned in Tehri jail, where he continued his fast. Meanwhile, a reading of the Bhagavada Geeta was started on the 26. Meeting with the determined resistance of the villagers even after the removal of their leaders from the scene, the contractor and FD officials had to admit defeat and abandon felling.

Participation

A feature of the *andolan* was the active participation of all sound groups. This was explained by the evident fact that all were equally affected by deforestation. The Bajgis, a caste of musicians, were solicited to mobilize villagers through their *dholaks* (drum), women played a prominent part, as did Government servents and defence personnel, though their support could only be covert.

Children, too, joined in a movement which recreated the atmosphere of joyous celebration in a fight against injustice. When police camped in Dhadi Ghandiyal High School, children went on strike in protest at the invasion of a "temple of knowledge" (*vidya mandir*). While the strike itself lasted for 4 days, all through the *andolan*, students skipped school with the connivance of the teachers. As the Principal recounted, he was placed in an awkward position, with the police harassing him, on the one hand, and on the other villagers imploring him to let his wards come to the forest. The school teacher, highly respected in Garhwal, symbolized in his person the conflict between the Government and the people. As a figure of authority, the State expected him to control people, while the people wanted sanction for their acts by that very same authority.

Moral Content of Chipko

Two further incidents that occurred after the successful completion of the *andolan* may serve to illustrate the strong moral content of *chipko*, When the contractor abandoned his labourers, locals fed them from village ration shops and petitioned officials to alleviate their plight. Only with the arrival of the Labour Commissioner could the grievances be redressed and the labourers sent home to Himachal.

The second incident relates to the wood fallen prior to *chipko* and which was not allowed to be carried away for conversion to sleepers. The Badyargarh Van Suraksha Samiti (BVSS) resolved to release the wood only after the local people their had fulfilled needs in the following manner:

The first claim would be exercised by those individuals and village who had not been granted rights on timber, following which the requirements of the other inhabitants of Badyargarh and its neighbouring *pattis* would be met on payment of nominal rates. It was proposed that the income so generated would be used to regenerate the deforested areas of Badyargarh. Despite stern official warnings the BVSS stuck to their stand (BVSS n.d.).

Chipko and Popular Consciousness

In this section we shall highlight some of the important characteristics of *chipko*, as it relates to popular perceptions.

Link between forest and man

During fieldwork, I found that almost all those interviewed

were aware of the importance of forest cover is regulating soil and water regimes. *Chipko* has contributed to a heightened awareness—the interesting question is the extent to which this ecological consciousness predates *chipko*. This, in Badyar village, no grass cutting has traditionally been allowed on the steep hill overlooking the settlement. The cliff has a thick crop of grass and shrubs, in the absence of which boulders would come tumbling down the hill during the monsoon-hence the ban. As we have argued elsewhere, (Guha, 1983:61-64) the link between man and forest that existed before the inception of commercial forestry has been eroded by the loss of community control.[3] In this context, *chipko* aims at halting the growing alienation of man from nature, an alienation with potentially damaging consequences.[4]

Chipko and Community Solidarity

An ecological consciousness, however attenuated, and the manifold benefits of forest cover to the hill economy (and ecology) can explain *chipko's* success in mobilizing all sections of the hill society. In response to criticism that the *andolan* depended largely on Bahuguna's appeal, the BVSS pointed out that if the movement did not enjoy popular support, it would have terminated with Sunderlal's arrest and removal (BVSS, n.d.). As villagers see it, efforts to put out forest fires (which they are obliged to do under the settlement) are made in the belief that their property was being destroyed. Thus, when the Government started indiscriminate feeling ("andhadhund katai") it was keenly resented.[5]

Attitude towards officials

The lack of fulfilment of basic needs of education, health, and employment found the accumulated grievances being crystalized in *chipko*. One BVSS activist put it,

> "Humme thoda sa anaaz mila, jab usse bhi
> nahin paka sake, to andolan karna pada."[6]

The implacable hostility towards state officials, particularly those belonging to the Forest Department, can be read as a symbol of such disillusionment. *Chipko* participants expressed delight in recalling the impotence of high officials (*ucchadhikari*) in the face of the *andolan*. Senior officials of the civil and forest administration, as well as the police, arrived but were powerless to resume felling operations ("Ucchadhikari pahunch gaye, lekin kuch nahi kar paye").

Women and Chipko

In the hills, all works devolve around the women, who in addition to household chores and rearing the children, have to perform physically strenuous tasks of cultivation and food and fodder collection. The drudgery of their lives and long hours of toil inhibit the recreation of a healthy social life (Sarala Devi, 1980). It is evident that today, in the absence of the adult male, the woman has to perform all the tasks. Some analysts see a direct link between the two. According to Sunderlal Bahuguna: "Due to washing away of fertile soil, the men folk were compelled to leave their families and wander in search of employment, thus making the women bear all the responsibilities, collecting fodder, firewood and carrying water, which form the main chores besides farming (1980a:5, cf. also Dogra, 1980).

However, the subjugation of the women and her having to perform hard tasks is culturally specific to the hill family and not merely a result of changed ecological or economic conditions. In his pioneering work, S.D. Pant (1935) shows how the hill woman has to perform every kind of agricultural job except the ploughing and harrowing. Thus her tasks include sowing, weeding, transplanting, reaping, pounding and threshing, manuring, fetching water, fuel and grass, grinding and cooking, as well as looking after the children. The menfolk, meanwhile, have reserved for themselves the less onerous and fatiguing tasks.[7] This unnatural division of labour has given rise to various social evils, (cf also Berreman, 1963).

Pant's account is clearly a description of a situation where the man of the house is present in the village (see also Nelson 1916: Appendix). According to him, 'at least 75% of the suicides are among the women; they destroy themselves out of disgust with their hard lot'. (1935:191).

An interesting conversation at a teashop in Badyar village

brought out the conflicts inherent in such a situation. One retired armyman was strongly of opinion that women's participation in *chipko* was a consequence of their inferior position in hill society. Observing the men gathered around the shop, he asked rhetorically, "we men are sitting and drinking tea, but can we see any woman here? Why not?" A look at the far hill side, where women were gathering firewood, provided the answer: "They are not here for they have work to do". This feminist stand brought forth jeers from fellow villagers, who later advised me not to take him seriously.[8] Nevertheless, the local women's leader, Sulochana Devi, was emphatic that the success of *chipko* depended on the women. *Chipko*, she argued, was only the first step—women needed to be educated and dowry banned in order that others did not fritter away women's wealth ("ladkiyon ka dhan na khoya jaye"). It may not be farfetched to see woman's participation in *chipko*, at least in part, as an expression of this historical subjugation at the hands of their own menfolk.

The Idiom of Protest

Protest in Tehri Garhwal has characteristically been expressed in a particular social idiom. In consonance with peasant movements elsewhere (Chatterjee, 1982), the immediate target of attack has been the minor Government functionaties who are perceived as the exploiters by virtue of their direct contact with village life. In the past, the attack on officials was accompanied by a call to the king to restore harmony by replacing corrupt and wicked officials. With the relationship between the peasantry and the king being defined in terms of mutual rights and obligations that have to be fulfilled (*dharma*) the transgression of this code—by the levying of extra taxes, for example, that breach the peasant's "subsistence ethic" (Scott, 1976)—have led to sporadic *dhandas*. Such *dhandas* have not sought to upturn the state machinery—rather, they have called upon the Raja of Tehri Garhwal to dispense justice, invoking his quasidivine status as "Bolanda Badrinath" (speaking god). Non-co-operation as a form of protest, and the notion of justice and a just Government (*sarkar*) that *dhandas* were strongly imbued with, are of course internal to the Hindu tradition (Dharampal, 1971: Introduction).

Chipko and protest in Badyargarh

Badyargarh was the scene of a wide ranging peasant movements in 1948 that culminated in the merger of Tehri Garhwal with the province of UP. Protesting against extortion of many by the king's officials, villagers gathered at a religious fair at Dhadi Ghandiyal, marched towards the capital, Tehri, capturing outposts on the way and symbolically replacing corrupt *patwaris* by their own men.

The 1948 *dhanda* remains vividly in the collective memory of the peasants of Badyargarh; and their heroism then was invoked by the *chipko* leaders in 1979. Apart from the participation of many in both, the movements itself have strong similarities—such as the identification of officials as the main exploiters, the belief that justice was on their side, and the forms of protest itself. In both instances, the act of protest was seen as having a moral-religious sanction. While in 1948 the peasantry was mobilized on the occasion of a religious fair held once in 13 years, an important event in *chipko* was the reading of the Geeta. Camped in the forests, *chipko* volunteers commenced the reading of the epic and the rendition of folk songs. The Conservator of Forests who opposed the ceremony, was firmly told that all *Vedas* were written in the forest. And when the *patwari* threatened one of the priests with arrest, the priest replied "arrest me under any section of the law, but what are the rules for the Nigam people".

Bahuguna and the idiom of protest

The idiom of *chipko*, then, can be understood in terms of the "moral economy"[9] of the Garhwal peasant who could readily comprehend tactics of the charismatic leader of the Badyargarh *andolan*, Sunderlal Bahuguna. Bahuguna concentrates his fire on the officials of the Forest Department who, in league with contractors, "do not leave a splinter of wood in the forests" (1980b: 35). Commercial forestry as practised by the profit-oriented Forest Department is seen as solely responsible for the deteriorating Himalayan environment (Bahuguna, 1980a;

1980b; 1981). The call to forest officers, to change their ways and serve local communities evokes a position reaction from a people exposed to extortion by officials during earlier regimes.

Bahuguna's method of functioning is far removed from that of the self-seeking politician. As a non-political person, he was able to strike a chord in the hearts of those disenchanted with the hypocrasy of popular representatives and the electoral process. Gandhian methods of non-violence and Bahuguna's personal asceticism were appreciatively responded to by the predominantly Hindu peasantry. The capacity for physical suffering (vide, the hunger fast in the bitter cold) and spirit of sacrifice (*tyaga*) in an age of selfishness were constantly marvelled at by villagers who read into these acts the renunciation of worldly ambition as extolled by Hindu scriptures.

Sunderlal's charisma is undoubted and his deeds are still an object of wonder in Badyargarh.[10] His success is clearly related to the distinctive character of social protest in Tehri Garhwal. The attacks of Forest Department officials can be understood in the content of *dhandas* aimed at the raja's minions. Sunderlal's remarkable physical endurance and sage-like appearance make him a natural leader whose followers look to him to restore a pristine state of harmony and just Government.

Conclusion: Whither Chipko?

The increasing confrontation between the hill people and the Government (primarily its wing, the Forest Department) has been mediated through the efforts of *chipko*. With *chipko* assuming different forms in the Bhagirathi and the Alakananda valley respectively, a brief examination of the differences between the two major groups working in the region, and the concommitant implications for the movement's future direction, follows.

Leader and led in Badyargarh

Bahuguna remains the unrivalled leader of *chipko* in the districts of Tehri and Uttarkashi (the Bhagirathi valley) and in the public eye the movement is synonymous with his name. His impressive (*prabhavshali*) appearance and capacity to influence people played a cruicial part during the Badyargarh movement.

However, his style of leading from the front, as it were, hampered the emergence of local level leadership. Bahuguna has returned only once to Badyargarh, and his brief visit was not noticed by many. There is thus a distinct feeling in Badyargarh that Bahuguna has forgotten the people who lent him such wholehearted support in 1979. His preoccupation with broader concerns (such as the 4000 kilometer footmark he completed in April 1983) has led to a relative neglect of Garhwal.[11] The absence of village leadership in Badyargarh is a lacunae that will severely constrain the peasantry's capacity to mobilize again.

Tehri and Chamoli: Contrasting styles

Bahuguna's relentless attack on the Forest Department goes hand-in-hand with his sharp rejection of the materialistic civilization of the west and its anthropocentric view of nature. His call for science to be guided by the "spirituality of the east" and the self-confessed attempt, through *chipko*, to "bring man to nature and dissuade him from the materialistic world" (as reported in *Indian Express*, 9-2-82), do occasionally assume mystical overtones.

In contrast, the Dashauli Gram Swarajya Mandal (DGSM) which is in the forefront of *chipko* in the Chamoli district (Alakananda valley), adopts a low keyed approach. As enunciated by DGSM leader Chandiprasad Bhatt, another charismatic figure, the aims of the *chipko andolan* are as follows: (i) Banning of felling in river catchments and other ecologically sensitive areas; (ii) replacement of the contractor system by forest labour co-operatives; (iii) involvement of villagers with forests through local small scale industries and afforestation drives (iv) correct assessment of the daily needs of the people in granting traditional forest rights; (v) afforestation of bare regions through joint co-operation of villagers and Government (Bhatt, 1980). Here, the restoration of the Himalayan ecosystem is organically linked with the reversing of the flow of raw materials and cheap labour out of the hills. There is an emphasis on the involvement of villagers in afforestation and on decentralization in the organization of production. Nor for Forest Department officials treated as enemies—the attempt being to "convert" them to the villagers' point of view (Interview with C.P. Bhatt, 2-5-81).

Undoubtedly, as some argue, there, is a degree of complementarity between the two approaches. The publicity oriented work of Bahuguna is not necessarily in conflict with the grassroots work of other individual or groups in Garhwal and neighbouring Kumaun region. But the deep enmity shown by the two groups towards each other (an enmity expressed only in private) preclude their coming together in a common cause.

Communal Management

Communal ownership of forest resources by village panchayats may be a way out of the present impasse in forest management. Historically, the panchayat forests in both parts of Garhwal have been well managed and in good condition (Gadgil et. al., 1982;) Johri, 1940). The strong sense of village solidarity and absence of sharp class differentials enable these forests to be managed equitably and without friction.

Although the state has consistently refused to encourage the growth of village forests, devolution of control over forest areas is a socially necessary imperative. As villagers see it, communally owned and managed forests could be run on part commercial lines, with money earned from felling operations utilized for items of lasting benefit such as education and health facilities. In the process the foundations of a self reliant economy geared towards local needs, could be laid.

In the hills, social ownership of forest resources can constitute the first step towards halting the disintegration caused by undirected commercialization. While the ecological debate had successfully contested western nations of programme and the "vision of infinite growth" (Guha, 1982a) an idyllic picture of man living in communion with nature tends to obscure the social origins of ecological degradation. The man-man and man-nature relationships, sometimes treated as being independent of each other, are infact mutuality determining. For, as young *chipko* activists in Kumaun argue (Pathak, 1983), can the forests be saved without simultaneously rescuing man from the oppressive web of social relationships he now finds himself in ?

Acknowledgements

I am deeply grateful to the people of Badyargarh for

their warmth and co-operation extended during my stay. In particular, I would like to thank Kunwar Singh Pundir, Sher Singh Rawat for their hospitality, and Thakur Sarop Singh for providing me access to the BVSS file. In Dehradun, Captain Shoorbeer Singh Panwar provided many insights from his unrivalled knowledge of Garhwali history and culture. Funds for fieldwork were provided by the fellowship programme, Indian Institute of Management, Calcutta.

NOTES

1. *Patti* is an administrative unit comprising a number of villages and administered by a *patwari*. In the period 1815-1949, Badyargarh formed part of the princely state of Tehri Garhwal.

2. Due to the impact of *chipko*, the system of auctioning blocks of forest to contractors was discontinued, and the U.P. Forest Corporation set up. But as the Corporation does not directly engage in forest operations, this has in effect meant only the elimination of one level of intermediary.

3. A link maintained through different social institutions that regulated the utilization of forest resources.

4. It is interesting to note that Badyargarh *andolan* was to save *chir* pine, a tree whose benefits in this locality are mostly ecological and to that extent indirect.

5. As we argue this solidarity can form a nucleus for effective community management of forest resources.

6. Freely translated: "when we could not cook the little grain we get (as the Nigam had taken away the wood) we did *chipko* to force the Government to notice our problems".

7. As a Garhwali friend, now settled in Dehradun, informed me, that the man's task is complete after the ploughing where upon he sits on the bed and smokes his *hookah* ("hal chalane ke baad ham charpay par beth ke hookah peete hein").

8. This is in keeping with the tendency, often reported by anthropologists, to minimize internal criticism in the presence of outsiders.

9. I am using the term in the sense of James Scott (1976).

10. On hearing that I had come to research *chipko*, I was invariably asked the whereabouts (and current activities) of Sunderlal Bahuguna. It may also be mentioned that Bahuguna is nationally and internationaly known through his visits and lectures and has done much to focus attention on the eco-crisis of the Garhwal Himalayas.

11. While admitting his failure to retain contact with the people in Badyargarh, Sunderlal contends that the Government's desire to localized *chipko*, forced him to reorder his priorities towards spreading tbe message outside Garhwal (interview with S. Bahuguna, 3-8-1983).

REFERENCES

Ashish, S.M.	1979	"Agricultural economy oi Kumaun hills: threat of ecological disaster. *Economic and Political Weekly*, Vol. 14.
Bahuguna, S.	1980a	*Chipko*, Silyara (Tehri-Garhwal).
Bahuguna, S.	1980b	Her Story: Women's non-violent power in the Chipko movement. *Manushi*, Vol. 6.
Bahuguna, S.	1981	Every tree is a friend, *Famina*, March 8-22.
Berreman, G.D.	1963	*Hindus of the Himalayas*, Bombay.
Bhatt, C.P.	1980	*Eco-system of the Central Himalayas and Chipko Movement*, Gopeshwar.
Brahmawar, R.N.	1932	*Working Plan for the Garhwal forest division, United Provinces, 1930-31 to 1939-40*, Allahabad.
B.V.S.S. (n.d.)		*Badyargarh Van Suraksha Samiti File*, Badyargarh.

Chatterjee, P. 1982 Agrarian relations and communalism in Bengal, 1926-35, In Ranajit Guha, Editor, *Subaltera Studies I*, Delhi.

Dabral, S. (n.d.) *Uttarakhand Ka Itihas,* Vol. 6, Dugadda.

Dharampal 1971 *Civil Disobedience and Indian Tradition*, Varanasi.

Dogra, B. 1980 *Forests and People*, Rishikesh.

Gadgil, M.; Rauf Ali, and Prasad, S.N. 1982 *Forests Management in India : A Critical Review*, Bombay.

Guha, R. 1982a Theories of man and nature. *PPST Bulletin* (Madras) Vol. 2, No. 2, November.

Guha, R. 1982b Ecological crisis and ecological movement: a bourgeois deviation?, *Economic and Political Weekly,* Vol. 17.

Guha, R. 1983 Colonialism, Capitalism and deforestation, *Social Scientist,* Vol. 119, April.

Gupta, P.N. 1980 Women, community forestry, and watershed management. Paper presented at the Seminar on *Role of Women in Community Forestry*, Dehradun, 4-9 December.

Hearle, N. 1888 *Working Plan for the Tehri Garhwal Leased Forests,* Allahabad.

Johri, C.M. 1940 *Working Plan for the Garhwal Forest Division, United Provinces, 1940-41 to 1954-55,* Allahabad.

Joshi, L.D. 1929 *The Khasa Family Law,* Allahabad.

Mobbs, E.C. 1926 *Working Plan for the Tons Forest Division, Tehri Garhwal State, 1925-46*, Allahabad.

Nelson, J.C. 1916 *Forest Settlement Report of the Garhwal District*, Lucknow.

Pant, S.D. 1935 *The Social Economy of the Himalayans*, London.

Panwar, S.S. 1982 Personal communication.

Pathak, S. 1983 Personal communicalion.

Pauw, E.K. 1896 *Report of the Tenth Settlement of the Garhwal District*, Allahabad.

People's Union for Democratic Rights (PUDR) 1982 *Undeclared Civil War*, Delhi.

Sarala Devi 1980 A blueprint for survival of the hills. Supplement to *Himalaya: Man and Nature*, Vol. 4, No. 6.

Scott, J.C. 1976 *The Moral Economy of the Peasant*, New Haven.

Stebbing, E.P. 1925 *The Forests of India*, Vol. II, London.

Uttar Pradesh Forest Department (UPFD), (n.d.) *Forest Statistics, 1978-79*, Lucknow.

SECTION THREE

THE WESTERN HIMALAYAN PERSPECTIVE

CHAPTER XX

THE GADDIS OF THE UPPER RAVI AS AN EXAMPLE OF A TRADITIONAL HINDU KINGDOM

WILLIAM H. NEWELL

One of the most long-term arguments in the history of Indian Anthropology concerns the relationships between tribes and castes. Distinctions between these two have been based on kinship differences, differences in the recruitment of members, the introduction of hierachical arrangements between different castes, the relationships to the king or chief and religious differences. In the census reports of the Himachal Pradesh Government concerning the inhabitants of Chamba, the Gaddis are always classified as a scheduled *tribe* in districts where they gain special administrative advantages. Yet I think it cannot be denied that they are clearly a caste for not only in historic times as far back as the 11th century were they definitely Hindu but they also have an endogamous hierachical system with some restrictions on interdining and intermarriage between the different subcastes. The gradual strengthening of caste barriers as a result of outside funds being pumped into the area by different government bodies such as Development Agencies and road building projects is an emphasis which has existed from the beginning, not a change from a "tribal" system to a "caste" system. (Newell, 1970)

The traditional term for the area which, at its widest

extent stretched from Chamba to Kugti, and from Dharmsala and the surrounding areas especially Nurpur to Tundah on the border of the Pangi range, is Gadaren. This cultural area is not identical with the boundaries of the former state of Chamba which included also the valley of the Ravi river below Chamba and the territory of Pangi which was annexed to Chamba in the early nineteenth century. The former rajah of Chamba at his coronation was separately crowned by each of the five cultural groups in Chamba State on five successive days. But since he himself considered himself a Rajput (Gaddi) the first day was entirely devoted to traditional Gaddi Hindu ceremonies. I cannot find in the records any description of the ritual accompanied the coronation but there is no doubt that the first day was totally Hindu.

On the first day's coronation delegates were sent from each of the main Gaddi cultural centres to the coronation, namely from Lil Bilj, Tundah, Holi, Brahmaur, Kugti and Chhatrari. In traditional times each of these areas was more or less isolated from the other sections by difficult paths, rushing rivers and mountain passes. At the very top of the Budl Nadl, a tributary of the Ravi, lies the village of Kugti adjoining Mt. Kailas and Lake Mani Mahesh. The mountain is considered a temple which enshrines Shiva and his consort, and a special group of Brahmin *pujaris* at Herser at the foot of the mountain, performs regular worship to Shiva on the mountain as well as being responsible for giving *tika* to all these pilgrims who intend to ascend the mountain on pilgrimage.

A myth dedicated to the Gaddi culture hero, Triloknath Dev, links the sacred mountain at one end of the valley with the palace of the rajah at the other end. Formerly various temples associated with this myth were sited at easy stages from top to bottom.[1]

In addition to the "national" culture represented by the rajah and by Lord Shiva certain villages also have a local religious culture represented by various sacred shrines usually associated with trees and inhabited by *nags, devtas* or *sidhs.*

It is clear therefore that notwithstanding the census classification of the Gaddis as "tribes" they are most certainly Hindus and have been so for a very long period.

In fact, the Gaddis regarded themselves as more Hindu than the various imigrants from the Punjab plains, government officials, merchants or pilgrims. Those visitors are regarded as heavily secularised and from a religious point of view not a very congenial to the Gaddi Hindu ideology. In one case the Gaddi (Rajputs) were horrified at the behaviour of certain illiterate local Brahmins, who in an attempt to curry favour with visiting government officials, started to criticise the drinking of a mild alcoholic beverage called *sur* which was locally made in the homes and was used for dedication to Shiva. They were ignorant of the dominant Gaddi Shaiva cult. Brahminic puritannical Hinduism which was often brought into the area by others was regarded as undermining the Gaddi Rajput dominant Hindu culture. The dominant and exclusive cult of Shiva, was regarded as true Hinduism. Outsiders should realise this. Although there was one shrine on the Brahmaur *maidan* dedicated to another manifestation of the Hindu trinity, I never heard of a Gaddi worshipping there. Shiva was above all a Gaddi god and the discovery that many plains Hindus did not recognise this but only placed his as part of the Hindu pantheon was, in a sense, an attack on the unity of the Gaddi life. Srinivas used the term sanscritization to illustrate the principle by which Hindu values became adopted from the Brahmins. But here in Brahmaur we have an example of 'Rajputization' which until recently even Brahmins followed. The Gaddis were the "dominant caste".

The Gaddis in the area about which I will speak from now on, the area round Brahmaur, consisted of about 80 per cent of the population. In accordance with the usual Hindu practice there was a pollution barrier which no one could cross. Above the pollution barrier were the Brahmins and the Gaddis (Rajputs, Thakurs, Ranas, Khatris). Below the pollution barrier were the Sipis and an extremely small number of the Hallis, etc. who had only entered this part of the valley in the last 100 years. Some scholars have argued that the Sipis were the descendants of early inhabitants of the valley before the upper castes, driven by the persecutions of Aurangzeb, emigrated from the Punjab plains. There is no doubt the Buddhist culture at one time spread very much further south than the present isolated monasteries in Kinnaur and Lahul would lead one to expect. When I first visited Gaddi land in 1952 at the bottom of the village of Goshen near the watermill there was a large Buddhist inscription which is now destroyed. The building of the jeep road to Brahmaur has resulted in a number of monuments of an earlier age (but not necessarily non-Hindu) being destroyed for road metal. A number of early three story fortress house still remain in use although the platform at the back of the Brahmaur *maidan* on which the former Rani's palace was built, has been gradually occupied by government buildings. As far as I am aware this royal platform has never been excavated. But with the exception of the Buddhist inscription all these archaeological remains seem to me to be quite consistent with the present Gaddi culture. Moreover although the Sipis have separate shrines in the villages where they live, the names of the gods they worship have Hindu names and titles. The sole evidence for an earlier culture seems to me to be based on the fact that the Sipis usually occupy the best land in the valley which implies that they were the earlier inhabitants. But I consider they are definitely Hindus within the Gaddi culture and are well integrated *as a caste* (and not as a tribe) within the valley systems.

Although the culture of the valley is clearly Hindu, as an ecosystem the whole area must be regarded as part of the Himalayas which stretch from Arunachal Pradesh to Leh via Sikkim and Himachal Pradesh. Some scholars have seen this whole area as being a sort of battleground between Buddhism and Hinduism. The 2500 year old ideological conflict seems now to be one where a third party is taking over, a sort of secularism following in the trail of government officials from the plains who are building dams and roads and importing music and dance. Culturally the Gaddis have their own style of dancing which is closely connected with the *narwala* ceremony given as a homage to Lord Shiva. Men and women dance separately in different areas although basically the dancing is the same. The introduction of schools has had the effect of also initially introducing non-Gaddi teachers who brought in secular film music which has become rapidly popular. This has mostly destroyed traditional dancing which is thought to be inferior.

The other cultural feature of the Gaddi cultural life was poetry. Capable poets were greatly respected. Original poems were however by no means exclusively on religious themes and the natural events of the Gaddi life were the most popular theme, especially friendship and unrequited love. These were rarely written down although some of the older Brahmin scholars have graduated from the former rajah's school which used the Tarkara script and would have been quite able to record it.

The cultural pattern that I am trying to convey to the reader is of a valley which because there were no through passes, over the course of a thousand years, retained a great deal of cultural identity. Nothing firm is known of the pre-Hindu period, but from the earliest period known there was a king, who originally occupied Brahmaur and who over the course of time subjugated other smaller Hindu rulers and eventually moved down the river to Chamba. This ruler was himself a Gaddi Rajput and gradually acquired the standard characteristics of a Hindu ruler, ultimate ownership of all the land in his kingdom, Brahminical priests and advisers and subjects who identified themselves with respect to the ruler both as citizens and also as belonging to particular horizontal classes. The system is very similar to the *jajmani* system on a national scale and the members of each group held their land by virtue of their status as priest or *parohit*, warrior or small ruler, or as peasant. Each group gave free service to the rajah as teacher, fighter or provider of labour, *begari* in exchange for the right to work in land. Land could not be alienated. This recognition of being a subject of the rajah applied also to shepherds who traditionally paid a much lower grazing tax on their own rajah's land than if they were wandering shepherds from elsewhere. Until about 20 years ago the Gaddis who grazed their sheep in Nurpur in the Kangra valley, paid a smaller amount of grazing tax than others on the gounds that Nurpur was once ruled by the rajah of Chamba.

Although the geographical features of the area undoubtedly was of assistance in supporting the integrity of the State's boundaries, basically it was the theocratic Hindu ideology which was systematically worked out and which was accepted completely by the valley's inhabitants. This was the real basis of continuity. However there was a difference between the Hinduism of the hills and the Hinduism of the plains. The Gaddis who for various reasons left the area, controlled directly by the rajah and who moved to the Kangra plains often became indistinguishable from the other plains peasants. The Punjab Board of Economic Enquiry has published a small handbook on Leuna, a village near Palampur about forty years ago (No. 12, 1940). The author however completely failed to understand that his villagers were all Gaddis. They were all regarded as plains Hindus. Yet in their own mountains there is an important cultural distinction between the Brahmaur area and the Kangra area, that between sanskritization and Rajputization. Many scholars have made the point that villagers in mountainous areas are much more equal than on the plains. The reason for this economically seems to me to be fairly clear. Where land is poor and limited in size there can be no landlords as the soil is just sufficient to support the actual farmer. Moreover, in Chamba at least the great increase in population is only a feature of the last hundred years and the preferred occupation formerly among men was that of hunting, cultivation for the most part being left to women. Hunters too are equalitarian by nature. In the highest part of the Budl Nadl in the village of Kugti, intermarriage took place between Brahmins and Gaddis both hypogamously and hypergamously although caste differentiation is now becoming more widespread. When I first enquired about intercaste marriage I was given a practical answer by a Brahmin. "The Gaddis and Brahmins are really the same and have the same occupation of cultivation. The difference is artificially created between us by religion. But here we are all the same." The Brahmins, none of whom in this village, were *parohits* and all of whom owned land, wished to emulate the Gaddis who were the majority group and who had a Rajput culture of goat eating, drinking and fighting. But in the Kangra valley there is no doubt that, hierarchically, Brahmins are at the top. But I have noticed in the last few years the rise of a sort of *bhakti* Brahminism in the hills with many families requesting to have a Brahmin perform the *Sat Narayan* family recitation. But a Brahmin was paid for it, whereas in traditional times the usual way of worshipping God collectively was by the *narwala* ceremony to Shiva where

Brahmins are not necessary. No Gaddi has ever become a *sadhu* or given a religious recital. But there are many Gaddi shamans (*chelas*).

To summarize my argument so far, this area of the Himalayas, being only marginally influenced historically by Buddhism and not being on any of the great through river valleys between north and south, is clearly Hindu. This Hinduism is however a form of Shaivism and it was the king and the Gaddi (Rajputs) which laid down the pattern of the Hindu society. Within the area of this kingdom however there are marked ecological differences and these ecological differences modify the application of the general Hindu principles of society. At high levels we have Rajputization; at low levels we have sanscritization. The latter tendency is increasing rapidly because of the pouring in of money and government officials, who are probably as much secular leaders, as leaders of Hindu thinking. Progress and development are connected with this invading secular pseudo-Hindu culture so that such cultural features and land ownership, dancing, education, poetry, relationship to the rulers, etc. all become changed with the final result that the unity of this Himalayan hill culture is being degenerated. However, it is the speed of the changing process which is most important. I believe that it has been possible to see the conflict between mountain and plains culture as a constant battle. In this part of the Himalayas it is, I think, a battle between Hindu Rajput culture and Hindu plains secular culture. Elsewhere it may have been a battle between Buddhism and Hinduism as in the area round Kulu and further north. The key issue in these struggles may well be the question of land ownership and use. In Berreman's *Hindus of the Himalayas* (1972), private ownership of land and the abolition of the rights of the rajah took place in Tehri-Garhwal about the 1870's. Reading through his book now about 100 years after the abolition of communal land ownership, I do not feel that his villagers are now anything more than the *paharis*, persons who are poorer than plains villagers round Dehra Dun but who live in slightly different type villages on the mountain side. But they are clearly part of the same cultural group as other UP villagers. In contrast, among the Gaddis, private property in land was introduced round about 1955 with individual inheritance even by women, thus changing equalitarian State allocation of landholdings. Cultural differences are still clearly visible between mountain and plains. Although it is now only about 30 years since this government rule was introduced, other later anthropologists have apparently found it difficult to acquire a feeling for the separate cultural identity of the Gaddis in Brahmaur and have tended to study special minor features of the ecology such as goat and sheep-herding or special features of the (introduced) administration like the *panchayat* system. But the total culture is no longer of interest to them.

It is the way in which distinctive features of a culture remain in existence after the general ecological features have been analysed which is really interesting for an area like the Himalayas. The cultural differences between different ecological levels have not been properly examined. This is more important than to force every tribe or caste to adjust to a dull and uninteresting niche in an introduced environment. All hail to differences.

NOTE

This information is highly condensed in this article. For more detailed information about the myth of Triloknath Dev and the politico-religious system see my book, *Report of the Scheduled Castes and Scheduled Tribes of Himachal Pradesh*, Census of India 1961, Govt. Printer, Simla 1967.

CHAPTER XXI

THE KHANDAN SYSTEM OF THE KINNAURA OF THE WESTERN HIMALAYAS

MANIS KUMAR RAHA

The Back-Drop

Kinnaur, the mountain-clad frontier district of Himachal Pradesh, is situated in the lap of the Great Himalayas. This district was created in May 1, 1960. Earlier it was a Tehsil of Simla (previously Mahasu) district. During pre-independence era, it formed a part of the erstwhile Bushahar state—one of the many small princely states reigned in the Himalayas during pre-independence time.

The district of Kinnaur consists of three sub-divisions, namely, Nachar, Kalpa and Pooh of which Nachar is situated in the lower Kinnaur adjacent to Simla district of Himachal Pradesh while Pooh is in the upper Kinnaur adjoining Tibet, Kalpa sub-division covering the central part of the district. A total of 77 villages are distributed in these three sub-divisions. Most of these villages are situated between 7,000 ft. to 14,000 ft. (approximately) above mean sea level.

The whole district is thoroughly mountainous, unkempt and quite inhospitable. "The face of the country presents high hills and low dales and is marked by precipitous skyhigh mountains with their peaks usually covered with perpetual snow". (Singh, 1965: 3). On the basis of the ecological conditions, the district is divisible into three eco-zones—(I) the moist zone covering the lower Kinnaur, (II) the dry zone spreading over central region, (III) the arid zone consisting of the part of upper Kinnaur (Raha and Mahato, 1985: 14; Raha, 1982: 4). Corresponding to these eco-zones, the district may also be divided into three culture zones. Zone—I covers the northeast part of the district or the upper Kinnaur i.e. Pooh sub-division (corresponds to the arid zone) and dominated by the Mahayan Buddhism; Zone II includes southwest part or lower Kinnaur i.e. Nachar sub-division (corresponds to the moist climate) which is wholly influenced by the local Hinduism and Zone III consists of the central part or Kalpa sub-division (corresponds to the dry zone) and is co-existed by both Buddhism and Hinduism. It is seen that in the arid zone of the district the people have mostly embraced Buddhism whereas in the moist area they have adopted Hinduism. In the central part which is dry, the people keep faith in both religions. (Raha et. al. 1976: 85; Raha 1979: 84; Raha et. al, 1980; 27).

The inhabitants of the district of Kinnaur are known as the Kinner, Kinnaura or Kinnaurese. The different Hindu mythologies and scriptures, have mentioned about the Kinnaura. In many of these books these people have been described as belonging to a divine race like Apsaras, Yakshas, Gandharvas, Guhyakas, Siddhas and others. (Raha and Mahato, 1985: 18-19; Raha et al., 1976: 86; Raha 1979: 84). According to 1971 census there are 49,835 souls in Kinnaur of which 26,407 are males and 23,428 females. Of the population 19,217 (38.56 per cent) live in Kalpa sub-division, 16,413 (32.93 per cent) in Pooh sub-division and the rest i.e. 14,205 (28.50 per cent) inhabit Nachar sub-division.

The Khosla System of Stratification

The people of Kinnaur is divisible into two distinct divisions—the *khosia* and the *beru.* While the former division includes exclusively the Khosia or Rajput (Kanet) people, the latter division consists of four artisan castes namely, the Lohar (blacksmith), the Badhi (carpenter and mason), the Koli (weaver, spinner and leather worker) and the Nangalu (basket maker) who are further grouped under three sub-divisions namely the

Zone I Zone II

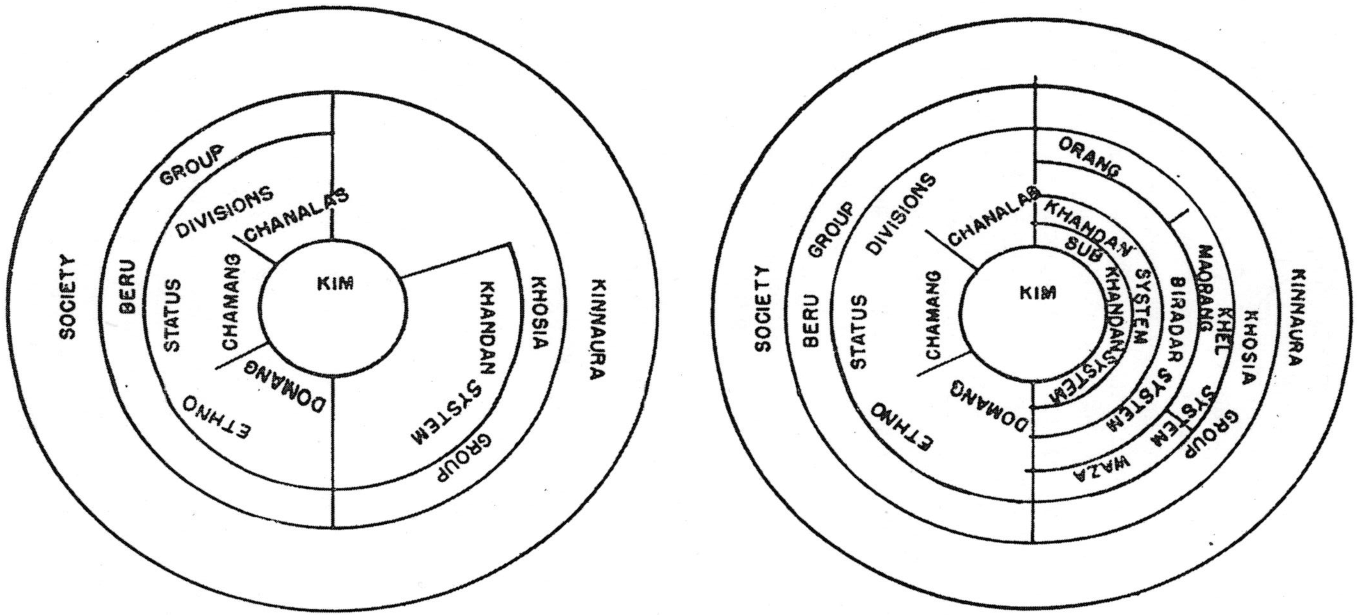

The Kinnaura System of Stratification

domang (includes the Lohar and the Badhi), the *chamang* (includes the Koli) and the *chanalas* (includes the Nagalu). However for my present paper I am considering only the former division i.e. the Khosia, as the members of this division only have the *khel* and *khandan* systems while the rest do not have any such systems. Only recently some rudimentary forms of segmentations on the basis of occupation have been started among the *koli* e.g. the *bonu* (weaving) and *sui* (stitching) (Raha and Mahato, 1985: 150; Raha, 1979: 88).

As already stated the culture zones in Kinnaur lead to two distinct types of stratification. As one moves from Zone—I to Zones II and III, one witnesses a drift from a comparatively simple type of stratification to a more complex type in the Khosia (Rajput) society (Raha, 1979: 88). The Rajputs of Kinnaur have two distinct divisions—firstly those who are Buddhists and secondly those who practise local Hinduism. While the former group is concentrated in Zones—I and III, the latter are found in Zones II and III.

In Zones II and III and some parts of Zone I the Khosia society is further divided into three distinct status groups called the *khel*. These three *khels* are the Orang, the Maorang (also known as Orang-Mech) and the Waza. While these *khels* or status groups are well developed in Zone-II and Zone-III, these gradually loose their importance as one moves in Zone-I where this system is not developed.

The three different *khels* of the Khosia society are further sub-divided into a number of smaller exogamous social unit called the *khandan*. The *khandan* system like the *khel* system, also has same type of distribution. It is well grown up in one culture zone but much rudimentary in different culture zone of Kinnaur. While this system is highly stratified and well developed in Zone-II and Zone-III, it is not so in north-eastern part of Zone-I i.e. in the Hangrang valley. It is rudimentary there.[1]

Some of these *khandans* in Kinnaur are further divided into the sub-*khandan*. But the sub-*khandans* are definitely not found in case of all *khandans*. Then comes the smallest social unit of the Khosia society, the *kim* or the household. A number of households come under a *khandan* or a sub-*khandan*. It is thus seen that the pattern of stratification of the Kinnaura society depends on the cultural and ecological designs of the areas. It is more complex in wet and the Hindu dominated areas. That is, while in the former area the society is well stratified, in the latter areas the stratification is much simpler or even rudimentary.

The Khel System

The *khel* or the status group may be defined as a set of locally united *khandans* each of which is linked with most of others by a common tie of *khelship*. This system perpetuates through both male and female members, unlike the *khandan*, because the *khel* is endogamous. It acts as a corporate unit in respect of certain common interests of its members who sometimes act together for certain common interest indicated by reciprocal rights, duties and obligations in the crises of life, conflicts and feuds etc. The *khel* system, unlike, the *khandan* system is not typical to a particular area or village but spread over different areas.

All these three *khels* have different positions in the society where these are arranged in hierarchial order. The Orang *khel* is considered as the superiormost and the Waza *khel* occupies the lowermost position. In between comes the Maorang or Orang-Mech *khel*. "These *khels* enjoy their respective status—not only in the social sphere but in the economic, political and religious spheres also" (Raha and Mahato, 1985: 138). It is usually seen that the members of the superiormost *khel*, in comparison to those of other two, have more landed and other property, hold more key positions in the village council and also act as the main *karder* or the temple functionaries. And again between the last two *khels*, Maorang and Waza, the position of the members of the former *khel* in the social, economic, political and religious spheres are undoubtedly far better than that of the latter.

All the three *khels* are further subdivided into a number of unilineal descent groups called the *khandan*. Each of the *khels* has got different set of the *khandans*. The identical *khandans* do not exist in two different *khels*. Like the *khels*, the *khandans* are also hierarchically stratified. That means the *khandans* of the superior *khel* enjoy the superior status. That means the *khan-*

dans of Orang *khel* have the highest social position while those of the Waza *khel* bear the lowest, keeping the *khandans* of the Maorang *khel* in the intermediate position. In a village in lower Kinnaur (Zone II) the Khosia society has been stratified in the following ways.

It is thus seen that the Orang *khel* of the Khosia of this village has got six *khandans*, the Maorang *khel* four and the Waza *khel* having only one *khandan*. The social status of the *khandans* are identically prescribed as prescribed for the *khels*. That means in this village, the *khandans* of the Orang *khel* i.e. Bhorya, Charas, Damesh, Rakyalu, Shabist and Tongku enjoy the highest status. The *khandans* of the Maorang *khel* viz. Bala, Kashu, Nagchan and Tui, share the next higher status. The only *khandan* of the Waza *khel*, i.e. Tewaza, is placed at the bottom of the ladder of social hierarchy.

Ibetson and MacLagan during first quarter of this century, found the Kenets (Rajput or Khosia) of Kinnaur also divided into three grades (*khel*). Each of these three grades of the Kanet had a number of septs (*khandan* ?) whose names did not appear among the Kanets of Bashahr proper. In case of first grade Kanet (Rajput), septs were different in different administrative units or parganas like Rajgaon, Inner Tupka, Outer Tupka, Pandrabis and Atharabis. Similarly the second grade Kanet (Rajput) also had different septs in different parganas. Ibetson mentioned about three parganas, Inner Tukpa, Shuwa and Rajgaon, where the septs were different. The third grade Kanets who worked as potters, also had a set of septs (Rose, 1911: 446-447).

Ibetson's classification of three different grades of the Kanets corresponds with three different *khels* of the Rajput namely the Orang, the Maorang and the Waza, the members of the last *khel* are potters.

Endogamy is the general marital rule for all the *khels*. The members of one *khel* must marry within their own *khel*. Marriage out side ones own *khel* is not approved. "In olden days all the three status groups were strictly endogamous. The members of one status group were not allowed to marry into other status groups. Marriage with lower status groups was considered as socially disgraceful and lowering of status" (Raha; 1979:89). If a member of one *khel* fails to find out his mate from same status group in his village or in the adjacent villages, he travels to a distant village to get his consort accepting much difficulty in a hazardous journey in the rugged inhospitable country. But even in spite of this difficulty he abstains from marrying a member of other *khel.* The main reason for avoiding such marriage is that the members of a *khel* are much conscious about their status. Marriage with lower status group means lowering of social status which they simply cannot afford while living in such status conscious stratified society. But in course of time, this restriction between the former two *khels,* that is, between the Orang and the Maorang, is gradually getting relaxed, and presently cases of marriage between these two groups are found. But in connection with their marriage with the members of the Waza, the former two *khels,* i.e. the Orang and Maorang, follow the same type of restrictions as was present in the past. That is no marriage alliance is possible between the Orang and the Maorang *khels* in one hand and the Waza *khel* on the other.

The Khandan System

In Kinnaur, as already stated all the three *khel* are divided into a number of smaller units called *khandan.* Like the people of some lower Himalayan region (Berreman, 1974: 178), the Kinnaura call their lineage a *khandan.* Each of these *khandans* is a 'consanguineal kingroup produced by unileneal descent' the members of which 'can actually trace their common relationship through a specific series of remembered genealogical links in the prevailing line of descent' (Murdock, 1965: 46). According to the Kinnaura a *khandan* :

> 'is an association of people of both sexes comprising of all the known descendants by a known genealogy of a single known and named ancestor putatively continuous male line. It is in other words, a strictly unilineal, agnatic descent group' (Fortes, 1945:30).

Following Evans-Pritchard, we may also define *khandan* 'as an agnatic group the members of which are genealogically linked' and 'trace their descent from a common ancestor and between whom marriage is forbidden and sexual relation considered incestucus'. (1940:192)

In the Rajput/Khosia society in Kinnaur, the *khandan* is patrilineal and exagamous in nature where descent is traced through a common male root or ancestry called the *jillang*. The persons or individuals who trace their relation from the common *jillang*, are considered to be related to one another (Raha & Mahato, 1975:385; Raha et. al., 1976:88). According to Sen, the *khandan* denotes 'a person's identity, his family of origin and his social position' (1970:109).

Following Tale lineage system (Fortes, 1945-32-33) it may be said that the *khandan* of the Kinnaura is also a temporal system.

> "Continuity in time is its fundamental quality. Its constitution and dimensions at a given time represent a phase of a process which... has been going on in (exactly) almost same way from the beginning of their social order and continuing into the future."

The other basic characteristic is that the contemporary phase of the *khandan* can be considered as a perpetuation of its past. It bears many of its past characters and changes. Identically some characteristics of its contemporary phase will roll down to its future organisation. The Kinnaura's view is that a *khandan* is a continuous social unit, perpetuates from time immemorial and exists at a given time. A Kinnaura always tells that the present status of his *khandan* was 'almost' same as it prevailed during his father's father's, even during earlier generations. Almost same duties, obligations, privileges, rules and regulations have been percolated through passage of time, though of course, some modifications have been incorporated time to time.

While the tribe Kinnaura is distributed throughout Kinnar district (a few of them are, of course, found outside Kinnaur district, in the adjacent districts of Simla, Kulu etc.) the *khandans* are usually found restricted in specific areas. Particular *khandans* are found in particular villages. Here the tribe is a territorial group with an unbroken social extension,.

the *khandans* are kingroups and also restricted to some specified areas (e.g. village).

Membership of the Khandan

The *khandan* is a birth ascribed social unit. In whatever *khandan* a man is born, that remains his *khandan* throughout his life. He can not change it nor does he think of changing it. The question of choice is irrelevant here. One retains no right to become choosy about the membership of his *khandan*. Even after marriage a man retains his *khandan* which he got from his father, and passes it to his progeny. Membership of the *khandan* gives him a particular meaning of life which he follows throughout his life. It demarcates the persons who belong to his own *khandan*, who are members of his closer *khandan* and who belong to the distant *khandan*. It has also helped him to understand and to realise his position and status in this society and also how he can maintain integrity in his society. To an individual the members of his *khandan* means:

> 'A particular collection of people taken severally in some situation, collectively in others, with whom he has certain kinds of known and regular social relations reflecting their common interest and based on the continuity and integrity of the group; and he submits to a number of restrains on wood and deed in order to maintain his relation with them. A man experiences this in a multitude of particular actions and events day by day'. (Fortes, 1945: 134)

The females, on the other hands, retain their parental *khandan* till they remain unmarried. On marriage they subscribe for their respective husband/husbands' *khandan*. While the males help in perpetuation of their *khandan*, the rule of the *khandan* exogamy compels females to marry outside their parental *khandan*, and as such they are unable to contribute to the perpetuation of the *khandan* and do not effect its organization significantly. But it is also true that on marriage a women's tie with her parental *khandan* is not altogether severed, in fact or theory, as found among the Garhwalis or Paharis of the Central

Himalaya (Berreman, 1974 : 176-177). It is clear from her post-marital relation with her paternal relatives.

When a married woman visits her parents' house she is well received by the members of her parental *khandan* as if she is a member this *khandan*. It may clearly be seen that at the death of her husband/husbands, she often goes back to her parents where she is given marriage with reference to her parents' *khandan* rather than that of her husband. Of course so long she remains with her husband/husbands in the latter's household, she takes part in various activities of her husband(s)' household—economic, social or religious, being a member of the household and *khandan* of her husband/husbands. As a member of a particular *khandan* one has definite right, duties and obligations towards ones *co-khandan* men, including 'amity for them, interest in them, common concern with them, simply and solely because they are in the same agnatic line'. (Fortes, 1945 : 134). The reason behind this is that a person is considered to be related to every member of his/her own *khandan*. It binds its members into a bond of co-operation which provides all *khandan* members with the opportunity to co-operate with one another collectively in all crises of life (Raha and Mahato, 1975 : 273). The *khandan* rules and also the rights, obligations, duties and privileges guide a member to identify and also to understand his position in the society, type of relationship he will have with the co-members of his *khandan* and also nature of reactions he will show towards his congeners. The norms of the *khandan* are absolutely binding on the part of the *khandan* members. Nobody can negate these. The *khandan* system also classifies related members into different categories and also as in case of the Hopi, 'regulates their social behaviour on the other. Towards each class of kindred, there is a definite relationship, expressed in term of duties, obligations, and privileges, which serves to order social life to a minimum of conflicts'. (Eggan, 1949 : 140).

Origin and Development of the Khandan

A number of legends are prevalent in Kinnaur narrating the origin and development of different *khandans* and the analysis of which reveals that this system is not connected with any sort of totem. On the contrary, in most of the cases, the *khandan* is found to have been derived from some individual or a family in the remote past. In course of time the name of the individual, or his surname or the place where from he had actually migrated, became the *khandan* name of the progeny of the individual. For example the *khandans*, Thongpen and Yongpen may be cited. These two *khandans* were originally derived from persons who came from Poari village of Kinnaur (Peari—Por—Pon) and settled in upper Sangla village (Thongpon, Thong=Upper) and Lower Sangla village (Yongpon, Yong =Lower) respectively. Identically the *khandan*, Mongtoan was derived from a person, called Megu, Chetha came from person, named Chethu, Repalto originated from a person Roy Pal (RoyPal—Repal—Repalto). Shongmathus was derived from a Mathus (Oracle) family who came from Shong village. Besides, in some cases a particular profession in particular family has also given birth to a particular *khandan*. For example, Ralpapong *khandan* was originated from a man who was the keeper of the store for rice (Ral=rice, Pal=keeper). Garpong *khandan* came from a worshipper (Gar) of a particular deity and so on.

It is also seen that some of the *khandans* have been originated and developed from the name of the ancestral settlement though of course, in some cases the *khandans* have been seen to have originated for some other reasons. In some cases *khandans* are mere titles given by the king or some other authority.

The Khandan Types

The *khandans* are usually of two types—firstly the original or core *khandan* of the village and secondly the immigrant or marginal *khandan*, the members of the latter type came to the village either by marriage or for some other reasons. The second type of *khandan* is further subdivided into two sub-types on the basis of the places wherefrom the members of those *khandans* have migrated. First sub-type consists of those *khandans* the members of which came from some other villages of Kinnaur. The members of other sub-type of *khandan* came from outside Kinnaur, mostly from neighbouring districts. Most of the cases, the members of the immigrant *khandans* have come by marriage as already stated, either as a wife of some person of the village or as a household son-in-law (*makpa*). In a village in central

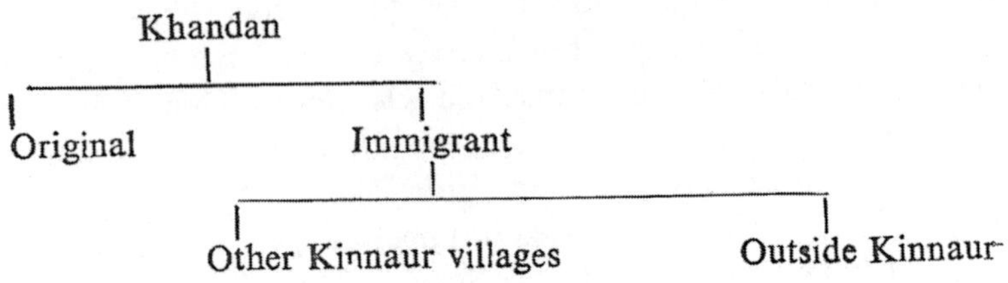

Kinnaur (Zone III) there are 42 *khandans*, (one immigrant *khandan* could not be identified) of which ten, viz., Ares, Braise, Dankas, Pangtu, Pirumathus, Potiyan, Sangchain, Surag, Surain and Turkian, are considered as the original *khandans* of the village. The other 31 *khandans* (one could not be identified) of this village, namely Barang, Charas, Damesh, Datiya, Gammar, Grokatperang, Ghar, Jatpang, Jamimathus, Kangsar, Kochaperang, Kochasong, Kambhi, Kotash, Khuralama, Kongsongmathus, Lamaperang, Lakhan, Mailash, Mathus, Prolaperang, Pancharas, Pranesh, Rapangcharas, Runga, Thakur, Tharangjaj, Uramathus, Yambur and Yarumathus are accepted as the immigrant *khandans*. Again of these 31 immigrant *khandans* two, namely, Kochaperang and Kochasong have come from outside Kinnaur (*kocha*=Kinnaura of other districts). Kochaperang has come from a village near Rampur in Simla district, and Kochasong also from some village of Simla district (previously Mahasu district). The person with unidentified *khandan* is a Kinnaura who has come to this village from outside Kinnaur. The members belonging to the immigrant *khandans* are all women and have come to this village on their marriage with the male members of this village and settled in their respective husbands' house.

Similar is the case with the *khandan* of a village in lower Kinnaur (Zone II). In this village also both original and immigrant *khandans* are found to reside. Here the *khandans* like Bala, Bhorya, Charas, Damesh, Kashu, Khajanchi, Nagchan, Rokyalu, Shabist, Tongku and Tui are the original *khandan* while those like Barang, Barchan, Borsan, Dilosha, Faga, Hinchoru, Indeja, Jangaya, Jengu, Kalya, Kocha, Mayan, Muta,

Olga, Pujar, Polmik, Rakhwan, Rigma, Sangdibakchang, Tupuck, Urchaiya, Wangchama and Yulam are all immigrant *khandans*. Here also Kocha is a *khandan* the members of which (two women) have come from outside Kinnaur. The members of these immigrant *khandans* are all females, and in this village they have come and settled by virtue of their marriage with the malefolk of the village.

In Zone I on the other hand, situation is somewhat different from that of both Zone II and Zone III. Here in a village there are 41 *khandans* belonging to both original and immigrant groups. Of these 41 *khandans* 21 belong to original group while the rest 20 to immigrant group. Some of the important original *khandans* are Chhokpa, Farmoba, Karfu, Kargutungpa, Kongma, Loctus, Nimapushi, Surkhang, Thalkang, Tograba, Youngma etc. Immigrant *khandans* are Chamba, Chumra, Dongbachche, Gyak, Kallalema, Kanhasoma, Khanna, Khary, Kogoma, Khemathengmu, Labrang, Lauphra, Nagchan, Nono, Suri, Talang, Tanzing, Thanga and Todrime. Seven of the immigrant *khandans* e.g. Dongbachche, Gyak, Nagchan, Khanna, Tatpa, Talang and Tokrimo have household in this village of which Nagchan, Khanna and Tokrimo have more than one household. Further, three of the above 20 immigrant *khandans*, viz. Chamba, Khanna and Suri are Kinnaura *khandans* the members of which have come from outside Kinnaur. Again of the 20 immigrant *khandans*, four (Dongbachche, Gyak, Khanna and Nagchan) have both males and females, three (Talang, Tatpa and Tokrimo) have males only and the rest have persons belonging to fair sex only. All of them have come to this village either on marriage or for some other purposes. Another interesting point by which this village differs from that of Zone II and Zone III, is that 276 individuals here who form 47.18 per cent of the total population of the village, do not have any *khandan*. Unlike villages of other two zones where all the households are covered by some *khandan*, here only 67 (57.75 per cent) out of 116 Rajput households are covered by one or other *khandan*, rest 49 (42.25 per cent) bear no *khandan*.

It is thus seen that the structural differences in the *khandan* system lead to distinct functional differences between those different types of the *khandans*.

> "The members of the original *khandan* can take direct part in the activities of various institutions and also other functions such as economic, social, political and religious, of the village while those of the immigrant *khandan* can not. Members of the former *khandan* only can become the functionaries of the temple and the *gumpha* (monastery). Most of the important posts of these religious institutions such as *pujar*, *grokch*, *mathus*, chief *lama* etc. are headed by the members of the original *khandan*. Never a member of the immigrant *khandan* can hold such an office. Similarly in their traditional village council, *charbhai*, all the important portfolios were held by the original *khandan*" (Raha and Mahato, 1975: 277; 1985: 143-144).

In between the two, the original *khandan* is, in every respect, considered as superior to the immigrant *khandan*. Again in case of the latter *khandans* (of other villages) are accepted as higher in status than the *khandans* (came from outside Kinnaur). Further within both original and immigrant *khandans*, a distinct hierarchy is maintained.

> "The *khandans* belonging to the higher status group or *khel* are treated as superior to those of the lower *khel*. That is the *khandans* of the Orang *khel* are superior to those of both Maorang and Waza *khels*. Again the *khandans* of the Maorang *khel* are considered to be superior to those of Waza *khel*". (Raha and Mahato, 1975 : 277-278; 1985: 144).

But this is true only in Zone II, Zone III and parts of Zone I. In a major part of Zone I where the *khel* system is ill-grown or absent the hierarchy is not maintained amongst the original *khandans*. All the original *khandans* here are given almost equal status.

THE KHANDAN SYSTEM OF THE KHOSIA

<table>
<tr><th colspan="11">Khosia
Of A Village in Zone III</th><th colspan="10">Khosia
Of a Village in Zone I</th></tr>
<tr><th colspan="6">Orang</th><th colspan="4">Maorang</th><th>Waza</th><td rowspan="2">Chhokpa</td><td rowspan="2">Farmoba</td><td rowspan="2">Kargutungpa</td><td rowspan="2">Loctus</td><td rowspan="2">Magchan</td><td rowspan="2">Surkhang</td><td rowspan="2">Tograba</td><td rowspan="2">Youngma</td><td rowspan="2">Other Khandans</td><td rowspan="2">No Khandan</td></tr>
<tr><td>Bhorya</td><td>Charas</td><td>Damesh</td><td>Rakayalu</td><td>Shabist</td><td>Tongku</td><td>Bala</td><td>Kashu</td><td>Nagchan</td><td>Tui</td><td>Tawaza</td></tr>
<tr><td></td><td>Pancharas
Ropangcharas</td><td>Dhami Damesh
Khono Damesh
Ladong Damesh</td><td colspan="18">No Sub-Khandan</td></tr>
</table>

Localization of the Khandan

Besides stratification on the basis of hierarchy, the *khandan* system in Kinnaur has another basic characteristic. These *khandans* are mostly localized and they are not universal in distribution. Particular *khandans* are found in particular locality or village. That means a particular locality or village has particular *khandans* which are usually different from those of other villages. Of course, in some cases a few common *khandans* are found located in different villages. In that case some members of those *khandans* of a village must have shifted to other villages and ultimately settled there retaining their original *khandan* name, though of course, in the latter villages they are treated as immigrants.

In two adjacent villages, X and Y in Zone II the only common *khandan* is Charas. And this is so because Charas household from village X got settled in the village Y. All other *khandans* of the village X are different from those of village Y. Again in villages A, B, C. under Zone III there is no identical *khandan* common to the villages A and B but between the villages B and C to only one common *khandan* is Charas. These Charas families were original settlers of the village X. Long back a few families came and settled in villages B and C. Between the villages A and C the common *khandans* are Kochaperang and Surein. The *khandan* Kochaperang has come to these villages from outside Kinnaur, and the *khandan* Surain has come to village C from village A and settled there.

Same identical picture is also seen in Zone I villages. In two Zone I villages (P and Q) the common *khandan* are Tatpa and Youngma. Here both Tatpa and Youngma are original *khandan* in one village (P) and immigrant in another (Q). Again between a Zone I (Q) and a Zone II (X) villages the common *khandan* is Nagchan. Long ago, one Nagchan family came to this Zone I village from the Zone II village and settled there permanently, and thereafter, it branched out to the present seven households.

Each village in Kinnaur as it is seen, has its own distinct set of the *khandans* which is usually different in different villages. When two or more villages project common *khandans*, there is reason to believe that these common *khandans* must have place of origin elsewhere or in some of these villages and thence migrated from the original village to the present villages.

Distribution of the Khandan

Erstwhile I have mentioned that the *khandan* system is not evenly distributed throughout Kinnaur. This uneven distribution of the *khandan* is mainly because of the cultural constraints. Kinnaur, as already discussed, has three distinct culture zones. "When one moves from south-west part of the district (Nachar sub-division and Sangla Tehsil) to north-east of the district (Pooh Tehsil and Hangrang sub-tehsil) one finds gradual degeneration of this system" (Raha and Mahato, 1975: 280). In its full-fledged form the *khandan* system can be found throughout Nachar sub-division (Zone II) and most part of Kalpa sub-division (Zone III). Beyond these areas it looses its importance. In the area of Kalpa sub-division adjoining Pooh sub-division, this system is not so well developed. The same is its condition in Pooh Tehsil; and in Hangrang valley of Pooh sub-division (Zone I) it is quite rudimentary in its formation. Reversely it may also be stated that while this system is characterised by its rudimentary growth in the north-east extremity of the district, it gradually developed in a complex form as it moves towards south-west of the district towards Zone II where it meets its full form. That means, this system may have possible link with the religion of the area. While Buddhism has restricted the development of the *khandan* system, the local Hinduism has nourished and nurtured it and made it into a well developed system in this society of the Western Himalaya, and that is why in the border between Buddhism and Hinduism dominated areas, it is in a transitory stage. It may also be otherwise. This system could be a part of the local Hindu social system and that is why it is found in its full form in Hinduism dominated areas. But as Buddhism of Kinnaur did not have any sort of stratification or hierarchical order; so this system has never been fairly developed in Buddhism dominated areas. Thus it may be inferred that the *khandan* system in Kinnaur is positively co-related with the local Hinduism, but negatively co-related with Buddhism prevalent in this district.

While inhabitants of the villages in Zone II and Zone III

have their own *khandans* in Zone I village all do not have *khandan.* In a village in Zone I as we have already seen, 49 (42.24 per cent) households out of 116 do not have *khandan.* It is also seen that in this village a large number of individuals (46.84 per cent) do not possess any *khandan.*

In another village under Pooh sub-division (Zone I) close to the international border also, all the inhabitants do not have *khandan.* Some of the Rajputs, of course, have *khandans* like Lamaperang, Donk, Kushak, Kanampa, Jawa, Meharperang, Youngma, Mathus, Shiaswa, Tatpa, Chhoreya, Phawanspa, Tongma, Donkthot, Riswa, Syaspa etc.

People of many Zone I villages bearing *khandan,* do not have much idea about rules and regulations, the privileges and prohibitions behind this *khandan* system. That the *khandan* is the guiding principle for their marriage, is also not much clear to them, though, of course, they do not like to marry in the same *khandan.* But a few cases are there in this region where marriage in the same *khandan* had taken place. Yet no punishment was given to the couples involved in the breach of the rule of the *khandan* exogamy. This laxity is primarily due to the lack of consolidation of the institution of the *khandan.* As the *khandan* system here is in its rudimentary form, no rigid rules have yet been framed as regards to the functioning of this system which is in contrast to the situation prevalent in lower and middle Kinnaur.

The Khandan Population

In the villages where *khandan* system exists, the original and superior *khandans* share the major bulk of the population. Moreover, the immigrant *khandans* are mostly peopled by the female folk whom the members of the original *khandans* have brought on marriage.

In a village in lower Kinnaur (Zone II) out of a total of 196 inhabitants 85.20 per cent belong to the original *khandans* and the rest (14.80 per cent) belong to the immigrant group. While the members of the original *khandans* have 59.88 per cent males and 40.12 per cent females, the members of the immigrant *khandans* are all females. Similar is the case in a village in middle Kinnaur (Zone III) where out of 310 villagers 83.87 per cent belong to the original and the rest 16.13 per cent to the immigrant *khandans*. Here also the original *khandans* have both male (58.46 per cent) and female (41.54 per cent) members, but the members of the immigrant *khandans* are all females except one. And this is true for almost all the villages in the lower and middle Kinnaur (Zone I and II) having the *khandan* system. This gives us the idea that in the lower and middle Kinnaur villages the *khandan* system is mostly peopled by the original *khandans*. Almost all the immigrant *khandans* have one member each, and she is a female and has come to the village on marriage.

In a upper Kinnaur (Zone I) village, on the other hand, the situation is somewhat different. Here out of 585 inhabitants 246 (42.05 per cent) have original *khandan* and only 65 (11.11 per cent) bear immigrant *khandan* i.e. villagers with *khandan* form 53.16 per cent. But quite a substantial number of inhabitants (274 or 46.84 per cent) have no *khandan* at all. Again the males and the females cover 58.13 per cent and 41.87 per cent respectively of the total original *khandan* population. In case of immigrant *khandan* population the males are comparatively smaller in number (28 or 44.77 per cent) but the females share the majority (37 or 55.23 per cent) of the people. This has caused a significant difference from the position of the villages in Zone II and Zone III where the fair sex forms almost the whole of the immigrant *khandan* population.

Again in a village under Zone II the *khandans* belonging to the Orang or the superior most *khel* (Bhorya, Charas, Damesh, Rakyalu, Shabist and Tongku) cover the majority (68.26 per cent) of the population of all the original *khandans* (167) of the village. The rest of the population of the original *khandans* (31.74 per cent) are shared by the *khandans* of the Maorang *khel*. Identically in the village under Zone III the overwhelming majority (93.85 per cent) of the population of the original *khandans* (260) belongs to the Orang *khel*. The rest of the population (6.15 per cent) are eaten up by the *khandans* of the Maorang *khel*. Both these villages do not have Waza population.

The condition of *khandan* system in Zone I villages is again much different from that of Zone II and Zone III villages. Here in a Zone I village the lack of status group or *khel* system (the *khel* system is either absent or very rudimentary in major part of Zone I) the *khandans* cannot be differentiated from one another on the basis of any hierarchical order. All *khandans* belonging to the original group, have almost equal status.

It is further seen that though most of the immigrant *khandans* have one member, a female each, the original *khandans* on the contrary, have multiple population of both sexes each. But definitely the numerical strength of population of the *khandans* is not equal but in variable number. In a village in Zone II Damesh with its three sub-*khandans*, covers 31.12 per cent of the total Rajput population of the village. Next comes Tongku with 8.16 per cent of the Rajput population which is followed by Shabist (7.65 per cent), Khajanchi (7.14 per cent) and Nagchan (6.12 per cent). Other *khandans* have still smaller population. Identically in a village under Zone III the *khandan*, Turkiyan bears the highest population (23.55 per cent) followed by Surag (22.90 per cent). The next higher population strength is shared by Sangchain (9.68 per cent) followed by Potiyan (7.10 per cent) and Surain (6.77 per cent). Rest of the original *khandans* cover less than 5.00 per cent of the total Rajput population of the village each. In a village in Zone I no *khandan* has got a very high frequency of population. Of the total population having *khandan*, Tograba has the highest member of people (30 or 12.22 per cent). Next to Tograba, Nagchan, an immigrant *khandan* bears the next higher frequency (7.40 per cent). It is followed by Youngma (6.11 per cent), Thalkang (5.79 per cent), Loctus (5.47 per cent), Surkhang (5.14 per cent) and Chhokpa (4.82 per cent). All these are original *khandans*.

The Sub-Khandan

Some of the *khandans* are found to be divided into a number of sub-*khandans*. These sub-*khandans* are differentiated by prefixing or suffixing some words before or after the core *khandan* name. The reason for the division of a *khandan* into a number of sub-*khandan*, is not always clear. In most of the cases members of the sub-*khandan* have forgotten any such reasons. But in certain cases it is due to the variation of social or economic status among different families of the same *khandan*. The position of different locality of the village and also the situation of the house of the members of the same *khandan* on different level of terraces in the village, also brings forth the formation of a sub-*khandan*.

Like the *khandan* members, the sub-*khandan* members also remain attached with the members of the original *khandans* or also with one another with a bond of relationship. Because of this bond, they always consider themselves as closely related to one another. For this close relation, no marriage is permissible between two sub-*khandans* of the same *khandan* or between a sub-*khandan* and its core *khandan*. Like intra-*khandan* marriage, intra-sub-*khandan* marriage is also considered as the worst kind of sin. As already stated some of the *khandans* are branched into a number of sub-divisions. For example the *khandan* Mathus can be cited.

This *khandan* is divided into a number of sub-*khandans* by prefixing or suffixing some distinguishing words before or after the core *khandan* name thus forming various sub-*khandans* like Barangmathus, Jamimathus, Kensangmathus, Shongmathus, Uramathus and Yarumathus etc.

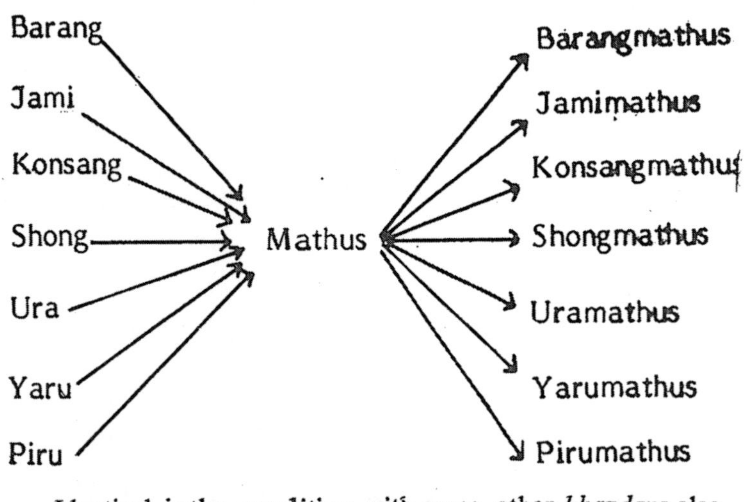

Identical is the condition with some other *khandans* also.

Charas is such a *khandan* and has got two sub-*khandans*, Pancharas and Ropangcharas

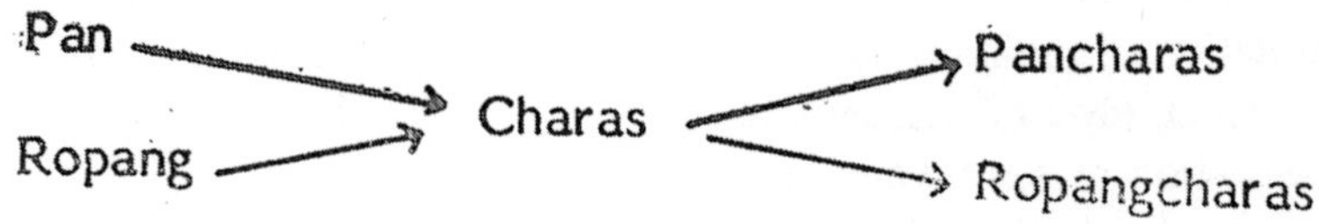

Here, two different sub-*khandans* of Charas have been derived from the core *khandan* Charas by prefixing two distinctive words, Pan and Ropang. Damesh *khandan* has been divided, in a similar way, into a number of sub-*khandans*.

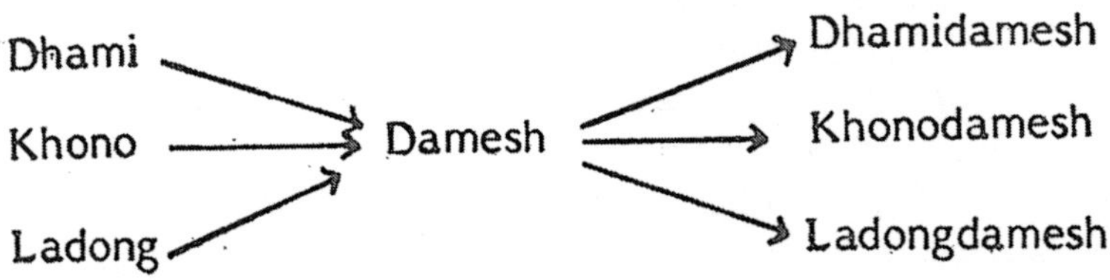

Thus, we get that some of the *khandans* both in Zone II and Zone III are divided into one or more sub-*khandans*. But the condition is not uniform throughout Kinnaur. In the major part of Zone I where the *khandan* system is rudimentary or ill-grown the sub-*khandan* is usually not seen to be present. In two villages in Zone I where we undertook our study no core *khandan* was found to have any sub-*khandans*. The reason seems to be obvious. Because of the lack of sufficient coherent conceptualization and structurization of this system in this region, the framing up of the guiding principles and various functions of the *khandan* system have not been sufficiently developed, and the non-formation of the sub-*khandan* here may have the same reason.

The Khandan and the Marriage System

The *khandan* among the Kinnaura is *par excellence*, a marriage regulating unit. Marriage within the same *khandan* i.e. with the *khandan* of the father (the *khandan* being patrilineal a descent), is strictly forbidden as the *khandan* is exogamous.

> "They consider the breach of this rule of the *khandan* exogamy is very formidable and injurious to the society.

> If any intra-*khandan* marriage takes place, the couple will then cause great annoyance to the deity of the household and also of the village, *ghori* and *khunt* who will definitely be shrew them." (Raha and Mahato 1975: 273; 1985: 149).

The curse of the deity and also of their ancestors and ancestresses will invite unhappiness, disease and even death not only in that family but also to their relatives and the co-villagers because of their inability to prevent the happening of such a sin. And this is the main reason why the Kinnaurs do not tolerate any breach of the *khandan* exogamy; and so they try their best to prevent the occurence of any such incident. "Even the fornication between the members of two different sexes of the same *khandan* is considered as sinful and incestuous. The root cause behind this prohibitory order is that the members of a *khandan* always consider themselves as related by blood" (Raha and Mahato, 1975:273). In a similar reasons the marriage between the members of two sub-*khandans* of a *khandan* or of a sub-*khandan* and its core *khandan* is prohibited.

There is another marriage rule that comes under the purview of the function of the *khandan* system. Under this rule the members of the *khandans* of the superior *khel* cannot marry the members of the *khandans* of the inferior *khel*, the *khel* being endogamous. Of course some relaxation is seen in recent years.

Another interesting rule in the Kinnaura society is that it shuns marriage in father's *khandan* as already stated. In an identical way the marriage in mother's *khandan* is also totally against the norm of the society. Marriage in any of the sub-*khandan's* of the *khandan* of the father or of the mother is identically shunned. That means, one considers both father's and mother's *khandan* at the time of marriage and carefully avoids *khandans* of both of them and also sub-*khandans* of those two *khandans*. But it is interesting to note that one always tries to marry in ones father's mother's *khandan* which is preferred over other *khandans*.

Descent of the Khandan

Among the Rajput of Kinnaur, the descent of the *khandan* is reckoned through the male line. Unmarried children always receive their father's *khandan*. Even after marriage, while the male child retains his father's *khandan*, the female child on the other hand, accepts her husband's *khandan*. So far as the descent is concerned the mother's *khandan* bears no importance.

> "Similarly, the *khandan* of the wife, father's, mother or of the mother's mother is without any importance when the descent is considered. In case of adoption, the adopted child usually gets its adoptive father's *khandan*. This rule is followed even when the marriage between the Rajput and some other ethnic group, takes place" (Raha and Mahato 1975: 276; 1985: 150).

The *khandan* of the Rajput is non-totemic in nature. But the members of each and every *khandan* trace their descent from a common ancestor, whom they always consider as a human being. That means, all families having a common *khandan* will have a common descent from a common ancestor. This is why members of a particular *khandan* are always considered as related to one another and recognize themselves as brothers and sisters. This has resulted in the prohibition of intra-*khandan* marriages. Similar is the case with the members of different sub-*khandans* of a *khandan*.

The Khandan and the Household

In Kinnaur village most of the Rajput households belong to the original *khandans* only. Only in a very few cases households belonging to the immigrant *khandans*, are found. Again the households are not evenly distributed among different *khandans*. Some *khandan* may have a larger number of households whereas some other may cover only one. In a village under Hangrang sub-Tehsil of Pooh sub-division (Zone I) the Rajputs have 116 households of which only 67 (57.76 per cent) households are covered by some *khandan* or other, but rest 49 (42.24 per cent) do not have any *khandan*. Of these 67 households which possess *khandan*, 51 (76.12 per cent) belong to original and the rest 16 to immigrant *khandan*. Tograba of these 28 *khandans*, covers the highest number of households (11 or 16.42 per cent). Next to it comes Nagchan covering 7 (10.45

per cent) households followed by Thalkang and Youngma (5.97 per cent each). It is further seen that 9 out of 21 original *khandans* cover 37 households, that means, these 9 *khandans* cover 55.22 per cent of the total households having *khandan.* In case of the immigrant *khandans* three viz., Khanna, Nagchan and Tokrimo hold 75.00 per cent of the total immigrant households.

In a village in Nachar sub-division (Zone II) on the other hand, there are a total of 40 households belonging to the Rajput. These 40 households are distributed among eleven original *khandans.* Immigrant *khandans* do not possess any household. The household without any *khandan* is non-existent here. In this village the *khandan* Damesh and its three sub-*khandans* (Dhami Damesh, Khono Damesh and Ladong Damesh) cover 14 or 35.00 per cent of the total Rajput households. And only Damesh itself covers 17.50 percent of the total number of the households. The next higher number of households belonging to different *khandans,* are Nagchan, Shabist and Tongku, each of which has 10.00 per cent of the total number of households. Rest of the *khandans* do have smaller number of households each. It is further seen that even among the original *khandans* only a few hold the majority of the households. In this village the *khandans* like Damesh (with its three sub-*khandans*), Nagchan, Shabist and Tongku share 65.00 percent of the total households.

Again a village in Central Kinnaur (Zone III) has ten original *khandans* which have households in the village. The largest number of the Rajput households (14 or 35.00 per cent) belong to Turkian *khandan.* The *khandan,* Surag, covers the next higher number of households (10 or 25.60 per cent). An immigrant *khandan,* Kochaperang has also got one household in its credit. That means out of the eleven *khandans* having household in the village all but one are original *khandans* of the village. Again like that in the village in lower Kinnaur, in this village too, out of the total of ten *khandans* five (Potiyan, Sangchain, Surag, Surain and Turkian) share majority (82.50 per cent) of the Rajpur households. Household without any *khandan* is also non-existent here.

Further, it is interesting to note that the superiormost *khandans* i.e. the *khandans* of the Orang *khel,* occupy larger

Table: Khandan distribution of Rajput households

Zone I Khandan	No. of Hh	Percentage	Zone II Khandan	No. of Hh	Percentage	Zone III Khandan	No. of Hh	Percentage
Chhokpa	3	4.48	Balo	3	7.50	Ares	2	5.10
Chongtut	1	1.49	Bhorya	1	2.50	Braise	1	2.50
*Dongbachche	1	1.49	Charas	2	5.00	Dankas	1	2.50
Dongringjingutpa	1	1.49	Damesh	7	17.50	*Kochaperang	1	2.50
Farmoba	3	4.48	Dhami Damesh	1	2.50	Pangtu	1	2.50
Gamphu	1	1.49	Khono Damesh	3	7.50	Pirumathus	1	2.50
Gungwa	1	1.49	Ladong Damesh	3	7.50	Potiyan	3	7.50
*Gyak	1	1.49	Kashu	1	2.50	Sangchain	3	7.50
Karfu	2	2.99	Khajanchi	3	7.50	Surag	10	25.00
Kargutungpa	3	4.48	Nagchan	4	10.00	Surain	3	7.50
*Khanna	3	4.48	Rokyalu	2	5.00	Turkian	14	35.00
Kongma	3	4.48	Shabist	4	10.00			
Loctus	3	4.48	Tongku	4	10.00			
*Nagchan	7	10.45	Tui	2	5.00			
Naidu	1	1.49						
Nimapushi	2	2.99						
Soshuma	1	1.49						

Zone I Khandan	No. of Hh	Percentage	Zone II Khandan	No. of Hh	Percentage	Zone III Khandan	No. of Hh	Percentage
Surkhang	3	4.48						
*Talang	1	1.49						
*Tatpa	1	1.49						
Thalkang	4	5.97						
Thalsara	1	1.49						
Tongpan	1	1.49						
Toglog	1	1.49						
Tograba	11	16.42						
*Tokrimo	2	2.99						
Youngma	4	5.97						
Yulpong	1	1.49						
Total	67	100.00		40	100.00		40	100.00

*Immigrant *Khandan*.

number of households in the village. In a village in Zone II 67.50 per cent of the households are occupied by the *khandans* like Bhorya, Charas, Damesh, Nagchan, Rakyalu, Shabist and Tongku, all of these belong to the *khel*, Orang. The rest belong to the other *khel*. In the village under Zone III the overwhelming majority of the households (90 00 per cent) are held by the members of the *khandans* like Areas, Pirumathus, Potian, Sangchain, Surag, Surain and Turkian. All these *khandans* belong to the *khel* Orang i.e. the superiormost *khel*. But as the *khel* system is non-existent in most of the Zone I villages, no such type of frequency can be available.

It is thus clear that three interesting points emerge out of the analysis of the *khandan*-wise distribution of the households. Firstly, the original *khandans* hold majority of the households of the village. Households belonging to the immigrant *khandans*, are either absent or only a few in number except in Zone I—village where 23.88 perc ent households are occupied by the immigrants. Secondly, even if a number of the *khandans* is present in the village, majority of households are occupied by only a few important *khandans*. Finally, the *khandans* of the superiormost *khel* Orang, occupy majority of the households of the village which is true for Zone II and III as most of the Zone I villages do not have *khel* system.

In Kinnaur the family (*kim*) is the growing point for the *khandan*. It is always patrilocal and simultaneously monogamous and nuclear, polygynous, polyandrous and polygynandrous too. While in nuclear monogamous families children are not differentiated from one another as they are born of the same parents. But in case of the polygynous families which are only a few in number, the children of the same father are differentiated from one another as they belong to different mothers whose status in the family always vary. But very interesting feature can be noticed in case of the polyandrous and polygynandrous families. Polyandry being the cultural profile of the Kinnaura, a good number of polyandrous and polygynandrous families are found here. In case of polyandrous families, children of same mother but different fathers (who are brothers) are not differentiated as the eldest of the husbands (also eldest brother) is treated as the 'father' of all the children. Here

KHANDAN AND KIM AFFILIATION

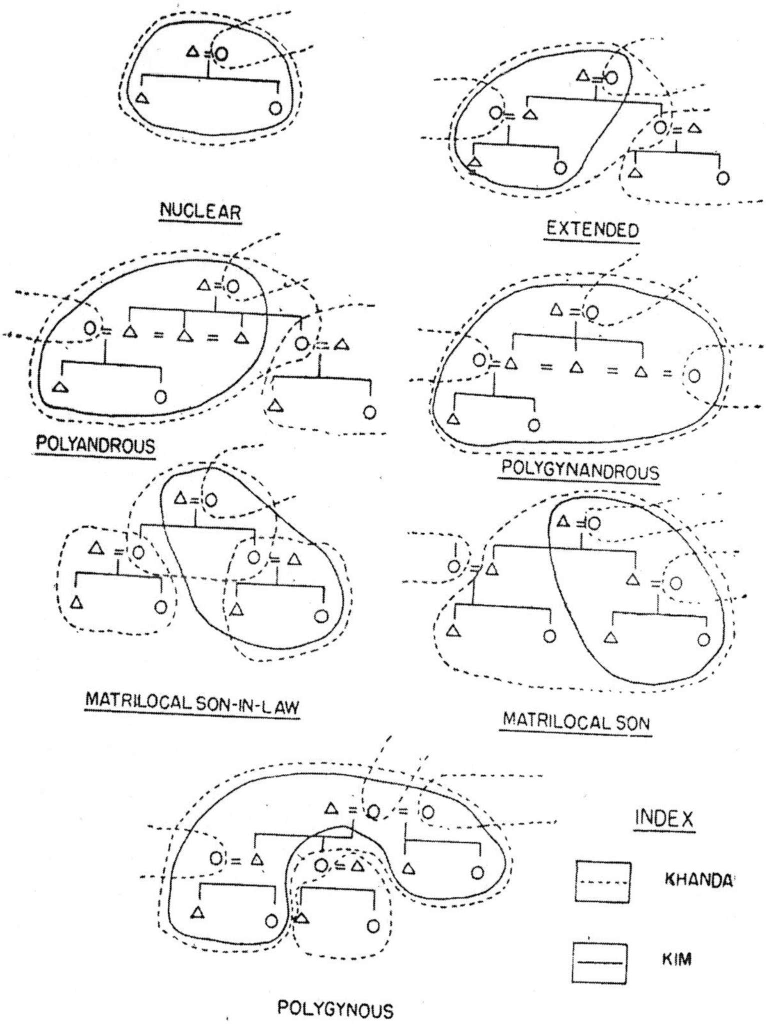

children differentiate their mother's husbands. Whoever may be the biological father, but children (of different brother-husbands) socially recognize the eldest husband (naturally the eldest brother) of their mother as their social father. Other brothers who may be termed as 'father' are not treated equally with the social father. The condition is almost same in case of the polygynandrous families. Here though eldest brother-husband is treated as the 'social father' (may not be biological) by all children of all mothers (here all the wives are wives of all the brother-husbands), but children differentiate the wives of their fathers. They only recognize their respective biological mother who has given them birth, as their 'own' mother. That means we get four different combinations.

1. Children of the same father and mother
2. Children of same father but different mothers
3. Children of same mother but different fathers recognizing one as 'father'
4. Children of different mothers and different fathers recognizing one as 'father'

These provide some scope for further criterion of differentiation within the *khandan* system. It is true that 'fathers' are always brothers and they have common *khandan*, and they keep no chance of differentiating the *khandan* (polyandry here being fraternal). But while the question of marriage of the sons of different mothers (polygyny and polygynandry) comes, differentiation becomes obvious in selecting the bride as marriage in mother's *khandan* is not permitted.

The Kinnaura Economy and the Khandan System

The traditional economy of the Kinnaura (the Rajput) was based on agriculture, animal husbandry and trade except the Waza section who were potters. Besides the Rajput, the Lohar had iron and silver works, the Koli professed agriculture, weaving, spinning and leather works, the Badhi practised carpentry and masonary works and the Nangalu were basket makers. With the passage of time, the traditional economy of the Kinnaura in general, show distinct changes, particularly from late fifties. The artisan castes, besides their traditional occupations, have accepted agriculture, daily labour, service etc. as addtional sources of livelihood. But distinct change in the Rajput economic life is noticed since the closure of the Indo-Tibetan international border in early sixty when one of their important economic persuits, the trade, particularly with Tibet, came to a halt. This political event also snatched the opportunity of their grazing facility in the alpine pastures of Tibet. Naturally, these reverses brought at least, a temporary set back in their economic condition which was gradually compensated when the Government came forward with a package programme of developmental and constructional works. This not only helped the people in developing their agriculture, horticulture, cottage industry and other existing sources of livelihood but also opened different new avenues of income such as daily labour, service, business etc. One of the significant achievements of the post-closure of the border period is the development of the market and cash economy which was hitherto almost absent. A number of markets has been developed in different areas alluring businessmen from outside Kinnaur to creep in. The Kinnaura are earning cash from the sale of fruits and vegetables and also from daily labour.

As already stated, agriculture forms one of the major economic resources of the Rajput. Most of them possess land for cultivation. But villages where the Rajput have the *khandan* system, do not show the uniformity in the *khandan*-wise distribution pattern of land. Though the households belonging to different *khandans* have land, there are *khandans* which possess more land while some others have very low acreage of land. "Usually the more important *khandan* have more land and less important ones have less holdings." (Raha and Mahato, 1985 : 106). As far as the quality of the land is concerned, the superior *khandans* own more fertile and better quality of land whereas less fertile and inferior quality of land is shared by inferior *khandans*. Of course, some exceptions are also found. In the village in Zone I all the original and seven immigrant *khandans* have cultivable land in varied acreage. Again in this village all but one of the 67 households belonging to 28 *khandans* (original and immigrant) have cultivable land. One of the immigrant households, a Khanna does not have any cultivable land. Further of these 28 *khandans* having cultivable land, Gamphu, Gungwa, Thalsara and Yulpong (all original) and Dongbachche (immigrant) have 20.00 or more bighas of cultivable land on an average and of them Yulpong has the highest holding (55.00 bighas). Further *khandans* like Dongringjing-utpa, Kargutungpa, Loctus (all original) and Gyak and Nagchan (both immigrant) have cultivable land in the range of 15.00 to 20.00 bighas on an average. All the other *khandans* have land below 15.00 bighas on an average.

One interesting point that needs to be mentioned here is that out a total of 116 Rajput households, in this village 49 have got no *khandan* and of these 46 have cultivable land with an average of 9.17 bighas. Three households having no *khandan*, have no land of their own.

The pattern is somewhat different in other two zones. So far as the cultivable land is concerned, a Zone II village depicts that only the original *khandans* of this village do possess cultivable land. No land belongs to the immigrant *khandans*. Here *khandans* like Bhorya, Tonku and Charas belonging to the superiormost *khel*, Orang have more than 20 bighas of land on an average. The *khandan* Khajanchi of Maorang *khel* occupying an intermediate position in social hierarchy, has an average of 17.46 bighas of land. Of course, some *khandans* of the Orang *khel* such as Damesh and Tui, also have land holding between 15.00 to 20.00 bighas on an average. Kashu *khandan* of the Waza *khel* with the lowest position in social hierarchy among the Rajputs, has an average of 29.00 bighas of land, but the quality of land as stated by the family members, is of inferior type.

Identically in a village in Zone III *khandans* like Turkiyan, Potiyan, Surag, Ares, Surain and Sangchain of the Orang *khel* have more than 20.00 bighas of cultivable land on an average. Of them Sangchain has got an average of 123.90 bighas of land on averge. Potiyan 50.67 bighas, Ares 42.00 bighas, Surain 39.00 bighas, Surag 31.30 and Pangtu 28.00 bighas, on an average. Pirumathus is the only *khandan* under Orang *khel* of this village having an average of only 15.00 bighas of cultivable land. The *khandan* Kochaperang, which came and settled in this village from outside Kinnaur, has the lowest average landholding—only 2.0 bighas of cultivable land.

The distribution of 'other types' of land shows a different trend. In the Zone I village out of 28 *khandans* only 17 possess 'other types' of land which include house site, pasture, fallow land etc. Of these 17 *khandans* of which 13 are original and 4 immigrant, Gomphu has the highest average of this type of land (50.00 bighas) followed by Dongringjingupta (15.00 bighas). Rest of the *khandans* have all below 6.00 bighas on an average. It is interesting to mention here that households having no *khandan* have on an average 0.65 bighas of 'other types' of land.

In Zone II village the Bhorya has the highest average of the 'other types' of landholding (10.00 bighas) on an average, All other *khandans* of Orang *khel* have below 3.00 bighas, on an average except Dhami Damesh which does not own such land. The *khandan* Khajanchi belonging to the Maorang *khel* has got an average of 4.34 bighas of such land. But Kashu, the only Waza *khandan* possesses no such 'other types' of land.

But in Zone III village more than half of the total *khandans* of the village do not own 'other types' of land. Only five out of 11 *khandans* have such land, and of these Sangchain has the highest (18.33 bighas) of land on an average per household and Surain had 6.33 bighas. Rest have less then 5.00 bighas on an average per household.

It is thus seen that the *khandans* belonging to original group and superior *khel* always possess bigger lands-holding and better type of land. The condition was also same in the past. The original *khandans* had the marked dominance so far as the land-holding was concerned. Identically, the *khandans* belonging to superior *khel* had highest share of land and also of better type of land.

Almost similar is the case of the other economic persuits also. Same dominance of the *khandans* of the superior *khels* in horticulture, animal husbandry and also in case of trade with the country across the border was found in olden days. The members of the original *khandans* and also those belonging to higher or superior *khels* had almost the monopoly in trade. Most of the Kinnaura traders belonged to the original *khandans* in all zones and to the Orang and Maorang *khels* in Zone II and III in particular. The members of the immigrant *khandans* and also the *khandans* of the inferior *khel* had very little share in this pursuit. Identically in case of animal husbandry, both in the past and in the present days as well, the majority of the animals (sheep, goat and cattle) are owned by the original and also *khandans* of the superior *khels*. The members of the original *khandans* and superior *khels* took the advantage of the horticultural development and are now reaping the benefits in a much better way.

The picture is not different in case of service and business. Here also dominance of superior *khels* and original *khandans* is seen. The Kinnaura Rajput who are in Kinnaur or who have gone out of Kinnaur for service, particularly for better service, are mostly belong to superior and original *khandans*.

The reasons behind this trend are that the number of superior and original *khandans* were and are in general, economically better than those of the inferior and/or immigrant *khandans*. And because they were economically well off, they could afford to be involved in trade in the past and to keep a good number of livestock and land. Even in the present day they are in a position to keep a large number of livestock or to plant improved varieties of fruit trees in an appreciable number and to apply improved knowhow in their agricultural field. Further because they are economically well off, they can afford to provide better and higher education to their children; and because of that their children could get better service. On the other hand, it could also be said that the members of the superior and original *khandans* are well off because they have bigger and better plots of land, more livestock and trades, and because they are well off, they are in a position to improve their condition in varied ways.

The Political Organisation and the Khandan System

The administrative set up which exists in Kinnaur today, is much different from what was prevalent in the long past. As already stated it was a part of the erstwhile Bushahar state, one of the many princely states of the Himalayas headed by a king.

The kingship here was heredictory. According to the Gazetteer of Bushahar State 1910, this princely state, in those days, had three tehsils namely, Chini, Rampur and Rohru, and the present day Kinnaur district was covered mostly by the tehsil Chini (1911 : 65). For the purpose of better administration, each tehsil of Bushahar state was divided into a number of pargana or *khunt*, each pargana or *khunt* was further divided into a number of *ghori*, and each *ghori* was constituted by a number of villages (*op. cit.*).

Kinnaur of the past was constituted of eight parganas namely, Sialkar, Shua, Bhaba or Wangpo, Parli or upper Rajgram, Warli or lower Rajgram, Pandrabis, Tukpa and Atharabis. Each of these parganas was headed by a *wazir*. The office of the *wazir* was hereditary. These *wazirs* used to run the administration through a number of sub-ordinate officials also called the *wazirs*. These latter *wazirs* were either elected or selected by the king every year, and their term lasted for only a year. They were authorized to assess and collect the revenues and settle minor disputes, but the king was always lord paramount. This has also been confirmed by Fraser over a hundred and fifty year ago (1820 : 269). The *wazirs* and the junior *wazirs* who headed various parganas of the Kinnaur of the past, belonged to the superior *khandans* and superior *khels* mostly. Besides, the king used to have two more sets of officials, *churriahs* and *hazrees*. The first set of officials consisting of sixty to eighty men, were led by three *pulsur*, *buttoonggee* and *negi* whose status was equivalent to subedar, jamadar and burkandase respectively. The duties of this set of officials were to collect revenue, to report any misconduct and to see that the people were equitably assessed. The other set of officials, the *hazree*, consisted of one hundred and forty men and was led by a *gooldar*. The duty of these officials who were paramilitary in nature, was to guard the king. Many of these two sets of officials who were deployed from the Kinnaura in the past, belonged to superior *khels* and original and superior *khandans*.

From the state if we look into the village level, we see that the same picture is prevalent. Most of the members of the village council or the *char bhai* belonged to the superior *khels* and also superior and original *khandans* of the Rajput. The head of the village council, the *mukhiya* never came from any household that did not belong to the original and superior *khandan.*

With the abolition of the old village council in 1895, the panchayats were replaced by a tehsil which with sixty three villages, were divided into five parganas, and these parganas were further sub-divided into fifteen *gories* each of which, in turn, consisted of a number of villages with common grazing ground. Each pargana was under the control of an official, called the *dashong* who was assisted by a number of *char* or watchmen in collection of revenue. Usually the original and superior *khandan* and superior *khel* used to hold the office of the *deshong* and the *char.*

In the present day Kinnaur the older administrative and judiciary systems have been totally changed, and the new statutory elective bodies, the *gram panchayat and the naya panchayat,* have replaced the older ones. Though the members of these two bodies are elected, still they come from the original and superior *khandans* and superior *khels* mostly. The *pradhan* and the *upa pradhan* of the *gram panchayat* and the *sarpanch* and the *nayeb sarpanch* of the *naya panchayat* invariably come from original and superior *khandans,* besides, the majority of the panchayat members also belong to the original and superior *khandans.*

Even in the modern political activities, the original and superior *khandans* have important contribution. Most of the village level leaders of different political parties are the members of the original and superior *khandans,* and being the leaders of different political parties, particularly of the ruling party, the *khandan* members exert their influence on the common mass.

It is thus seen that the original and superior *khandans* have, as in the past, very effective political control over the people of Kinnaur.

The Religion and the Khandan System

As already stated two religious faiths are found to be prevalent among the Kinnaura of the present day—the Mahayan Buddhism and the local Hinduism. While the influence of Buddhism is marked in the Zone I, the dominance of local Hinduism is apparant in Zone II, Zone III on the other hand, being influenced by both religions simultaneously.

In the areas with the influence of Buddhism, people keep faith on a large number of Buddhist deities, saints, spirits etc. who reside in the monasteries run either by the *lama* (monk) or by the *zomo* (nuns). Both the *lama* and the *zomo* have enough influence over the common people. They conduct all functions, both sacred and secular. As in the past, in the present days also the *lamas* in this district, belong to

> "three sects, Geloopa, Dookpa and Neengma. The Geloopas or Gelookpas...wear yellow cloth garments and caps of the same or various shapes. The Dookpas are dressed indifferently, but have red caps; and the Nengmas wear the same or go bareheaded; the two former do not marry but there is no restriction on the Neengma" (Gerard, 1841 : 117).

Of the above three sects, the latter two are more numerous in Kinnaur. Here the *lamas* are of two types-*gyalong* (celibate) who are strict followers of lamahood, remain unmarried, shave their head and live in the monasteries, and *dugpu* who may live in the house, may marry but do not shave their head. Besides, there are some monasteries in Kinnaur which are under the control of the *zomos* (nuns.)

Each of the monestaries has got a specified area over which it exerts its influence, and the *lamas* of that monasteries have influence on the people in that area. The *lamas* come from the Rajput group. Nobody other than the Rajput can become the *lamas* here. Even among the Rajput, usually the members of the higher *khels*, that is, the Orang and the Maorang, become the *lama*. Rarely a member of the Waza *khel* is seen to become a *lama*. At all a Waza becomes a *lama*, he usually does not hold any important office in the monasteries. All important positions of the monasteries are usually held by the *lamas* of the Orang or the Maorang *khel*.

In the Hinduism dominated areas, each of the deities has a defined area over which the deity concerned has absolute jurisdiction. The deity exerts authority and power on the people residing there. Nothing important can be done without the approval of the deity. The territorial jurisdiction usually coincides with the traditional socio-political or administrative divisions like *khunt*, *ghori*, *gaon* and *kim* (household) (Raha and Mahato, 1985 : 302-304; Raha, 1979 : 95-97). Each *khunt* has a *khunt* deity; under each *khunt* deity there are several *ghori* deities; under each *ghori* deity there are a number of *gaon* (village) deities and in each household in a village a *kim* deity is worshipped. And over all these deities is the *pradesh* deity (Bhimakali), the presiding deity of the whole of the erstwhile Bushahar state. Bhimakali has the abode in a temple at Sarahan, the summer capital of the erstwhile Maharaja of Bushahar (at present in Simla district).

Each of the above dieties has an abode in a temple (*santhang*). The administration of the *santhang* is run by a group of functionaries called the *kardar*. "They actually serve the deity and control the socio-religious administration of the socio-political units like the *gaon*, the *ghori* or the *khunt*...." (Raha and Mahato, 1985 : 320: 324).

These *kardars* are the *pujaris* (the priest), the *grokch* (oracle who ascertains the will or the verdict of the deity and relays it to the villagers), the *mathus* (who speaks to the deity on behalf of the villagers) the *kaithus* or *khajanchi* (accountant who keeps the temple account), the *chalia* (carrier of the palanquin of the deity), the *kroshya* (temple guard), the *halbandi* (messenger), the *baijantri* (musician) etc. Of these former four are the most important functionaries of the temple.

As stated elsewhere a villager does not have the right to approach the deity directly and again he cannot do any important work without consulting the deity. He has to depend on the above four important *kardars* for this purpose. If he has any problem he has to tell it to the *mathus* who is the person who only can narrate the problem to the deity on behalf of the villager. The deity's verdict can only be had from the *grokch* who is the mouth-piece of the deity. That means a villager is totally dependant of these *kardars* for any solution to his problem; and whatever solution is prescribed by the deity, he has no option but to accept it. Of course before he or she approaches the deity, he or she has to offer worship to the deity through the *pujar* and also make payment, if any, to the *khajanchi*. Nobody has any right to disobey the will of the deity which is to be accepted at any cost. So, it clearly indicates that the *kardars* play very significant and important roles and have enough control over the people, and often act as the key-figures in the village politics. The offices of the *kardars* particularly of the formar four (i.e. *pujar, mathus, grokch,* and *khajanchi*) are always held by the members of the superior *khels* and superior and original *khandans.* None other than them can ever hold these important and key positions. The selection of these functionaries are done by the deity itself. For the selection of the *kardar* when any post falls vacant, the deity is approached by the *mathus* and the verdict of the deity is spelt out by the *grokch* to the assembled villagers. Even about the selection/election of the members of *char bhai,* the former village council, deity's approval was required, and this approval came through the same procedure.

It is thus seen that the members of the superior *khels* and thereby the members of the superior and original *khandans* had enough authority and control over the village affairs and also on the villagers. They had enough control over the village economy (they were the main landowners, traders and keepers of livestock), social system (they remained on the top of the ladder of the social hierarchy), political activities (they used to hold the post of village headman and also the important members of the village council which was totally under their control) and also in the religious affairs (they used to hold the offices of the key religious functionaries).

Almost the same condition prevails in the present days. Over and above the members of the superior *khel* and *khandan* are enjoying some more privileges of the present day. Their children are getting higher education and thereby have got good services (Government and private) both inside or outside the district. On becoming educated they get involved in modern politics and capture the political leadership of the area. Thus, they have every opportunity to improve their condition and also have secured the capability of controlling the fate of the other villagers.

NOTE

1. In my previous article (Raha, 1979) I have mentioned that the khandan system in Zone I (Pooh sub-division) is non-existent. But further analysis of later data shows that the said system is in existence there but definitely ill-developed or rudimentary in nature.

REFERENCES

Bajpai, S.C.	1981	*Kinnaur in the Himalayas*, Concept Publishing House, New Delhi.
Berreman, G.D.	1962	Sib and clan among the Pahari of North India, *Ethnology*, Vol. I.
Berreman, G.D.	1974	*Hindus of the Himalayas : Ethnography and Change*, University of California Press, Berkley, USA, New extended Edition.
Eggan, F.	1949	The Hopi and the Lineage Principles, in *Social Structure*, Ed. by M. Fortes, Oxford University Press, Oxford.
Eggan, F.	1950	*Social Organization of the Western Pusbles*, Chicago.
Evans-Pritchard, E.E.	1940	*The Nuer*, The Clarendon Press, Oxford.
Forde, Daryll	1970	Ecology and Social Structure, The Huxley Memorial Lecture, 1970.
Fortes, M.	1945	*The Dynamics of clanship among the Tallensi*, Oxford University Press, London.
Gerard, A.	1841	*An Account of Koonawar in the Himalayas, etc.* London.

Government of Punjab 1911 *Punjab State Gazetteer*, Vol. VIII, Simla Hill States, 1910, The Civil and Military Press, Lahore.

Mahato, S.N. and M.K. Raha 1975 The Kinnaurese of Western Himalaya, *Bulletin of the Cultural Rasearch Institute*, Vol. XI, No. 1 & 2, Calcutta.

Mamgain, M.D. 1971 *Himachal Pradesh District Gazetteer, Kinnaur*, State Editor, District Gazetteer, Simla.

Murdock, G.P. 1965 *Social Structure*, The Free Press, New York.

Raha, M.K. 1974 The Highlanders of Western and Central Himalaya, *Vanyajati*, Vol. XXII, No. 3, New Delhi.

Raha, M.K. 1979 Stratification and Religion in a Himalayan Seciety in *Himalayan Anthropology*, Ed. James Fisher, Moutan & Co. The Hague.

Raha, M.K. 1981 Urgent Anthropology of the Himalayas in *Journal of Social Research*, Special number on Himalayan Studies, vol. XXIV, No. 11, Ranchi.

Raha, M.K. 1982a Subsistence Economy, Environmental Involvement and Survival Strategies in the high Himalayas. (Unpub.)

Raha, M.K. 1982b Economic Strategies, Religious Pluralism and change in Diverse Ecological Setting: A case from Western Himalaya in *The Himalayas and the Himalayans : Bio-Cultural Aspects*, Ed. M.K. Raha, Anthro-

		pological Survey of India, Calcutta, (forthcoming)
Raha, M.K.	1982c	Environmental Diversity and Polyvalent Economy in the Western Himalayas (Paper presented in the seminar on Environmental Anthropology)
Raha, M.K. and S.N. Mahato	1975	The Kinnaurese of Western Himalayas, Anthropological Survey of India Memoirno 63 Calcutta.
Raha, M.K., J.C. Das and S.C. Mondal	1980	Village Structure in Kinnaur, in *Journal of Social Research*, Vol. XXIII, No. 1, Ranchi.
Raha, M.K., S.N. Mahato and R.S. Negi	1976	The Kinnaurese Kinship System: A Termenological Analysis, in *Bulletin of Anthropological Survey of India*, Vol. XXV, Nos. 3 & 4, Calcutta.
Rose, H.A.	1911	*A Glossary of the Tribes and Castes of the Punjab and N.W.F.P.*, Vol. II, Civil and Military Gazette Press, Lahore.
Sanskrityan, R.	1956	*Kinner Desh* (in Hindi), Allahabad.
Sen, B.	1970	Social Changes in the Himalayan Villages: A case study of the three villages in the Kinnaur District (Unpublished Ph. D. dissertation).
Singh, A.C.P.	1965	*District Handbook : Kinnaur District*, Himachal Pradesh Census 1961, Simla.

CHAPTER XXII

CHANGING PATTERN OF POLITICAL LEADERSHIP AMONG TRIBALS OF KINNAUR

D. B. NEGI

The Problem

The contemporary tribal people of India is passing through a period of transition and a sense of bewilderment has been caused at that. The new social and economic forces generated by the large scale developments and planned changes have shaken up the social structure and are beginning to alter the old values and attitudes as well. We believe that such changes are bound to impinge on social and political processes of the tribal communities. New networks of political powers, institutions, procedures and practices have either emerged or are required to cope up with such historical change. The introduction of parliamentary form of government, universal franchise, party competitiveness, Panchayat institutions, community projects, modern education, mass communication and land reforms etc. have greatly affected the natural process that gives rise to the phenomenon of political leadership. As a consequence of such changes, the traditional leadership is being challenged and new leadership is coming out to meet the changed situation with different combination of skills as well as techniques of mobilisation of support. Traditionally, caste, age and wealth were considered to be the major determinants of the village leadership. But in the wake of modernization process, do they still continue to be major criteria for village leadership ? What are the bases and roots of existing leadership? How do emerging leaders differ from traditional ones? The attempt of this paper is to give answers to this broad set of questions as well as to go into few related issues that are closely bound up with such an inquiry.

Leadership Theoretical Aspects

While the leader may be understood in terms of corporate body (person) with certain distinct qualities, leadership is the activity of leader i.e. influencing the behaviour of others to realize common goal or goals. Ordway also thinks that the leadership is the activity of influencing people to co-operate towards some common goal which they have come to find desirable (1935 : 20). For the leader personal relationship is utmost important. Allport makes special emphasis on personal relation of leadership. "Leadership according to our present usage means the direct face to face control between leader and followers; it is personal sociol control" (1924 : 419). It is also seen that the leadership is an 'inter-personal influence exercised in situation and directed through communication process towards the attainment of specific goal or goals' (Tannenbaum and Massarik, 1961 : 24). Glenn D. Paige while defining leadership, emphasised that the political leadership is the behaviour of those, "in position of political authority, their competitors and the interaction between them" (1977 : 1).

During the past few decades the concept of leadership is shifting focus in theoretical orientation. During the first decade of twentieth century, leadership research was guided by the 'trait of greatman approach'. It was assumed that leadership could be explained by isolating psychological and physical characteristic, which were presumed to differentiate the leader from other members of his group. However, this theory ended in unsatisfactory results due to difficulty in defining universal traits.[1] As a result, it has been recognised that leadership must be seen in the background oı cultural, social and physical context. The concept of leadership, then, came to be viewed as a function of situation. Thus, the 'situationist approach' has attempted to look personality traits in social situations containing common elements. However, it was soon realised that no concept of leadership would be complete unless it considered the structure of the group in which the interactions among members had taken place. This gradually took the form of another approach, the 'group-follower approach.' This approach underlines the assumption that leadership is a set of functions required by group under various conditions (Nagpal, 1967: 58-59).

In fact, leadership is such a complex social phenomenon that we cannot characterise leader and deal with leadership traits apart from group and situations in what the leadership occurs. Thus leadership is taken to be a combination of the factors of the persons, groups and situations.

Typology : Traditional and Emerging Leaders

For the present study the leadership concept has been conceived to cover the traditional and the emerging leaders. The leader has operationally been defined as formal or informal. A formal leader is an authority figure holding an elective or appointive office or offices. An informal leader is an influential person without holding formal position but is still considered a person of great political prestige because he controls 'power exercise'. Both sets of leaders were carefully classified into traditional and emerging leaders. The traditional leaders come from the families which have tradition of displaying leadership of generations. Their leadership is invariably based on ascriptive criteria, namely, caste, age and wealth. Such leaders are locally pronounced as *sainas* (elders), *shukars* (wealthymen), *lamberdar* (village headmen) and *chares* (village messanger). Apart from the above types of leaders, the introduction of new institutions and organizations, i.e., *gram panchayats, yuva mandals, mahila mandals,* co-operative societies etc. has given rise to emerging leaders. In contrast to traditional leaders, the emerging leaders acquire leadership position on the basis of personal achievement and merit. Also, they are largely differentiated and specialized in roles as compared to traditional leaders. The leaders identified from the sample villages have been carefully classified into two categories. Of the 154 total leaders, 51 of them were identified as traditional leaders and 103 were emerging leaders.

Methodology

Universe of Study : This paper concerns with village leadership among tribals[2] of Kinnaur in Himachal Pradesh. Kinnaur is an isolated region, rugged and mountaineous to an extra ordinary degree, and lies on the both banks of the Sutlej. It is situated at the height between 1,220 and 3,050 metres above the mean sea level. The district consisting of 77 villages, spreads over 6,530 sq. kms. and stands divided into five tehsils and one sub-tehsil. Prior to the merger of princely states, Kinnaur was a tehsil of the erstwhile Bushahr State. However, it finally became a separate district on 1st May, 1960. According to census report of India 1971, Kinnaur has 49,835 souls of which 34,090 are indigenous scheduled tribes and 9,669 scheduled castes.

The people of Kinnaur belong to two principle endogamous caste groups called the *khosia* and the *beru* and the former in terms of caste heirarchy, is considered superior. The *khosia* includes the Kanets and the Jads who are called the Rajput or Negi[3]. The *beru* castes are primarily consisting of three sub-groups : (i) The Domang and Ores; (ii) The Chanals; and (iii) Chamang and Sumi. Because of their past and present impure status, the *beru* people are treated as untouchables. Also, numerically they are dominated by the *khosia* group.

The nature of family system is patrilineal in which authority is exercised by the elderly male, and the woman occupies subordinate position. Since the institution of polyandry is the central factor to family system, the joint family system continues to exist. However, to some extent, exposure to the outside world has disturbed both polyandry as well as the joint family system. Above the family level, the families of both caste groups are organized into diffenent patrilineages called the *biradar*. The membership of the *biradar* is based on patrilineage. Hence the *biradar* members can easily be traced back to single family. They observe common rituals and ceremonies relating to death-birth pollution. Further, two or more *biradar* groups form single exogamous unit known as the *khandan*. But it is interesting to note that the *khandan* system is not well developed among the Jads of Upper Kinnaur and the *beru* caste.[4]

Identification of Leaders

A review of the studies on rural and tribal village leadership conducted in India shows variability in methodology and approaches relating to identification of the leaders. Researchers in their studies have mostly used three main approaches. These are : The Positional approach, the Reputational approach and the Decision-making approach. The basic assumption of the positional approach is that those who hold vital positions in the community are also the key decision-makers (Bonjen and Olson, 1964 : 282). The Reputational approach, by which members of the community are asked to name the most influential person of the village, perhaps the most commonly used method of designating leaders, underlines the assumptions that the members of the community understand the question well, and they are able to perceive the power structure accurately. (Hunter, 1953 : 13). The decision making efforts involve the history of a particular public decision about some community issue thereby locating the leaders of the community (Freedom et al, 1963 : 791-798). Here the emphasis is on the decision-making process and various decisions-maker's location of participation in decision-making process is viewed as an act of leadership.

It is seen that no one method can give the complete picture of community leadership as each method has its own short comings (White, 1950 : 50-60). But a combination of approaches is required to gain a deep insight. We have, however, modified them to suit the demands of our study and local conditions. The following procedures have been followed

1. The community members were asked to name those who they think, as most influential persons in the village. Those who were mentioned by the respondents, were considered as the leaders of the village.
2. The leaders were also identified by asking respondents to give positive sociometric choices for individuals on the following activities. (a) Taking active interest in village development activities, (b) organizing sports, fairs, etc. (c) taking part in political affairs (d) repre-

senting village in the wake of inter-village disputes (e) mediating in intra or inter-caste disputes.

3. In addition to above methods, various records and registers of panchayats, co-operatives and voluntary organizations were also consulted for the identification of formal leaders.

Socio-Economic Bases And Roots of Leadership

It is widely accepted in the political sociology that leadership position of a person is greatly determined by his socio-economic background and up-bringing. In fact, each of the leaders belongs to one group or the other in relation to social heirarchy. The attitudes and values of leaders undergo changes over a period of time and the accumulation of experiences may bring about new patterns of acculturation. Yet one never fully frees oneself from one ssocio-economic background in which one has been brought up and socialized. That socially influential persons emerge from the upper echelon of socio-economic status, has been well documented in a number of rural and tribal studies in India. Village studies conducted in India has used age, family size, caste rank, land ownership, income, education etc, as major elements that constitute the index of socio-economic status (Dube, 1955:161; Lewis, 1958:127; Abraham, 1973: 45-55). In the forthcoming pages the pattern of socio-economic status of village leaders in general, particularly to what extent emerging leaders differ from the traditional ones, has been attempted.

Age Structure

The information on actual age reported by respondents, has been divided into four categaries. These are : 24-35 years; 35-45 years, 45-55 years; and over 55 years, and may be termed as lower, middle, higher and old age group.

It is found that out of 154 leaders, 42.20 per cent belong to middle age group, 27.27 per cent to higher age group, 25.32 per cent to lower age group and 5.19 per cent to the old age group. If we distribute the same age groups between traditional and emerging leaders, it will be seen that as compared to traditional leaders, majority of emerging leaders belong to lower and middle age groups. Our evidence shows that out of 130 emerging leaders, 51.45 per cent belong to middle age group while 33.98 per cent to lower age group and only 14.56 per cent to higher age group. In contrast, of the 51 traditional leaders, the largest number (47.05 per cent) belong to higher age group. Of the rest 23.52 per cent belong to middle age group, 15.68 per cent old age group and only 13.72 per cent belong to lower age group.

The above analysis suggests that in general leadership tends to be more defused in middle age group than to the higher and lower age groups. But when we contrast the emerging leaders with traditional leaders we also notice that younger elements predominate among the emerging leaders as compared to the traditional leaders. On this basis we can say that leadership is no longer entirely based on one of the ascriptive values —"Wisdom of the Age".

Sex

Politically, women have been most unrepresented group in the traditional village society. However, our data reveal that out of 154 leaders, 19 (12.34 per cent) are women leaders, and all of them have been performing formal leadership roles in Panchayat institutions and *Mahila Mandals*. In fact preponderance of male leaders in village leadership in Kinnaur is the reflection of the cultural tradition. Women here do not feel encouraged to take up leadership roles in public life; rather they are expected to play secondary and supportive roles in the social institutions.

Caste

Despite the new forces, which to some extent have undermined the rigidity of caste system, it is still a potential force in determing political life of Indian society. This is largely because in the absence of well articulated interest groups, caste provides a base for politics (Kothari and Maru, 1965: 33-50). In the traditional village structure generally persons of high caste rise to the leadership position.[5]

Our data indicate that out of the 154 leaders, 93.91 per cent belong to the *khosia* caste. The caste composition of leaders shows that leaders identified from the *beru* caste in much less than their numerical strength (19.40 per cent) in the total population of Kinnaur. However, in the light of their past and present inferior social position in the Kinnaur society, the identification of 14 emerging *beru* leaders is significant. Traditionally, the *beru* caste has been an unprivileged group in the village power structure. The traditional village panchayat, the *sainas* or *char bai* (council of elders) were represented by the *khosia* caste to which the other caste groups, the *beru* was subjugated.

Social Status

No study on village leadership in terms of caste is complete unless the status order of the social groups to which the leaders belong, is examined. During the course of our field work it was found that unlike the *beru* the *khosia* caste people are organized into different status groups. These are broadly: (i) higher status group; (ii) middle status group; and (iii) lower status group. Our data on the subject show that out of 140 *khosia* leaders, 37.14 per cent of them come from higher status group, 56.42 per cent belong to middle status group and 6.42 per cent come from lower status group. Our analysis vouches for significant shift in village leadership i.e., ftom higher status group to middle status group. This view is further supported from the fact that of the 51 traditional leaders, 64.70 per cent of them come from higher status group where as 35.29 per cent belong to middle group. On the other hand out of the 89 emerging *khosia* leaders, only 21.34 per cent belong to higher status group, 68.59 per cent to middle and 10.11 per cent to lower status group. Thus, it clearly shows that the leadership in terms of social status has moved down upto middle status families and gets blocked at that point. This is perhaps due to the fact that the social status of a family remains to be an important factor for the acquisition of village leadership position.

Family Structure

The institution of family is also another important agency of political socialization. It is more so when a family has a tradition of displaying leadership. It is believed that the struc-

of the family in some respect enhances one's social prestige and influence. Family structure may be defined in terms of nuclear and extended families and the latter, by definition, is larger in size than the former. We look at our leaders in terms of these two types. We have, therefore, hypothesized that village leaders come from large families which have support of an extensive network of lineage.

Our data show that out of 154 leaders, 66.23 per cent of them come from extended families and 33.76 per cent leaders come from nuclear familes which was less prevalent in the past because of the practice of strong polyandrous system. Further, analysis of data focuses that emerging leaders coming from nuclear families are relatively higher in number (35.92 per cent) than the traditional leaders coming from the same family base (29.45 per cent). But leaders belonging to extended families are less among emerging leaders (64.04 per cent) than the traditional leaders (70.58 per cent). These analyses lead us to believe that leadership is still greatly related to the extended family system. However, there is an indication of its decline as our evidence shows that leaders coming from extended families are less among emerging leaders than the traditional leaders.

Occupation

In Kinnaur, a large number of leaders remain engaged in various allied occupations such as small business, sheep rearing, tailoring, carpentry and various other jobs, apart from the primary occupation, agriculture. This phenomenon reveals one important fact that such allied occupations have become a part of their agro-pastoral economy. Though all our leaders are primarily land owners and have agriculture as their main occupation, yet there is also the fact that some people have other sources of income. It is more so in the region like Kinnaur where very limited arable land is available.

It is seen that of 154 leaders, 82 (53.24 per cent) are having allied occupations. Out of these 82 who are having allied occupations, 63.41 per cent are engaged in small business activities, 12.19 per cent in traditional sheep-rearing and the rest in other areas such as carpentry, tailoring etc. The data further indicate that higher proportion of emerging leaders are having allied occupations in comparison to traditional leaders. It seems that this is an indication of their enterprise and efforts to overcome the inherited disadvantages of socio-economic status as compared to traditional leaders.

Education

In early times education and leadership were not much related in Kinnaur. However, today in many ways education tends to increase the capacity for empathy and mediates in shaping the configurations of values, attitudes, and skill patterns of leaders. Several studies have illustrated that education is positively correlated to village leadership (Abraham, 1973: 50-51).

Our data on the subject indicate that out of 154 leaders, 14.28 per cent are illiterate, 21.48 per cent literate without having any formal education, 44.80 per cent educated upto middle standard, 14.89 per cent educated upto matric and 4.54 per cent are educated upto graduation and above.

The variation in educational attainment is not found very significant between traditional and emerging leaders. However, leaders having middle standard education (49.51 per cent) and graduation or above (5.82 per cent) are comparatively higher among emerging leaders than among the traditional leaders (35.29 per cent and 1.96 per cent respectively). Not unexpectedly, traditional leaders educated upto matric are (19.60 per cent) more than the emerging leaders with same educational standard (12.62 per cent).

On the basis of this analysis we can say that some level of formal education tends to be important factor for village leadership position. This extent of educations seems to be determined by the role requirements of leaders at village level politics i.e. an ability to use and determinate information at that level. If so, then, this is significant enough to suggest that leadership which was once based on ascriptive criteria is gradually being replaced by achievement factors like education but with the qualification noted above.

Land Ownership

Land ownership is a crucial factor in establishing social

status, power and influence in the village society.[6] The system of land tenure in rural India is such that a small group of land owners enjoys the lion's share of the arable land whereas the majority of the people are either landless or subsistence farmers. The nationwide survey reported by Sen and Roy found that almost 60 percent of leaders in Indian village possess atleast 10 acres of land (1966: 57). The presence of limited arable land available in the mountaineous area like Kinnaur, persons with more than 25 bighas[7] of arable land could surely be considered rich.

Out of 154 leaders, 10.78 per cent are found owning more than 40 bighas of land, 38.67 per cent possess 25 to 40 bighas of land, 39.65 per cent have 10-24 bighas and 10.88 per cent own less than 10 bighas of land. Analysis of data relating to land ownership suggests that village leadership is largely dominated by persons who own fairly large size of land. However by making comparison between traditional and emerging leaders, our data show that leadership has moved down to medium, and, to some extent, small land owning groups. This is evident from the fact that out of 103 emerging leaders 6.79 per cent own above 40 bighas of land, 28.15 per cent have 25 to 40 bighas of land and 49.51 per cent possess 10 to 24 bighas and 25.24 per cent carry less than 10 bighas of land. In contrast, out of 51 traditional leaders, 17.76 per cent own above 40 bighas of land, 56.97 per cent have 25 to 40 bighas of land, 19.38 per cent are having 10 to 24 bighas and only 5.88 per cent possess less than 10 bighas of land.

Income Status

It is generally accepted that more prosperous people are more likely to be active in politics. Sometime politics becomes a monopoly of economically well off class of society. Many studies have demonstrated that there is a positive relationship between income status and leadership (Lewis, 1958: 16; Blau, 1967: 108-109). Taking a lead from these studies, we have hypothesized that those who are economically better off, are most likely to be in the leadership positions.

What follows under this section has certain limitations. There is no possibility of the verification of income stated by respondents. Some of the observable discrepencies concerning the income have been brought out by way of consulting with knowledgeable villagers besides assessing the size of land, orchards, allied occupations, live-stock wealth and other material possession.

For the present study, leaders have been divided into three income categories: (1) higher income group (over Rs. 12,000 p.a.) (2) middle income group (Rs. 6,000 to 12,C00 p.a.); (3) lower income group (upto Rs. 5,000 p.a.). This has been calculated on the basis of information provided by the respondents and cross-checking this with other villagers. Our data on the subject indicate that out of 154 leaders, 40.24 per cent belong to middle income group, 32.48 per cent from higher income group and 27.27 per cent leaders come from lower income group. A point of significance to be noted here is the close relationship between income status and village leadership. In other words, economic status of a person tends to be an important determinant of power and influence in the village community.

Further distribution of data between traditional and emerging leaders shows that leadership has considerably moved from higher income group to middle income group. This is evident from from the fact that out of the 51 traditional leaders, 60.79 per cent come from higher income group, 31.37 per cent from middle income group and 7.84 per cent belong to lower income group. In contrast, out of 103 emerging leaders, 44.63 per cent belong to middle income group, 36.89 per cent from lower income group and only 18.47 per cent come from higher income group.

Discussions and Conclusions

We shall now try to recapitulate the major findings of our study:

1. Our investigation shows that under the new trends of formulation and implementation of the various welfare and development programmes and introduction of new organizations and institutions, there has been a significant shift in the existing leadership pattern among the Kinnaura. This is evident from the fact that out of 154 leaders located from the sample villages,

51 (33.11 per cent) are identified as traditional leaders and 103 (66.88 per cent) emerging leaders.

2. In terms of age, as we have seen, leadership positions in the villages are not confined any longer to older people as was the case in the past. When we compare the age structure between traditional and emerging leaders we also notice that comparatively younger elements tend to predominate among emerging leaders as compared to traditional leaders.

3. The village leadership seems to be still dominated by males. This is supported from the fact that out of 154 leaders, 135 (87.66 per cent) are men and only 19 (12.34 per cent) women.

4. The caste composition of leaders indicates that the *khosia* caste (higher caste) continues to be dominant in the village leadership structure. This may be attributed to their numerical strength, economic power and ritual superiority. They are not only strategically located in the village social system with access to power but also considered superior and powerful because of their economic position and social standing.

5. In terms of occupation, our evidence shows that apart from agriculture, some allied occupations, viz., petty business and sheep rearing etc. have become an important factor for the acquisition of village leadership position. However, such activities are partly due to the peculiar ecology of the area as there is very limited arable land and that too with low productive fertility.

6. Although joint family continues to be strongly related to village leadership, but there are signs of its decline. Our evidence shows that as compared to traditional leaders, more emerging leaders tend to come from nuclear families.

7. Our findings on the education show that formal education tends to be assumed important for the village leadership status. Despite the lower economic status of emerging leaders, there is no significant difference in terms of institutional education between traditional and emerging leaders, but the emerging leaders tend to be in general a little more educated.

8. Land ownership remains to be crucial factor in the village power mechanism. However, the land holding pattern of the traditional and emerging leaders indicates the village leader-

ship has considerably come down to medium land-owning families.

9. From the point of view of income status, the village leaders tend to come more from higher and middle income groups. The comparison of data between traditional and emerging leaders reveals that leadership has significantly moved down upto middle income groups. But the downward mobility is blocked at the "middle" level as is the case with land holdings; this is largely due to the importance of property in our socio-economic system.

NOTES

1. Referring to the "Trait Approach", Gouldner remarks, "at this time there is no reliable evidence concerning the existence of the universal trait". Alvin W. Gouldner (ed.), *Studies in Leadership*, New York: Harper and Brothers, 1950, p. 31.

2. Under Government of India, Ministry of Home Affairs, Scheduled Caste and Scheduled Tribe List Modification Order, 1956, the local inhabitants of Kinnaur were recognised as "Kinnaura Tribe".

3. The Khosia people of Kinnaur, unlike others, use the suffix "Negi" after their names.

4. In the study of kinship system in Kinnaur, some anthropologists also noted the absence of the *khandan* system in Pooh sub-divisions. See Manis K. Raha, Satya Narayan Mahato and Raghunath Singh Negi, "The Kinnaurese Kinship System: A Terminological System". *Bulletin.* The Anthropological Survey of India, Vol. XXV. No. 3-4, July-Dec., 1976, p. 87.

5. The same view has been expressed by many social Anthropologists in the studies of traditional Indian village. For example, Bailey in his book, *Caste, Tribe and Nation* (1960) proposes the model that village community is ruled by one dominant caste. Srinivas also views that usually the leaders of locally dominant caste are elected to panchayats, (in *Caste in Modern India*), 1962, Bombay.

6. According to Srinivas, three conditions facilitate for caste to be dominant, namely, considerable amount of land,

strength of numbers and high status. See M.N. Srinivas, *Social Change in Modern India*, University of California Press, Barkeley and Los Angels, 1972, p. 10.

7. In Himachal Pradesh land is measured in terms of bighas i.e. 5 bighas is equal to one acre.

REFERENCES

Abraham, F.	1973	*Dynamics of Leadership in Village India*, India International Publication, New Delhi.
Allport, J.H.	1924	*Social Psychology*, Houghton Mifflin Co., Boston.
Bailey, F.G.	1960	*Caste, Tribe and Nation : A Study of Political Activity and Political Change in Highland Orissa*, Oxford University Press, Bombay.
Blau, P.M.	1967	*Exchange and Power in Social Life*, John Wiley & Sons Inc., New York.
Bonjean, C.M. and D.M. Olson	1964	Community Leadership: Direction of Research, *Administrative Science Quarterly*, 9 : 3.
Dube, S.C.	1955	*Indian Village*, Routledge and Kegan Paul, London.
Freeman, L.C., et. al.	1963	Locating Leadership in Local Community: A Comparison of some Alternative Approaches, *American Sociological Review*, Vol. 28.
Gouldner, A.W. (ed.)	1950	*Studies in Leadership*, Harper & Brothers, New York.
Hunter, F.	1953	*Community Power Structure*, University of North California Press, Chapel Hill.
Kothari, R. and R. Maru	1965	Caste and Secularisation in India, *The Journal of Asian Studies*, XXV: i.

Lewis, O. 1958 *Village Life in Northern India*, University of Illinois Press, Upana.

Nagpal, H. 1967 Leadership in a Frame of Reference in *Leadership in India*, L.P. Vidyarthi (ed.), Asia Publishing House, Delhi.

Paige, G.D. 1977 *Scientific Study of Political Leadership*, Free Press, New York.

Raha, M.K., S.N. Mahato and R.S. Negi 1976 The Kinnaurese Kinship System. A Terminological Analysis, *Bulletin*, *Anthropological Survey of India*, XXV: 3-4.

Sen, L.P. and P. Roy 1966 *Emerging Leadership: An Awareness of Community Development Programme*, National Institute of Community Development, Hyderabad.

Srinivas, M.N. 1962 *Caste in Modern India and Other Essays*, Asia Publishing House, Calcutta.

Srinivas, M.N. 1972 *Social Change in Modern India*, University of California Press, Barkeley & Los Angels.

Tead, O. 1935 *The Art of Leadership*, Willesey House, London.

Tennenbaum, R.P. and Fred Massrik 1961 Leadership: A Frame of Reference in *Leadership and Organisation*, R. Tennenbaum, et. al. (eds.), McGraw Hill Book Co. Inc., New York.

White, J.E. 1950 Theory and Methods for Research in Leadership, *American Sociological Review*, Vol. 15.

CHAPTER XXIII

KINSHIP ORGANIZATION OF THE POLYANDROUS LAHULAS

D.D. SHARMA

Owing to its important characteristics of binding different individuals into a compact social system and defining their duties and rights with regard to other individuals of that organization, the kinship organization has strongest hold on its members and has a significant bearing on all spheres of their social activities. For the duties and obligations arising out of kinship bond exercise an all round influence on the social life of an individual, right from the cradle to the grave. In short, 'the system of kinship can be looked at an arrangement which enables persons to live together and co-operate with one another in any orderly social life' (Sreedhar, 1982). As such, a study of the kinship organization to understand the social structure of a community has its own sociological and anthropological importance. The community selected here for this purpose belongs to the Gahr valley of the Lahul sub-division of Lahul and Spiti district of Himachal Pradesh. The area is adjoined on its eastern border by Spiti sub-division and to its north lies Ladakh district of Jammu and Kashmir. On its western and southern borders it is bounded respectively by the Chamba and Kulu districts of Himachal Pradesh. There are high mountain passes on its northern, eastern and southern boundaries which remain closed for more than half the year, on account of heavy snow on them, and thus it remains almost cut off from the rest of the world during this period, though now a fortnightly helicopter service, depending on weather, operates between Simla and its headquarters, Keylong. Formerly, it was almost inaccessible to the outside world, even during summer season. It has four valleys situated on the banks of the rivers, the Chandra and the Bhaga. The Gahr valley is situated on the banks of the river Bhaga. The other valleys of this sub-division are the Tod, the Tinan (Chandra valley) and the Pattan (Chandra-Bhaga valley).

At present, the absence of authentic historical records of this region provides no definite idea about the ethnic affinity of the inhabitants of this region though, linguistically, traces of austro-asiatic words exist in the dialects of the region. Religiously, too, like the Ladakhis and the Tibetants, they are followers of Buddhism.

In this paper we have briefly discussed both the internal (consanguineal) and external (affinal) aspects of the kinship organization of these polyandrous Lahulas. In fact, as yet the polyandrous family system of the Lahulas has not received the notice from anthropologists. Only a few know that the polyandry functioning among them, particularly among the Lahulas of the Gahr and the Tod valleys, is far more complete and tenacious than in any other society, so far reported. Though polyandry is on the decline now, yet it was practised in its purest form in the past.

The unique feature of the Lahula society of the Gahr valley is this that it is homogeneous without any stratification based on castes and creeds. Religiously, they are all Buddhists and socially do not recognize any caste.

The basic unit at the social level is the family. It is an acknowledged fact that family is the bed-rock of all social organizations. In fact, in India family and caste are the most important social groups to which an individual is intimately related and which ultimately determine his/her rights and duties in that particular social group.

Family : A family among the Lahulas, as in other societies, forms the basic unit of kinship organization. Basically, a Lahula family, on account of polyandry, is a joint family with patrilocal residence, patrilineal descent, patrinymic designation, and patriprotestal authority. There can rarely be a nuclear family. Consequently, a Lahula family unit is always headed by a senior male member who may not necessarily be, but usually is, the oldest male member of the senior generation living in the family. He commands authority in the family and is known as *yunda* etymologically meaning 'the owner of the property', and his wife is *yundamo*. Generally, under this system he attains this position automatically by virtue of his being born first among living male members of his generation. But in case of his incapability of discharging his duties as a patriarch, be on account of informities of old age or for some other reason, he may transfer this authority to any other male member of his generation or to the oldest male member of the next generation or to his eldest son. Seniority in age, in comparison with the seniority in other matters, is highly honoured among the Lahulas, and that is why the seniormost member of the family, even if he has relinquished his authority for day to day affairs, is still a highly respected member of the family or clan; and his advice is sought for on all important matters concerning the family or the social group to which he belongs.

Clan : The next higher unit in the social structure of the Lahulas is the clan, locally termed as *rhus*. It is this unit that divides the Buddhist community of this valley into smaller groups, which form the bases for establishing affinal relationship. For, the choice of a spouse is strictly forbidden within the same *rhus*.

In the matter of selection of spouses the main consideration of the Lahulas of the Gahr valley is the avoidance of the same *rhus* or clan. As per rule of descent a person whether male or female, invariably belongs to the clan of his/her father. As such, even flirting with a clansman/woman is an unpardonable sin. Some of the groups forming such an exogamous unit are: Lenchenpa, Khingopa, Langzipa, Chepapa, Darnapa, Mehrupa, Kisingpa etc.

Marriage

In every human society marriage and inheritance are the two important subjects which are regulated by certain written or unwritten social codes. Needless to say that these codes of conduct vary from one community to another or even stand to change in the same community from one period to another period. The Lahulas also have certain social codes to regulate marriage and sex relations.

Selection of Spouse

As already stated, the Lahulas avoid selecting their spouse from the same clan or *rhus*. But, on the other hand, there is no taboo in selecting a spouse from the family of mother's parents or from the family of father's sister. The custom of cross-cousin marriage though exists in this society and is fully confirmed by their kinship terminology, is not a preferential one. The only taboo next to one's own clan (*rhus*) is the family of mother's sister in which one cannot choose a spouse for oneself. However, owing to the prevalence of the exchange marriage system there is no taboo in having a spouse from the family of sister's in-laws or from their village.

Moreover, the members of this community though strictly adhere to the code of clan exogamy, yet are fully different towards village exogamy. There are instances in which the spouses from the next door neighbours, belonging to different clans, have been selected and these have got approval of the village community.

In the matter of giving or receiving a bride there is, on account of absence of caste-like stratification, neither a sense of superiority or inferiority, nor any directional trend, though some regional considerations had been there in the past, mainly on account of some cultural differences existing in different valleys, hence a preference for local marriages. Besides, linguistic barriers seldom allowed youths from different valleys to have verbal exchanges on love affairs. Another reason of the Lahulas of the Gahr valley for not giving their daughters to the grooms from the Pattan valley was also that the inhabitants of the Gahr valley were strictly polyandrous whereas polyandry was loosely practised in the Pattan valley. Hence they never wanted that the exclusive right of the mistress of the house of their daughters be shared by another woman or women in the house.

In the polyandrous system of the Lahula all brothers

belonging to the same parentage are legitimate husbands of the common wife. Moreover, in this system a woman never becomes a widow, unless her husband is the only son of his parents. There is neither any taboo, nor any social stigma attached to the remarriage of a widow. It is as normal a marriage as the first one. There can, of course, be a scope for sororate (in case the wife dies).

It may be interesting to note that though no rituals are performed in a marriage ceremony, yet marriage is a must among the Lahulas. According to their religious beliefs, a normal man/woman, unless embraces the monastic order (i.e becomes a *lama* or *chomo*), cannot have salvation or a good post-death life without having performed this sacrament. Consequently, if a woman dies as a spinster or a man as a bachelor, his/her marriage ceremony is performed by a special ritual before litting up his/her pyre in the cremation ground.

FORM OF MARRIAGE

Polyandry

From the time immemorial, polyandry is an honourable sacrosanct and socially approved custom of marriage among the Lahulas. It was widely practised in the past but now it is on its speedy decline. The practice of polyandry, prevalent among the Lahulas, is of the adelphic fraternal type, in which only the eldest brother weds a woman ceremoniously, and she becomes a *de facto* joint wife of all the brothers having a common parentage. This principle has been formulated by Goldstein as 'monomarital principle'. According to this, only one marriage should be contacted in a given generation, and that all the offsprings of the marriage shall have full jural right in the corporation (cf. Moodey, 1978: 3).

Thus among the Lahulas of the Gahr valley we come across a form of polyandry different from the type practised by the Khasas of Jaunsar-Bawar, where it has more or less, assumed the form of polygynandry i.e. two or more brothers may begin with only one or two common wives and may subsequently add more wives when they can afford to this (Majumdar, 1982: 75), nor the type of the polyandry that is prevalent among the

Ladakhis, in which the conjugal right was given only to two younger brothers next to the elder brother in age.

In the Gahr valley it was so rigid a social custom that no younger brother was allowed to have a separate wife or to bring a second woman in the house even if there was vast difference in the age of the elder brother's wife and of the youngest brother. Gill has given an instance in which the youngest household was so young that the wife of the elder brother suckled him, and when he himself grew up he took her as his wife and fathered children by her (1972: 143).

The reason of the introduction and according sanctity to this system in Lahul and elsewhere in the Himalaya was probably due to the socio-economic compulsion under which, on the one hand, the people of these extra-ordinarily rugged snow bound hilly region had to prevent further fragmentation of their meagre, low productive agricultural holdings, and, on the other hand, to keep the population under control. It is well understandable that in a region where there was an acute scarcity of cultivable land, vegetation, irrigation facilities, exploitation of natural resources or any indigenous industry, prevention of fragmentation of agricultural land and strict control over population were must for the survival of the people living there. This custom was found effective enough to serve both purposes and so was adhered to rigidly. Further, in this very inhospitable region their experience made them aware that the existence of more than one wife under the same roof would invariably lead to frequent separation of brothers and division of family estate ultimately, under the conditions they were put by the Nature, creating a disastrous situation for the whole society. On the other hand, they had also noticed that under this system the sense of partnership among brothers would not only help in consolidating family estate, but also ensure a cordial co-operation among all members of the family. For, the lady of the house would help regulating the sexual affairs of brothers in such a way as there would hardly be any conflict of their interests leading to sexual jealousy. It is a well blended harmonious union.

But, now on account of all round advancement and consequent to it, with the opening of many fresh avenues for livelihood and with the development of new social consciousness and changed outlook towards life and social customs, this age old edifice of polyandry is crumbling down. There is a visible struggle between the older and the younger generations for upholding the time honoured custom and for discarding it altogether.

Divorce

In the Lahula society though cases of divorce are not very frequent, yet when it is sought, it is accomplished in an extremely simple manner. For divorce (*kudpa chadche* or *tshud-thwagtsi*, meaning 'breaking of thread') couple sits in the presence of some elderly persons or relatives and a woollen thread is tied to the little fingers of both partners. It is pulled apart proclaiming that henceforth they will have nothing to do with one another. and with the snapping of the thread the marriage bond also is snapped for ever. Dissolution of marriage can be sought by any partner but the initiator has to pay a compensation to the aggrieved party. If the husband initiates the proceedings of divorce then he has to return the entire dowry to the wife which she might have brought at the time of her marriage. But in case a wife seeks divorce the husband is paid compensation only if she remarries some other person; otherwise no compensation is required.

Inheritance

In the polyandrous Lahula society the law of inheritance is very simple. If one of the brothers dies the family estate is inherited by all other surviving brothers with equal proportion. No son or the widow is allowed to succeed him till any one of the brothers of this union is surviving. The sons are entitled to this right only after the death of all the brothers of such a union. But it is only the legitimate son/sons who are allowed to enjoy this right. An exceptional point in the custom of inheritance among the Lahulas is this that in the absence of a male heir the family wealth is inherited by an unmarried female heir in preference to other male kinsmen. She can hold the property for life as a maid and can marry a person of her own choice but the husband must live with her at her father's place. In case she changes her residence and goes to her husband's place to live with him, she automatically forfeits this right. But the husband, called *makpa* (household son-in-law) has no right on the property of the father of his wife.

Moreover, the right of inheritance is extendable to a married daughter as well (of course in the absence of a male heir only), if she is living with her husband in her father's house. Although in a polyandrous society there are rare changes of a woman becoming widow, yet if there is one then, according to the law of the land, an issueless widow can inherit the property of her husband/husbands on his/their death but she has no right to dispose off it or to gift it to any one. She can only sustain her livelihood out of it during her lifetime, provided she remains chaste and does not marry any one inside or outside the family of her deceased husband/husbands. In case of marriage she automatically forgoes this privilege. This property, after her death or on her contacting sexual relations with any person, reverts back to the nearest collectoral (*zagospa*) of her deceased husbands/husband.

Interpersonal Relationship

In a kinship web every individual, both with reference to consanguineal and affinal kin, has a definite place for himself/herself in the organization and a code of conduct to follow. In the family unit, too, one's behaviour with regard to different members of the family is, more or less, fixed by convention, and one is simply expected to learn it in order to become a respectable member of the society.

The patriarch and other members of the family : The kinship behaviour pattern of the tradition ridden patrilineal polyandrous Lahulas is somewhat different from that exists in the monogamous societies. In the former area a family which is essentially a co-operative unit, functions under the supreme authority of the patriarch who is the head of the family. The patriarch is the seniormost male member, usually the eldest brother, of the polyandrous union. Because of his position and status he is the most revered person in the family, and all other members, including younger brothers, hold a subordinate position. He is the social father of all the children born to the polyandrous union and as such commands the highest respect from them, though they duly respect their other fathers as well. His authority in all matters is supreme and his wishes are carried out almost ungrudgingly by all members of the family. Obedience to him is the first thing learnt by all the junior members of the family. On his part the patriarch, too, is kind and considerate towards his younger brothers and other members of the family. He sees that the justice is done to all in all matters. In the assignment of duties as also in other matters, he tries to become impartial so that there is no chance for complaint from any member; it is very essential to avoid conflicts which are very potential dangers to the unity of the family.

Husband(s)-wife : In fact, relationship between spouses in a polyandrous union is a complicated affair and the most important of all interpersonal relationships. All the partners have to take it in the spirit of mutual care and co-operation, and the common wife has to handle it in such a way as the sense of interpersonal jealousy, arising out of sexual interest, does not germinate among the husbands. For regulating the household affairs in a smoother way and for maintaining the tradition of keeping the family intact in a polyandrous union a wife has definitely much greater responsibility than that of a wife of a monogamous union.

The conjugal relations between a wife and her husbands are quite cordial and of mutual trust, yet in it, the sense of unbreakable bond of pre and post births is totally missing. In fact, a Lahula marriage is basically a partnership between two equals. Traditionally or ritualistically there is nothing which may suggest that a Lahula wife should regard her husband as her lord or venerable godling. Besides, the easy dissolution of the marriage bonds and remarriage also bears out that the marital bond is not very strong and lasting. But, even then it is the duty of a husband/husbands to provide all possible comforts to his/their wife and in return the wife is expected to be loyal and obedient to her husband/husbands.

Customarily, though the eldest brother is the 'real' husband of the common wife and he is also the social father of all the children born to this union, yet it is the duty of wife to see that none of the brothers is deprived of his conjugal rights. Like the patriarch, the common wife, too, commands a fairly respectable position in the family. She controls all household affairs and regulates the marital affairs of all of her husbands. In this regard she has to be very cautious and tactful, because in a polyandrous union sexual rights are exercised through a tacit understanding among the brothers and the common wife. To avoid the rivalry among brothers for keeping the family and the land holdings intact, she has to regulate the whole affairs in such a way as there is no clash of sexual interest of any partner. Moreover, she has also to see that no husband ever thinks of bringing another woman in the family. For this she has to keep her every husband satisfied so that none of them has any complaint about her favour or disfavour to any partner.

Sibling-Sibling : In a polyandrous system general relationship of mutual consideration and co-operation among the brothers is very essential. In the absence of mutual love and affection the union is likely to be broken up and the sole purpose of polyandry is defeated. In the Lahula society there is more understanding than rivalry among brothers. However, being the potential head of the family, the eldest brother, in comparison with other brothers, commands more respect and higher social position in the family. It is because in the Lahula polyandrous organization the eldest brother is not only the traditional representative of his generation in the family line, but also the rightful husband of the common wife and social father of all the children born to the union. Even then other brothers, too, have a say in family matters. In personal matters they have equal status, and after the death of the eldest brother the next seniormost in the line takes his place and discharges the duties of the patriarch. Personal conflicts and bickerings, on account of clash of interests, are not very common among brothers. The relationship between brothers and sisters is of love and non-interference.

Parents-in-law and daughter-in-law : As in other societies, in this society, too, a daughter-in-law who is a new member to the family, regards her parents-in-law as her own parents and treats them with respect and awe. The custom of *purda* or 'avoidance' is completely unknown to this society. A daughter-in-law is always benign and submissive to all commands of her parents-in-law and is reserve in her verbal expressions. For a few years, after her marriage, she even avoids meetings or conversing with her husbands in their presence. Even a loud laughter in their presence is considered to be an indecent act on her part. Though they can call her by her first name yet she has to address them always with honorific terms of address. A father-in-law seldom interferes in the affairs of a daughter-in-law, though a mother-in-law has a full right to do so, and at a later stage mother-in-law's interference leads sometimes to conflict.

Grand-parents and grand-children : The relationship between grand-parents and grand-children is that of reverence and affection. Elders are always shown proper respect by their juniors in all walks of life. Besides, obedience to them in a sober and benign manner is a must for younger people. In social and private gatherings, seats are provided in accordance with the seniority of age of the participants and the same principle is followed with regard to serving tea and food. Sometimes the grand-parents cut jokes, play with their grand-children and take them to different parts of the village thus providing them many new ideas of this big world. This creates a very affectionate relation between the two.

Agnates : Among agnates the father's sister is the most important member of the family. She is duly respected by her brother's wife and sons and invited on all ceremonial occasions if she is a married one. On matrimonial affairs her advice is sought and sometimes negotiations are carried through her. On the occasion of New-Year day (*Loser*) her visit to her parents is a must. She brings with her a *kalchur* of *chhang* alongwith a particular number of *basyachi* (a sort of *puri*) for her brothers and *marjyak* (prepared with *sattu* and butter) for her nephews. In return she is offered a bottle of *arak* and added a number of *basyachis*. On the other hand a *chomama* aunt has a place of authority in her brother's house. She is addressed as *ane* (mother-in-law) by the wife of her brothers and is given the same respect. With their children her relationship is that of respect and affection.

Affinal kins : On account of the prevalence of marriage by elopement as the most popular form of marriage among the

Lahulas, there are no frequent visits to the house of in-laws or daughters. By nature, too, the Lahulas are indifferent to inviting their daughters to their place or visiting them occasionally. A visit from the son-in-law or a daughter also is not an event for them. As such in this system we find neither a meticulous differentiation in the kinship terminology (most of them being covered by classificatory terms) nor any conventional prescription for kinship behaviour. Still, on some ceremonial occasions, when invited, the general pattern of kinship behaviour is of respect to elders and affection to youngers, there being no custom of saluting elders and blessing youngers in this society.

Almost the same is the position with regard to maternal relations, with whom the relationship is almost the same. The maternal uncle does not play any important role in the life of his nephew or niece. He can only be requested to act as emissary to reconciliate the parents of the girl on the occasion of her being eloped by his nephew. All the relations belonging to this class of avanculates are equated with relations of various other classes, terminologically. However, a maternal uncle, his wife or his parents receive due regard from their nephews or grand-sons and in return are treated affectionately, though mutual visits among these relations are very infrequent.

Taboo of naming : The name taboo in case of certain relationships is prevalent among the Lahulas. There are only a few such relations. The parents-in-law, generally, avoid calling their daughter-in-law by name and vice versa. The sons-in-law also do not take the names of their mothers-in-law and fathers-in-law. In fact, calling any senior relation by name by a junior relation is tabooed.

Joking relationship : The joking relationship is mostly confined to affinal kins only. But on account of the polyandrous character of the kinship organization the scope of exchanging jokes is very limited. In the absence of younger brothers-in-law (HyB) there is no scope for exchanging jokes betwen the sister-in-law (eBW) and the brother-in-law (HyB). However, this can take place between husband's sister and wife's brother and between wife's sister and her brother-in-law (SH).

Kinship Terminology

The study of kinship terminology is one of the most reliable and authentic parameters for understanding the intrinsic structure of the kinship organization in a social group, for it not only reflects various levels of social reality, but also manifests a definite socio-cultural ethos of the society concerned.

Within the framework of kinship organization the social relationship is established on two counts, viz., by birth and by marriage. All the studies conducted on this aspect of the various societies confirm that there is a socially recognized ordering of the consanguineal and the affinal relations in every society independent of others, and for relations of every order there are separate sets of kinship terms. Whatever may be the form but the system is basically ego-centric. In fact, 'kinship terms are category words by means of which an individual is taught to recognize the significant groupings in the social structure into which he is born.' (Leach, 1958:143).

Owing to the absence of a number of relationships, the kinship terminology of the patrilineal polyandrous Lahulas is remarkably simple in comparison with the very complicated categories of kinship nomenclature attested among many Hindus in the plains of northern India. For their kinship web the Lahulas primarily recognize their consanguineal relations (agnates) only, known as *rhuspa* or *zagospa*, and that, too, upto two ascending and two descending generations from the ego. No definite status is given to the 'avunculars'; and most of the affinal relations, not directly related to the ego, are left unspecified. Moreover, the practice of cross-cousin marriage has further eliminated the scope of using specific kinship terms pertaining to the mother's brother's descendents and father's sister's descendents.

Now, we shall take up the kinship terminology of the Lahulas of the Gahr valley for its analysis groupwise, viz., the members in a nuclear family, the agnates of the lineage, the avunculars and the other kin.

Kinship terminology in a family : Owing to its polyandrous character the interpersonal relationship in a Lahula family differs from that of a monogamous nuclear family, as well as from the usual type of monogamous joint family. Here first we take up primary kinship terms used in a nuclear family and then those connected with the polyandrous family of the Lahulas of the Gahr valley :

(a) Kins in a Nuclear Family

Sl. No.	*Relationship (Abbri)*	*Term of Kinship*	*Term of Add.*	*Term of Ref.*
1.	Husband (H)	dagpe	by name/father of so and so	dagpo
2.	Wife (W)	byanme/ digsag	by name/father of so and so	byanmo/ digsag
3.	Son (Z)	bucha	by name	bucha
4.	Daughter (D)	chomed	by name	chemed
5.	Father (F)	awa	awa	awa
6.	Mother (M)	ama	ama	ama
7.	Elder brother (eB)	achho	achho	achho
8.	Younger brother (yB)	chocho	chocho/by name	chocho
9.	Elder sister (eS)	achhe	achhe	achhe
10.	Younger sister (yS)	apu	apu/by name	apu

Besides the kinship terms, the above table also shows that there are three distinct ways of addressing a kin:

1. by term of kinship itself, as in the case of father (*awa*), mother (*ama*), elder brother (*achho*) and elder sister (*achhe*).
2. by name of the person addressed as in the case of son, daughter, younger brother, younger sister. It may be noted here that in the Lahula society addressing by spouses to each other by personal name is not a taboo. Formerly in many cases the wife used to be elder than her husband as well.
3. by the use of an interjection or a teknonymic term as in the case of husband and wife.

In short, all the kins who are elder or senior to the ego are addressed by the corresponding kinship terms and those younger or junior to the speakers are addressed by their personal names. But in the case of spouses though, generally, addressing to each other by his/her personal name is avoided and the use of the teknonymic terms (i.e., father or mother of so and so) is preferred, yet there is no social restriction or taboo for calling each other by his/her personal name.

Another notable point with regard to spouses in a fraternal polyandrous family is this that while for the wife all the husbands are her *dagpo* but for the husbands she is either *byanmo* or *digsag*, i.e. she is *byanmo* with reference to her real husband, who is invariably the eldest brother, but is *digsag* to all other husbands of this polyandrous union. Consequently, while referring her to someone else indirectly, she is referred to with these two distinctive terms by her respective husbands.

The most interesting aspect of kinship terminology in an ideal type of polyandrous family is the use of multiple distinctive kin terms to denote each individual of paternal category. In Gahri dialect (Lahula) the patriarchal hierarchy in a polyandrous family is indicated as under:

1. *awa* i.e. real or assigned father
2. *tyawa* (*teji*+*awa*) i.e. father elder to *awa* or eldest father
3. *bawa* i.e. father immediately younger to *awa*
4. *bara* i.e. father younger to *bawa*
5. *phechawa*/*pheche* i.e. father younger to *bara*
6. *acha* i.e. father younger to *phechawa*
7. *awa-kyugchi* i.e. father younger of all
8. *au* i.e. that brother of the parental category who does not join the polyandrous union but embraces the Buddhistic monastic order.

From among these eight terms *tyawa* (*teji*+*awa*=elder father), *phechawa* (*pheche*+*awa*=younger father) and *awa kyugchi* (the youngest father) are descriptive. These are, moreover, readjustable according to the number of brothers belonging to the union of fraternal polyandry.

In an ideal type of polyandrous family there is no scope for a co-wife or step-mother. However, among the Lahulas of Gahr stray instances of such a situation rarely occur. In such a situation the first wife is termed as *tyama* (elder mother) by the children of the polyandrous union and the second wife as *phechama* (*pheche+ama*) i.e. younger mother. There is no term for co-wife or step-sons. The children are common to all fathers and mothers, therefore, no distinction is made among them. All the children born to the same polyandrous union are addressed as well as referred to, by all mothers and fathers in the same way as they do with their own issues. The co-wives have a relation of elder (*achhe*) and younger (*apu*) sisters. This is determined in accordance with the kinship status they are having in their paternal family, irrespective of their age, and one is to treat the other as one's younger sister and address her by her personal name.

Kins in a polyandrous joint (extended) family : The pattern of joint family among the Lahulas is that of a lineal or vertical order and the extension of kinship terms is normally attested upto two degrees in the ascending order and two degrees in the descending order from the ego. Kins beyond that are addressed and referred to if necessary, by the term used for the last kin in that order. For instance, the term for grand-father (FF) is extendable to great-grand-father (FFF) and the term for grandson (ZZ) for great-grand-son (ZZZ). These may be illustrated by the following table.

Sl. No.	*Relationship*	*Term of kinship*	*Term of address*	*Term of reference*
1.	HF	shu	azang	shu
2.	HM	yug	ane	yug
3.	He/yS	digsag/ ngidmo	ane	digsag/ ngidmo
4.	e/y BW (w.s.)	digsag	digsag	digsag
5.	BZ (w.s.)	pi	by name	pi
6.	BD (w.s.)	pimed	by name	pimed
7.	ZW	nam	nam/by name	nam

8.	ZZ	khod/chhao	by name	khod/chhao
9.	ZD	khodmed/ chhamo	by name	khodmed/ chhamo
10.	FF	tete/meme	tete/meme	tete/meme
11.	FM	apa/abi	apa/abi	apa/abi
12.	ZZW	khodmedchi	by name	khodmedchi
13.	HFF	tete/meme	tete/meme	tete/meme
14.	HFM	apa/abi	apa/abi	apa/abi
15.	FFF	tete/meme	tete/meme	tete/meme
16.	FFM	apa/abi	apa/abi	apa/abi
17.	ZZZ	X	by name	ZZZ
18.	ZZD	X	by name	ZZD

With reference to grand/great-grand parents *meme* and *abi* are restricted to parents who observe celebacy in life and embrace the monastic order by becoming *lama* and *chomo* respectively. However, among the Thakurs of the upper Gahr valley a non-lama FF or HFF is also addressed as *meme*. In the Pattan valley this term refers to the maternal grand-father. The term *meme* and *abi* are terms of respect and veneration, and are commonly used by villagers for persons of their grand-parents' generation. It may also be noted here that the kinship terms used for HF and HM have a very wide range. The term *azang* besides HF, refers to WF/MB/WB (when older in age) and the term *ane* refers to HM/HFS/SHM/HMS/HS/WM/WMBW/WMS etc. Further, no distinctive kinship terms are attested beyond two ascending or descending generations from the speaker.

A notable point in the above table is the term *digsag* which is used both for BW and HS. Because under the custom of exchange marriage husband's sister can be a potential wife of her brother. Hence the prevalence of this term for both the relations.

Kinship terminology among agnates : The most remarkable feature of a polyandrous joint family is the absence of many terms for both male and female agnates which otherwise form an integral part of kinship terminology of a joint family pattern. From among these relations there is no term for FB (e/y), and FBW (e/y). For, they are all fathers with specific terms, as noted earlier and consequently, there is no scope for aunts as well. Similarly, owing to the polyandrous union, in which all brothers share the same wife (wives), there is no term for BW(e/y). A 'lama' brother who does not join this union also refers to her as *digsag* (wife), the same term which is used by all other younger brothers of this union. Moreover, in a system in which brothers of a single parentage cannot have more than one common wife, there is no scope for kinship terms like HBW (e/y)/BZ/BD/HBZ/HBD. For, there cannot be any 'nephews' and 'nieces' in a perfect polyandrous joint family. The terms for BZ and BD are, however, attested in the case of a woman speaker.

However, outside the family all such consanguineal male members of the same generation, who are cousins in a broad sense are regarded as one's brothers and sisters and are addressed as *achho/chocho* or *achhe/apu* according to their age, as is the case with one's own brothers or sisters. Reciprocally, the male or female ego is regarded as one's own brother or sister with reference to his/her age. In the *rhus* (clan) all male members of the father's generation are regarded as brothers of one's own fathers and are addressed or referred to as *aku* (fathers). Similarly, their wives are regarded as mothers and are addressed as *chichi.*

Female agnates : This system recognizes only a few kinship terms for female agnates. The term of address and the term of reference for the FS and HFS are identical with the term HM and WM, i.e. *ane*. The currency of identical terms in this respect is due to cross-cousin marriage among the Lahulas. Similarly, the term *apa* for FFS is identical with the term used for FM/HFM/FFM, etc. There are no kinship terms for BZZ (w.s.) and BZD (w.s.). They all are addressed with their personal names and are referred to as son or daughter of so and so. In fact, in case of female agnates there are no kinship terms beyond the second ascending or descending generation from the ego.

Kinship terminology among the avunculates : The kinship web among the Lahulas recognizes only a limited number of avunculates. These may be described as under :

Affinal kins through mother : Of the affinal kins, through mother, the term for mother's brother is *azang*, which may be qualified by prefixes like *teji* (elder) and *pheche* (younger) and for MBW, is *mechung*. The other two terms available in this regard are *tete* (MF) and *apa* (MM).

Some of the notable points in this regard are :

(1) a woman in the Lahula society does not recognize the kins of her husbands; consequently, there are no terms for HMB/HMBW/HMF/HMM etc.

(2) on account of the cross-cousin marriage the term for MB, viz. *azang*, is identical with WF and for this very reason there are no kinship terms for MBZ/MBD/MBZW/MBDH etc.

(3) the terms for the maternal grand-parents, viz. MF/MM are the same as for paternal grand-parents. The same terms are also used for FFF/FMM/HFF/HFM etc.

Affinal kins through marriage (or wife) : The kinship web of affinal kins may be illustrated as under :

1. *azang* (WF), 2. *ane* (WM), 3. *sagpa/azang* (WeB), 4. *sagpo* (WyB), 5. *tete* (WFF), 6. *apa* (WFM).

Some of the points in this regard are :

(1) terms for WF and WM are identical with the terms MB and FS respectively, on account of the prevalence of cross-cousin marriage.

(2) currency of identical terms of address for WBM and one's own e/y sisters is an indicator of the practice of exchange marriage in this society. Moreover, the term *azang* for the WeB also indicates that matrimonial relations is possible with his daughter, perhaps in the case when his wife is not the sister of the ego, but not with WyBD as WyB is *sagpo*, a term which is identical with the term for ySH and DH.

(3) complete absence of term for WBW/WS and WSH is inexplicable. While introducing to some one, the WS is referred to as 'wife's husband'. The term of address for WBW is identical with the term for one's own sister, viz. *achhe/apu* again an indicator of exchange marriage.

(4) the relations in the senior generation, i.e., two generations ascending, as usual, have same classificatory terms as used for grand-parents.

Affinal kins through the son : In this system no affinal kin is recognized through the son. There is a complete absence of kinship terms for the relationship of ZWF/ZWH/ZWFF/ZWFM/ZWB/ZWBW/ZWS/ZWSH etc.

However, the point of interest in this relationship is that the parents of the boy and the girl address each other, reciprocally, as elder brother and younger brother or elder sister and younger sister, in accordance with relative age of the addresser and the addressee. This is again an indicator of the system of cross-cousin marriage.

Kins through the father's sister : In the Lahuli kinship system no relation is recognized through father's sister, except her husband, who is termed as *pechung* (FSH). Owing to prevalence of cross-cousin marriage system, no term is attested for FSZ/FSD/HFSH or beyond that, either in the ascending or descending generation.

Kins through the sister : The kinship terms used to denote nepotic kins through a sister are as under :

1. *chhau* (eSH, m.s.), 2. *sagpo* (ySH, m.s.), 3. *chhau* (SH, w.s.), 4. *chhao* (SZ), 5. *nam* (SZW), 6. *chhamo* (SD), 7. *magpa* (SDH), 8. *azang* (SHF), 9. *ane* (SHM).

Some of the notable points in this regard are : the term for ySH is the same as for WyB which is again an indicator of the system of exchange marriage. What is pertinent with regard to the kinship term for SH is that it is identical with WB i.e. these are mutually interchangeable. In both relations the brother-in-law (SH or WB) whosoever is elder in age is addressed as *chhau* and the younger as *sagpo*, irrespective of their marital positions. Moreover, the sex of the speaker does not make any difference in kinship terms for SH. Further, the terms, viz., *azang* and *ane*, are identical with the terms used for WF and WM which further confirm that marriage with SHS is permissible in this system. No kinship term is available for HSH. In this framework the use of a common term for ZZ/DZ/SZ, viz. *chhoo* and for ZD/DD/SD, viz. *chhamo* is somewhat inexplicable on account of a generation gap between them. However, the use of the term *magpa* for SDH is in agreement with the use of this term for DH/ZDH/DDH. Similar is the use of the term *nam* for SZW.

Kins through daughters : Some of the interesting points in this respect are :

(1) there are no kinship terms for ascending generation of the in-laws of the daughter.
(2) no kinship relation exists beyond two generations from the daughter.
(3) the term for DH (i.e. son-in-law), viz. *magpa*, is identical with the term used for SDH or DDH/ZDH. Though he is referred to as *magpa*, yet he is addressed by his personal name.
(4) the terms for DZ and DD are the same (*chhao/khod* and *chhamo/khodmed* respectively) as are used for ZZ and ZD respectively.
(5) no affinal relationship is recognized with DHS/DHF/DHM etc. However, the parents-in-law of both spouses address one another as brother and sister reciprocally.

Kins through the mother's sister : Various kinship terms denoting relations through MS are as follows :

tyama (MeS), *phechama* (MyS), *chomama* (Me/yS if *chomo*), *aku* (MSH), *au* (MSH if *lama*), *ane* (HMS), *achho/chocho* (MSZ), *achhe/apu* (MSD), *digsag* (MSZW), *sagpo/chhau* (MSDH), *tete* (MSHF), *apa* (MSHM).

Notable points in this regard are :

(i) since MSH is a potential husband of the mother of the ego, consequently, as a potential father to the ego, therefore, he is termed as *aku*, not *azang*, a term for FSH. The term *aku* besides MSH also denotes FB/FMSH and step-father. However, if any one of her husbands is a *lama* then he will be called *au*. The terms of address and reference are the same as are the terms of kinship.

(ii) The terminology for MSA is parallel to that noted with reference to mother. The eldest one is *tyama*, younger to her is *barama*, then *phechama* and then *kyugchiama*. It is *chomama*, if she is a nun (*chomo*).

(iii) There is no correspondence between the children of MB and MS. While the children of MS are treated as one's own brothers and sisters and have the same terms of kinship i.e. *achho* (eB), *chocho* (yB), *achhe* (eS), *apu* (yS), there are no kinship terms for the children of MB because of prevalence of cross-cousin marriage.

(iv) The parents of MSH are addressed with the same classificatory terms which are common for the people of older generation.

Kins through the Wife's Mother

Following terms have been recorded in this connection :

1. *azang* (WMB), *ane* (WMS), *azang* (WMSH), *tete* (WMF), *apa* (WMM).

Here we notice that the husband regards his WMB as his own MB and treats WMS and WMSH as her parents. Similarly, the parents of his WM are treated at par with his own grand-parents. Though there is no kinship term for WMBW yet the term of address viz. *ane* indicates that she is given the same status which is accorded to a mother-in-law.

Variation and adoption of kinship terms : No variation or adoption of kinship terms from other systems is seen among the polyandrous Buddhists of Upper Lahul. On the contrary, the kinship terms of the Buddhists of Lower Lahul, i.e. of the Chandra-Bhaga valley, who are gradually resorting to monogamous form of marriage, show both variations and adoptions in many cases. They have borrowed many distinctive terms from their neighbours, and these terms otherwise do not fit in the polyandrous system, e.g. independent terms for HB, HBW, and distinctive terms for consanguineal and affinal grand-children as in ZZ (*potra*), ZD (*potri*), DZ (*jhotra*), DD (*jhotri*) which otherwise are altogether missing in a polyandrous system or in BZ (*yo*), BD (*myo*), SZ (*bhanja*), SD (*bhanji*), HeS (*chhamo*), HyS (*bhau*) etc. It is evident from these terms that these have been borrowed from their Swangla (Hindu Brahman) brethrens to meet the necessity of changing pattern of the society.

Conclusion : From the above analysis of kinship system it may be concluded that the kinship system of a polyandrous society differs both behaviourally andt erminologically from a monogamous society significantly. Among the Lahulas of the Gahr valley the most universal behaviour pattern is respect for seniors by juniors of all kinship categories. The criterion for seniority among these people is seniority in age and generation and not by certain kinship relations as is found in some societies. Reciprocally, all juniors belonging to all kin categories are treated with love and affection, though there may be variation in the degree of it, depending on intimacy of relationship between them.

Another notable feature of kinship behaviour in the Lahula family is that of co-operation and equality that make the polyandrous family run smoothly. All male and female members are treated on equal footing and are assigned their duties in domestic affairs according to their age and capacity. In all matters of family welfare there is a spirit of co-operation; jealousy and selfishness are strikingly low, particularly in conjugal relationship. In fact, this spirit of the polyandrous Lahulas has enabled them to stick to their peculiar ways of life through all these ages. But, in recent years, the century long isolation of Lahul is breaking down and an all round change is paying its way into the socio-cultural ethos of these people of the Himalayas. Owing to a distinct family structure and its polyandrous union there are only three terms (F,M,FS) in the parental generation and four (H/W/B/S) in the ego's own generation. Similarly, because of the practice of cross-cousin marriage the matrilateral and patrilateral cross-cousins are not terminologically recognized, and the cross-cousins related through MS are recognized as siblings, because of the taboo of marriage between them. The prevalence of polyandry and cross-cousin marriage has further reduced the scope of the terminology for parallel cousins from both sides. Lineal separation is only partial. For, ego's line is separated from the collaterals only in the parental generation. Categories in all other generations are lineally merged. Affinal relations beyond second generation are terminologically equated with consanguineal relations of the same category. It distinguishes kinsmen of four generations only, the first for senior persons of ego's own generation (eB/eS), the second for persons of parental generation, the third for the persons of second or more ascending generation, and the fourth for the second or more descending generation. The kinship system of the polyandrous Buddhists of Upper Lahul valley differs partially from the monogamous Buddhists of Lower Lahul or Pattan and significantly from the Hindu Swanglas and Chahns of the Chandra-Bhaga valley.

The picture of the inner structure of the society revealed by the above analysis is, perhaps, more authentic than by any other source. A thorough socio-linguistic analysis of dialects of this region is sure to unveil many hitherto unknown socio-cultural aspects of the people of these Himalayan regions.

REFERENCES

Bohannam, P. 1963 *Social Anthropology*, Holt Rinehart and Winston Inc., London.

Bose, N.K. 1963 *Cultural Anthropology and Other Essays*, Indian Associated Publishing Co., Calcutta.

Bose, N.K. 1971 *Tribal Life in India*, National Book Trust, New Delhi.

Dube, S.C. (ed.) 1971 *Tribal Heritage in India*, Vikas Publishing House Pvt. Ltd., New Delhi.

Fox, R. 1967 *Kinship and Marriage*, Panguin Books Ltd., England.

Firth, R. 1951 *Elements of Social Organization*, Watts & Co., London.

Fisher, James F. (ed.) 1978 *Himalayan Anthropology*, Mouton Publishers, The Hague.

Gill, M.S. 1972 *Himalayan Wanderland: Travels in Lahaul-Spiti,* Vikas Publishing House Pvt. Ltd., Delhi.

Goldstein, M.S. 1971 Stratification, Polyandry and Family Structure in Central Tibet, *South Western Journal of Anthropology*, Vol. 27.

Goody, Jack (ed.) 1973 *Kinship,* Panguin Books Ltd., London.

Gover, Geoffrey 1938 *Himalayan Village: An Account of the Lepchas of Sikkim*, Michael Joseph, London.

Hsu, Francis (ed.) 1971 *Kinship and Culture,* Aldine, Chicago.

Hymes, Dell 1964 *Language in Culture and Society*, Harper & Row Publishers, New York.

Kapadia, K.M. 1955 *Marriage and Family in India,* Oxford University Press, London.

Karve, Iravati 1965 *Kinship Organization in India,* Asia Publishing House, Bombay.

Leach, E.R. 1958 Concerning Tobriand Clans and the Kinship Category Tabu in Jack Goody (ed.), *The Development Cycle in Domestic Groups,* Cambridge University Press, London.

MacDonald, David 1978 *Cultural Heritage of Tibet* (photoprint), Delhi.

Moodey, R.W. 1978 Kinship and Culture in the Himalayan Region, in *Himalayan Anthropology* (ed.) James, F. Fisher, Mouton Publishers, The Hague.

Majumdar, D.N. 1962 *Himalayan Polyandry,* Asia Publishing House, Bombay.

Parmar, Y.S. 1975 *Polyandry in the Himalayas,* Vikas Publishing House Pvt. Ltd., Delhi.

Sreedhar, M.V. 1983 Clan, Marriage Practices and Kinship Terms amongst the Ao and Sema Naga, *International Jn. of Dravidian Linguistics*, Vol. XII, No. 1.

Tanaka, Masako 1976 Kinship Terminologies: The Okinawan case, in *Language and Thought : Anthropological Issues* (eds.) William McCormack and Stephen A. Wurm, Aldine Publishing Co., Chicago.

CHAPTER XXIV

CLASS FORMATION AND CONFLICT IN A POLYANDROUS VILLAGE OF HIMACHAL PRADESH

B.R. RIZVI

This paper deals with the emerging patterns of social stratification and class formation of the Bodhs of Spiti that leads to a conflict between the old and the new emerging social systems which is a direct result of the weakening of the institution of Lamaism, the matrix of the Gelukpa culture and ideology.

This article is an outcome of the study of society and culture of the people of Spiti, a sub-division of Lahul and Spiti District of Himachal Pradesh. The above study was initiated by North-Western Regional Office of the Anthropological Survey of India at Dehru Dun. The area was visited by me in October, 1973 when I could study the village Tabo.

The Spiti valley is named after the river that drains a large area behind the Great Himalayan Range and is a principal tributary of the Sutlej. The Spiti or 'Piti' as called by the local people, flows through a deep and narrow valley scarcely more than a mile across. On either side of which steep rocky mountains rise to a height of 20,000 ft. or more. The length of the Spiti valley is about 80 kms. Other valleys of the sub-division are the Peen, the Purang and the Lingti.

Table 1: *Distribution of Village Population*

Sex	Age Groups								*Total*	*percentage*
	0-14 No.	*age percentage*	*15-34 No.*	*age percentage*	*35-59 No.*	*age percentage*	*60+ No.*	*age percentage*		
Male	26	35.61	25	34.25	19	26.03	3	4.11	73	100.00
Female	25	34.25	29	39.72	15	20.55	4	5.48	73	100.00
TOTAL	51	34.93	54	36.99	34	23.29	7	4.79	146	100.00

The inhabitants of Spiti are Bodhs, who speak Bodhi and owe their allegiance to the Gelugpa sect of Buddhism.

Tabo is accessible through Hindustan Tibet road which runs via Simla, Rampur Bushahr, and onward to Kaurik. A 36 kms. long westward brittle track the only link from Sumdo to Tabo via Hurling and Lari villages took me to my destination. The village was the seat of a famous monastery built by Richen Zangpo, who lived 900 years ago. Innumerable *chortens* (receptacles of worship) scattered all around the village and longitudinal *mane* walls littered with 'Om mani-padme-om' inscribed pebbles of all sizes welcome visitors as they approach towards the village and the famous monastery.

The village is situated in the lower Spiti valley the average height of it being 10,662 ft. above the mean sea level. Rainfall is trace and vegetation scarce. Low juniper shrubs provide a change to brown, buff and white landscape.

The total population of the village at the time of investigation was 146. Distribution of the village population on the basis of age and sex is shown in the table on page 414.

It is evident from Table No. 1 that the male and female population is equal in size but a slight variation is visible in different age groups. The male members dominate in the age groups of 0 to 14 and 35 to 59 years while female population is slightly higher in 15 to 34 and 60 and above age groups. Hence, the general pattern of population in Tabo is not different from other populations in spite of the fact that adelphic polyandry was widely practised till the recent past. The total number of households in Tabo is 35 with an average size of 4.17 individuals. The area of the village is 91 acres out of which 67 acres are cultivable and 24 non-cultivable. Each household in Tabo possesses 2.6 acres. In terms of cultivable land the average size of landholding possessed by a household is 1.9 acres.

The houses are built low with small windows due to absence of rains but because of high velocity wind. Sun-burnt bricks are used for raising walls and thatching is done with wood, twigs and mud. The flat top of the roof is used for storing fuel, keeping wicker baskets and agricultural implements. The houses of the *khangchen* are clustered together and are bigger and more elaborate while those belonging to the *hinjung* are smaller and scattered in a separate part of the village.

The arctic climate in Spiti forces the inhabitants to wear a dress which consists of a woollen cloak, made of hand-woven woollen bands called *pattoo*, the undergarments, also made of *pattoo*, a shirt and a petti-coat. Caps with a large flap to cover the neck and ears are worn by both men and women. A man ties a girdle around the waist in a knot which lies just below their belly. The women wear a woollen jacket over a coloured woollen *paijama* or a petti-coat almost touching their feet. Footwears, made of *pattoo* and goat-skin, are manufactured locally for self-consumption. Contact with the outsiders has brought about a substantial change in the dress pattern of the male. Discarded army clothes like woollen monkey-caps, jerseys, trousers, overcoats and leather shoes have replaced the traditional items of dress. This change is more marked among the poorer section of the population. The rich still stick to traditional dresses. Festive occasions, however, provide an occasion when all villagers, rich or poor, don their traditional dress.

Parched barley flour (*sattoo*) is the staple diet. It is usually mixed with salted tea till it becomes a thick paste and then eaten with a spoon. Another method of consuming *sattoo* is to moisten it with hot water and prepare a dough (*khulaq*). Small balls are made out of it and are eaten by soaking them with butter (*skew*). *Chang*, i.e., home made beer, is brewed in almost every house and consumed by all irrespective of age and sex.

The major crops are wheat (*tso*), barley (*meh*) and millets (*che che*). Sowing starts immediately after the melting of snow and crops are harvested by the middle of October. Before threshing operations begin, the villagers worship the village deity Yulsamanjyong, whose shrine is situated in the western border of the village. The deity is implored to blow strong winds enabling the straw blown out of the grain. Horse polo (*chaugen*) provides a grand finale to the festival. The game is played in the evening and villagers are invited by the head of the village council (*sarpanch*), who was also the traditional head of the village in the past (*nambardar*), for drinking *chang* which is brewed from the funds collected from each household of the village. The festival is known as Namgan.

Till the recent past the people of Spiti maintained trade links with Ladakh and Central Asia. The Spitian traders used to carry barley, wheat, cotton, tea, etc. and exchanged them with silver ingots, wool, *pasham*, goats, sheep, salt and borax with their counterparts coming from the cities across the border famous for wool. After the expiry of Sino-Indian Trade Agreement in 1961, all trade stopped across the border. This gave a serious jolt to village economy but soon it was recovered through job opportunities thrown open by the Government.

Social Stratification

Spiti lies in the polyandrous belt of the Himalayas where adelphic polyandry is observed. This custom in Spiti in the past derived its strength from the people's strict adherence to the law of primogeniture which allowed only the eldest male issue to marry and inherit the real estate of family. Parents used to retire to a separate household. Other male issues who were neither supposed to marry nor to attain the status of social fatherhood, could share their eldest brother's wife. The youngest brother was sent to monastery for the attainment of religious learning. The sisters used to make an exit either through marriage or by becoming nuns (*chomo*).

The group of households, established by the eldest male issue after his marriage, was known as the *khangchen*. The parents then retired to a separate household constituting the *khinjung* group of households. The head of the *khangchen* used to provide maintenance to all members of the *khinjung* and to donate a part of the paternal land to the village monastery (*gompa*) for the maintenance of his youngest brother.

The core of a *khinjung* household consisted of the two spouses. When either of the two spouses died, the life of a *khinjung* household came to an end and the surviving member of theh ousehold joined its respective *khangchen* household. Thus, *khinjung* was not a permanent and stable unit as its component households were unstable and short-lived. The fission and fusion of households in Tabo occurred in the following three stages :

Diagram 1

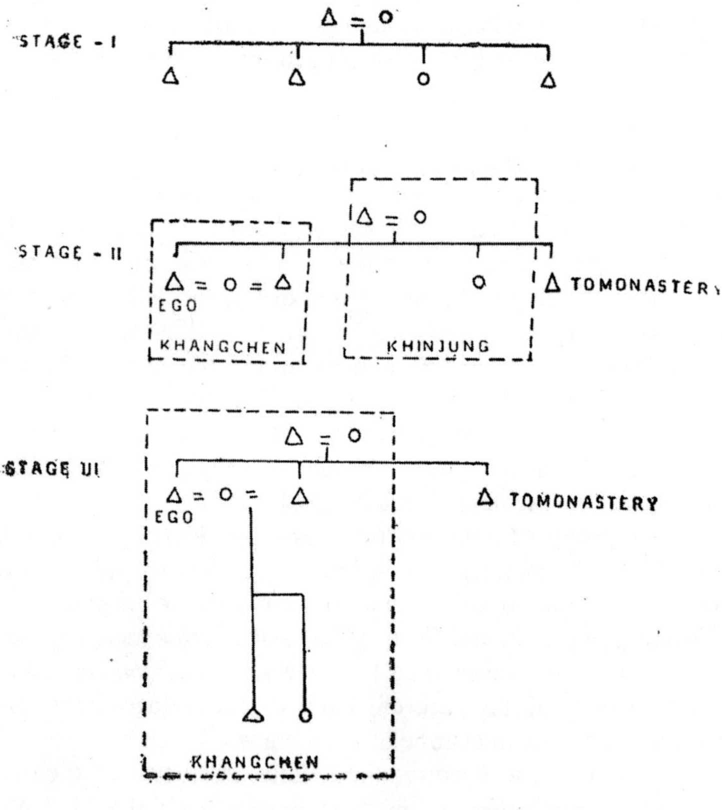
STAGE - I
STAGE - II
EGO
KHANGCHEN
KHINJUNG
TOMONASTERY
STAGE III
EGO
TOMONASTERY
KHANGCHEN

The three stages in Diagram No. 1 portray the transformation occurred in a domestic group. A nuclear family in Stage I broke into two segments of household i.e. *khangchen* and *khinjung*. A *khangchen* household consisted of the ego, his wife and his younger brother, who was also the co-sharer of his wife while a *khinjung* consisted of the ego's parents and unmarried sister. The ego's youngest brother joined monastery for religious learning. The ego was responsible for the maintenance of the members of the *khinjung* and of his youngest brother who had joined the monastery (Stage II). When the ego's father died and sister got married and lived with her husband, the ego's mother joined the *khangchen*. Thus the *khinjung* household lost its existence due to death of one of its members and marriage of the other.

The above arrangement worked well till introduction of anti-polyandry laws in early forties of this century. Soon afterwards fissures appeared in the polyandrous arrangement of the *khangchen* household. The younger brother of ego in the *khangchen* household who was not allowed to marry but to share his elder brother's wife, started asserting his right to marry of his own and to get a share in familial property. Later on when they got married, they established a separate group of households known as the *hinjung*. *Lamas* abdicated their avowed celibacy and rigours of monastic life and swelled the ranks of the *hinjung* as having committed a grave sin against religion they could not get a place in the *khangchen* segment. The transformation has been portrayed in Diagram No. 2 shown on page 420.

In Diagram No. 2 ego's parents form the *khinjung*. Ego himself forms the *khangchen* and ego's younger brother(s) the *hinjung* household. Ego's two younger brothers may or may not share the same house but their membership with the *hinjung* household is indisputable.

The *khangchen* group of households in Tabo assumed an air of superiority due to political and social reasons. Politically, the rulers of Spiti known as the Nonos, belonged to the *khangchen*, and the Nonoship, like family estate, ran in the line of first male issue. As a result of this socio-political process, most of the village chiefs (*numbardars*) belonged to the *khangchen*

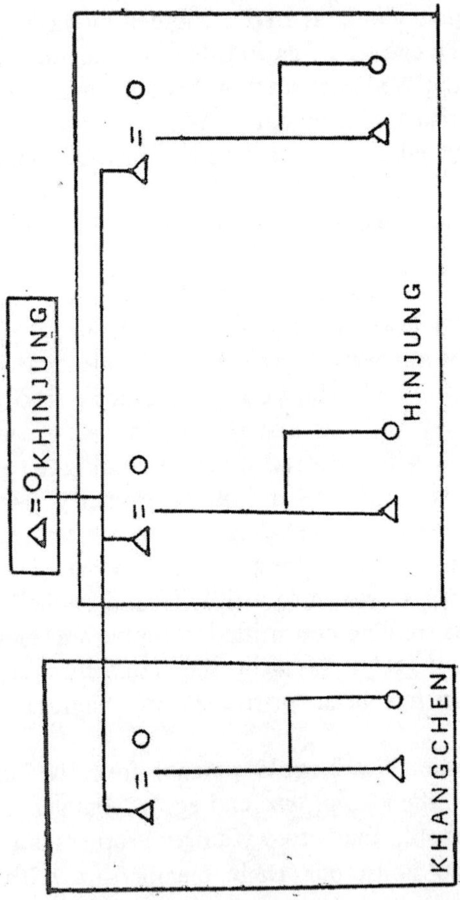

Diagram 2

group. The duty of the *numbardars* was to collect revenue from the village and to deposit it in the treasury. The *numbardar* of Tabo belonged similarly to a *khangchen* household. After the merger of Spiti in Himachal Pradesh, the *numbardar* was divested of his traditional duties and his influence eroded considerably. The inception of the statutory village council (Panchayat) opened up fresh avenues for the head of a *khangchen* household in Tabo to assert his traditional authority through elections based on adult franchise. In Tabo the *numbardar* and two other persons belonging to the *khangchen* households were elected as members of the village council. The former after sometime, was elected as head of the village council (surpanch) in spite of the fact that majority of the village, as we shall see later, belongs to the *hinjung*, who are economically dependent on the *khangchen*. Hence the latter still enjoy both economic and political control over the *khinjung* and the *hinjung*.

The rule of primogeniture seems to have helped the *khangchen* unit not only in monopolising and accumulating politico-economic powers in their hands but also in attaining a higher position in the hierarchical ladder of the society.

Though, treated at par with the *khangchen* unit socially and ritually, the *khinjung* unit was placed in the middle partly due to the latter's economic dependence on the former and partly due to the impending danger of fission of *khinjung* household leading to the ultimate fusion of its remaining members with the *khangchen*.

The *hinjung* unit of households found the lowest place in the hierarchical ladder because members of this group breached the vow of monastic celibacy; they abdicated their religious throne and indulged themselves in temporal activities. Some members acted against the age-old system of polyandry fortified by the strict observance of the rule of primogeniture. On the occasion of Namgan all villagers were invited by the *sarpanch* (still known as the *numbardar*) for listening the declaration of Yulsaminjyong, the village deity, regarding their personal and collective welfare through a priest, possessed and in trance. After the ceremony, people sat down and were offered *chang*. They sat in the as shown in Diagram No. 3 manner :

Diagram 3

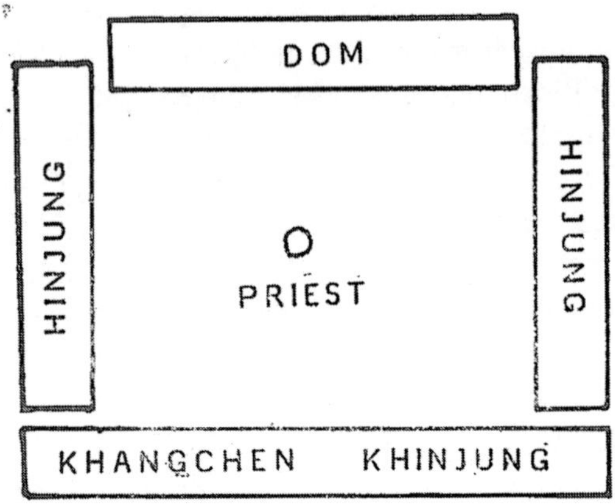

The *hinjung* members sat in the two vertical rows and were served in the cups that they brought themselves while the members of both the *khangchen* and the *khinjung* sitting together horizontally, were served in cups of silver, brass and porcelain provided by the host. The maximum spatial distance visible in the diagram is between the *khangchen* and the Dom whose main profession is drumming and playing music on festive occasions. The Doms are considered as lowest in the group hierarchy. The *hinjung* and the *khangchen,* though sitting closer than with the Dom, did not sit together as the *khangchen* seemed to observe spatial differentiation with the *hinjung.* The priest stood facing the *khangchen* and even in the course of conversation he did not turn even once towards the *hinjung.*

There is no possibility for a member of the *hinjung* segment as stands today, to change his status and join *khangchen* excepting through the *makpa* marriages in which a male member of the *hinjung* marries with the female member of the *khangchen.* The status of the newly inducted member into the *khangchen* is never treated at par with the other members of this group. He works for his wife's brother as long as the two live together in the *khangchen.* Afterwards the couple leaves the *khangchen* and joins the *hinjung.* The children born out of the *makpa* marriages also join the *hinjung* segment. This situation can be portrayed in the following diagram :

Diagram 4

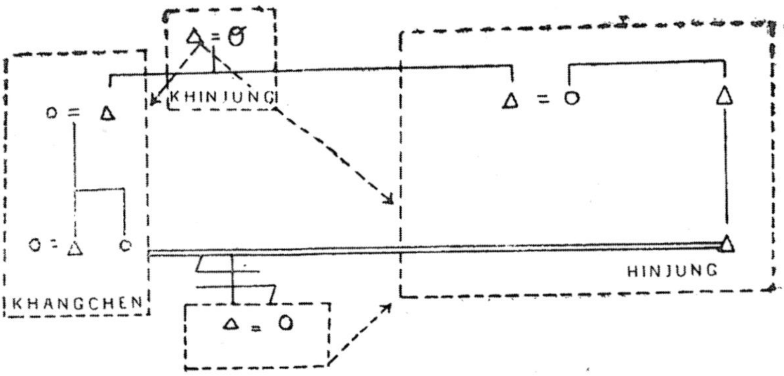

In the above diagram the processes of the formation of three segments from a single nuclear family and intergroup mobility have been depicted. After the marriage of the eldest male issue, the parents retire to a separate residence and form the *khinjung* leaving behind the former to become the head of the *khangchen*. But the *khinjung* is a transitory unit which breaks up with the death of either of the two spouses who form the core of the unit. The surviving spouse either shifts to the *khangchen* or to the *hinjung*. The members of the *khangchen*, now, resent the inclusion of the members of the broken *khinjung*, treating them as a sort of economic liability. Thus the latter have no option but to seek alliance with the *hinjung*. Hence, it was observed that the size of the *khangchen* is decreasing and the *hinjung* increasing. The members of the *khangchen*, however, have evolved a mechanism to induct new members in their labour force through uxorilocal (*makpa*) marriage but this arrangement is again temporary because the newly inducted members, now, no longer work as sincerely for their hosts as they used to do a decade earlier. As a result of the unwillingness on the part of the *khangchen* to keep the *makpa* entrants in their group, the *makpa* have no alternative but to form neo-local families leading to their ultimate merger into the *hinjung*. Hence the size of the *khangchen* is shrinking and that of the *khinjung* swelling. The *khangchen* thus can be termed as the donor group for both the *khinjung* and the *hinjung* who can be treated as recipient groups. The *khangchen* constitute 22.86 per cent, the *khinjung* 8.57 per cent and the *hinjung* 68.57 per cent of the total village population. Out of 35 households in the village, all the eight *khangchen* households depend solely on agriculture. Out of the three *khinjung* households, two depend on agriculture and the third on labour and agriculture. Out of the twenty-four *hinjung* households, eighteen earn their livelihood by working in the fields of the *khangchen*, five through agriculture and one through government service. Hence 20 households belonging to the *khinjung* and the *hinjung* work for their *khangchen* masters.

The modern forces of change, viz., presence of armed forces and extension of communication network to the border villages is bringing about a new development in socio-economic relationship between the *khangchen, khinjung* and the *hinjung*.

The *khangchen,* being traditionally dominant in the regional economy and politics, are reluctant to the endeavours of planned development aimed at the upliftment of weaker segments of the society. The *hinjung*, on the other hand, are receptive to the processes of change. They are not only going ahead in the field of education but are joining Government services in increasing numbers. This has brought about a measure of prosperity among the *hinjung*, who now oppose and resist the *khangchen's* authority in the village; and the latter's economic hold on the former is fast receding. The *khangchen* still like to live in their past glory and try to resist the idea of integrated rural development. The labour resource of the *khangchen* is drying up fast. Now, the *hinjung* families in Tabo do not work willingly in the fields of the *khangchen*. As a result of former's unwillingness to work for their age-old patrons, an open confrontation started between the two groups of the village.

The head of the statutory council in Tabo, who belongs to the *khangchen,* refuses to retire after the marriage of his eldest son and is holding the property against the traditional rule of primogeniture. The son and father have a strained relationship, and it is difficult for the son to get justice. Hence acquisition of power through statutory village council has been responsible for bringing about a change in local relationship. Many people belonging to the *khangchen* complain about the attitude of their respective fathers who refuse to relinquish the *khangchen* at the desired moment. The deprived ones affiliate themselves with the *hinjung* but such affiliations are not openly demonstrated due to fear of reprisals.

Thus, a discordant note in the relationship between the *khangchen* and the *hinjung* is clearly discernible. The *khangchen* resist the modern forces of planned development least the *hinjung* gain an economic superiority over them, depriving them of their traditional status which they have been enjoying till the recent past.

The Government officials complain bitterly about the indifferent attitude of the *khangchen* who resist innovations. When the idea of potato cultivation was mooted by the village level worker, most of the *khangchen* members of Tabo resisted it with tooth and nail while the *hinjung* were more receptive and enthusiastic about it. The same story was repeated when a primary school was opened in Tabo. The *hinjung* sent their children in large numbers but the *khangchen* remained indifferent to the newly opened school. Later they yielded and sent their children to the village school. At the time of investigation it was observed that a large number of children belonged to the *hinjung* and the rate of literacy among them was also found higher than that of the *khangchen*.

Lately, however, Sonam Dorje of the *khangchen* group who lives in the neighbouring village, Lari, is trying to bring about a measure of reconciliation between the two groups in Tabo. His advice is fairly respected by both groups of the village. Working as an army contractor, Sonam Dorje owns a fleet of horses for transportation. He is responsible for organizing Pony Drivers Association in Spiti. He is the first person among the *khangchen* who cultivated potatoes in his fields and found encouraging results. Others followed him. Now, they earn a sizeable income from potato cultivation. Thus, a large area in Spiti has come under potato cultivation due to the lone efforts of Sonam Dorje.

In short, social stratification in Tabo, manifesting itself in three district status-oriented segments, is an outcome of the age-old custom of polyandry fortified by the people's strong adherence to the rule of primogeniture. The rules were framed with a view to preserve the group solidarity and its religious order and to stop fragmentation of land into small and economically unviable parcels.

The arrangement worked well for centuries so long as the basic fabric of the society remained intact and the traditional norms of the society were adhered to. After the introduction of anti-polyandry legislation and the subsequent decline of religious authority as the governing factor of life, rapid changes occurred. The extended *khangchen* households were replaced by the nuclear *hinjung* households whose size grew at the cost of the *khangchen* population leading to spatial discrimination and to conflict between the two major segments of the village population. The modern processes of socio-economic development and the presence of armed forces in the area for protection of national borders, however, are bringing about a measure of prosperity and reconciliation between the two major segments of the village.

CHAPTER XXV

MUSLIMS OF THE KASHMIR VALLEY AND KARGIL

A STUDY OF CULTURAL CONTINUITY AND CHANGE

B.R. RIZVI

Introduction

Indian Muslims have recently become a focus of interest for the social scientists. While to some of them the Muslim societies in India have been branded as an unchanging monolithic lot, some other social scientists, on the other hand, have portrayed them changing under the impact of Vedic religion with which the former came into contact as historical compulsion.

Some of the questions that arise at this moment should be treated objectively and empirically rather than on subjective assumptions and pre-conceived notions.

Whether the Muslims in India resist changes ? If so, why ? If they are prone to change what aspects of society are more conducive to change ? In order to have an objective view of this situation and to answer these queries we may have to differentiate between the 'content' and 'form' of the Muslim culture. With 'content' I mean the continuous and irreducible system of values with which the society adheres tightly, a set of fundamental religious principles that provides a 'collective representation' to society. These contents are widely and universally distributed and are easily distinguishable from the 'contents' of other societies and cultures. The contents of the Muslim societies, in other words, may be termed as the basic religious philosophy, which is too well known to elaborate here and a system of basic rituals that surround the life of an individual from his birth to death and even after.

The term 'form' of the Muslim societies is meant a 'form' that is more varied in dimensions of time and space. Like a cacoon, it is spun around the 'content'. 'Form' is a summation of chronological events viz., the history of conquests, of migration, ecology and the culture-contact situations. It is subject to vast variations of dimensions of time and space unlike 'contents'.

Viewing the Muslim society in the light of 'content' and 'form' dichotomy, the elements of which are combined with each other like a silk-work and cacoon, we notice that Muslims all over the world have a firm faith in Unity of God, the Faculty of His Justice, the mechanism of His guidance to His creatures by a stream of 1,24,000 Prophets and their deputies and the last day of Judgement. The manifestations of this system of faith are the observance of five daily prayers, thirty days of obligatory fast, a pilgrimage to Mecca, payment of levies and striving for the establishment and expansion of Islam. This is a uniformly observed system of values to which the Muslims in all the continents are strictly conformed to. This is a continuous static and unchanging aspect of Muslim society. Variations and changes occur on the other hand in the resultant form of the society, as there are Muslims in America, Asia, Europe, Africa and elsewhere speaking different languages, wearing different attires, ethnically different in looks and appearance being subjected to varied historical processes and culture contact situations but all of them share the common 'core' of culture.

In short, there is a similarity in the contents amongst all the Muslim societies in the dimensions of time and space but they differ each other in form. In other words, a concentric structure emerges wherein contents are enveloped by form.

Against the background of the above proposition only the Shia Muslims of the Kashmir valley and Kargil have been studied in order to maintain uniformity and bring into relief the continuity of content and changes and variations in form.

This study is based on the Shia Dards of Karkit, Shia Baltis of Hardas and the Shia Purgis of Wakha. All the above mentioned three villages are situated in Kargil. The Shias in Kashmir have been studied from the village Balahama situated in Srinagar district. Studies in Kargil were conducted in the year 1973-75 and in Kashmir in 1981.

KARGIL

The Area and the People

Kargil, now a district recently carved out from the erstwhile district of Ladakh is situated 11,000 ft. above the mean sea level. It is a vast expanse of brown mountain bereft of all types of vegetation excepting sporadic and spontaneous growth of juniper bushes. The river banks, however, are carpetted with moderate vegetation. Willow and Poplar trees, planted in the recent past, provide a feast to eyes otherwise tired of the monotonous barrenness of the region. The cloud, unable to cross Zo-ji pass, the gateway to Ladakh, gets exhausted and freeze into snow. Hence the rainfall is trace and snowfall copious. The area experiences prolonged arctic winter when it remains cut off well above six months in a year from Kashmir valley, its only link with the rest of India. Kargil town experiences a relatively mild climate hence it falls under double crop zone but in high altitude village only a single crop is possible. Wheat, barley, *grim*, peas, and turnip are the main crops in the double crop zone whereas millets are the main crop in the single crop areas.

There are four major distinct ethnic groups in Kargil : the Dards, locally called as the Broq-pa and amicably referred to as the Shin, the Baltis, the Mongoloids and the mixture of the three—the Purgis. The Mons, the earliest settlers of Kargil and also referred to as the Dom, are a small population having an age-old profession of singing and playing musical instruments on festive occasions.

Religion-wise the majority of the people in Kargil are Muslims of the Shia faith with the sporadic sprinkling of the Sunnis and the Nurbakhshis. However, the Shias form a 95.00 per cent strong majority.

KASHMIR

The Area and the People

Situated in the western flank of the Himalayas at an average height of 6,000 ft. above the mean sea level, the valley of Kashmir is a basin 136 kms. long and 40 kms. wide. The valley is well fed with the monsoon rains. Rice, lentils, careals, millet, oilseeds, fruits, saffron, maize, etc. are the main crops. The verdant forests of mixed variety offer rich economic resources to the people who live in relative prosperity enjoying its salubrious climate.

The percentage of the Muslim population in the Kashmir valley is 94.00 per cent of the total population. Unlike Kargil, the Shias in Kashmir form a small minority.

Social Stratification

One interesting aspect of the Muslim societies in the two regions is that in Kargil the Muslims are in close interaction with the Buddhists whereas in the Kashmir valley they interact with the Hindus. There appears to be no trace of caste system among the Kargil Muslims whereas Muslims in Kashmir are clearly divided into caste type professional groups. Thus the picture of social stratification in Kargil is a bit different from that of the Kashmir valley. A scheme of social stratification among the Shia Muslims in Kargil and the Kashmir valley is depicted below :

Table 1 : *Social Stratification among the Shias in Kashmir valley and Kargil*

Social Stratification among the Shia Muslims of Kargil	*Social Stratification among the Shia Muslims of Kashmir valley*
SYED (Agha) Mujtahid (Ascribed status)	SYED (Ascribed status)
Immigrants	SHEIKH (Ethnic group) (Ascribed status)
SHEIKH (Priest)—Mujtahid	Higher occupation groups

Social Stratification among the Shia Muslims of Kargil	*Social Stratification among the Shia Muslims of Kashmir valley*
(Ascribed status) AKHUND (Priest) Non-Mujtahid (Ascribed status)	(Ascribed status) (Goldsmiths, masons, butchers, oil pressers, carpenters, vegetable sellers, weavers, potters, etc.)
HAJI (Ascribed status) (Persons having returned as the pilgrims from Iraq and Iran)	COBBLER (Ascribed status)
ZAMIDAR (Ascribed status) Ron Raj-Shin, Kacho-Saget	SCAVENGERS (Ascribed status)
DOM or MON (Status in transition)	

Table No. 1 shows a greater amount of group mobility among the Muslims of Kargil. The Doms are slowly merging themselves with the agrarian class. A peasant from the agrarian group possesses all the potentialities of achieving the status of a Haji or a Sheikh. Hence, with the singular exception of Syed, all other groups enjoy an achieved status with a strong trend of an upward group mobility. In other words the Muslims of Kargil, as we will see, have a more or less open class oriented society in comparison to the Muslims of Kashmir who show a strongly closed status oriented society with no or very little chances of upward group mobility. Unlike the Muslims of Kargil the status of each group on the hierarchical ladder is ascribed and therefore fixed. This variation should be considered as a variation in the form of the society not in the content as both groups share the similar religious philosophy handed down to them by their common prophet Mohammad and the common deputies of the Prophet, and of course, the holy Quran.

How this variation in form has come about ? For a satisfactory answer of the above question we may have to look back into the history of the pre-Islamic ages in Kashmir and then of Kargil.

Hinduism in Kashmir

In the unknown remotest ages the worship of Naga or Snake God was in vogue. Buddhism was introduced in the valley around 250 B.C. by the Emperor Ashoke. Caste hierarchy was established by Jaloka, his successor. The snake worship was followed by the Tartar princes and the Brahminical or Vedic religion was introduced by Abhimanyu in B.C. 73. The snake worship, however, was subsequently revived under Gonerda III. Shankaracharya established the present form of Shaivaism in Kashmir which remained under the rule of the Hindu kings till Islam came to stay as the main religion of the Kashmir valley.

Islam in Kashmir

Syed Sharafuddin alias Bulbul Shah is credited with laying the foundation of Islam in Kashmir valley. As a saint from Turkey, he came to Kashmir and established a monastery (*Khengah*) near Chattabal in Srinagar. His call for prayers (*azqqh*) once attracted the attention of a mentally dormanted fugitive Buddhist Prince Rinchen who, being dissatisfied with the brand of Buddhism practised in Ladakh, wanted to change his faith and become a Hindu. His request was, however, turned down by the Hindu clergy as Rinchen was not a Hindu by birth. Hearing the call for prayers of Bulbul Shah one morning, Rinchen decided to be the follower of the caller for prayers (*muazzin*). He met Bulbul Shah and soon became very intimate with him who bestowed on Rinchen the title of Sadruddin, the chief of the religion.

On assuming the throne of Kashmir, as the first Muslim ruler of Kashmir, Rinchen, now known as Rinchen Shah, built the first mosque in Kashmir, known as Awwal-masjid. He also constructed a free boarding for the poor who had neither food nor shelter and named the complex after his mentor's name, 'Bulbul-Lankar'. Thus Rinchen's rule in Kashmir, though short, paved the way for establishment of Islam in the valley. After Rinchen's death his widow, Kota Rani assumed the regency but was very soon dethroned by one of her most trusted lieutenants and her Prime Minister, Hasan Shahmir, who laid the foundations of the longest Shahmiri dynasty in the recorded history of Kashmir. During the reign of Shahbuddin, a king of the same dynasty, entered into Kashmir valley a Persian saint named Syed Ali Hamadani and his son Mir Hamadani with a train of 1000 followers. Though the seeds of Islamic faith were sown by his predecessor Bulbul Shah but the arrival of Syed Ali Hamadani, affectionately referred to by the Kashmiris as Amir-e-kabir, seems to have fixed Islam as the major faith of Kashmir. The history of Islam in Kashmir suggests that the new faith came mainly through the peaceful persuasion of saints and missionaries through the cruel and compulsive methods of conversion of the local populace cannot be ruled out. Sikendar Shah, also known as Sikendar Butshikan (Sikendar, the iconoclast), Mirza Haider Douglat and some Afghan invaders have written chapters of the Islamic history in Kashmir with blood. The conversion of the Hindus in Kashmir did not effect the social hierarchy of the Kashmiri Hindus who even after their conversion to Islam remained attached to their respective professional occupation giving rise to a stratified form of the Muslim society. Here is a case where contents of one culture were transmitted into another in the form of the change over one religious faith to another, preserving the form of culture intact. But once Islam came as the main religion of the people, the cultural contents since then remained uniform and continuous. Such changes occur very rarely when the whole society shifts over from one set of cultural contents to another. The situation in Kargil, however, is quite similar to that of Kashmir. The Buddhist faith here was replaced by the Muslim faith. But the overall form of the societies in Kashmir and Kargil differ in many respects though both populations follow more or less the similar faiths. Another very important factor determining the cultural form of the two areas is the ecology.

Ecology and Culture

As it has already been stated that the Muslim societies sharing the same contents of culture differ greatly in form by way of sharing vastly different ecological niches having a different set of symbiotic relationships between culture and the echo-system. The variation in cultural forms of the Kashmir and the Kargil Muslims is clearly discernible more in material forms of culture than in ideational. It will not be amiss to portray the differences in material aspects of culture of the Muslims of Kashmir and Kargil.

The monsoon fed Kashmir valley, as already stated, is rich in all economic resources like water, forests and a wet paddy cultivation that determine the dietary habits of the people. Wet cultivation is prevalent in the central valley whereas dry cultivation is resorted to in the periphery. The riverine system of the Jhelum offers an effective waterway linking various places of the valley. Lakes and rivers breed baffling varieties of vegetables, ducks and fish that take care the food requirements of the people. The houses made of wood are elaborate and multi-storied. The people's economy has got a boost especially after the state's merger with India, and the bestowal of ownership of land to the tenants. The Japanese method of paddy cultivation, new scientific techniques adopted to expand horticultural, silvi and piscicultural activities, the expansion of saffron and hop-cultivation in selected areas and an unending stream of tourist, which is the biggest single industry in Kashmir, brought a further strength to the economy of the people. The newly begotten wealth was used like Kargil, for strengthening the faith by way of visiting Mecca and other pilgrimages in the Middle East more frequently and by starting new or strengthening the existing religious educational institutions known as *Madarsahs*. A part of income was further invested into converting the mud-plastered wooden house into the reinforced concrete structures.

The Shia Muslims of Balahama, a village in Srinagar, found themselves divided into two parallel politico-religious groups—one led by the Agha Saheb of Badgam having its mooring in the ruling party and the other following Maulana Iftikhar Husain Ansari, a prominent member of one of the major opposition groups. In the past, all religious performances were conducted collectively but after the political division came the two rival groups were reported to have fought pitched battles during Mohurram observances (Rizvi : 1982a). The district authorities intervened and stopped all public religious processions and observances. The hardening of attitudes of the two sides had its reflection on marital unions which saw an abrupt stoppage of inter-marriage between the two groups. The village Imambara (Rizvi, 1973: 73-82) was locked by the administration apprehending a breach of peace in the village. That was the situation when the village was last visited in 1981.

Hence it may be observed that the people sharing the same set of fundamental religious principles differ in their political ideologies though adhering to different forms of culture.

Ecology and Culture in Kargil

The Muslims of Kargil share a vastly different ecological niche vis-a-vis the Kashmiri Muslims, Kargil, a part of the vast Himalayan desert i e. Ladakh, was always deficient in agricultural produces due to scanty rainfall and it is basically a mountainous snow fed area. The surrounding ring of mountains fall under a perennial snow line making agriculture only as a subsidiary occupation as there is simply not much land available to support the entire population of the area, though thin in density. Thus, pastoralism and trade emerged as the basic means of eking out a livelihood by the people. Kargil eases out a part of its population during winter (Rizvi, 1982b: 52-57) to the neighbouring Kashmir, Punjab, Uttar Pradesh and Himachal Pradesh more as an ecological compulsion than to seek a livelihood as stated by Drew (1875: 357) and Hashmatullah (1939: 677-751).

Unlike Kashmir villages, where houses are clustered, the settlement pattern in Kargil is of dispersed type. Members of a particular lineage (*quaum*) live nearer to each other.

Non-availability of timber for house construction has compelled the people to evolve their own architectural genius by which they construct multi-storied houses with stone masonry and sub-baked bricks.

The traditional trade routes, which once hummed with the footstep of traders and jingling of the caravan bells, are now silent as trade activities having been stopped. The people faced this economic catastrophe quite stoically. The cessation of trade activities was followed with the national efforts of defending and strengthening the borders in the three successive wars that were fought in and around Kargil. The influx of new job opportunities gave a fillip to the people's economy in Kargil. The Kashmir story was repeated in Kargil once more : the newly acquired wealth was invested more on efforts of reviving faith that remained dormant during the Punjabi and Dogra rulers under whom the people enjoyed only a subsistence economy and could not possibly pay much attention to the dwindling adherence to the cultural core. In the post 1947 era the number of the people going to the Middle East on pilgrimage and for imbibing religious learning had gone up considerably. Some of the alleged non-Islamic practices, earlier resorted to by the people, were discouraged and discontinued. In the process, the Dom musicians catering to the needs of their clients lost their traditional occupation of music and dance and turned artisans. The Kargil peasantry, on the other hand, have come closer to a higher degree of conformity to the fundamental values of Islam.

Islam puts a definite emphasis on puritanism and a frugal style of living with the least emphasis on exhibitionism and consumerism. The Muslims of Kargil followed this emphatic fiat in its true spirit whereas many Kashmiri Muslims could not withstand the charm of western oriented culture of consumerism e.g. many villagers in Balahama acquired bank loans and purchased trucks and taxis plying to and fro Balahama. At the time when the present study was conducted, Kargil was out of bounds for the tourists but since the area has now been thrown open to the tourist traffic, only further studies would reveal whether or not Kargil is also following the same trends which were set earlier in Kashmir. However, there are indications of rising bride price among the Brog-pa Muslims and an increasing number of *makpa* marriages among the Baltis and the Purgis. With the spread of secular education the Muslims of Kargil too are aspiring to attain better living conditions.

Islam came into direct contact with Hinduism in Kashmir and with Buddhism in Kargil. Naturally, the Kashmiri Muslims inherited a culture with Hinduic overtones whereas the Muslims of Kargil have a Buddhistic blend in their culture. Although Islam was propagated by more or less the same missionaries of Sufistic creed, one still finds an intact hierarchical caste structure in Kashmir which is missing in Kargil as there are no indications to suggest the Buddhists ever had a hierarchical arrangement based on the Hindu caste model.

It will, therefore, be not out of place to present a comparative picture of the Muslims of Kashmir and Kargil as to show how effectively the following major determining principles of Hindu caste system have influenced the two cultures under study. Before a comparative assessment is made a brief elucidation on the governing caste principles will be essential.

(I) *Ascribed caste status* : Looking at the social stratification in Kashmir, it is evident that all groups, hierarchically arranged from Syed down below to cobblers (*watal*) and scavengers have ascribed status through birth without any scope for upward group mobility. In Kargil, on the other hand, excepting the Syeds all other groups from the Sheikhs to the Doms have achieved caste status. The autochthories have all potentiality to move upward to the level of the Sheikhs from down below.

(II) *Purity and pollutions* : The concept of pollution is absolutely fundamental and governs the relations between castes among the Hindus (Srinivas : 1952). This concept operates among the Muslims of Kashmir valley specially in case of untouchables like cobblers and scavengers with whom intermarriage and interdining found absent. In Kargil no such concept is present in the Muslim society. The Syeds may be considered as an exception who enjoy an ascribed caste status by virtue of their consanguineous proximity with the Prophet Mohammad (Rizvi: 1978).

(III) *Occupational specialisation* : Caste groups are identified through their respective occupations. Among the Kashmiri Muslims there are set caste groups with specified occupations like goldsmiths (Zargar), oilmen (Teli), carpenter (Takhan), cook (Waza), potters (Kraal), cobblers (Watal) and scavengers for which there is no specific term. In Kargil all the functions of the occupational caste groups are performed by the people themselves irrespective of their respective states through specialist either in one or many occupations. Scavenging caste does not exist in Kargil as the entire quantity of human refuse is administered to the fields (*sum*).

(IV) *Commensal taboos* : In Kashmir, interdining and sharing of hubble-bubble is allowed only upto the level of clean professional groups but sharing of smoke and water between the high castes and untouchable Muslims viz., Watal and scavengers, has not been noticed. The Muslims of Kargil, on the other hand, do not impose any restrictions in interdining within the community. The dietary taboos, however, are observed with the non-Muslim communities as the Muslims in Kargil do not accept anything cooked or wet from non-Muslim viz. a Hindu or a Buddhist. Even if a Muslim relative is invited by a Buddhist relative in a marriage or a mourning ceremony, the former is offered with dry and uncooked food. The Buddhists on the other hand do not observe any commensal taboos with the Muslims.

(V) *Spatial differentiation* : One of the many traits of the peculiar Hindu caste system is to maintain a spatial distance with the lower caste groups. It has been observed that the Muslims of Kashmir have minimal social interaction with unclean caste groups which are mostly economic in nature. The cobblers and scavengers live away from the centre of Muslim population in the peripheral hamlets of the village. Akura, in Anantnag district, may be cited as an example. In case of the Muslims of Kargil the notion of spatial differentiation does not hold good.

(VI) *Jajmani system* : The jajmani system envisages the economic relationships between the high caste Hindus and low occupational caste groups. These relationships which are mainly hereditary in nature are maintained among the Muslims of Kashmir. The Muslim occupational groups serve not only the Muslim high caste groups but also the Kashmiri Pandits (Madan, 1972: 106-139). Kargil does not have any notion of the jajmani system.

(VII) *Endogamy* : Group endogamy is usually resorted to by various Hindu caste groups. The Kashmir Pandits are strictly endogamous with the provision of *gotra* exogamy. Cases of hypergamy do not occur and hypogamy is strictly prohibited. The Muslims of Kashmir, on the other hand, tend to observe group endogamy but there are no hard and fast rules for marrying with a woman of low caste but marriage with a woman of high caste Muslim by a male member of low caste especially the unclean caste is a remote possibility. The Muslims of Kargil, on the other hand, have not set any limits on marriage distance excepting one's own mother, brother, or sister, and between one and the children of a woman who have nursed the former.

(VIII) *Upward group mobility* : Looking at the stratification among the Muslims of Kashmir and Kargil one can infer that the upward group mobility is not possible at least in theory among the Muslims of Kashmir as a Watal cannot become a Zargar or a Sheikh whereas in Kargil the Doms have entered into the ethnic boundary of the agrarian classes and have established marital alliances even with the priestly class of the Sheikhs. Thus group mobility among the Muslims of Kashmir is much more slow than that of the Muslims of Kargil.

The list of the above mentioned traits is no way exhaustive. There may be some more important traits which might have been overlooked in the suggested list. Here only some of important significant traits have been listed as per field situations. On the basis of the eight listed traits it is evident that the Muslims of Kashmir have seven traits of the Hindu caste system whereas the Muslims of Kargil have a single trait, that is, upward group mobility. The table on page 440 sums up the above mentioned proposition.

It is evident from the table that the Muslims of Kashmir are nearer to the Hindu caste model than the Muslims of Kargil, who never had an immediate contact with Hinduism. The scoring has been done on the basis of the significance of the respective traits. Hence the most significant trait, i.e., Ascribed caste status which is determined by birth on the basis of the concept of Brahma, Karma, and Dharma (Ansari : 1961) has been given a maximum score of eight. All other traits have been scored in a receding order in accordance with their receding significance. After summing up all scores on the basis of their presence, a quantitative picture emerges that suggests the proximity of the Kashmiri Muslims to the Hindu caste model in contrast to the Muslims of Kargil who are nearest to the Islamic model of society by virtue of their winning a minimum score of 1 only.

Sl. No.	*Traits of Hindu caste system*	*Score in order of significance of traits*	*Muslims of Kashmir*	*Score on the basis of presence or absence of traits*	*Muslims of Kargil*	*Score on the basis of presence or absence of traits*
1.	Ascribed caste	8	Present	8	Absent	—
2.	Status Purity and Pollution	7	Present	7	Absent	—
3.	Occupational specialization	6	Present	6	Absent	—
4.	Commensal taboos	5	Partially Present	2.5	Absent	—
5.	Spatial differentiation	4	Present	4	Absent	—
6.	Jajmani system	3	Present	3	Absent	—
7.	Endogamy	2	Present	2	Absent	—
8.	Upward group mobility	1	Absent	1	Present	1
Score		36		32.5		1

The same picture may be put on a bipolar scale in the following manner :

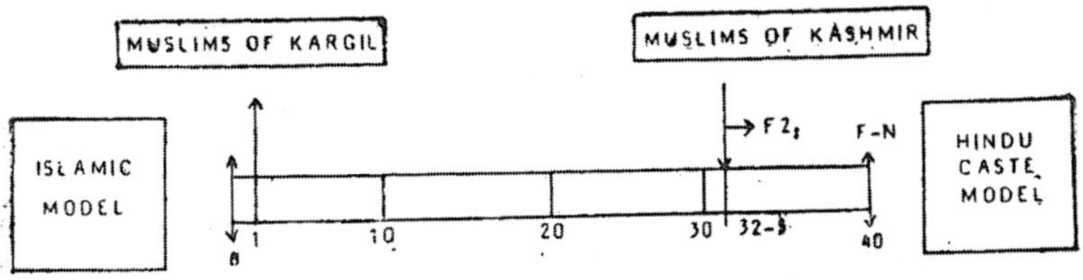

In the above diagram Islamic model has been put on the left side at the 'zero-end' as the Islam is against any type of social inequality. The Hindu caste model, having a strong belief in a hierarchical order, has been put on the opposite end of the scale. Theoretically it is impossible to come across with any Muslim society having a zero score as each of them has been influenced by exogenous factors in the dimensions of time and space. Similarly no Hindu society is likely to be 100.00 per cent caste oriented. Hence all Muslim societies are likely to find a place betwen 0_+ to 40 in the above scale. F-1 as indicated above is the particular form of society of the Muslims of Kargil and F-2 is a different form of society representing the Muslims of Kashmir valley. F-n denotes the infinite numbers of Muslim societies that can be put on the above scale between 0 to 40. On the basis of scores each one of them can be assigned by observing the presence or absence of the traits of the Hindu caste system.

Thus one can observe that the two groups of the Muslims, sharing the same set of religious tenets, differ considerably in form within a limited area of Kashmir valley and Kargil. It has further been observed that the variation of the forms between the cultural profiles of the Muslims of Kashmir valley and Kargil is the result of ecological, historical and ethnological factors.

REFERENCES

Ansari, Ghous 1960 *Muslim Caste in Uttar Pradesh*, Lucknow Ethnographic and Folk Culture Society.

Drew, Fredrick 1875 *The Jammu and Kashmir Territories*, Delhi: Oriental Publisher (Reprint 1971).

Gazetteer of Kashmir and Ladakh 1974 (Originally 1890) Delhi: Vikas Publishing House (Reprint).

Hashmutullah, Moulvi 1939 *Mukhtasar Tarikh - e - Jammu* (Urdu), Lucknow: Nawal Kishore.

Madan, T.N. 1972 "Religious Ideology in a Plural Society: The Muslims and Hindus of Kashmir", *Contribution to Indian Sociology*, No. 4.

Rizvi, B.R. 1973 Resistance to an Innovation: A case study from a North Indian village", *Folklore*, XIV (2).

Rizvi, B.R. 1978 "Caste among Muslims with special reference to Kargil", *Abstract*. Xth International Congress of Ethnological and Anthropological Sciences, New Delhi.

Rizvi, B.R. 1982 (a) "Peasantry and Secularism in India", *Uttarayan*.

Rizvi, B.R. 1982 (b) "Ecology and Nomadism: A study of some migratory groups of Ladakh", *Nomads in India*. Eds. P.K. Mishra and K.C. Malhotra, Calcutta : Anthropological Survey of India.

Srinivas, M.N. 1952 *Religion and Society among the Coorgs of South India*, Oxford: Clarendon Press.

CHAPTER XXVI

DE-ENCAPSULATION AND CHANGE IN LADAKH

MELVYN C. GOLDSTEIN
P. TSARONG

Introduction

Ladakh was first opened to outsiders in 1974 and from the perspective of the energetic but naive travellers and writers who flocked there, appeared a traditional society which modernization had bypassed. These "observers" took the quaint and traditional physical appearance of Ladakh and Ladakhis to reflect the persistence of traditional social and cultural structures. They were mistaken. In point of fact, substantial changes have and are transforming the social, cultural and environmental fabric of life in Ladakh.

The emergence and sustenance of a sophisticated civilization for roughly 1,000 years in the frigid and arid high-altitude mountain region of the Ladakh represents one of the great victories of human adaptation to an extreme environment. This successful human-environment relationship is all the more impressive when we consider the extreme sensitivity of mountain systems to even small disturbances and the tendency for such disturbances to be irreversible (UNESCO, 1974 : MAB Series 14 : 132).

Not surprisingly, the problems of the Himalayan physical environment e.g. soil erosion, the elimination of forest cover, and the overuse of pasture areas are well known. While this environmental focus is important and necessary, a different, and perhaps more basic, dimension of the problem—the social dislocation deriving from the indirect impact of change and modernization in these areas—has not received adequate attention. This paper suggests that the traditional Ladakhi social adaptation was no less fragile than the physical environment and that the impact of modernization in areas adjacent to the Tibeto-Himalayan region has dramatically transformed the social structure of the high-altitude inhabitants.

An Encapsulated Environment

The adaptation of the Ladakhis to the high-altitude environment of the Himalaya involves the cultivation of cereal grains and the husbandry of bovines and ovines. Although it is difficult to generalize for the entire geographic area, it is possible to delineate a high-altitude arid zone and to characterize the traditional socio-economic organization found there as an adaptation to what is here termed environmental encapsulation.

Encapsulation refers to a situation in which the potential for increased production of energy by agricultural exploitation of new areas and by internal intensification of production is virtually nil. Unlike most of the monsoonal parts of the Himalaya, cultivation in the high-altitude arid zone is extremely limited, typically between 3,600 m and 4,200 m but usually extending only a few hundred metres in any single area. Early frost and late thaw combine to restrict severely the amount of land suitable for agriculture. Furthermore, within the narrow arable zone, extreme aridity and the subsequent need for irrigation render a sizable portion unsuitable for cultivation due to the absence of a secured source of water. Poor soil composition and steep slopes in the river valleys further reduce this potential. It is not surprising, then, to find that only 0.48 per cent of the total area of the Tibetan plateau is under cultivation (Li, 1980: 7).

Intensification of cultivation is also limited. Tibetan and Ladakhi agricultural technology traditionally used fertilizers, irrigation, crop rotation, and weeding and in most areas arable was carefully husbanded on well-kept terraces. It is difficult to imagine how the Ladakhis could have farmed more intensively than they traditionally did. Despite their agricultural skill, however, yields were low and throughout the Himalayan arid zone yields of only ten times the seed sown were considered excellent.

Thus, the ecosystem is encapsulated in the sense that there is a limited potential for energy extraction and the population must adjust to this reality. This situation is very different from that found in the lower regions of the Himalaya where expansion of agriculture into forests and onto steeper slopes has continued up to the present in some areas.

The inelasticity of the environment, however, has another dimension. For centuries, the Tibetans and the Ladakhis not only have had to extract their own subsistence from the delicate and inelastic physical environment but have had to generate substantial surpluses in order to maintain in luxury the elites that dominated their society. These surpluses comprised not only foodstuffs and products but critically also labour (corvee tax obligations). Peasants, for example, had provided animals and humans to transport their goods, and it is clear that such labour obligations were among the most onerous. The traditional Ladakhi and social structure was as much an adaptation to this exploitation as it was to the climatic and geomorphological limitations of the high-altitude environment.

Modernization and De-encapsulation in Ladakh

Despite the lack of sufficient development and the unchanging utilization of traditional agricultural and pastoral technologies, the people in Ladakh have undergone substantial and fundamental changes that have de-encapsulated the environment by (1) offering new economic opportunities that do not require significant initial reserves of capital and (2) by eliminating the exploitive politico-economic system with its heavy labour obligations. As is discussed below, these new forces reduced the importance of concentrating labour in the family and provided younger brothers new opportunities for obtaining income outside the traditional system. The result has been the disintegration of the traditional fraternal polyandrous family and marriage system (2 or more brothers sharing one wife) which functioned to reduce both population growth and fragmentation of land. While these areas appear traditional and undeveloped at first glance, in reality, their key social and economic structures have been, or are in the process of becoming, fundamentally transformed. This paper suggests that this transformation of the traditional social milieu is a very important component of the current social and ecological situation.

Ladakh

Ladakh is the northeasternmost district of Jammu and Kashmir State. It is divided into three Tehsils, two of which, Leh and Zanskar, are overwhelmingly Buddhist, while the third, Kargil, is predominantly Muslim. In Ladakh as a whole, 52 per cent of the population is Buddhist, 46 per cent Muslim, and 2 per cent Hindu and others (Census of India, 1973 : 83).

The village of Kyilung (pseudonym) is a predominantly agricultural village located at an altitude of about 3,597 m near Leh, the capital of Ladakh. According to the 1971 Census of India, it has a population of 1,056. Roughly 75 per cent of the people are Buddhists (who are the original inhabitants) and 25 per cent Muslims most of whom are of the Shia sect.

A basic structural unit in the traditional Tibetan and Ladakhi societies was the corporate polyandrous stem family. As alluded to earlier and discussed in detail in previous papers (Goldstein, 1971 : 64-74 ; 1976, 223-233 ; 1977 : 481-489 ; 1978 : 325-337), because of the nature of the feudal corvee (labour) tax system, the inelasticity of the environment and the need for male labour to fulfil tax obligations and utilize the disparate economic niches traditionally exploited, the basic adaptive strategy of such corporate families was to retain the land intact and maintain a core of males in the family. Fraternal polyandrous marriages and stem families were the main vehicles by which this was achieved.

Traditionally, all males in Tibet had demand rights to their family's land. This produced a fundamental structural contradiction in that prevention of land fragmentation was considered essential yet the legal system permitted any male to fission from his family and to take a share of the land on demand. Fraternal polyandry, the sharing of one wife by two or more brothers, was the main mechanism by which this structural contradiction was overcome. It provided for gratification of the sexual and emotional needs of all the brothers without forcing them to marry monogamously and produce separate sets of heirs. Land stayed within the family unit and the most effective cost-benefit equation ensued. Fraternal polyandry, however, is not without problems and many younger brothers clearly preferred to many monogamously and establish independent households. They generally did not do so because there was a series of legal, economic and labour constraints that traditionally reduced their ability to achieve a satisfactory style of life if they split from their natal family.

In Ladakh, however, the conservation of land principle was carried to its logical, and most rigid, extreme in that inheritance went according to the principle of primogeniture, i.e., the eldest son inherited the land and control of the family corporation (called a *khangchen*). Younger sons could not legally demand nor did they obtain any portion of the family patrimony unless their elder brother agreed. Unlike Europe, however, in Ladakh, primogeniture was linked to fraternal polyandry. Consequently, when younger brothers reached maturity they were not sent from their natal household to seek their livelihood elsewhere but rather were brought into the polyandrous marriage of their elder brother(s). The Ladakhi social structure, therefore, eliminated the underlying contradictions of the Tibetan social structure by linking primogeniture to fraternal polyandry. By this strategy, land fragmentation was precluded and labour concentration was assured.

The manner in which fraternal polyandry acts to reduce aggregate fertility has been discussed briefly above and in detail in (Goldstein, 1976 : 223-233). Suffice it to say that because of the prevalence of fraternal polyandry, substantial numbers of the Ladakhi Buddhist females of reproductive age remained unmarried unless they could find husbands outside the Buddhist community, in which case their offspring were not heirs to the land of their mother's family. While this movement of the Buddhist females to non-Buddhist husbands was common until recently, in 1980, 13 per cent of Kyilung's Buddhist females 45 and over were unmarried and had not reproduced.

Traditionally, therefore, the Ladakh social structure was very well adapted to the limiting features of an encapsulated environment.

The end of World War II marks the onset of a series of different and often unrelated events that affected different parts of the Himalaya in similar ways. In India, independence was attained in 1947 and after a brief conflagration in Kashmir, Ladakh joined with Kashmir to become part of the new Indian nation. As such it was subject to the Constitution of India including laws concerning corvee taxation, inheritance, and land tenure. According to Indian law, primogeniture was not legal and corvee and other "serf" taxes were not allowed. Although no special effort has been made to eradicate primogeniture in Ladakh, gradual realization of its illegality has totally transformed the nature of family organization in the Buddhist sector of Ladakh, since younger brothers who grudgingly remained together with their older brother(s) began to demand a share of the family patrimony. As their demands were sustained in government courts, the integrity of the corporate family dissolved, and land and family fragmentation began to prevail. The resultant population explosion has irreversibly altered the nature of the human adaptation.

The case of the Pichu family illustrates this transformation. Figure 1 sets out genealogically the last three generations of this family. Until about 1957 the Pichu family had maintained its land intact and was well-to-do, holding about 150 *khal* (in this area roughly 7.5 *khal*=1 acre) of land. In generation I there were three brothers, two of whom married polyandrously while the third became a monk. The marriage resulted in nine surviving children, five of whom were males and four females. The two eldest males (aged 44 and 42 in 1980) were initially married polyandrously but this did not work out, and the younger brother demanded a share of the land to set up an independent household. He was given about 20 *khal* of land and is Family III in the figure. The third son was made a monk and got no land but the son who is now 38 separated taking with him another 20 *khal* of land.

Finally, about ten years ago, the two fathers decided to split from their eldest son (aged 44) because they could not get

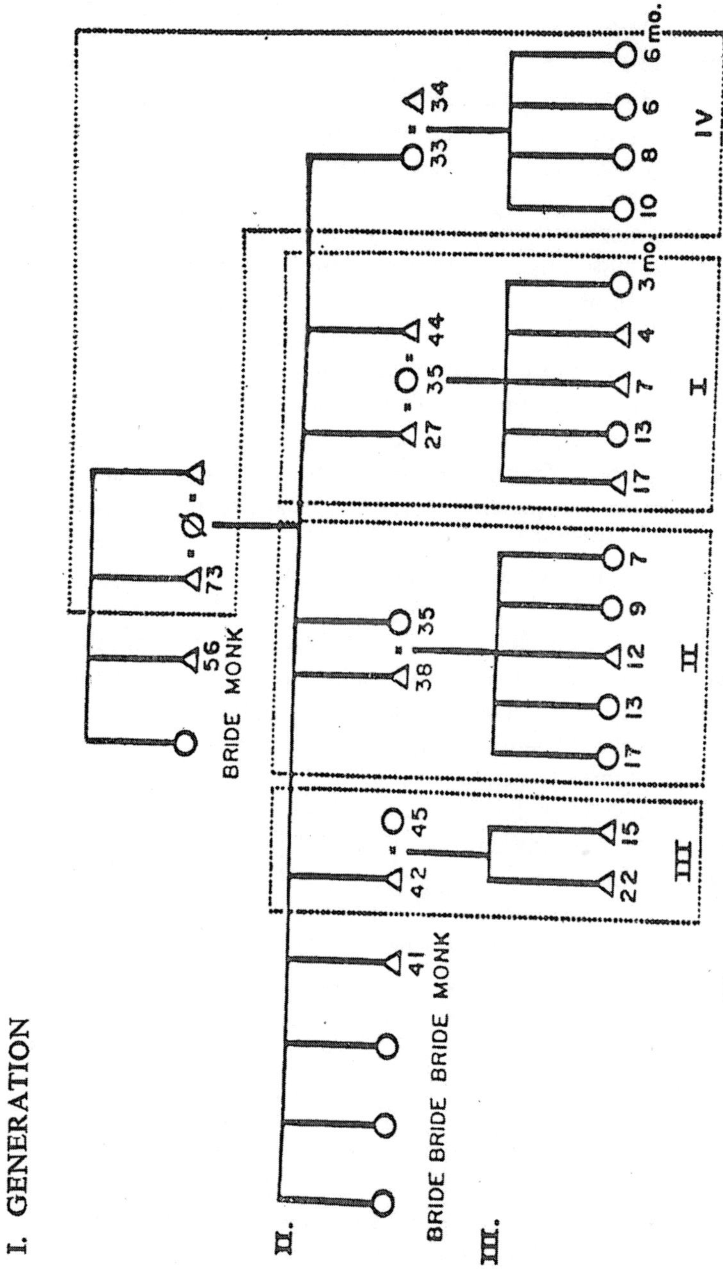

Figure 1: *The Phichu Family through Three Generations*

along with his wife. They took their daughter with them and received 30 *khal* of land. She then took an "adoptive" bridegroom, and this is Family IV in the figure. This left the main family (in Ladakhi, the *khang chen*) with 60 *khal* of land and a polyandrous marriage linking the eldest and youngest brothers.

Thus, from one large and wealthy family, there are today four families comprising 28 persons (9 parents, 2 grandparents, and 17 children). Assuming, however, that the traditional system was still intact and that fraternal polyandry would have been the form of marriage for all four of the brothers (one male would still be a monk), and if their wife had five surviving offspring (i.e. the most children surviving to any of the actual females), the total number of persons in the one polyandrous stem family would have been only eleven (4 parents, 2 grandparents, and 5 children). The per capita land size would have been 11.8 *khal* per person versus the actual average which is 4.6 *khal* per person; that is to say, it would have been 157 per cent greater than the actual per capita amount. Not only is the total number of persons more than twice what it would have been with polyandrous stem family, but the actual number of offspring produced is over 3.4 times greater (17 versus 5) than it would have been if polyandry had been retained.

This type of family and land fragmentation has become extremely common and today fission is the expectation and fraternal polyandry the exception. Because the Ladakhi corporate families have names and because fissiparous families are known as the *khang bu* ("little house") of the main family (*khang chen*). It is easy to determine the degree to which fission has occurred in the village. About one hundred years ago there were 64 main families (*khang chen*) who held virtually all the land and were the basic taxpayers. Today there are 143 households, including the 64 original main houses. The additional 79 families are all "little houses" (*khang bu*) that have come into existence in the period since Indian independence. This represents an increase of 123 per cent in the number of families in the course of roughly three decades. Modernization in the plains India, therefore, has had somewhat different impact on the traditional Ladakhi social structure despite the fact that no much special effort was made in this direction.

The transformation of the traditional social organization in Ladakh has another element that must be mentioned. Even though primogeniture could be legally circumvented in modern India, younger brothers still had to weigh the costs of fission versus fraternal polyandry in the sense that they had to determine whether they could survive economically if they split off. Although before Indian independence there normally were no "extra" resources, a series of events occurred after 1947 that made fission feasible by providing new and alternative sources of income for village Ladakhis while eliminating corvee labour obligations.

Indian independence also ended the feudal-like corvee transportation tax that had been imposed on all families (i.e. all taxpayers). In Kyilung, this tax obligated each family to send one adult male with food and animals for four months of the year (one month every three months) to a nearby Transport Station where authorized travellers and goods were assembled for transportation to the next station either toward Leh or Srinagar. This was a very costly and difficult obligation and those who were negligent or inefficient were often punished physically, when, for example, animals or people were not ready to leave on time. Several old Ladakhi men told me that the night or two before their turn came to move to the station they could not sleep because of their apprehension. This requirement, even without primogeniture, would have made it extremely difficult for a young man to marry monogamously and to succeed on his own. The elimination of the corvee transportation tax was another factor, therefore, underlying the structural transformation in Kyilung.

At about the same time that India obtained her independence from Britain, Tibet came under the direct administration of the People's Republic of China. The result of this was an economic boom. The Ladakhi villagers obtained jobs in road building, construction, in the army, and in the complex infrastructure that was necessary to maintain a bureaucracy and a sophisticated modern army in a backward, extraordinarily harsh environment. For the Ladakhis, the Indians' awareness of the strategic importance of Ladakh has provided a golden opportunity, and they have not been slow to take advantage of it. Not surprisingly, the overwhelming majority of families which split off (*khang bu*) have one or more individuals working for wages, either for the government or for other establishments. It is these new economic opportunities that have afforded younger brothers and sisters the economic viability to be independent of the traditional family structure.

One further aspect of modernization should be mentioned, namely the influence of politics on fertility. As indicated earlier, the traditional Ladakhi social structure was oriented to land conservation which had the consequence of reducing population growth. This, however, was not the case for the Muslims of Ladakh. The majority of the Muslims in Kyilung are Baltis, that is, Shia Muslims who speak Ladakhi as their native language. The Baltis never utilized polyandry and instead followed patterns wherein each son married and stayed in a joint family. Sometimes before, and almost always after, the father died, these families typically split up with each brother taking a share of the land. Theoretically females also had rights to own land and appear to have sometimes inherited it. From the beginning, therefore, Muslims followed a system wherein land was continually fragmented and also one which resulted in maximal reproduction since females were not systematically removed from the breeding pool. Moreover, because there was always a pool of unmarried Buddhist females, each Muslim male invariably married and reproduced. Thus, whereas the number of Buddhist families in Kyilung has increased 1.3 times in the past thirty years, the number of Muslim families has increased seven or eight times.

Since these Muslims were immigrants, they had traditionally only small landholdings, most of which they held on permanent lease from the larger Buddhist families. Consequently, they depended to a great extent on outside wages; in particular, on employment in the government. The breakdown of fraternal polyandry among the Buddhists has placed them in a situation analogous to that of the Muslims since they also have come to depend on outside income to maintain their quality of life. Because most of the more lucrative economic opportunities are in the government, or at least controlled by the government, political organization has become an economic issue. The composition of the Kashmir government, the control of the seat of the Member of Parliament for Ladakh, the amount of political influence in Srinagar and Delhi—these have become critical issues in Ladakh. Not surprisingly then, the Buddhist leaders support pro-natalist values arguing that the Buddhist females should not be permitted to marry non-Buddhists and that all good Buddhists should marry monogamously and reproduce maximally. This has given broad-based sanction to anti-polyandrous ideas that were already present in the rest of India (where it is actually illegal) and among the younger Ladakhi who were more influenced by the Indian ways. Thus, within the last decade, fraternal polyandry has been actively attacked within the Buddhist community for political reasons and passively derecognised by Indian law. Its total demise seems inevitable by the next generation.

The result of these factors has been a rapid transformation of the traditional encapsulated socio-economic system into one dependent on the world economic and political system for its subsistence. No longer are the Ladakhis part of a more or less homeostatic system in which population, technology, and environment are roughly balanced. The traditional environmental encapsulation has been destroyed by the explosion of new ideas and influences generated from outside. The Ladakhis now have high population growth rates (estimates of current population growth are over 2 per cent per annum), and decreasing per capita land holdings. Their future well-being is inexorably linked to events and processes beyond their control. Traditional norms and values concerning conservation of the environment are no longer efficacious in this new situation and western-type notions that the environment is something to be used and manipulated rather than conserved is becoming the dominant idea. Education and governmental employment are the new long-term strategic values. The future of Ladakh, therefore, appears somewhat less than sanguine since large inputs of capital and technology will be necessary to maintain the present quality of life there. As long as opportunities for outside employment are maintained, the local economy can cope with the ecosystem disequilibrium, but should there be a decline to uncontrollable political events, the local situation could deteriorate.

The social matrix of the Ladakhis has been irreversibly transformed as an indirect consequence of modernizing influences in India; and the Ladakhis are now locked in a struggle which they are unlikely to win without substantial assistance. That assistance, however, must not only examine the arid physical environment, but also the social environment to which it is inexorably linked.

CONCLUSION

This paper suggests that the populations inhabiting Ladakh have adapted to the inelasticity of the physical environment and the "encapsulation" of the total environment by developing social mechanisms that (1) prevented (or decreased) the fragmentation of arable land; (2) concentrated male labour in family units; and (3) decreased aggregate fertility (and thus overall population growth) by relegating substantial numbers of reproductive age females to a status of "unmarried". The main vehicle for accomplishing this has been the fraternal polyandrous stem family.

Despite their remoteness and inaccessibility, over the past thirty or so years a series of different, but structurally analogous, events have impacted on the life of these people and, in essence, have altered the traditional homeostatic adaptation. This transformation has produced a situation of instability and dependence that emerges as one of the most salient characteristics of current high altitude population in the Himalaya.

In Ladakh (Kyilung) modernization and development in areas adjacent to them have produced a new situation in which rapid population growth and land fragmentation are the norm. Because of this, the future of life at high altitudes in the Himalaya in not sanguine and it may not be possible to sustain the current quality of life in the near future. A particularly distressing effect of transformation is a shift in attitude toward the environment from one focused on long-term conservation and adaptation to one focused on short-term exploitation and manipulation.

REFERENCES

Goldstein, M.C. 1971 Stratification, Polyandry and Family Structure in Tibet. *Southwestern Journal of Anthropology*, 27 (1).

Goldstein, M.C. 1976 Fraternal Polyandry and Fertility in a high Himalayan Valley in Northwest Nepal. *Human Ecology*, 4 (3).

Goldstein, M.C. 1977 Culture, Population, Ecology and Development: A view from Northwest Nepal. Proceedings of the 1976 C.N.R.S. International Conference on the Ethnology of the Himalayas, Paris.

Goldstein, M.C. 1978 Paharia and Tibetan Polyandry revisited, *Ethnology*, 17(3).

Govt. of India 1973 Ladakh District Handbook, Census of India 1971, Government Press, Srinagar.

Li, Wen-hau 1980 A brief introduction to the Ecological Research on the Qinghai-Zizang Plateau by Chinese scientists. Unpubl. Manuscript.

UNESCO 1974 Programme on Man and the Biosphere (MAB), Working Group on Project 6: Impact of Human Activities on Mountain and Tundra Ecosystems, Lillehammer, 20-23 November 1973, Final Report. MAB Report 14, UNESCO, Paris.

CHAPTER XXVII

STRATIFICATION AND CHANGE IN THE CONTEMPORARY LADAKHI SOCIETY

SANDHYA GOKHALE—CHATTERJEE

Introduction

The typical Himalayan ecology may be partially responsible for building up diverse social systems exist among the various ethnic groups inhabiting there. Of the different societies functioning throughout the length and breadth of the Himalayas, the Ladakhi society is unique being in a region where a typical Buddhist cultural tradition is still in vogue and where this Buddhist tradition co-exists with other religious faiths. The stratification in the society is based on typical arid high altitude ecology present there and the economy in which the people there are involved. Religion is also a determining factor for the pattern of stratification exists there.

But with the passage of time when the area was thrown open to the outside world, the Ladakhi social system typical for an isolated rugged highland arid ecology, accepted the forces of change. The communication with the rest of the country which allowed an easy contact of the Ladakhis with the people of the rest of the country and also outsiders, has almost broken down the age old isolation and altered the uniqueness of the Ladakhi social stratification and pattern of interaction.

Situated within the trans-Himalayan ranges at an altitude over 10,000 ft. from the mean sea level, Ladakh can aptly be called the land of mountains and monasteries and till 1979 was the largest district of India with an area of 95,876 sq. km. Earlier Ladakh had tehsils namely Leh, Kargil and Zanskar (Padam). In 1979 Ladakh was subdivided into Leh and Kargil districts. In 1971 there were 109 villages in Leh tehsil, 104 in Kargil tehsil and 25 villages in Zanskar tehsil. The only two towns of the area, Leh (Class V) and Kargil (Class VI) form the headquarters of the respective districts.

Ladakh is totally rugged mountainous country with only a few fertile patches along the river banks, giving the whole area a barren and desolated look. The main factors responsible for the isolation of Ladakh were its remoteness, inaccessibility and its extreme inhospitable climate though in last two decades this isolation has much been overcome with the opening of this district to outside world.

Ladakh is characterised by a curious co-existence of different ethnic, linguistic and cultural groups for centuries. Various ethnic groups like the Argon, the Baltis, the Bhot or Bodh, the Dards, the Kashmiris, the Nurbaxis, the Tibetans and some from plains India are living side by side. They also belong to different linguistic groups like Brokpa, Dardi, Gilgiri, Hindi, Kashmiri, Ladakhi etc. Identically these people have embraced various religions like Buddhism, Christianity, Hinduism and Islam.

The Ladakhis keep themselves busy primarily with agriculture and animal husbandry. In the past trade with some Central Asian countries and parts of India used to play a very important role in their economy. After independence when the Government introduced package programmes for the development, the Ladakhis accepted various other jobs and services. Waged labour is one of the most important sources of livelihood of these people. Both men and women are found to work in different constructional projects. Some educated Ladakhis are found happy with Government and other services. Various other occupations these people have as secondary sources, are brick-making, carpentry, masonry, spinning, shoe making, weaving etc.

During the last couple of decades the Ladakhi society as already stated, has put itself before various dynamic forces which the modern world can provide.

The first major impetus to change came in 1947 when Ladakh became part of India. In 1949 the Chinese occupied Tibet, and this surely affected the trade of the Ladakhis with Central Asia and Tibet. Leh which had been an important market place and trade centre, dwindled in importance and lost its erstwhile glory. The second major impetus to change followed the Indo-Chinese conflict in 1962 when China illegally occupied a substantial portion of Ladakh. The complete suspension of trade with Central Asian countries particularly with Tibet resulted from this conflict.

The years following the 1962 Indo-China conflict, the strategic importance of Ladakh forged into focus, and was followed with the influx of the Government officials including military and para-military personnel, businessmen and others. The subsequent introduction of industrial technology also brought about major changes. The turning point, however, came in 1974 when the Government opened this restricted strategic zone to tourism, and thus to diverse socio-economic influences. After enjoying centuries of comparative isolation the Ladakhi society, within the span of the past two decades, has been subjected to major economic and cultural upheavals. Though the traditional Buddhism is still a living religion, tradition has thus begun to undergo changes, and economic and political powers have changed hands.

The most important change brought about by military presence and constructional works, however, is the demand for wage labour for construction and services and the demand for local resources like horses. These lead to the inflow of cash capital that has spread throughout the region. This has enabled the local population to purchase previously unavailable industrial commodities and changed their consumption pattern. It has also increased the opportunities of earning wages through a different occupation.

Since then the pace of change has been phenomenal, both in the type of transition and the extent of its assimilation within the socio-economic milieu. The fast changing way of life in rural Ladakh in terms of personal values and peaceful uncomplicated existence still lie somewhat near to the ideal ones.

Nonetheless, the material life is not much developed, and economically these villages are poor. Since the tendency to improve the material basis of life is intuitively desirable, and the process of change has already begun and cannot be reversed, it becomes all the more important to channelise the direction of these changes by a planned process, that will assimilate them into the existing structure without provoking new forms of discontent that are socially disruptive or form an uneasy superstructure over the existing system.

The following pages have thus dealt with the traditional stratification of the Ladakhi society, of primarily the Buddhist communities of Leh and Zanskar tehsils, and also changes in the socio-economic system and those brought about through the growing importance of tourism.

II. *Traditional System of Stratificatian*

Ladakh is an epitome of a high altitude arid cold mountainous land and has a unique ecosystem. The harsh environmental constraints of this region largely determine the broad pattern of human activity. The villages constitute individual units which are almost self-sustaining in rural Ladakh. The environmental rigours perforce require a large amount of communal work especially in agricultural operations at the village level. This has resulted in a close kinship ties and a well-knit social fabric. The family structure is all important, social ties range from family to ceremonial *phaspun* groups which have a common god, to the village and *gompa* (monastery) affiliations.

As already stated, Ladakh focuses a curious blending of different ethnic groups with varied customs, languages and religions. The two major religious groups, Buddhists and Muslims, dominate in different areas. While the Buddhists cover above 86 per cent and 95 per cent of the inhabitants of Leh and Zanskar tehsils respectively, Muslims predominate in Kargil tehsil.

The Ladakhi society of the past was broadly classified into four different strata. These are the *rgyal-rigs* (royalty), *sku-drag* (nobility), *dmans-rigs* (common peasants) and the *rigs-nan* (outcastes). In terms of the administrative hierarchy, the king or *rgyal-po* was the highest authority who and also other *jo* lords were of royal descent, followed by the hereditary local (often a few villages) governor or prime minister called the *bka-blon.* He was known as *blon-po* also if he had a slightly lower status. He was followed by the *nan-so* or revenue officer, affiliated to the royal court and the *go-ba* or village headman, both belonged to the *dmans-rigs* class.

Lower downin the hierarchy were various local lower titles carried by various *dmans-rigs* class officials like the *lha-rdag* or the temple guard, the *mkhar-dpon* or master of the castle and others. These and other court titles used to elevate the family bearing these above the rest of the *dmans-rigs* i.e. middle class. Similarly the Ladakhi *am-chi* (doctors) and *on-po* (astrologers) and *lha-pa* (oracles) were given a special respected status for their specialized profession even though they belonged to the peasantry; for sometimes they are either *sku-drag* or lamas.

Even though for social functions, the hierarchy was strictly adhered to, there had never been a very clear cut difference between the *sku-drag* and the *dmans-rig* households. In case there was no *sku-drag* in a village an outstanding *dmans-rig* would take over the leading role. Further, there were numerous levels within the *dmans-rig* class itself such that in a village families could be placed at a higher or lower level. Again the division between the *rigs-nan* and *dmans-rig* was much more accentuated than the division between the *dmans-rigs* and the *sku-drag* or the notability. Within the *rigs-nan* three further sub-divisions were identified. These were the *mgar-ba*, the *mon*, and the *be-da*, each identified by their occupation. The *mgar-ba* were the village blacksmiths who worked with metal and manufacture plough shares, arrows, knives, pots, tea cups etc. The *mon* were basically carpenters and musicians, while the *be-da* were the lowest caste of wandering ministerials. The *mgar-ba* and the *mon* belonged to a village, in that they could own land and livestock but the *be-da* were basically wanderers moving from place to place with their tents making a living often by begging.

On the whole, the lower classes of *rigs-nan* were socially segregated, and norms had to be strictly adhered to, but it was enough for the Ladakhi to recognize the low class of a person without making an issue of it. In fact the presence of the *mon* musicians was a must for most festivities, as were the metal products of the *mgar-ba* for daily life.

The past decade has seen a number of changes in social stratification, values and norms in this society following the widespread monetization of the Ladakhi economy (though the barter system still predominates in many parts of rural Ladakh in terms of local transaction). A new class of entrepreneurs has emerged, and their status irrespective of class has considerably risen. Most of them are employed in the service sector dealing with trade, transport, tourism affiliated services and in government administrative etc., offices. These days more and more Ladakhi youths develop the feeling that making money means becoming the *sku-drag*.

III. *Stratification in the Contemporary Ladakhi Society*

The present day Ladakhi population is constituted of a number of ethnic groups both artisan and non-artisan. These are the Ladakhi or Bodh, the Mon, the Gara, the Beda, the Balti, the Kashmiri, the Argon, the Changspa, the Dogpa or Brokpa, the Dard and the Tibetans. Besides some Hindu castes, Sikhs and Christians are also found to inhabit. Mann found these ethnic groups as distributed in the following order (1972: 1):

Buddhist	*Muslims*
1. Ladakhi or Bhoto, Boto, Bhautta etc. (also known as Mangric)	1. Balti
	2. Argon
2. Gara } also known as Dolba	
3. Mon } also known as Dolba	
4. Beda } also known as Dolba	

The Ladakhis are basically agriculturists. Earlier they had trade for which they used to remain busy for a period of time in the year and to keep a close link with their counterparts across the border. But trade does no longer play any role in their economy particularly after the closure of the Indo-Tibet border. Animal husbandry is an additional source of their livelihood. They keep large number of livestock including cattle, sheep, goat, etc. During summer they move in the high altitude areas with their animals while during winter they come down to the lower hills and low land. They are Buddhists and occupy the highest position in the ladder of social hierarchy.

Blacksmithy is the traditional occupation of the Gara. They prepare a variety of agricultural implements and other tools and supply them to the villagers, particularly to the Ladakhis on a symbiotic basis almost similar to the *jajmani* system of the plains. Agriculture and wage labour are subsidiary sources of income of some of them. While their position in the contemporary Ladakhi society is just lower than the Ladakhi or Bodh as the latter consider the Gara inferior to them, but the Gara consider their position higher than other ethnic groups.

The Mon are village musicians. They play flute in village festivities. Unlike the Gara they do not have land but sometimes earn cash by selling their labour. Their position is just below the Gara. They profess Buddhism.

The Beda are also musicians and serve the village folk with their expertize. They are drum beaters and take part in village festivities as musicians. They are also landless but earn wages by employing themselves in different constructional projects as labourers. They profess Islam and their position is inferior to that of the Bodh.

Though both the Baltis and the Argons are believers of Islamic faith and are land owners and agriculturists, in the social hierarchy the Baltis consider themselves superior to the Argon. Their status is higher than the Argon because they acknowledge the Argons to have born from the Kashmiri Muslim father and Ladakhi mother (Mann, 1972: 4) though Featherstone feels that the Argons are 'the result of cross between a Turkestan father and a Ladakhi mother' (1926: 213). Both the Baltis and Argons have much cultural similarities with the Ladakhis or Bodh.

The Changspa are on the other hand, a pastoral group and follow a transhumant life. They move with their livestock and tents from one place in the unkind desolate arid highlands to another. They depend on the products of their animals as they do not have any other pursuit.

The Dards who are found only in a few villages, are basically agriculturists. They also keep animals like cattle, sheep, goat etc. A section of the Dard is Buddhist by religion. They are also known as the Brokpas or Dokpas. But the other section has adopted Islamic way of life.

The role of religion in determining the hierarchical social status within the monastic order is also quite complex. The most revered monk is the *rin-po-che* or the reincarnate monk, who is the spiritual head of the monastery. Next to him in rank is the *tschag-dzog* or manager in charge of administrative affairs, followed by *khan-po* or abbot. Then come older *lamas* and other younger novices. In terms of social hierarchy, the nobility or *sku-drag* ranks below the *rin-po-che* and other *lamas* (monks).

As already stated, the Ladakhis consider other ethnic groups as inferior to them. As regards the status of the three ethnic groups, the Gara, the Mon and the Beda, the Ladakhis describe in the context of an arrow. "A Gara's position is comparable to the iron head of an arrow; a Mon's to the thread work, in between iron head and the shaft; and the Beda's position is equivalent to the shaft, the last portion of the arrow" (Mann, 1972: 5). This social position of these different groups is reflected in various aspects of their life and activities. The sitting arrangements in the place of ownership and feast are fixed for various groups as per their social status which is clearly reflected by the arrangement of seats and the heights of the table and cups (of *chang*), besides the quality of the carpets underneath and tapestry on the wall behind supplied at different socio-religious ceremonies. The person of the highest rank sits at the head of the room on the largest seat in front of the highest table. All the other people sit to his left with the next highest ranking next to him and so on, with the size of the seating cushions and tables diminishing in size and quality towards the end of the row. The place situated to the extreme right nearest to the door, a little away from the rest, is occupied by the lower caste of the *rigs-nan*. Similarly, in smoking, drinking, dancing etc. some sort of restriction on equality is there. But in some other aspects commensality does not seem to exist. There is no bar to the entry into the monastery and also making offerings to the deities. Entry into each other's house and also inter-dining are not prohibited.

Changing Social Order

The dynamics of social systems can be studied through the dimensions of economic, socio-cultural and power change.

Taken in the recent historic perspective, three broad impetuses of change can be identified in Ladakh. The first came with the independence after 1947 and then breaking up of traditional religious and trade ties with Tibet post 1959. The next major impetus to change came along with the presence of the military and para-military forces and civil officials following the Indo-Chinese conflict in 1962 and with the introduction of industrial technology. Even though the military personnel do not intermingle freely into the traditionally existing socio-economic structure, they nevertheless have brought numerous changes by the introduction of widespread demand for wage-labour and local materials, besides introducing various industrial items thereby changing the Ladakhi economy and consumption pattern.

It is rare these days even in the more remote parts of rural Ladakh to find a household that does not own an army disposal jerrycan (used for storage of water), items of army woollen clothing, etc. Trade links with the rest of India have also been strengthened and numerous goods previously unavailable or very difficult to obtain have come within reach. These include items like torches, lanterns, aluminium and other utensils, pens, plastic goods, mill-made cloth and clothes, spades, and many other items. Another major type of consumption change is visible in the Ladakhi diet. The use of new food commodities like sugar, rice, tea (the local brew is green tea) etc. and kerosene has become widespread, and now their use is one of daily consumptions not only in the towns of Leh and Kargil, but also in a large number of villages.

In post 1961 period the district and tehsil level administration has been streamlined and a number of developmental activities and programmes have been initiated. These include the setting up of schools, dispensaries, various civic amenities, agricultural and veterinary centres, and a number of shops supplying essential commodities to remote parts of Ladakh. Transport and communications have been developed and mobility from and to Ladakh, and within Ladakh itself have greatly been increased. This has greatly increased the sphere of social mobility and interaction as well, and intra and inter-personal ties within the social structure are no longer confined to the village or the neighbourhood. The increased opportunity for other occupations apart from agriculture and pastoralism have brought about another very important shift in the role of monasteries and various religious norms.

Montasteries had been and still are a vital part of the social structure with very strong ties with its affiliated villages. These not only do own land within different villages, but also keep strong links with the villagers; the *lamas* living in the monastery belong to the affiliated villages. Further, various religious ceremonies are required to perform before and during the process of village economic activities. These range from determining the auspicious date of sowing crops to various other decisions. Besides, the religious services rendered during different crises of life and other ceremonies are indispensable.

But in recent decades distinct changes in the role of monasteries are seen. Many families now prefer to send their male children to the government-run schools instead of to the monastery. This enables the young men to aspire for jobs beyond the traditional ones associated with agriculture and livestock. This is reflected by the increase of literacy among the population in the undivided Ladakh district from 12.7 per cent in 1971, to 17.06 per cent for Kargil district and 24.18 per cent literacy for Ladakh district in 1981.

The third and the most important impetus to change came in 1974 when Ladakh was opened to tourism. From 495 tourists arrived at Leh in 1974, the number jumped to 1980 in 1975, 4580 in 1976, 7150 in 1977 and 10,000 in 1978. With the exception of the villages and monasteries lying along the Leh-Srinagar road, Zanskar tehsil has been the most attractive to tourism. In 1977 there were 306 tourists arrived at Padam, the tehsil headquarters of Zanskar, followed by 435 in 1978, 405 in 1979, 549 in 1980, and 819 in 1981. This clearly brings out the growing impact of tourism—one that is bound to further change the traditional socio-economic structure. As a result, there has been a boom in the construction of new hotels in Leh and Kargil and many rooms in the village houses are given out on rent during the summer season. In 1979 there were 66 registered hotels in Leh as the demand for rooms with a minimum standard of comfort increased with the number of visiting tourists. Gradually, a large number of restaurants has been opened, and shops, geared to sell Ladakhi, Kashmiri and Tibetan arts and crafts like *thang-khas*, carpets, necklaces, statures etc. have been grown like mushroom. Most of these shops and pavement stalls are owned by the Tibetan and the Kashmiri traders with the goods produced either in Kashmir or in the Tibetan colonies spread in different parts of the country.

A number of local Ladakhis (specifically in Leh) have opened their own tourist agencies, though a larger number of branch offices of international and national agencies predominates. During the peak tourist season in the summer months from May to October, a number of local Ladakhis gets employment in tourist affiliated services including hotels, restaurants, shops, in transport, as guides and porters, and other jobs. These have created a new source of income and generally those connected with the world outside Ladakh through tourism, own a number of high technology goods like watches, cameras, trekking equipments, radios, calculators etc. Most of these items are bought or obtained either as gifts or for services given (for guides and porters etc.) or bartered tourists. It is not unusual to see a Ladakhi barter a coral and turquoise necklace for a watch or camera with a tourist and to find both equally satisfied with the bargain.

Tourism has undoubtedly been instrumental in the monetization of the Ladakhi economy. Nevertheless the major proportion of profits accruing from tourism goes outside Ladakh to the airlines, outside travel agencies and shopkeepers. The process of modernization has greatly strained and altered the traditional social hierarchy and norms.

The traditional rank of many *sku-drag* families is lowering in esteem with changing social values. Most of them are, however, comparatively better off, literate, and thus able to switch to the new emerging class of entrepreneurs. Numerous *dmans-rigs* families have grown in status and importance with the growing commercialization of the economy. Similarly some low caste *rigs-nan* have acquired education, and work in the newly created ocupations and have thus considerably gained in social status. These socio-economic changes have marked impact on the functional role of individuals in the Ladakhi society as well. Family ties are still very strong and even though separate households have been established by brothers of the same family, financial aid is still given to help promoting education, business etc. The head of the family, however, is no longer as important in economic decision making, especially if he is not educated and is employed in agriculture as he was in the past.

The traditional Buddhist socio-religious practices of the past also show distinct changes. Especially around Leh and Kargil, the two towns of Ladakh, the pomp and grandeur of these ceremonies has much been reduced. During the Buddhist New Year (*losar*) and during birth, death and marriage ceremonies, the distribution of *thab-zan* and *paba* has been reduced and now the presentation of the white *khatak* scarfs is the most common practice.

There has also been a concomitant increase in political awareness during the past two decades. During the pre-independence days Ladakh was ruled by a *Gyal-po* or king whose capital was at Leh. Numerous vassal kingdoms like Zanskar, Nulbeck etc. came under the Leh suzerainty. The break-up of the old feudal system meant the cessation of taxes and the change of political power to the State and Central governments. In the recent past the National Conference and Congress (I) have emerged as the most important political parties. There is a growing awareness among the people of their social and economic problems and status, and various agitations have been held to secure scheduled tribe status for the Ladakhis. This changing political awareness has further reduced the importance of the royalty and noble *sku-drag* families.

REFERENCES

Cunningham, A. 1970 (Ori. 1853) *Ladakh—Physical, Historical and Statistical,* Sagar Publications, New Delhi

Drew, F. 1971 *Territories of Jamoo and Kashmir*, Oriental Publishers, New Delhi

Featherstone, B.K. 1926 *An Unexplored Pass*, Hutchinson & Co. Ltd., London

Franke, A.H. 1977 *A History of Ladakh* (with critical introduction and annotation by S.S. Gergan and F.M. Husshain), Sterling Publishers Pvt. Ltd., New Delhi

Husshain, F.M. 1974 *Ladakh, the Moonland*, Sterling Publishers Pvt. Ltd., New Delhi

Mann, R.S. 1972a "Intra and Inter Family Relations among the Ladakhis of Ladakh", *Bulletin of Anthropological Survey of India*, Vol. XXI, No. 1 & 2

1972b "Social Stratification and Interaction in Ladakhi Villages", *Bulletin of Anthropological Survey of India*, Vol. XXI, No. 3 & 4

ERRATA

Page No.	*Line No.*	*Existing state*	*To be changed to*
4	3-4	Wanghans	Wanghams
12	4	Monogamy in the general rule	Monogamy is the general rule.
32	15	When Mara the Evil one	Put comma (,) after When Mara the Evil one,
33	20	The rest of the day thel ayman	The rest of the day the layman (keep gap between the and layman)
35	14	because as one monk put	because as one monk puts
35	19	The *mangal sutta* is	The *mangala sutta* is
38	10-11	does no include	does not include.
41	20	attain enlightenment	attained enlightenment
42	14	*Kalpataru*	*kalpataru*
43	32	Nang Vasundari image	put full stop (.) after Nang Vasundari image.
43	33-34	Chowdham	Chowkham
45			Delete inverted comma (') after Arunachal Pradesh from the title of the article.
45	3	Das 1945	Das, 1945
49	2	Catagories of the kin	Categories of the kin
49	6	*Kamou*	*kamou*
54	2	the Kacharis of the plan	the Kacharis of the plain
66	1	state of Sikkim emcompassing	state of Sikkim encompassing

70	10		delete comma (,) after Executive Councillor
74	22		delete gap in between 'the'
74	24		delete comma (,) after 22nd state of India
77	33	woods are avaiable	woods are available
78	10	The Bhutias are all	The Bhotias are all
84	30	worship like amulet	put comma (,) after amulet,
86	26	context of these chages	context of these changes
92	17-18	If his father was recal-citrant and indolent, he was weak, ineffec-tive and retiring nature	delete the whole
	29	border af India	border of India

ILLUSTRATIONS